BARGAINING FOR HEALTH

Labor Unions, Health Insurance, and Medical Care

BARGAINING FOR HEALTH

LABOR UNIONS,
HEALTH INSURANCE,
AND MEDICAL CARE

Raymond Munts

THE UNIVERSITY OF WISCONSIN PRESS
Madison, Milwaukee, and London, 1967

Published by
The University of Wisconsin Press
Madison, Milwaukee, and London

U.S.A.: Box 1379, Madison, Wisconsin 53701
U.K.: 26–28 Hallam Street, London, W.1

Printed in the United States of America
by NAPCO, Inc., Milwaukee, Wisconsin

Library of Congress Catalog Card Number 67–13555

Preface

In recent years the voluntary health insurance movement has come under careful scrutiny by students concerned with its inner problems and future prospects. As the "engine" of the health insurance movement, collective bargaining has played a key role; and study of its influence is indispensable for the evaluation of what has been accomplished. With almost two decades of union bargaining on health insurance behind us, it should be possible to look at both accomplishments and failures with some objectivity.

More health care for more people seemed, in the late 1940's, to be a simple matter of removing the dollar sign from between the patient and the medical services he needed. That was an age of innocence, because the kind and extent of services needed raise a whole series of problems. Negotiating health insurance has drawn labor and management into one of the most complex of economic markets. Unlike many commodity markets where the single-price principle operates, the marketing of medical services lacks uniformity in quality or prices. The standards for good medicine, let alone its financing, are not readily recognizable to the consumer.

There is no need to underestimate now the accomplishment of the many thousands of negotiated prepayment plans which have helped raise the medical standard of living of the entire nation, but the wisdom and sophistication that come with experience force some humility. Labor feels increasingly pressed by the problems on the supply side inefficient use of facilities, shortage of good quality medical centers— and inflated costs. How far can prepayment be extended without cost and quality controls over the disbursement of medical care? If these controls provide the answer, what is labor's role in their establishment?

Even asking these questions jars the old-line trade unionist who thinks he should stick to labor contracts rather than poke his nose into other people's business, a view that also has substantial support in the medical profession. Of course, labor should not be a blind instrument for medical reformers, but the problems are persistent and urgent. The obstacles that stand in the way of prepaid medical care of good quality cannot be wished away. If controls offer an answer, they should be tested and appraised. This study is designed to analyze the obstacles and to review the solutions that have been invented to overcome them.

The organization of the chapters requires some explanation. Chapter 1 is historical; Chapters 2–6 are studies of health bargaining in particular industries—men's and women's clothing, coal, autos, and steel. These chapters preserve the particular economic and industry context in which collective bargaining is conducted. In Part II, comprising Chapters 7–14, the union movement as a whole is considered in relation to other institutions operating in the medical market. In these chapters the evidence from Part I and more fragmentary evidence from other industries is used to develop the implications of "community health bargaining" for insurance carriers, hospitals, doctors, and medical service plans as well as for labor and management. The last two chapters, which comprise Part III, define the stages of health bargaining, summarize its contribution to the medical market, and suggest implications for public policy.

Four overlapping objectives motivated the study and helped shape it. I have tried (1) to summarize the "minutes" of the labor movement's experience with health insurance and medical care; (2) to provide a guide to union leaders on health bargaining and its implications; (3) to evaluate the more significant programs in which labor is involved; (4) to interpret for institutional economists the present inter-relationships of the labor and medical markets.

Critically-minded readers may question whether the central idea—community health bargaining—is descriptive, prescriptive, or predictive. Objectivity in research requires these distinctions, of course, and I have been acutely aware of them throughout. The selection of unions, the abstracting of their insurance and medical care activities, the choice of supplementary evidence in Part II, and the organization of material around certain chapter headings have entailed many crises of conscience.

My method is to search out all available information and sift with skepticism, to note differences among unions and within the same union where traditions, economic setting, and community context alter the results of bargaining. There is here no pretense of omniscience. It has been difficult enough to keep value judgments explicit and to find the relevant facts.

I respect activists dealing with social issues and want to help them: this is one good purpose for research. For this reason I have stated the results in conceptual terms that are familiar to the participants themselves: to the trade unionist, "bargaining" means the use of counter vailing power; he understands "bargaining" in its social and political meaning as well as in its economic sense. Above all, I respect the methods of democratic decision-making where goals and experience are constantly rubbing away at each other, and if this study helps to eliminate unnecessary arguments, and sharpens the alternatives, it will accomplish its purpose: it will show where the opportunities lie.

Many persons have helped me in ways unknown to themselves. Problems of welfare bargaining troubled my associates in the Textile Workers Union of America in the late 1940's. In the middle 1950's I worked with union leaders in Wisconsin on health and welfare issues through the facilities of the School for Workers of the University of Wisconsin. Later at national AFL–CIO headquarters I was exposed directly to problems of policy development and the thinking of elected and staff leadership. My associates in all these years have developed my understanding of what the labor movement is and how it looks at welfare issues. Looking back I feel particularly indebted to the encouragement I have received from Lawrence Rogin, Selig Perlman, Edwin Witte, Nelson Cruikshank, and Jack Barbash.

The following persons have read all or parts of the manuscript and have made valuable suggestions: Lisbeth Bamberger, Jack Barbash, Michael Davis, Warren Draper, Don Landay, Jerome Pollack, Morris Sackman, Richard Shoemaker, and Louis Segadelli. I want particularly to thank Dr. Herbert Abrams who gave most generously of his time on repeated occasions. I also owe a special debt to John Brumm for allowing use of his files, and to the excellent labor collections at the University of Wisconsin Memorial Library and the library of the State Historical Society of Wisconsin.

My wife, Mary Louise, helped to put the manuscript in final form.

Without her encouragement from the beginning, this book could not have been completed.

RAYMOND MUNTS

Madison, Wisconsin
December 17, 1966

Contents

Preface   v

Part I: *Background and Setting*
1   Wages, Health, and History   3
2   Health Experiments in the Needle Trades   13
3   Miners and Their Powerful Fund   29
4   The Mainstream: Beginnings in Autos and Steel   48
5   The Partnership in Steel   53
6   The Vocal Auto Workers   67

Part II: *Toward Community Health Bargaining*
7   Bargaining with Employers: Benefits and Costs   81
8   Bargaining with Employers: Administration   101
9   Bargaining with the Insurance Business   116
10   Bargaining with Hospitals and Blue Cross   131
11   Bargaining with Doctors: Fees and Quality   144
12   Bargaining with Doctors: Prepaid Group Practice   159
13   Bargaining for and with Medical Service Centers   177
14   Administering Medical Service Centers   204

Part III: *Implications*
15   Rationalizing the Medical Market   223
16   Community Health Bargaining   231

Notes   247

Index   311

Part I

Background and Setting

1

WAGES, HEALTH, AND HISTORY

The origins of health and welfare bargaining do not start with the contract settlements under World War II wage stabilization policies, nor with the first welfare agreement in the mid-20's. Trade union interest in welfare goals started with the beginning of unionism itself. There has always existed a strong desire among workers for security on the job *and* for security against the hazards of illness and death. The drive for welfare benefits in the middle of the twentieth century is a reassertion of one of labor's first goals.

The Union Tradition

The first benefit plans were indistinguishable from the first unions or local associations.[1] The societies of printers organized between 1794 and 1815 laid great stress on welfare purposes—"the beneficiary functions were regarded as equally important with trade regulation activities."[2] The Pennsylvania Society of Journeymen Cabinetmakers of Philadelphia was established as a benefit society in 1806; not until 1829 did it include settling disputes with employers among its purposes. The Philadelphia Typographical Society incorporated in 1810 as a benevolent society; it was 23 years later that it reorganized for the primary purpose of raising wages of journeymen printers. A student of this early period has concluded that, "American trade unionism owed its origin as much to the desire to associate for mutual insurance as to the desire to establish trade unions."[3]

There are evidences of this at a later date also: the Iron Molders' Union and the Brotherhood of Locomotive Firemen and Enginemen were originally formed as benevolent societies, in 1859 and 1873,

3

respectively. But by this time most workingmen's organizations were confronted with severe employment problems—job security in the long depression, wages and inflation in the Civil War boom, the emergence of big industry. Far-sighted union leaders were considering how to deal effectively with management under the new conditions, how to build effective bargaining units and national unions. By 1860 the prevailing view was that dues should be low to encourage membership, that local benefit plans were a hindrance and should be discouraged.

But the growth of mutual insurance companies after the Civil War caught labor's interest. Several national unions set up their own insurance associations, with membership limited to the members of the union. One of these, the Granite Cutters' Union, is usually cited as establishing the first national union sick benefit program, in 1877. The Iron Molders and the Printers also established their own insurance associations, but only in the railway brotherhoods did insurance associations develop into a permanent feature.

Mutual insurance and the unions' desire for stable organizations led, about 1880, to a new theory on the relation of the beneficiary and trade functions of a labor organization. For the first time it was argued that benefits were a direct aid to accomplishing trade purposes. Some older leaders continued to emphasize the danger of benefit plans to union functions, but the greater number of leaders who came into positions of authority after 1880 advocated the establishment of benefits. In 1895 the Barbers' Union organized a sick benefit program, as did the Tobacco Workers in 1896, and the Plumbers' Union in 1903.

Samuel Gompers was a vigorous promoter of the new theory. He held that benefit plans, whether or not they attracted members, undoubtedly retained them.[4] Past experience had shown that depression periods always brought wage cuts, defensive strikes, and unemployment. Workers would be more likely to continue to belong to the union and pay dues if failure to do so cancelled their equity in the union benefit program.[5] The panic of 1893–97 decimated the International Typographical Union and the Brotherhood of Carpenters but left the Cigar Makers virtually untouched. Adolph Strasser, the Cigar Makers' President, credited the union's highly developed system of benefits with maintaining membership and pulling the union through with only a slight reduction in wages.[6]

The International Ladies' Garment Workers' Union started its tuberculosis benefits and medical care plan also as mortar for union strength. One of the union's officers, Nathaniel Minkoff, has described the situation vividly:

In the early stages of the I.L.G.W.U., its membership was in a constant state of flux. The industry in all its branches was sharply seasonal. Shop strikes would break out on the eve of every season. The workers would obtain some wage increases here and there, only to see them disappear several weeks later. There was nothing to bind the garment worker to his union. He would join and drop out at frequent intervals. The turnover was tremendous. With the introduction of the benefit system, conditions changed radically. Today the person who joins the I.L.G.W.U. has every good reason to maintain his membership even in slack periods. He no longer drops his membership at the end of the busy season as he did formerly, because today his membership is a form of security against illness, unemployment, accident, and death. This makes for stability, organizational strength, and effectiveness on the industrial field and gives the union real capacity for expansion.[7]

By the 1930's the pendulum was swinging back again. Matthew Woll, a vice president of the AF of L, warned that "benefit systems are a constant source of trouble—all the troubles that beset unscientific institutions. Their assessments must be raised constantly to meet rising wages, and increases of assessments are always resented."[8] Dan Tobin warned his Teamsters' locals to save money and keep away from benefit plans: "Remember, there are lean days ahead of us."[9] These AF of L leaders were dubious and those who formed the CIO completely eschewed any payments that might discourage new membership, including union dues on occasion. There are no recorded instances where a CIO union inaugurated an intra-union benefit program.[10]

In retrospect, we see a pulsating response in union policy, an alternating emphasis between welfare and trade goals. After the workingmen's benevolent societies, there was a de-emphasis during the building of national unions, followed in turn by the American Federation of Labor's theory that benefit plans had organizational value, especially in recession times. But welfare matters were later subordinated, and particularly by the Congress of Industrial Organizations. In the search for the greatest appeal to workers, the discussion has shifted back and forth between low dues as incentives to join and benefit systems through higher dues as incentives to stay, between wage and job security on the one hand and security against the expenses of illness and death on the other. One of the implications of this pattern is that so long as union dues were the primary source of financing welfare benefits there would be a conflict between welfare and employment objectives. Obviously a new way of financing welfare benefits would have to be found. This is a major reason for the beginning of welfare bargaining in the 1940's.

This union interest in welfare matters is most apparent in the history of benefit and sickness plans. These plans simply replaced wage loss, but some of them also provided medical care. Union interest in this area was undoubtedly stimulated by the experience of the fraternal societies, many of which had health prepayment plans where, for a dollar a year, members could have the service of a physician (a system known among doctors as "lodge practice").

Workers also got medical care through their employee associations or through their unions. The International Typographical Union established a Printers' Home for sick and aged printers in Colorado Springs, Colorado, in 1892. Locals of the United Mine Workers sponsored prepayment hospital plans in some areas. The Ladies' Garment Workers opened its medical clinic in New York City in 1913 to provide entrance examinations for new members and to aid in administering sick benefits; it was later expanded to provide diagnostic and treatment services. The Mine, Mill and Smelter Workers owned a hospital in Silverton, Colorado, to which members contributed monthly dues for medical, surgical, and hospital care for illness or disability whether incurred in the mines or not.

Pierce Williams in a study done in 1932 reported that at that time medical and hospital services were being provided by the union of letter carriers in New York, by public utility workers in Milwaukee, by engraving and printing trades in Washington, D.C., and by local unions in Los Angeles.[11] The Milwaukee program provided periodic health examinations and dental services as well as medical and surgical services for members and their dependent families. The letter carriers' plan in New York covered hospitalization in any one of five hospitals, and the union employed eight physicians. In a recent survey of the history of prepayment, Jerome Schwartz says that, while not numerous, these early plans "were experiments which called for initiative and imagination, and they represented attempts by individuals with little education and limited income to provide medical care for themselves and their dependents by using the prepayment principle."[12]

The Management Tradition

Company-sponsored medical care plans in isolated areas and hazardous occupations such as lumbering, mining, and railroads came into operation after the Civil War, and some then established still survive. The lack of badly needed medical care suggested prepayment as a way of attracting doctors and nurses, and providing medical facilities. Sometimes the employer took the whole financial responsibility but usually there was some deduction from the employees' wages; the employer may have provided a hospital facility or contracted with doctors who established a proprietary hospital that otherwise would never have entered the remote areas.[13]

The oldest major industrial medical care prepayment program still in existence is that which the Southern Pacific Railroad Company started in 1868. Other early railroad programs still in operation are the Missouri-Pacific Hospital Association, established in 1872, and the Northern Pacific Beneficial Association, begun in 1882. In 1887, the Homestake Mining Company of Lead, South Dakota, established a company-financed medical department with full-time staff to provide complete medical service to its employees and their families. In 1897, at Roanoke Rapids, North Carolina, a medical fund for employees of Patterson Mills and Rosemary Manufacturing Company was established under joint employer-employee sponsorship. Other instances of prepaid, jointly sponsored medical service plans were the health department of the Tennessee Coal, Iron and Railroad Company, at Birmingham, Alabama, begun in 1913, and the Stanacola Employees' Medical and Hospital Association, Inc., organized by the Standard Oil Company of Louisiana in 1924. How many employees participated in all these plans is not known, but it was estimated that in 1930 over a million workers were covered in railroads, mining, and lumbering.[14]

In these cases it was primarily the absence of local facilities that suggested prepayment as a way of attracting doctors and nurses and building hospitals. It was for the same reasons that Henry Kaiser during World War II built a medical program for the thousands of employees in his mushrooming California shipyards. Not all the early plans achieved the same standards of quality attained in the Kaiser hospitals, and some were very poor indeed.

It is difficult today to recapture a feeling for the period of rapid growth in manufacturing that preceded World War I. The social consequences of industrialization were little appreciated until the strident voice of Upton Sinclair described *The Jungle* in which packing house employees worked. The horror and danger of industrial working conditions finally became a major subject of indignation. Workmen's compensation laws were enacted ostensibly to promote safety and to assure more speedy justice. Industrial toxicology became an important study, and considerable interest developed in programs of government health insurance.[15] During World War I it was touch and go in some states whether the private or governmental route would be taken, but in the end health insurance was left for private development.

To these social problems and public concerns, the business community responded with new welfare plans for their employees. Public-spirited business leaders actively promoted death benefit plans, disability pay programs, and industrial medical care. Montgomery Ward in 1911 bought the first group life insurance contract for its employees. Sometimes employers helped "bail out" employee mutual benefit associations (which were rarely organized on actuarial principles) either by offers of clerical assistance or by some assumption of the risk; there was seldom any significant financial contribution and workers, suspicious of management's objectives, frequently refrained from joining such associations. But with the wartime growth in unionism, employers moved in vigorously to sponsor and finance employee benefit plans fully. These plans were "good business":

They relieved the employer of the solicitations for aid for the destitute dependents of deceased employees; also, it was not necessary for the employees to "pass the hat" among themselves during working hours for the same purpose; the program assisted in attracting better employees and in retaining those already employed, employee morale was enhanced, job relations improved and the public relations of some firms favorably affected.[16]

This view, which flowered in the 1920's and persists in vestigial form even now, has been called "welfare capitalism."

Both unions and management pursuing their economic objectives had to give much thought to workers' health and welfare needs; and in the climate of the 1930's, when unionism nearly foundered only to return with a new strength that panicked the business community, the battles over wages and work rules frequently spilled over into contests for control of employee benefit plans. When company unions were declared illegal, employee benefit associations substituted nicely with their health, welfare, and recreational facilities which the employees were unwilling to surrender.[17] This gave CIO organizers trouble, because they had decided not to emphasize such functions: they sometimes had to promise to continue welfare features, where the employees were accustomed to them, in addition to higher wages and shorter hours.[18] Later the unions raised questions about the employee benefit plans. A few plans persist today in unaltered form, but most of them had to be absorbed into collective bargaining before the union could feel that it was not challenged from within.[19] The Auto Workers, for example, vigorously opposed employee benefit plans, on the grounds that benefits could be raised most effectively through collective bargaining and that employer domination of employee benefit plans hampered the union as a spokesman for the employees. For the companies, however, to have to bargain on welfare and employee benefit plans was to relinquish a fountainhead of employee loyalty. For neither side was the issue primarily one of who paid for the benefits, company or employee; it was a question of who was to control the plan's administration. The dispute was over "management prerogative."

Welfare Bargaining Emerges

Most accounts of the origins of health and welfare bargaining emphasize the role played by World War II wage stabilization policies, which stimulated a search for non-wage forms of remuneration. In addition, the postwar business prosperity, excess profits taxes, and tax exemptions for health and welfare contributions, which reduced the additional cost of insurance and pension programs, created a favorable climate for union demands. These factors provided the opportunity, but the motivations for postwar welfare bargaining are best seen in the confluence of the two separate traditions described above: the long history of union welfare activity, and management-sponsored employee benefit and medical care programs.

The history of health and welfare plans before World War II shows very little collective bargaining on these questions;[20] it was either exclusive management or exclusive union control, and the merging of interests was a matter of much travail.

It should first be made clear how Congress, perhaps not entirely with intention, gave the green light to welfare bargaining. Whether or not management had to bargain on welfare matters had never been settled under the Wagner Act, although the Act's requirement that management bargain on "wages and conditions of employment" was probably intended by Senator Wagner to be broadly interpreted. The battles over employee benefit and pension plans had, in a number of cases, ended up in the courts on the issue of whether they were management prerogative or "wages and conditions of employment." The Inland Steel Case in 1948 decided that pensions were within the latter category and the issue was settled in favor of the union. While these cases were still in the courts, the issue was also before the public eye. The 80th Congress had set about rewriting labor law. In fact, it was welfare bargaining as much as any other subject which produced the public fear and outrage that brought about the Taft-Hartley Act. Why then did Congress decide simply to repeat the ambiguous "wages and conditions of employment" of the Wagner Act? Why did Congress avoid a clear decision on such an important policy issue as that posed by welfare bargaining?

The attitude of Congress was a reaction to the wartime growth and the new-found confidence of unions. Prodded by the search for ways of offsetting the War Labor Board restriction on wage increases, and reasserting labor's historical interest in welfare goals, the CIO Convention in 1946 declared high priority for "pension plans, health insurance plans, group hospitalization, and the guaranteed minimum annual wage."[21] Union members were increasingly hard pressed by rising medical costs, for which insurance offered the only apparent protection, and the economic conditions were favorable to union demands. By 1948, ten unions, some AFL and some CIO, had negotiated health and welfare plans, even though the legal requirement of management to bargain had not been established.[22]

But pattern-setting companies in the heavy industries—steel, autos, rubber, and coal—presented a solid front of opposition to the new demands, and got substantial support in Congress.[23] John L. Lewis in 1946 had outraged the public with his demand for a welfare plan paid for by the operators and administered by the union. "It is not in the national interest," said a House Committee, "for union leaders to control these great, unregulated, untaxed funds derived from exactions upon the employers." It proposed to forbid "employers to conspire with unions to mulct employees, without their consent, of huge amounts that ought to go into the workers' wages." Welfare plans would be excluded from the list of subjects on which management must bargain, and no union could "compel any member to agree to contribute to, or participate in, any insurance or other benefit plan."[24]

These extreme views did not prevail in the Senate or in the Conference Committee compromise. Both Houses did agree that unions should never have sole authority to administer trusteed welfare funds to which employers contributed (this became Sec. 302 of the Taft-Hartley Act), but the Senate would not exclude insurance and pensions from mandatory bargaining. There was, nevertheless, some strong feeling in the Senate against welfare bargaining. The original bill introduced by Senator Joseph Ball, a Republican from Minnesota, had substituted "other working conditions" for "other conditions of employment," which some thought would have narrowed the scope of collective bargaining to exclude welfare plans. Along with Ball and Senator Harry Byrd of Virginia, Senator Robert Taft of Ohio had serious doubts about welfare bargaining:

. . . it is questionable how far we should go in the matter of private welfare funds. We have a general social security system. We have a separate fund for the railroad employees. There are a number of other special funds. . . . There should be a requirement that such funds fit into and supplement the ordinary social security system. The subject calls for long and involved study.[25]

The ensuing debate, however, indicated that Taft's margin of votes in the Senate for a new labor law was close. Limiting the area of mandatory bargaining to exclude welfare plans would run the risk of defeat in the Senate and consequently no legislation that year (1947). In the final bill that Taft reported to the Senate, the Wagner Act's "other conditions of employment" was restored. It was this language that appeared in the new Labor-Management Relations Act, better known as the Taft-Hartley Act.

This interpretation of Taft's strategy is an effort to answer the question of whether Congress intended to avoid the issue of mandatory welfare bargaining by simply passing the old wording along to the courts for interpretation, or to reaffirm the Wagner Act's apparent inclusion of welfare bargaining. The meaning of the Wagner Act language was not established until the Inland Steel Case of the following year and even lawyers among the congressmen might have had some difficulty predicting the outcome. But Senator Taft's doubts about welfare bargaining suggest that his decision was the purely strategic one of not raising another issue that could imperil the entire legislation. If the Wagner Act language meant that employers had to bargain on welfare issues, this price was not too great a compromise. At the same time, he and others would have had good reasons for thinking the court might have some difficulty in interpreting this language to permit welfare bargaining.

If so, they were wrong. The court unequivocally found that welfare bargaining was included in the "other conditions of employment" on which management had to negotiate.[26] The Inland Steel Case broke the dike and ended the long history of unilateral employer control of employee benefit plans. Management had lost the big issue, but proceeded to fight on the secondary issue of who should finance welfare benefits, or, in the words of the steel fact-finding board, whether "social insurance and pensions should be considered a part of normal business to take care of temporary and permanent depreciation in the human 'machine' much the same way as provision is made for depreciation and insurance of plant and machinery."[27] A six-week strike resulted. Within a few months after the settlement on November 11, 1949, the engine of the voluntary health insurance movement was under a full head of steam.[28]

To get close to the real character of health bargaining, it is important to understand that the major decisions about voluntary health and medical plans have been made in the context of different industries. In the next three chapters we will show how labor and management in the women's garment industry, in men's clothing, in coal, and in autos and steel have created new weapons for the old enemy of ill health, and how, even by 1950 when the big decade of health bargaining was just beginning, these industries had already furnished an arsenal of ideas.

2

HEALTH EXPERIMENTS IN THE NEEDLE TRADES

From needle trades unions, particularly the International Ladies' Garment Workers and the Amalgamated Clothing Workers, have come such inventions as the union medical care plan, the multi-employer welfare fund, the industry-wide welfare fund, and the union insurance company.

Pioneering in the Ladies' Garment Industry

The infamous sweatshops of the ladies' garment industry—or more technically, the "contract shops" where cloth was farmed out for assembling after it was cut to pattern in a central plant—were a product of the late nineteenth century. This form of economic organization created a jungle of hopeless competition, and it spread a blight over 80 per cent of the industry, grinding down wages and working conditions, producing overcrowding, ignorance, and poverty. Tuberculosis, rheumatism, and skin diseases from cloth dyes produced "galloping old age" for men in their thirties and forties.[1] With this shared misery as a bond, the garment workers set about to "take care of our own." Even before the ILGWU was formed in 1900, its predecessors, the International Cloakmakers' Union and the Gotham Knife Cutters' Association, urged their locals to establish sick benefit funds that paid from $3 to $7 a week for up to ten weeks. The Pressers established a Tuberculosis Benefit Fund in 1913 that provided, in exchange for a $1.00 a year contribution, $100 in cash or a sojourn in the country for ten weeks for a member who contracted tuberculosis. These plans and their successors, mutual benefit funds that sometimes included death payments to survivors, suffered a precarious existence, and many disappeared as a result of strikes and lockouts, lack of actuarial planning, and the rapid turnover in the industry.[2] However, some have survived to this day.[3] In 1938, the ILGWU established a death benefit fund paid by union dues which is still in operation. In general, these plans served both to cement the union in a highly seasonal industry that was difficult to organize and also to help workers caught in the occupational diseases of the sweatshop system. Health and welfare programs are a significant part of the stability, rationality, and humanity that unionism has brought to the industry.

Multi-employer Welfare Funds

The first multi-employer welfare fund in any industry originated when Children's Dress Local 91 proposed in 1938 that vacations be paid through a pooled fund to which employers would contribute a fraction of their payroll. Previously, many workers had lost vacation pay if they changed jobs or if the employer went out of business. The idea of employer-paid vacations had been accepted by many of the employers for six or eight years; the pooled fund was merely a good way to eliminate hardships and inequities. The next step was taken in 1942, when the Dress Joint Board in Philadelphia signed a contract providing for a single pooled fund from which not only vacation pay but also sickness, hospitalization, and other welfare benefits were to be disbursed to all workers. Multi-employer funds have also been established to provide retirement benefits and severance and supplemental unemployment benefits.

In 1966 there were 71 health and welfare funds (and, in addition, 55 retirement plans and several severance-unemployment benefit funds) which cover 98 per cent of the membership, located mostly in New York but with concentrations in Philadelphia, Boston, Chicago, St. Louis, Kansas City, Los Angeles, and San Francisco.[4] They range in size from the 22-member plan in a Seattle local to New York's giant Cloak and Dress funds, covering 34,000 and 45,000 members each. The union wants all employers to contribute from 3 to 5 per cent of payroll for health and welfare, although several locals have negotiated as much as 6.5 per cent contributions.[5] (Where retirement and severance-unemployment benefits have been negotiated, additional contributions are made to these funds.) Even the 3 per cent for health and welfare is sometimes difficult to negotiate, particularly in such areas as the Midwest and Southwest where there are great numbers of unorganized shops, and the union may be forced to settle for less. Because wages are often close to the federal minimum allowed, whenever the minimum is raised by Congress there are many employers who object that they should not have to increase their welfare contributions proportionately. At these times they seek concessions from the 3 per cent union standard.

The health and welfare plan is usually coterminous with the local or joint board contract. The International sets bargaining policies in a general way, but the negotiation and administration of big and little funds is decentralized, unlike the industry-wide funds in men's clothing, but very much like those in the hat and millinery and the fur and leather businesses. Administration proceeds through the union and management trustees who control the funds at the local union or joint board level.

The smaller welfare funds lead a precarious existence in slack times when employers want concessions in their contribution rate. More flexibility in contributions may be possible with consolidated funds that have a broader base and more reserves. Some consolidation has been achieved by reducing the 87 funds existing in the 1956 to the present 71. The ILGWU has been studying the possibility of merging many or all of its funds, but the variations in claims experience, resistance of employers to more union control, and the guarding of autonomy by large joint boards in the union will probably postpone for a long time any such unification.

Within the framework of this decentralized structure, the International does exert influence on the investment policies of the funds and provides regular auditing and statistical comparisons of experience and costs. The ILGWU prides itself on the scrupulousness and the efficiency of its financial operations.[6] Union funds are completely separated from welfare funds. Annual reports show the costs of administration as a per cent of total receipts average between 5 and 6 per cent for all funds, with fewer than ten funds running over 8 per cent.

Caution characterizes both reserve and investment policies. Most of the funds' reserves have reached two and a half times yearly benefit disbursements, but the union urges that reserves should be equal to three times the annual payments; with benefit costs going up, most funds have to establish an 85 per cent relationship between annual disbursements and annual contributions to maintain the desired reserve policy. In the investment of assets, the union has, until a few years ago, required all holdings to be government securities, but government-insured mortgage loans have been purchased in recent years, and since 1958 so have corporate bonds.[7] Some funds are invested in co-operative housing and union health centers. Of the invested assets in 1964, approximately 53 per cent was in government bonds, 20 per cent in insured mortgages, 16 per cent in corporate and other bonds, 10 per cent in ILGWU co-operative housing, and 1 per cent in ILGWU health centers.

The most significant feature of the ILGWU welfare funds lies in the fact that they are self-insured and that claims are administered from the union office. All benefits—vacation, medical, surgical, and hospital care, life insurance, disability and maternity benefits, and eye care—are paid directly from the funds without resort to outside insurance carriers. For verifying disability claims, the union health centers are frequently used; the center doctors either examine the claimant or screen the certification by other doctors. (A notable exception is the Dress Joint Board in New York, which, when it left the Union Health Center in 1955, turned over to employers and their carriers the administration of disability benefits.) In 1964, close to $50 million were paid out of 60 health and welfare funds through the union offices. Only 11 funds, mostly in Canada, are not administered through the union offices.

The union's desire to assume the headaches of claims administration is best understood as another case of building the union through membership services in order to achieve worker solidarity in a low-paying, seasonal industry where many workers are recent immigrants (now Puerto Ricans). Distribution of welfare benefits through the union office builds one more bond against the centrifugal forces of disorganization. Employers recognize the union's contribution to stability in the industry by allowing this practice, although they retain authority to review the nature and scope of benefits paid.

Is the union as an interested party capable of meeting the requirements of sound administration, and how can it avoid, for internal political reasons, giving more consideration to the claimant than to the merits of his application? Officials of the ILGWU's Welfare and Health Benefits Department point to the intimate knowledge of the membership held by the officers and sick benefit committees which makes them quite effective in dealing with malingering.[8] In general, the union has skillfully met the problem by educational methods: a denied claim can become an opportunity to explain more about qualifying requirements and limitations of the plan. One study reports that "pooling employer contributions on a local basis and administering the benefit provisions at the local level, has the advantage of impressing local officers that payment of unjustified claims would lead to insolvency, since unwarranted drains upon the fund would not be compensated by the contributions of employers in other localities."[9] In short, prudence is assured through the principle of placing responsibility for fund performance with the same people who administer claims.

Union Health Centers

The cloak and suitmakers' strike in 1910 had just been settled, in part by setting up a union-employer Joint Board of Sanitary Control to improve working conditions, when the country was shocked at the tragedy of 147 girls being burned to death in a locked dress shop. Following investigations of the Triangle Shirt Waist Company fire, a plan was proposed by the medical director of the Joint Board of Sanitary Control for improving the health of garment workers, and by 1913 a union-sponsored medical service program had been inaugurated. In 1917, the Union Health Center was incorporated and it is still in operation. At first the Center was jointly financed by employers and the union, but after a short time the ILGWU locals in New York assumed all financial responsibility. Until 1943, the Center was supported by contributions from union members and their locals. Since 1943, a large part of the Center's funds has come from employer contributions negotiated by the union.

During most of its life, the Health Center has served several purposes, with changing emphasis. Its most significant function is to furnish certain limited ambulant services. For example, diagnostic work is performed, including clinical examinations, consultations with specialists where necessary, X-rays, and such laboratory tests as may be required. The report of findings, however, is sent to the worker's physician for whatever treatment is required. In one respect, at least, the Health Center goes beyond this. Rehabilitation of union members with chronic diseases is an important objective, and there are special clinics for control and treatment of diabetes, allergies, rheumatism, heart conditions, and gastro-intestinal ailments. Emphasis is on the garment worker and the industrial ills associated with the industry. Complete medical services are not provided the member, nor is his family covered by the program. Members are not recruited for annual diagnostic exams in the New York Health Center as they are in ILGWU Health Centers elsewhere. Utilization of the services tends to be about 25 per cent, that is, about one in four of the covered members goes to the clinic during the year. The New York locals all use the Center, except the locals of the Dress Joint Board, which have entered other arrangements that provide a broader range of medical care.

Another function of the Health Center, the supervision of the medical aspects of the sick benefit plans, including verification of claims, has, since 1952, been delegated to the local unions. Only a small portion of sick-plan administration is now done at the Health Center.

An important original purpose of the Center has been revived. It examines candidates for membership in the union, particularly to detect tuberculosis, in order to safeguard the health of workers already employed. In 1955, the Center discovered a sudden and dangerous rise in tuberculosis and an increase in tropical diseases, especially in locals with a high percentage of Puerto Rican members, and it has been urging locals to revive the practice of pre-membership examinations. In this and other matters, the Health Center co-operates with the New York City Department of Health.

From its New York experiences, where the ILGWU learned that low-income workers are reluctant to spend money for medical care and particularly for preventive medicine, the union evolved a program of diagnostic health centers in other garment districts.[10] Thirteen full-time Health Centers on union-owned premises are located in Allentown, Boston, Chicago, Cleveland, Fall River, Kansas City, Los Angeles, Montreal, Newark, New York, Philadelphia, St. Louis, and Wilkes-Barre. Through special arrangements with hospital outpatient clinics or other organizations, health services are also being rendered ILGWU members in Baltimore, Dallas, Houston, Laredo, Minneapolis, San Antonio, and San Francisco. These services cover about 90 per cent of the membership. In addition, there are nine mobile units which travel to union shops and give a battery of diagnostic tests.

All of the Health Centers, with the exception of that in New York, employ the services of a local physician as a director, usually on a part-time basis. He in turn hires other local physicians on a part-time basis. Garment workers come to the clinic for diagnostic check-ups, usually once a year; if it is necessary to bring the members from nearby towns, special buses are chartered. Except in New York, Philadelphia, and St. Louis, local medical societies and the AMA do not allow the ILGWU to do any treatment at these Centers; all diagnoses and findings must be sent to the member's personal physician. A physician may refer a patient to the Center, if he belongs to the union, so that he can save the costs of expensive work-ups; but the personal physician must provide the therapy. The doctors are remunerated according to the length of time they put in at the Health Center each week.

In St. Louis, where the prestige of two fine medical schools dominates the medical community, the ILGWU has been able to extend its medical center into more than a mere diagnostic program.[11] Nearly all the doctors participating in the St. Louis Health Center are from the staff of the medical schools. They have shown great concern about the quality of treatment, perhaps, in part, because they do not have the general practitioner's doctrinaire views about "third parties" in medicine. The St. Louis Health Center has broadened its services to provide for therapy given union members in hospitals when they are referred there and treated by a doctor on the Health Center staff. The Health Center reimburses the doctor for his services at the hospital. The record of each patient is open to review by any doctor on the staff. Where such features are present there is a heightened sense of group responsibility and unnecessary surgery is less likely to occur.

In Kansas City, where the union tried to establish a Health Center on the St. Louis model, the union was notified a few days prior to the opening that the medical society was forbidding any but diagnostic practice and that if the union persisted in including in-hospital medical services on anything but an open-panel basis, the clinic would not open at all. The Center was opened and is operating on a purely diagnostic basis.

The mobile units, the most recent addition to the union's program of health service, were developed by Dr. James Bloom of Harrisburg, Pennsylvania, on the principle that where a union cannot build a health center to which the member is brought, a technical team should be trained and equipped to go to the members. The equipment is housed in a "healthmobile" at a total cost of $35,000 each. The technical team, traveling to plant gates with the healthmobile, performs all of the usual clinic procedures for diagnostic purposes on those workers who are willing, usually a high proportion of all workers. The tests include urinalysis, blood count, Wassermann test, eye screening, blood pressure, and weight; a medical history is taken. The results are reported to the office of the doctor in charge of the program, any abnormalities which may be uncovered are immediately classified, and the worker involved summoned to the office of the doctor for further study and examination. The full findings are then evaluated and a report transmitted to the patient's family physician.

Beyond Tradition

Some questions have been raised about the ILGWU Health Centers that have influenced their development and their usefulness as models for other unions. Dr. Richard Weinerman, for example, has bluntly concluded, "The earliest labor health center organized 40 years ago in the sweatshops of the garment industry, is not necessarily a good model for more recent union efforts—as far as its design of limited service, part-time staff, and exclusion of dependents is concerned."[12] His perspective here is the total family financial burden for medical care and the disciplined demands of modern medicine, requiring careful coordination between diagnosis and treatment, between specialists and "generalists," between union health efforts and community facilities. Such a total view of the problem finds the ILGWU policies narrowly oriented to only a portion of the health needs of its membership.

In appraising the union's contribution, we should not overlook some of the obstacles it has encountered, including the strictures of organized medicine. In 1948, the union's executive secretary told the American Medical Association, "Speaking to you frankly, I can say that if the Medical Societies of certain areas had been a little more cooperative and a little more alert and aware of changing concepts in this field, a greater number of ILG health centers could have been established."[13] Other unions have had similar experiences, as we shall see, but to some extent the modest goal of the ILGWU—to build diagnostic centers—has, by limiting the union's perspective, also limited the vigor of its stance. In the union there are some who want to make an accommodation with the medical profession on the latter's own terms. For example, Dr. Bloom, founder of the healthmobile program, has been quoted by the director of the union's Welfare and Health Benefits Department, in this vein:

. . . We do not feel that we can develop the type of organization that will be prepared to render an adequate and complete general medical service, nor do we believe that it would be wise even if it were possible. Let it not be forgotten that the patient-doctor relationship in smaller communities is rather sacred. For this relationship there is no substitute. A ready antagonism would greet any plan which would presume to threaten this set-up. From a practical consideration, too, it would be rather difficult if not impossible. There would be many occasions when medical care would be needed, maybe urgently needed, for acute illnesses. Local physicians would be reluctant to respond, if indeed they would respond at all, if our activities encroached upon their sovereignty.[14]

While it is true that the ILGWU cannot itself command the extensive resources required for a reform in medical economics, it has shown little inclination to work along with other unions and community organizations.[15]

A notable exception to the union's desire to "go it alone" is the New York Dress and Waistmaker Joint Board, which in 1955 shifted to a community-wide health program.[16] Employer contributions were raised from 4 to 5 per cent of the payroll, and the responsibility for payment of disability benefits was transferred to the employers, making available an additional $3,000,000 to finance a broad range of health and medical services. The result was a great extension of the amount and kind of hospital and medical services provided. Blue Cross was to provide hospitalization, and medical services were made available either through the Health Insurance Plan of Greater New York or Group Health Insurance, and later through United Medical Service (Blue Shield). Selection of one of these alternative programs was permitted to each union member. Thus, the Dress Joint Board not only abandoned the Union Health Center but entered an alternative choice arrangement, one of the more interesting experiments in group prepayment plans (see discussion of alternative choice plans in Chapter 14). Here we only note that by joining other community health innovations, the Dress Joint Board has challenged a forty-year tradition, and by so doing has greatly extended the range of health protection for its members.

Hillman's Legacy

The Amalgamated Clothing Workers has contributed two ideas in health and welfare—the industry-wide welfare fund and the union-controlled insurance company. The first of these has been widely adopted in other industries, but the Amalgamated's two insurance companies have not been imitated. In recent years the Amalgamated has developed medical service plans in some urban centers.

Industry-wide Plans

The core of the Amalgamated has always been the men's and boys' clothing industry, much of which is in New York and Chicago. Sidney Hillman began his union career at Hart, Schaffner and Marx in Chicago, and he negotiated with the company's president, Meyer Kestnbaum, the first employee benefit fund in the industry.[17] This plan, established in 1923, provided unemployment benefits from employer contributions of 2 per cent of wages and employee contributions of 1.5 per cent. Later, the fund was extended to Rochester and New York City but was abolished in those cities in 1939, after the enactment of unemployment insurance.

Instead of abolishing the program in Chicago, however, the union took the lead in converting the fund to provide weekly disability and death benefits. This fund, known as the Amalgamated Social Benefit Association, now provides life and health insurance for all Amalgamated members in the Chicago area, regardless of the kind of industry in which they are employed.

A second fund was from the outset an industry-wide plan. In 1942, the Amalgamated negotiated 2 per cent of payroll from the Clothing Manufacturers' Association (covering all men's and boys' clothing workers under contract everywhere except in Chicago). This is called the Amalgamated Insurance Fund and is the largest of the thirteen funds now in existence. Benefits were improved in 1952 with the negotiation of an additional 1 per cent of the payroll. In addition to life insurance and weekly disability payments, both the Chicago and the national funds provide hospitalization and surgical coverage for union members and for their dependents. The Amalgamated Insurance Fund has also provided, since 1945, retirement and disability benefits.

This pattern of industry-wide, centrally controlled welfare funds has been extended to other industries and trades organized by the Amalgamated: cotton and garment, neckwear, laundry, washable clothing and sportswear, retail, cleaners and dyers, and journeymen tailors. Each of these groups has a separate fund.

The industry-wide funds facilitate coverage of union members when they move from job to job and from city to city. Furthermore, there are reciprocity arrangements between the funds so that they can provide continuous coverage even when workers move from one industry to another.

Union Insurance Companies

In 1943, the Amalgamated Life Insurance Company was licensed to do business in New York. It originated when the union and employer trustees of the newly formed Amalgamated Insurance Fund described above asked insurance companies to bid for the privilege of underwriting the benefits. There was no bid that was considered satisfactory, and it was decided to organize an insurance company whose stock would be entirely owned by the Amalgamated Insurance Fund.

It was at this point that an administrative structure developed that is unique among multi-employer welfare plans. The employer trustees of the Amalgamated Insurance Fund were unwilling to assume the financial responsibility of such an insurance company, and as a result the board of trustees of the fund reorganized to include only union representatives. The employers were to participate as a top-level advisory committee, operating within the fund, with the power to veto any decision of the board of trustees concerning three matters: any increase or change in benefits; investment of funds in anything other than United States Government securities; any unusual expenses. Under this arrangement the employers considered that they held essential controls without the full financial responsibility of trusteeship. The union was certain of the success of the insurance company and, further to guarantee its solvency, passed a resolution agreeing to buy the stock of the insurance company at face value at any time that the trustees and the advisory committee decided to dispose of it.

The Amalgamated Life Insurance Company is non-profit and limited by its charter to underwriting union funds. It now provides insurance for all the union welfare funds except the Chicago Amalgamated Social Benefit Association. But there the pattern is repeated and that fund owns the Amalgamated Life and Health Insurance Company of Illinois, which underwrites the benefits.

Except for their non-profit character, the union's insurance companies are in all other respects business-like operations; the union leaders want good administration. The main concern of the trustees of the insurance companies is low costs and rigorous financial accountability. They do not carry on a "crusade" against the commercial insurance business, although it was dissatisfaction with that business that prompted establishment of the Amalgamated Life Insurance Company. The union does not publicize details of its insurance activities, keeping its experience pretty much to itself for its own welfare bargaining purposes.

From the beginning it was an objective to separate insurance clearly from union administration. The relationship of the insurance company to the union is seen in this report of an interview with James J. Shoaff, the manager of the insurance company and acting director of the fund:

" . . . His attitude toward the Amalgamated and unions in general was sympathetic, but not markedly so. He obviously regarded himself as an independent executive, hired by the trustees to administer an insurance program without fear or favor. It was clear that he did not regard himself as a member of the union's staff, nor did he wish to be so regarded. . . ."[18]

Except for the filing of sick benefit claims, where the local must verify the employee's absence before forwarding the claim to the insurance company, the claimant deals directly with the insurance company on all matters, including the direct submission of claims for hospitalization and medical care benefits. To the union member, the union insurance company is just as distant and impersonal as any commercial carrier.[19] This method of handling claims contrasts sharply with that in the International Ladies' Garment Workers' Union, because the different character of the industry has never compelled the Amalgamated to regard its welfare program as day-to-day mortar for union organization.

The advantage of a union insurance company is that all cost information about the union's welfare program is readily available. The Amalgamated had "explicit financing"—direct knowledge of benefit costs—even before some unions realized that getting this information was going to be a problem. In addition, there are the savings that go with non-profit underwriting and with eliminating the "middleman." This arrangement also makes it easier to invest accumulated health and welfare funds in socially useful activities, such as workers' housing and medical care centers, which the union has done.

The big disadvantage is that a union insurance company can only write cash indemnity health insurance, with all the limitations inherent in this method of buying medical care—inflationary impact, absence of cost and quality controls, and significant but unknown out-of-pocket expenses for the members. The union insurance company precludes the use of limited-service (e.g., Blue Cross) or direct-service programs. A conflict of interest can develop between using the insurance company and buying the best medical care.

New Medical Centers

Soon after World War II, considerable interest developed in the major men's clothing centers for union-sponsored medical care programs. The shortcomings of the union insurance company's policies were too apparent. In 1950, the union's research department estimated that the average claimant received in insurance benefits only 45 per cent of his total hospital expenses and only 30 per cent of his surgical costs; furthermore, there was no provision for medical care in the home or doctor's office, for dentistry, for pre- and post-natal care, or for innoculations.[20] In 1951, a Sidney Hillman Health Center was opened in New York, and another center of the same name opened in Philadelphia. In Chicago in 1955, the Joint Board there established a health center. In 1954, the Amalgamated Laundry Workers' Health Center was established in New York City; Local 169 Amalgamated Washable Clothing, Sportswear, and Novelty Workers has since joined and so has the New York Joint Board of Neckwear Workers. Members of Local 169 who are outside New York City proper are serviced by a mobile medical unit. In eastern Pennsylvania, members can obtain diagnostic examinations paid for by the Local 119 Health Fund of the Male Apparel Industry. About 110,000 members are covered in all these direct-service programs.[21]

The Sidney Hillman Health Centers

The New York and Philadelphia Centers attracted much interest when they were established.[22] Although they belonged to the pattern of health centers established exclusively for union members in one industry, they were also a major reorganization of health care facilities, going far beyond diagnostic care. In part to symbolize complete departure from "clinics," the stereotype of free care for the indigent, the Philadelphia Center was built as a spectacular, ultra-modern brick building with semi-private waiting rooms outside each physician's office. A large staff of general practitioners and a wide range of specialists, all of whom are on a part-time basis, provide diagnostic, therapeutic, and preventive services for ambulatory patients. Hospitalization and surgical insurance are provided separately through negotiated health insurance.

These Centers have made some major contributions to union thinking about prepaid group practice, and these will be noted in subsequent chapters. For example, there was an early recognition here that health is a family affair. Since 1953, wives have been allowed to use the New York Center for the same $10.00 annual fee as union members; and in Philadelphia, about the same time, the union negotiated Health Center services for wives and dependent husbands. From this beginning, some other unions have negotiated full medical benefit coverage for all dependents.

One significant limitation in the Sidney Hillman Health Centers is that there are no services provided for the patient in his home. This accounts in part for the fact that medical societies, while not pleased, at least tolerated these ventures in "third-party medicine." The exclusion of home visits builds in a discontinuity of care which obviously affects its quality. However, Amalgamated members are entitled to technical and diagnostic services from the Center on the request of their "outside" or non-staff physician, and the Center makes great efforts to work harmoniously with these doctors.

Utilization is not high in either Center by the standards of comprehensive direct-service plans, and while there are insufficient data available for an analysis of this, it is probably due in part to the absence of home care as part of the coverage.

There are problems inherent in the administration of medical centers with part-time staff appointments, as we will see in Chapters 13 and 14. Although the use of part-time staff is a limitation of the Amalgamated Centers, their significance lies in the effort they have made to cope with the problems of poor quality that beset even the best indemnity or compensation prepayment programs. The project is geared to bring the most advanced techniques of medicine to bear in a way that best serves the workers. In such a setting, the principles of good care can be developed with responsibility resting on both the patient and the medical staff. The patient is encouraged to select a general practitioner who acts as his personal physician, outlines whatever diagnostic work-up may be needed, and watches the progress of treatment. The specialists are consulted as needed, and their work co-ordinated by the personal physician. Referrals for surgery or hospitalization are subject to review of the Medical Director or Clinic Chief. The staff are urged to treat patients not as humble recipients of free care, but as members to whom the Center belongs and whom the staff has been engaged to serve.

The New York Sidney Hillman Center received a federal grant in 1961 for the rehabilitation of physically disabled and sick workers. It was found, however, that when workers had problems of mental health, treatment of their physical ailments was not enough. Grants of $500,000 from the National Institute of Mental Health and $150,000 from the Vocational Rehabilitation Administration were made in June, 1964, to further this effort by establishing the union as a source of aid in coping with mental health problems; developing methods to encourage the union member and his family to use mental health services for "average" as well as for severe problems, and new ways of providing such services; experimenting with techniques for keeping a worker with emotional problems on the job or restoring him to his job; and testing new ways of working with existing community mental health agencies.[23]

Anyone looking for answers to the health problems of industrial workers must study the contributions of the needle trades, which were already substantial even before most unions first started health bargaining.

By identifying with both the job problems and the health problems of their members, these unions played a significant role in developing health and welfare funds, both the decentralized type in the ladies' garment industry, and the industry-wide fund in different segments of the men's clothing industry. The ILGWU preferred a strong role in administering these funds within sight of the membership, whereas the Amalgamated established non-profit insurance companies for underwriting benefits. Despite these differences in "closeness" to the membership, both unions show a strong family sense of taking care of their own.

The ILGWU Health Centers were conceived before a public health service had assumed a policing role in control of contagious diseases, and even today the union Health Centers are doing much to educate garment workers in an area that the medical profession has generally neglected—the practice of preventive medicine. These programs will continue not only because they weigh heavily in the tradition of the unions but also because they fall within the limits of what a small capital industry of poorly paid workers can provide.

The needle trades unions, however, are responding to new concepts of financing and providing medical services. Where their membership is concentrated in urban centers, both the ILGWU and Amalgamated Health Centers have gone far beyond detection and diagnosis. Health Centers such as those of the ILGWU in St. Louis and Philadelphia, and those of the Amalgamated in New York, Philadelphia, and Chicago, are important experiments.

The tradition of caring for their own members has given needle trades unions both the vision and the motive for their considerable accomplishments. It is noteworthy that only the New York Dress Joint Board of the ILGWU has sensed the potentialities for better health care by joining community-wide efforts to extend medical care. In the future, will needle trades unions and employers work to provide more medical care facilities just for garment and clothing workers? Or will they decide that they should work for the reform and reorganization of community-wide health services? Other unions, too, are trying to answer this question.

3

MINERS AND THEIR POWERFUL FUND

Miners have always looked primarily to their own meager resources for help in crisis. The earliest welfare plan was no plan at all: in the isolated mining communities where the company owned "everything in town except the railroad and God,"[1] assistance came from collections taken up among the miners to help a stricken family with burial costs. Later on, this sort of informal aid was systematized through death benefit funds supported by dues and assessments, usually on a local basis, though in 1916 the United Mine Workers made a constitutional provision for benefit funds.[2] In Harrisburg, Illinois, the miners got tired of the high cost of burials and started their own funeral home, and soon could report that it had "conducted 87 funerals at a saving of approximately $2,000."[3] Self-help characterized the meeting of medical costs also. At first it was "pass the hat"; the union sometimes contributed when money was available. The District 12 ledger for 1903, for example, shows an entry: "St. John's Hospital for James Buchanan and Peter Zerovich . . . $12.15";[4] and similar entries are found at later dates and for other districts. This method of meeting the costs of injury and illness was recognized as unsatisfactory, however, depending as it did on the solvency of the union. In some areas contracts were made with local hospitals, and in 1915 a miner's wife in Iowa described what may well be one of the first prepayment plans:

We have a very nice little hospital here in Albia for the benefit of the miners. It only costs us a small sum of 50¢ a month and when we are paying that we always have a place to go in time of need of medical and surgical care. . . . Now this little hospital at the sum of 50¢ a month is there for all the miners families, mothers, wives, sons and daughters, all are one. . . .[5]

29

In a few places the union owned a hospital and operated it as a co-operative venture.[6] The only other resource for medical care was the "check-off" doctor, hired by the coal company but charged to the workers through deductions from their wages.[7] These doctors made no regular examinations, and the medicine they practiced was sometimes gruesome: there was one man who coated his scarlet fever patients "with axle grease from head to foot to keep the germs sealed up and eliminate quarantining."[8]

Today, the miners still uphold the tradition of caring for their own, but they manage it through a national Welfare and Retirement Fund financed from the sale of the coal they produce. The fund is the country's biggest private buyer of medical services (second only to the federal government), spending around fifty million dollars a year ($52,836,432 in 1966).[9] The fund uses no insurance middlemen since these are not in the miners' tradition of self-help and distrust of outsiders. The fund not only buys medical care directly, but it insists on good medicine and pays huge amounts in rehabilitation cases. To all objections on the scope and cost to the fund, and to pleas for prudence, cost accounting, and the niceties of actuarial method, Lewis' attitude in the early years of the fund was probably one he expressed several years later: "Would you put a price on the value to you of your own life?"[10]

The new era of welfare bargaining was born in the strife and outrage of this pension and medical care revolution in the coal fields. The UMW's determination agitated the United States government, the general public, the officials of organized medicine, and the miners themselves, not to mention the operators. The rest of labor has never quite decided to what extent it should follow, or shun, the miners' approach. But in any case, there was to be much that could be learned from them.

The Launching of "Private Social Security"

The United Mine Workers is an old union. Why did it take so long for the central administration of an international union whose members worked in continual danger to develop a health and welfare program? The answer probably lies in the uphill fight the union has had for its very existence. As we have seen, the rank-and-file were at work on their welfare and medical care problems, but they were not satisfied with the results. Time and again they expressed the desire that the international union help out through some overall program, but the union leadership was beset and harassed by the most fundamental organizational and economic problems and preferred to emphasize the local traditions. The union problems in coal were not of a seasonal nature, as they were in the ladies' garment industry, where medical benefits were seen as an important aid to organization. In 1916, the union leadership did show concern with the wide variation in plans to cope with old age that existed in the districts, and proposed a union-wide retirement system with permanent and total disability benefits.[11] The subject was under consideration for several years but because of the high cost of living and the total paralysis of industry following World War I, it was postponed—for twenty-six years.

From 1918 to 1945, Lewis showed little interest in welfare plans. Survival of the union itself was in question until the mid-'30's. The union had been unable to organize the southern coal fields, and in 1928 faced a showdown with the organized portion of the industry. The failure of the strike at that time and the return of the bituminous coal industry to cut-throat competition and wage-cutting almost spelled the end of the United Mine Workers. With the resurgence of unionism in the '30's and Lewis' leadership of the CIO, welfare considerations were ignored because they were regarded as an impediment to organizing. In mass production industries, Lewis urged low dues to attract industrial workers, and would have none of the old intra-union welfare programs. But it is interesting to note that in the 1938 and 1944 conventions of the United Mine Workers, a number of resolutions were presented concerning welfare and retirement. Some of these resolutions suggested that the union establish a system of retirement or insurance to be supported by assessments on the total membership. However, while the Resolutions Committee approved a resolution suggesting federal or state legislative action, it rejected, probably in accord with Lewis' wishes, all proposals for union action on pensions or welfare programs. This recurrent interest in welfare and retirement in the ranks, a kind of persistent feeling that unionism is a broad way of life which extends the hand of brotherhood in sickness and in tragedy as well as on the job, is a significant phenomenon in trade unionism. A revival of union interest in welfare was due to come when CIO leaders felt they were on a more secure footing.

In addition to the local and district efforts, there was only workmen's compensation to help fill the need. It is doubtful that Lewis ever had much interest in social insurance. Basically, he was conservative in his social outlook and even in the New Deal period he was a Republican on vacation, but the country and the miners had been watching this first of the social security programs and it left much to be desired. Had it been more successful, there would have been less pressure among the miners for a union-wide health and welfare program. "There is not a single coal mining state," said Lewis, "that provides compensation payments adequate to maintain a widowed family or fairly compensate the injured. Inefficient compensation laws have aided in the perpetuation of so-called company doctors' systems, a scourge foisted upon mine workers representing well over half of the total annual production of coal. . . ."[12] If Lewis ever had any hopes for the federal social security program, they were dispelled by 1945: "Let me make no suggestions about social security as such, except that it is totally inadequate to meet the problems of an incapacitated man in industry."[13] The coal industry rather than the government, he said, should take over the problems of welfare and retirement and "eliminate the necessity for government to build up huge, inefficient and costly administrative bureaus to try to do the task in a less efficient way."[14]

The year 1945 marks the end of Lewis' long neglect of miners' health and welfare problems. The timing was related to four factors: with his repudiation of Roosevelt, Lewis had returned to the ranks of those scornful of the welfare role of government; union leaders were interested in the possibilities opened up by the health and welfare fringe benefits allowed by the War Labor Board; rank-and-file pressures repressed in the '30's and increased by the disillusionment with workmen's compensation could not be ignored indefinitely; and the union at last had a firm footing in the economy. With his genius for organization, Lewis saw a dramatic role for himself and his union as implementers of a new approach which has come to be called "private social security." So, in 1945, he demanded of the coal operators that they finance a health and welfare plan.

Strategy in Bargaining and Administration

The Events of 1945–1952

The 1945 negotiations reached no agreement on welfare and retirement but the union's proposal was put forth again in 1946. Following a complete deadlock on May 21, 1946, and several weeks of strikes and diminishing coal stocks, the government seized the mines under authority of the War Labor Disputes Act. Secretary of Interior Julius A. Krug and Lewis signed an agreement, Item 4 of which established a health and welfare program, including a welfare and retirement fund, a medical and hospital fund, and provisions for co-ordination of these two funds. Also included were provisions for a mine safety program and a survey of medical and sanitary conditions in coal mining areas, to be conducted under the direction of Admiral Joel T. Boone. The funds were to be supported by a five-cent royalty for each ton of coal and administered by a union trustee, an industry trustee, and a neutral trustee.[15]

This agreement between the Krug mine administration and the UMW was an uneasy one, characterized by strikes and court action against Lewis and the UMW. During this period the fund was inoperative, largely because the government as administrator of the coal mines and the union did not agree on a neutral trustee. Shortly after the Centralia mine explosion on March 25, 1947, in which 111 miners lost their lives, the third trustee, Thomas E. Murray, was named. The first act of the three trustees (Captain A.T. Collisson, administrator of the mines for the government, Lewis, and Murray) was to authorize death benefits of $1,000 to the survivors of the miners who had died in that disaster.

When the War Labor Disputes Act expired on June 30, 1947, the mines were returned to the operators, who entered into an agreement with the union approving the welfare fund and increasing the royalty payments to ten cents a ton. Ezra Van Horn became trustee for the operators.

Up to this time all benefit expenditures of the fund had been limited to the payment of death benefits and distress benefits for relief and disaster cases. Payment of pensions had not been initiated because the trustees were unable to agree on the salient features of a pension program, the chief issue being whether the pension plan should be funded or operated on a pay-as-you-go basis. On January 17, 1948, Murray resigned as the neutral trustee. On March 15, 1948, the miners again stopped work, charging that refusal by the operator's trustee to activate the pension plan was a refusal to honor the agreement.

The failure of mediators' efforts to end the work stoppage led President Truman to invoke the Taft Hartley Act, and on April 13 he ordered the Attorney General to seek an injunction against Lewis and the UMW. U.S. District Judge T. Alan Goldsborough issued an order restraining the strike and scheduled a hearing directing Lewis and the UMW to show why they should not be held in contempt because of the miners' refusal to return to work. A few days later Goldsborough found the union and Lewis guilty of civil and criminal contempt of court and fined them heavily. Meanwhile Lewis and the operators had agreed on Senator H. Styles Bridges, a Republican from New Hampshire, as neutral trustee and the miners had returned to work.

The trustees had agreed on pensions of $100 a month to men who were at least sixty-two years old, who had twenty years service in the industry, and who had retired after May 29, 1946, the date of the Lewis-Krug Agreement. The actual payment of pensions was held up because of various suits which had been filed by Van Horn.

In the 1948 wage settlement, the royalty payments were raised to twenty cents per ton and in September, 1948, the fund issued its first pension check. At about the same time, the medical program began operation. Dr. R. R. Sayers, formerly head of the Bureau of Mines and previously of the United States Public Health Service, had been appointed Chairman of the Medical Advisory Board for the fund in July, 1947. The trustees asked the Board to study the types and standards of medical and hospital service to be furnished to miners in their communities, to suggest policies for physical rehabilitation, and to develop plans for carrying out the recommendations in Admiral Boone's medical survey of the industry. Miss Josephine Roche was appointed director of the fund in 1948, and Dr. Warren F. Draper was appointed Executive Medical Officer of the Medical Health and Hospitalization Service of the fund in September, 1948. In the beginning, the medical program consisted of hospital care and physician's service in the hospital, office, or home for miners who had been disabled for six months or more and for their families; hospital and in-hospital medical care for working miners and their dependents; and a program of public health and preventive medicine. It was decided that the fund itself should administer the medical benefits.

When the contract expired on June 30, 1949, no agreement had been reached. The miners slowed down to a three-day week; then the operators stopped their royalty payments. In protest against non-payment of royalties, the miners stopped work altogether. Finally an agreement was reached in March, 1950, which, in addition to a wage increase, raised the royalty for the welfare fund to thirty cents a ton. This agreement provided that Lewis would be chairman of the trustees, that Miss Josephine Roche, the Fund Director, would be the neutral trustee, and that the operator trustee would be Charles Owen. Pension payments were resumed on June 1 and hospitalization and medical service became available on July 1, but were limited thereafter to hospital care and physician's services *in the hospital* for both disabled and working miners. On October 1, 1952, the bituminous coal wage agreement of 1950 was amended by raising the royalty to forty cents a ton.

Interpretation of UMW Strategy

Some interpretation of the preceding events will throw light on welfare bargaining and administration, and show that Lewis' strategy was more rational than was thought at the time.

An experienced organizer once said that bargaining is 10 per cent education of the employer and 90 per cent education of the workers. To achieve its goal of shifting welfare costs to the industry, the UMW leadership had first a tremendous job of proving, to the miners themselves, to the employers, and to the public, the need for a complete revolution in the traditional ways of providing medical, old age, and survivor care.

The Lewis-Krug Agreement stipulated a survey of medical conditions in mining communities. After studying 260 representative mines and mining communities, the Boone Commission concluded their report with these telling criticisms:

. . . at the majority of the mines . . . dispensaries and offices range from adequate to very poor; practitioners are overburdened and there are evident tendencies in a number of places to give less consideration to the quality of medical care than to profits. . . . Physicians were not selected primarily on the basis of professional qualifications and the character of facilities and services that were offered, but on the basis of personal friendships, financial tie-ups, social viewpoints, and other non-medical considerations. . . . Several instances were noted where poorly qualified physicians or others not appropriately licensed are receiving the payroll deductions for medical care. . . .

And on hospital care:

It is estimated that less than 20 per cent of the mines are served by hospitals characteristic of those in metropolitan centers, such as Pittsburgh or St. Louis.

. . . The evidence is convincing that three-fourths of the hospitals are inadequate with regard to one or more of the following: surgical rooms, delivery rooms and nurseries, clinical laboratories, and X-ray facilities. . . .

As for the rehabilitation of thousands of miners with lost limbs or broken backs, the Commission concluded that there was "not any program at all for rehabilitating the disabled within the bituminous coal industry."[16] To make any improvement at all it would be necessary completely to reorganize the medical and hospital practices in the coal fields.

A major undertaking of this sort was bound to be costly. The operators would have to be educated in a series of steps to their responsibility and the miners would have to develop a sustained concern and willingness to strike and sacrifice.

Education, in order to be effective, needs drama as well as facts and logic, and here Lewis moved with the confidence of a master playwright. It was apparent that he wanted to keep the operation of the fund and its meager resources constantly in the public eye. He wanted to retain for himself the power to select those two basic ingredients of drama—issues and timing. For these reasons it was essential that he control the administrative decision-making. So long as his purpose was to build the fund, Lewis could not relegate decisions on benefits to actuaries or to other prudent men. He had to build the fund without letting the operators know the full scale of his objectives. It presumably aided his purpose to provide benefits more grandiose than the fund in any successive period could afford. Then when the solvency of the whole program was in question, the miners, if they liked what they had been getting, would be willing to strike for a bigger royalty on coal. This interpretation of Lewis' role has nothing to do with actuarial science or funding principles. But it has much to do with the principles of power and social change and explains why the administration of the fund was made completely subservient to the bargaining process.

To repeat, then, it was essential to Lewis' strategy that he keep control of the administration of the program. In the first place, the fund had to be run effectively and in terms miners would understand. "No other agency could operate the fund as efficiently or as cheaply as the Mine Workers," he argued in 1946; the fund "could not become a tripartite fund and simply another bureaucratic governmental agency with the overhead eating up a major part of the revenue of the fund, clogging it with red tape and with its awards delayed after the manner of other governmental agencies."[17]

In the second place, it was necessary to veil the subservience of administration to his bargaining intentions. It was no business of the operators, he stated, to supervise the fund, but they would continue to have the control that comes with periodic review:

> . . . the operators' veto power on this fund rested in the fact that at the end of each contract period they could, if they would, discontinue it by refusal to continue it; that the amount of aid that could be extended to the miners was necessarily limited by the contracting limitations of income; that the mine workers should be constantly on trial before the joint conferences of the industry and before the public at large as to the manner of its administration. . . .[18]

It is obvious now that Lewis was willing to run the risk of a charge of extravagant management if the threat of discontinuance of benefits could be used to build up the bargaining strength of the miners.

The coal operators were suspicious. They felt that the union would use the welfare fund to build support for the union, to discipline union members. (The Southern Coal Producers' Association still thinks so.)[19] The attitude of the public vacillated between skepticism and downright fear. In the Congressional debates on the Taft and Hartley Bills, the view was expressed that Lewis and James A. Petrillo of the Musicians' Union (who wanted a royalty fund for unemployed musicians) were power-hungry leaders who wanted to use the employers' money (or worse, the public's money by a royalty or tax on the product) in order to build their own personal empires. While the operators and the public were right about aggrandizement of power, they overlooked an essential part of the purpose. The UMW wanted to administer the fund to enlarge it so that it would grow and become a powerful tool for advancing human welfare in the coal fields.

But pressure from the employers and the public was too great and Lewis never got exclusive union administration, at least in the formal sense. The Lewis-Krug Agreement itself was a compromise: the Welfare and Retirement Fund would be jointly administered, and the Medical and Hospital Fund would be administered by the union. This latter fund would be financed by deduction from the miners' wages, and was to include the amount they were currently having deducted for medical and hospital prepayment. In the next contract in 1947,

Lewis gave up the separate Medical and Hospital Fund and agreed that the practices in existence with regard to "wage deductions and their use for provision of medical, hospital and related services shall continue during the term of this contract or until such earlier date or dates as may be agreed upon by the United Mine Workers of America and any Operator signatory hereto."[20]

Thus the 1947 agreement extended the existence of the "check-off doctor," consolidated the program into one fund, and made the national program entirely non-contributory. Lewis had to give up unilateral union administration, but he increased the employer contribution, got a portion of the fund set aside for pensions, and established the principle that the industry should bear the cost.

How does this development—Lewis' actually giving up unilateral union administration—square with our claim that control over the administration was the *sine qua non* of bargaining strategy? Lewis had to be able to determine the benefits in order to select the issues, and he had to develop the dramatics by influencing the timing. Why then did he give up control over the administration, even for valuable concessions? The answer is that he never did. Under the jointly administered program the key to control was the neutral trustee and here Lewis never compromised: he never agreed to a neutral trustee who would oppose him on the main issues.

The clue which reveals Lewis' bargaining strategy is his handling of the pension issue. The 1947 agreement provided that some of the fund would be set aside for pensions, the exact amount to be decided by the trustees according to actuarial computations after eligibility and the amount of benefit had been decided. Lewis, as UMW trustee, insisted on $100 a month pensions (a good round figure that could capture a miner's imagination) and got the support of the "neutral" trustee. The operators' trustee regarded this as impossible; his actuary showed that a $100 a month pension would require twenty-two cents a ton (the fund only received five cents per ton at the time) and if such a pension were added to the death, disability, hospital, and sick benefits, the total required would amount to forty cents a ton on the rate of production as of December 17, 1947. The actuaries later proved that they were right about the cost of the pension program and that Lewis was wrong.[21] But this is not to the point, because Lewis was looking ahead toward enlarging the fund. Men will strike for good pensions, and strike again if more is needed to keep them from being terminated. Lewis was leading the miner down a difficult trail and he had to make the incentives justify the sacrifices. Very few unions have succeeded in really standing by the principle of "fully funded, actuarially sound pensions" that later became the cry in autos and steel, simply because the benefits obtained under such a principle are, at least in first agreements, too meager to fight for. It is clear that Lewis never was interested in actuarially sound financing, because, presumably, he was occupied with a strategy for building the fund. A small fund could never be substantial enough to effect a welfare revolution in the coal fields. Judgment on Lewis must be passed with reference to his goals as well as to his methods.

Judge Goldsborough became Lewis' strategical ally when the court ignored the funding principle and declared that the need of the miners justified $100 a month pensions and that benefits could be adjusted as experience dictated:

There seems to be nothing that shocks the mind at the idea that the members of the United Mine Workers who have worked for twenty years under the ground and who are sixty-two years old should get $100 a month pension. Of course, if the fund won't stand it they will have to change it but it is meager, just enough to keep them from being objects of charity in their old age; it is just to give them a little dignity. The court does not think that there is any justification in law or in sound reason for this complaint.[22]

Lewis was fighting for control of the administration in order to build up bargaining strength against the operators. But he also had to consolidate the miners' support for the Welfare and Retirement Fund. He regarded the local and district operation of medical and hospital plans as inimical to the grand design and took his case to the 1948 convention, which eliminated from the Constitution Article XXI, which had provided for local and district benefit funds. It was explained that permitting the continuation of such funds would provide the operators with an argument against higher royalties.[23] The benefit funds would be liquidated gradually and their function taken over by the Welfare and Retirement Fund. As the local and district benefit programs were liquidated and as the fund provided arrangements for medical care other than the company-doctor systems, the check-off prepayments were eliminated; some check-off arrangements are still in effect to provide home and office medical service for the miners, but the number is greatly reduced. Persuading local leaders in the United Mine Workers to give up local and district benefit funds they had built must have been for them a rather unwelcome lesson in their welfare "education."

We have not yet pointed to the second lesson in the miners' welfare education. They were taught to want more and better welfare care, but they also had to learn to accept the limits necessary at any time. These limits—the eligibility rules and benefit durations—led to some grumbling, even though they were overly liberal, given the resources of the fund. In some instances the rules had to be tightened up, bringing more dissatisfaction in the coal fields.

At one time or another, the fund has had six different benefit programs: (1) pensions; (2) hospital and medical care; (3) distress and disability benefits for disabled miners and subsequent rehabilitation and maintenance-aid cash benefits to miners disabled for more than six months; (4) death benefits (now called funeral expenses and widow and survivors benefits); (5) widows and dependent children cash-aid benefits; and (6) disaster benefits. However, the fund is currently limited to (1), (2), (4), and (6). The other programs were discontinued on April 1, 1954; the fund could not support all of its benefit programs and it was found that some of the benefits paid often took the place of assistance which would otherwise have been provided from various sources.

In both the pension and the medical care programs there have also been curtailments. The eligibility requirements for pensions have been tightened.[24] In medical care, dental benefits were cut back because they caused continual trouble and dissatisfaction; the miners could not understand the limitations of the program. Some doctors referred considerable numbers of patients for dental care, others practically none. The cost of this program mounted and at one time reached $2.5 million a year. In 1952, the fund decided to eliminate all dental care except for injuries and in certain diseases, and payment under these conditions must be approved by the Washington office.

The bitterness felt by those union members who think they have been unjustifiably denied or deprived of a benefit can be of serious concern to any union, even a union whose internal procedures are not democratic. The union has suffered loss of prestige from the pitiable pleas of widows who had been receiving continuing maintenance-aid cash benefits, only to have them terminated in 1954, and from miners over sixty who have been ruled ineligible but who would have been eligible prior to 1953, or who have been in the industry for many years but were not in 1946. Some feel that the fund was managed entirely by Lewis—that the miners themselves had very little to say about it.[25] Curtailing benefits and changing eligibility requirements made Lewis appear arbitrary and cruel.

It has never been Lewis' method to educate by developing leadership in others and assigning responsibility. The complaints about the Welfare and Retirement Fund are a small mirror reflecting the union's tradition of high-handed and autocratic administration. But it is also true that a less secure national union leadership might never have dared pioneer so extensively in an area where all mistakes become big ones.

The fund's efforts to get along with the medical profession constituted an entirely different form of "bargaining." In these "negotiations," the impressive authority of the Welfare and Retirement Fund has been very useful in improving medical care, at times in direct opposition to the wishes of some doctors.

Buying Medical Services

There are about one million persons—bituminous miners who are working, retired, or unemployed, and their dependents—for whom the fund is prepared to cover the entire cost of hospitalization and medical care in a hospital. This protection applies regardless of how old the beneficiary may be, of how often or how long he must be hospitalized, or of the length of time the condition may have existed before his eligibility was established. Payment is also made for specialists' services whether or not the patient is hospitalized, and the patient may be sent for special care and treatment any distance necessary. During the last ten years, 500,000 miners have received in-hospital care and there have been 8,000,000 office and outpatient clinic visits to specialists for diagnosis and treatment. The current annual (1966) cost to the fund for all services is about $53 million.

In the twenty-six states served by the fund, existing facilities are used whenever the fund determines they are of high enough quality and do not involve exorbitant charges. Hospitals which serve only a few fund cases are paid as far as possible on the basis of their billed charges; those with an appreciable volume of care to miners are reimbursed according to daily cost as determined by cost formulae developed by the American Hospital Association and several federal agencies. When local facilities are inadequate, a patient needing highly specialized services may be sent across the country if necessary.

Any physician selected by the miner can participate in the program by applying to the fund, provided he is in good professional standing, is willing to provide treatment at a charge that is reasonable, and is willing to abide by the regulations of the fund in regard to the submission of clinical records and data required for payment of services. (Non-participating physicians may also be remunerated by the fund but only after prior authorization in each case from the area medical office.) Each area medical office has developed a list of participating physicians, a total of over 7,000 doctors in all areas. Nearly all the physicians except those in the Miners' Memorial Hospitals were at one time paid on a fee-for-service basis. Now, with the development of group practice clinics in a number of areas, slightly more than half are reimbursed on some kind of prepayment basis. Exceptions are doctors who do much of their work for the fund and who have agreed to reimbursement on a fee-for-time basis. In a few areas a specified fee schedule known to the doctors is being used, either the local Blue Shield schedule, Veterans' Administration schedule, or some other guide. In general, it is the practice of the fund to pay "reasonable fees," depending on the situation in different parts of the country rather than to publish any schedule. There are a small number of physicians whom the fund will not pay; for example, those whom the fund has found abusing the fund or providing an unacceptable level of care, or whose past charges to the fund were unreasonable. The fund reserves to itself the decision to pay for only those services it considers necessary to provide the medical benefits authorized.

Until recently, the fund operated a chain of ten hospitals from Middlesboro, Kentucky, to Beckley, Virginia. In 1963, five of the hospitals were sold to the Board of National Missions of the Presbyterian Church, which acquired the remaining five in 1964. The hospitals were constructed by the fund to attract doctors and provide a quality of care well above that which previously existed in the area. These hospitals were models of planning: there were central accounting and purchasing, standardization of personnel policies, division of labor among them for maintenance and services, many facilities for outpatient care, nurses' training programs, etc. They were open to the community, although beneficiaries of the fund were given preference, and local doctors in good standing were given admitting privileges. Each hospital had full-time salaried doctors as chiefs of the medical, surgical, pediatric, and obstetrical services, and some of the larger hospitals had full-time men in other specialties; the total medical staff numbered about a hundred. Many of these features will be maintained by the new owner. The fund had to sell the hospitals because, with the decline in coal production and the rising volume of pension payments, it was financially impossible to keep them. The Area Redevelopment Agency and the State of Kentucky assisted in the purchase and operation of the chain, which is administered by a new hospital authority called the Appalachian Regional Hospitals, Inc., a non-sectarian, non-profit organization. Although the hospitals proved to be too ambitious for the fortunes of the fund, they fulfilled a prophecy made by Louis Reed in 1955, when he said that "there is little doubt that the presence of these hospitals, with their well-qualified staffs, will improve the whole level of medical practice in the area."[26]

That medical care in many coal mining areas was inadequate has been acknowledged by the medical profession. There never has been real free choice of doctors in these areas, and the check-off doctor frequently undertook to care for too many patients or to do surgery for which he had insufficient training. A committee of the American Medical Association studied conditions in the southern part of West Virginia and parts of Kentucky and Tennessee in 1952 and concluded:

General practitioner services should be greatly expanded and strengthened in these areas. . . . The further development of community type hospitals based on recognized standards, and open to all qualified physicians including general practitioners should be strongly encouraged and supported by the state medical societies and by the A.M.A. and the A.H.A.[27]

Dr. Draper, Medical Director of the fund, has in his discussions with the American Medical Association always been able to furnish precise documentation of the low level of care. For example, he pointed out that

out of 54 appendectomies performed, the pathological report confirmed the diagnosis of appendicitis in 25 and reported normal appendices in the other 29. In the case of one physician who performed 11 appendectomies, only three were confirmed by the pathologist. Another physician who had performed 12 appendectomies, five of which were confirmed by the pathologist, did not obtain more than one white cell count during the hospitalization of any of these 12 patients, and did not obtain a urinalysis on five of these patients.[28]

In medically blighted areas the fund has been able to police the quality of care in a way that the medical societies themselves are unable to do. Physicians, Dr. Draper commented, frequently perform unnecessary surgery because they know that if they don't the patient will go to someone else who will, and this situation is difficult for local medical societies to cope with.[29] State medical societies are reluctant to take decisive action, although admitting the deficiencies alleged, "for fear that it might result in general questioning by other patients of the standard of medical care available."[30]

Until 1955, Dr. Draper's professional prestige, his acceptance of the fee-for-service principle of remuneration, and his willingness to work with established medical societies tended to minimize conflict with the AMA and helped establish the UMW program on a working basis.[31] However, the UMW's efforts to secure high quality care at reasonable prices angered some doctors. Unnecessary hospitalizations and undue length of stay were questioned. The fund challenged any failures to make specialist referral and any services performed by physicians not best qualified to render them. And it questioned continuation of care by specialists when the family physician could perform the service satisfactorily. These policies caused some doctors to feel aggrieved. Some felt that by publishing its lists of "approved" physicians the United Mine Workers was setting itself up "as a judge of professional qualifications of doctors; and in so doing was damaging the non-approved doctor's reputation and professional standing."[32] They objected to "the UMW disqualifying doctors as participants in the medical program without bringing charges, either through established medical-society or hospital-staff channels."[33] And they claimed that "the miner-patient's free choice of physician is becoming more and more limited," that they themselves were spied on by UMW officials, and that the UMW was moving in the direction of "monopoly medicine."[34] The grumbling reached a climax in 1955 when Dr. Draper announced a new policy requiring consultation with a UMW–approved specialist when any miner was committed to a hospital, so that unnecessary surgery might be prevented and prolonged hospitalization avoided. At the meeting of the AMA House of Delegates in June, 1955, five state medical societies introduced resolutions condemning this decision, and Dr. Draper backed down on this issue, but continued his surveillance of quality. By November, a meeting of fund officials and the Medical Society of the State of Pennsylvania suggested that some of the turbulence had subsided.[35]

Because the UMW is primarily concerned about quality in medical care and knows what it is talking about, the AMA has been unwilling to fight the program head-on. Its Committee on Medical Care for Industrial Workers denies the UMW the right to pass judgment on the qualifications of doctors, and overlooks the fact that the UMW's objections are to general practitioners who want to do surgery or in other ways exceed their capacities. The Committee maintains that physicians should be paid on a fee-for-service basis except under "unusual circumstances," but leaves these decisions to local medical societies.

The last ten years have brought stability in the fund's relations with organized medicine. There have been flare-ups in some states, particularly in Pennsylvania, Colorado, and Illinois.[36] In 1958, the Pennsylvania Medical Society scrapped its agreement with the fund and established a fee-for-service code. The Colorado House of Delegates of the AMA threatened to bring any doctors participating in a medical plan that "denies its beneficiaries the right of free choice of physician" before a medical tribunal for unprofessional conduct.[37] And in Illinois, a resolution was adopted which stated that the medical society would not "look with favor" on doctors who do business with the UMW.[38] Despite action in these three states, "we have continued our program and pretty much on our terms," says a fund official.[39] Controversy can be expected when disaffected elements take control of the state society but the AMA clearly wants to contain these disputes at a state level. In the *Journal of the American Medical Association,* Dr. Draper was allowed to thank those physicians who have co-operated with the fund although they have been criticized and "hampered in their work by less understanding colleagues because they believed in the Fund's objectives."[40]

Toward Comprehensive Care

The UMW has had a significant role in upgrading medical care in the coal mining areas. It is true, of course, that there are places where the check-off doctor is still at work, perhaps over-extending his abilities but carrying primary responsibility for the care the miner and his family receive outside the hospital; since the UMW program has concentrated on hospitalization, the general practice has been affected only indirectly. The main limitations of the UMW's early efforts were those inherent in any plan that covers only the more infrequent and more expensive cases of hospitalization and specialist services. Not only does the absence of office and home coverage encourage excessive hospitalization, but it sets up discontinuity in the doctor-patient relationship. In recent years, however, the fund has been directing more and more of its attention to these limitations.

The real prod in this direction came with the financial pressures on the fund from declining coal production and the increasing demands of pension commitments. The fund has had to look for ways to cut its medical expenditures without curtailing services, and fund officials decided hospital services could be reduced by developing in the mining areas a network of health centers staffed with general practitioners who would work in close contact with visiting or full-time specialists.[41] Such an arrangement, by broadening the health services available, offers a more integrated medical program and helps screen out cases that otherwise might have to go into the hospital.[42] To encourage local health centers, the fund has provided medical advice to locals willing to finance ambulatory clinics, and has loaned them money in some cases. One of the first medical groups with which the fund did business was the Russelton group in New Kensington, Pennsylvania, some of the staff of which is from the University of Pittsburgh Medical Center. Excellent groups have developed in Centerville, Pennsylvania; Fairmont, West Virginia; and Birmingham, Alabama. Altogether, the fund is purchasing services from twenty-two separate groups of physicians at this time, and thus it is again in the forefront of efforts to achieve the efficiency and the better services that come with reorganizing medical care facilities.

We conclude that the miners' program provides the most extensive union-sponsored medical services in existence. It was developed at the cost of antagonizing the public, which had little understanding of the strategy required, but which now lauds the program as an outstanding accomplishment. In the words of the American Public Health Association, when it presented the Lasker Award to Dr. Draper: "The bold, comprehensive medical care program you have developed has demonstrated that private physicians and organized labor can work together in harmony for the good of the patient."[43]

What lessons in the miners' experience are there for other unions?

First, the fund has, by insisting on high standards of quality, necessarily developed a restricted panel arrangement. This surveillance of quality was a direct confrontation of the medical profession, but by using existing facilities (except for the hospital chain in the southern coal fields) and working out acceptable bases for reimbursing hospitals and doctors, the fund has avoided a head-on clash over organized medicine's economic-ethical principles.

Nevertheless, it took considerable "muscle" to undertake a program of quality surveillance. Concentration of authority in the national fund has been absolutely necessary for the enforcement of standards upon local doctors who want to practice medicine in their own way and who are beyond effective policing by their professional association. Union members' allegiances to local doctors are frequently violated when the fund enforces its standards. Since to administer such a program requires so much centralized authority, and since the UMW under Lewis succeeded in developing that dominance over the union and over the industry to a degree seldom achieved in other unions, it may well be that the lessons here are of limited practical value for other labor organizations.

Other unions are also aware that there are distinct limitations to the UMW program, which basically concentrates on covering the less frequent and more costly cases of hospitalization and specialist services. However, a more unified comprehensive medical care program for miners may yet be achieved by adding out-of-hospital care through clinics sponsored by the local unions.

An important question about the UMW fund is whether the base of coal on which it is built is a base of sand. The UMW initiated the era of "private social security," but can such programs, built as they are on single industries, really endure in an age of automation? With the sale of the UMW hospitals and the curtailment in eligibility and benefit amounts for both medical care and pensions, are we witnessing the beginning of a proof that "private social security" is really a contradiction in terms, that a program cannot be both private and secure?

4

THE MAINSTREAM:
BEGINNINGS IN AUTOS AND STEEL

Unionism came late to heavy industry, and welfare bargaining in autos and steel has no early history like that in the needle trades. The auto and steel unions, in the years following World War II, were still grappling with the giants of heavy industry over questions of prerogative. But their contribution, if late, was nonetheless decisive for the labor movement's welfare goals. By undermining the unilateral foundation of employee benefit plans and by breaking the legal obstacle to welfare bargaining in the courts, the auto and steel unions paved the way for many other unions. The needle trades unions and the United Mine Workers were the inspiration for health bargaining, but the United Auto Workers and the United Steelworkers planted it firmly in American industry.

From Benefit Plans to Bargained Plans

The huge companies in autos and steel established employee benefit plans in the 1920's and 1930's.[1] General Motors started a group insurance program in 1926 with $1,000 life insurance per employee at a cost to him of fifty cents a month; two years later weekly disability benefits were added, and in 1939 health insurance benefits. The United States Steel Company in 1935 had established a program of life insurance equal to one year's wages, at a cost to the employee of sixty cents per $1,000. So it was elsewhere; some companies even had pensions. The employee benefit plans were usually financed in whole or part by employers but sometimes entirely by the employee. The unions skirted or fought these plans, as organizing strategy dictated, because employees as well as employers had vested interests in the plans as

48

they had been operating. The unions' main problems were to achieve recognition and a measure of union security. There were times when they could ignore the employee benefit plans; there were other times when they could not.

Many employers established or improved these plans during World War II under War Labor Board policies that encouraged fringe benefits. The unions became involved in bargaining on these plans after World War II, when some companies wanted to reduce benefits or terminate them. Frequently, the contract provision merely bound the company to keep the unilaterally established insurance plan in force during the contract term.[2]

After the war, some companies which under wartime manpower needs had not enforced compulsory retirement features in their unilaterally established pension plans began to try to compel employees to retire. The United Steelworkers protested such action by the Inland Steel Company, which claimed that this issue, and anything else about a pension plan as well, was not subject to collective bargaining: thus began the famous Inland Steel Case. In a similar case, the W. W. Cross Company argued that bargaining was not required on insurance benefits.[3] Nearly all the big steel companies opposed welfare bargaining (though United States Steel had agreed in 1947 to join the union in a study of pension costs), but the courts held against them in both the Inland Steel and W. W. Cross cases, and clearly established the companies' obligation to bargain on both pensions and insurance.

In the United Auto Workers, where organizing was a grass-roots movement, the rank-and-file members were asked to re-evaluate the employee benefit plans. A program of education began, as in coal, with surveys of the need. In 1948, Harry Becker, Director of the UAW Social Security Department, announced the results of a public opinion poll conducted in Detroit by the Columbia University Bureau of Applied Research in co-operation with the union.[4] This "demonstration project" revealed, he said, that the principal worry among auto workers was how to support their families and pay hospital and doctor bills in case of illness. Throughout the union, local bargaining committees began collecting data: how many workers and their dependents are not covered by company plans; what are local hospital charges and what is the gap between the charges and insured coverage; what has happened to local union members with prolonged illness in their families; and how many elderly people are on relief because Social Security's old-age insurance is inadequate to support them? Urgency was added by the rising cost of being sick: in Detroit hospital costs reached an average of $20 a day!

The employee benefit plans could not meet the need, the union argued, because "these plans have been developed by the employer in consultation with his insurance broker—not in consultation with his employees."[5] As with other so-called "prerogatives of management," company-controlled plans were regarded as a degrading paternalism; there could be no progress until workers had a voice in the planning and operation of the program. Why did the union insist on more employee participation?

First, the employee benefit plans were financed at least in part by payroll deduction; the worker's ability to finance his benefits was very limited. The union argued that company and insurance representatives always estimated a benefit package small enough to assure participation of a sufficient number of workers. So long as the dominant consideration was the attractiveness of the benefits as a "sales package," paid for by the employee, the benefits were bound to be inadequate. Second, these low-benefit employer plans were defended by company and insurance spokesmen as adequate to cover average hospital and surgical bills, an argument completely missing the point that the burden of illness falls very unevenly, ranging from minor to catastrophic losses. Furthermore, to cover up low standards, the group insurance packages frequently contained items of "window dressing" that had little value and cost only a few cents a month. They had excessive restrictions on eligibility, the effects of which were not readily apparent when the plans were being sold to the workers. Since the heart of the problem was a financial one, according to the UAW, the company-controlled plan could not be the agency for improvement: "Insurance company agents and employers often will defend low standards of benefits because if they admit that present benefits are inadequate they would, thereby, admit the necessity for an improved method of financing."[6] Only through collective bargaining, the union argued, could the company be made to finance the programs with enough money to provide health security to the auto worker.

The Patterns are Set

As we have seen, steel's big contribution to the preparations for welfare bargaining was in the courts; auto's was in educating the employee's perception of the problem. With the groundwork laid, the bargains had now to be struck.

The UAW had begun its welfare bargaining a little prematurely with the Ford Motor Company in 1947. The workers were not ready for such a step, and they turned down the retirement program negotiated by the union, preferring instead a straight wage increase. The UAW learned here a lesson that it never forgot—whether bargaining for insurance, pensions, or guaranteed annual wages. Welfare bargaining requires advance preparation and reflection before the issues become clear to the membership. The new awareness of this led the union to develop its "demonstration survey" of health needs in Detroit, to publish a *Collective Bargaining Handbook for Workers' Security Programs,* and generally to educate members on the questions involved and generate interest in them.

On June 11, 1948, the UAW obtained its first major employee welfare plan under collective bargaining when the Kaiser-Frazer Corporation agreed to put five cents for each hour worked by its employees into a jointly administered social security fund.[7] The stage was set. In 1949, UAW President Walter Reuther announced, "This year we can and must bring into the lives of our members a substantial measure of security against the hazards of old age, illness and disability."[8]

Meanwhile, the United Steelworkers was headed for a showdown strike on welfare issues with the large companies of the basic steel industry. It demanded pension and insurance benefits fully paid by the companies. By August, 1949, the union had negotiated insurance provisions in all contracts covering 180,000 members; for 127,000 of these the employer paid all insurance costs. But again the big companies were adamant; they contended that bargaining on pensions in 1949 was not permitted by the agreement then in effect. The steel fact-finding board appointed by the President reached an opposite conclusion, but this did not change the companies' viewpoint. Nor were they persuaded by the fact-finding board's recommendation for company-financed pensions, life insurance, temporary disability payments, and hospital and surgical benefits. After a six-week strike the union settled for an employer-paid pension program and contributory insurance program—2½ cents per hour each by employer and employee—in addition to wage and other benefits.

Subsequent negotiations, conducted separately with each steel company, established insurance benefit levels with some differences. For example, at Republic, Youngstown, and Inland Steel the hospitalization and surgical benefits were underwritten on a cash indemnity basis although the union had pressed hard everywhere for Blue Cross–Blue Shield. With many variations, these agreements in basic steel, including the contributory financing of group insurance and emphasis on Blue Cross–Blue Shield coverage, were copied in the rest of the industry.[9]

As for autos, Kaiser-Frazer suggested the possibilities, but it was not until after the steel strike in the summer of 1949 that a pattern was set in autos. Within the year, Ford, General Motors, and Chrysler had settled. By the summer of 1950, all of the major automobile producers had incorporated such a program into their union contracts, and by 1951, at least 90 per cent of all workers in the industry were under some type of collectively bargained welfare program.[10]

5

THE PARTNERSHIP IN STEEL

"The time has come," said United Steelworkers President Philip Murray in 1949, "for industry to stop treating its machines better than its workers."[1] The union's objective was company-financed insurance and pensions—the maintenance and "amortization" of employees. For the right to bargain on these issues, the union challenged the legal bastions of employer prerogative and then went to the picket line.

Extending Insurance Benefits

The 1949 strike did not establish company obligation to pay the full cost, but it did establish a firm basis for a health program. Hospitalization and surgical benefits were provided not only for the employee but for his dependents as well. The emphasis in the program was to be on benefits in the form of services, rather than in cash form. The union was to be entitled to all information necessary to keeping it properly informed on the operation of the program, but the company retained responsibility for its administration.[2]

The original benefit levels have been improved in successive negotiations. In 1954, along with improvements in the life insurance and temporary disability benefits, hospitalization was extended to 120 days; the company and the employees each raised their contributions to nine cents per hour. By 1956, accumulated reserves at U.S. Steel and Bethlehem permitted further improvements in hospitalization and surgical benefits.[3] In the negotiations of that year, the union wanted all the companies to assume full cost of insurance and health benefits, to provide full coverage for medical, hospital, surgical, and dental costs, and to increase weekly disability benefits to $70 and life insurance to one year's earnings. Actually, the modest improvements adopted cost the companies only an additional one and a half cents per employee-hour. The weekly disability benefits were liberalized and put on a graduated basis; the health insurance added diagnosis to the in-hospital coverage, and was extended to provide for expensive laboratory tests on an outpatient basis; the surgical schedule was raised to a maximum of $300 and the family income limit for Blue Shield service benefits was pushed up to $6000 in Pennsylvania. But, in general, insurance and health coverage took a back seat to wages, supplemental unemployment benefits, pensions, union shop, and overtime pay for week-ends. One union accomplishment in 1956 was the achievement of greater uniformity in insurance benefits throughout the steel industry.

In the 1959 negotiations, the union established its long-sought principle—full employer-financing of the insurance program. The strike in that year was at least partly over this issue; and shifting this cost meant an increase in income, averaging $9.50 a month, the typical employee-contribution toward insurance. Full employer-financing had already been established in the can industry as early as 1956, and this, along with the defection of Kaiser Steel during the negotiations, helped bring additional pressure on the basic steel companies to pick up the employee contribution.

The union also won life insurance and disability increases, company-paid insurance for the first six months after lay-off, and conversion rights under which retired workers could continue health insurance by paying a premium as individuals. (The union had originally demanded fully paid health insurance for retirees.) Further uniformity was achieved and over two-thirds of the membership was included under the standard health insurance program.[4] The leading companies would have liked to substitute major medical insurance of the so-called "comprehensive type," but the union would have none of it.

There were no changes in the insurance program under the 1962 agreement, but insurance was included in the "re-opener" clause of May 1, 1963. Group life insurance was increased, depending on the worker's job class; accident and sickness benefits were increased; and hospital coverage was extended from 120 to 365 days per year. In 1966 bargaining was delayed by the union elections in which A. W. Abel, then serving as Secretary-Treasurer, unseated David J. McDonald as president. Weekly sickness and accident benefits for workers with 2 years or more of service were increased to an average of $80 a week and their duration extended from 26 to 52 weeks. For employees with 10 or more years' service length of hospitalization was increased from 1 to 2 years with full rather than partial reimbursement for in-hospital doctor's fees, surgical fees, and maternity benefits. Life insurance was raised again (it ranges from $5,000 to $7,500 depending on the company). For disabled and laid-off workers with 10 or more years of service, insurance coverages were extended from 26 to 52 weeks.

The Steelworkers believes that it has done considerably better than most other mass production industries which have bought insurance from standard carriers. The union is particularly proud of its record of extending the more liberal benefits to smaller companies.[5] The standard steel plan has an exceptionally broad program of outpatient hospital benefits and ancillary doctor's services. The union also feels it has done better than other unions in providing for the continued coverage of laid-off workers, while conceding that others have done better for retired workers. But the leadership doubts that much more can be done within the framework of the established insurance plans, and, as will become clear, it has been studying new approaches in the organization of medical care services.

Financing and Administration

Bitter battles have been fought to unionize the steel industry, but in some big steel companies—most notably the United States Steel Corporation—the union strategy of winning over the company unions established collective bargaining in 1937 without a strike. This history helps explain why labor relations in the larger companies sometimes has the tone of a joint partnership. In the particular case of insurance bargaining with the larger companies in basic steel, there are some "partnership" characteristics, at least by contrast with experience in the auto, rubber, and electrical industries. Far more than in these other industries, the union in basic steel has been privy to the costing and financial administration of group insurance. With the first insurance agreements in 1949, bargaining was on both a cost and a level-of-benefits basis. Dividends are not returnable to the company, but accrue to the insurance account for furtherance of the benefit plan. Since their financial obligation is fixed, the companies are willing to provide information on financing and experience.[6] U.S. Steel provides quarterly reports and Bethlehem monthly reports, while most of the others are on an annual basis. These reports include claims paid, claims incurred, accumulation of contingency reserves, expenses, accounting transfers, conversions, etc.[7] Not until March 4, 1955, did the union ask for information on administrative expenses and commissions, and on the parties receiving such payments. The union also asks for special information on claims experience, as in its request to Jones and Laughlin and Republic Steel in 1954 to study the insurance indemnities paid for surgical benefits in order to ascertain the extent to which those indemnities reimbursed the employees for their actual bills.[8]

While the approach of the larger companies, the so-called "Big Steel" group, does set patterns for the basic steel industry, the majority of smaller steel companies and steel fabricators bargain only on the subject of benefits; the employer's contribution is not specified and he merely assumes an obligation to maintain the benefits negotiated.[9] Dividends are returnable to the company, and the union does not usually know the precise insurance cost; this must be estimated from experience with other companies where the union does have access to information.

But by being "behind the scenes" in the basic steel companies, the union has had an interesting exposure to the problems of financing health insurance. One of these problems was that of estimating what the company and employee contributions would actually be over the year; this depended on the number of hours to be worked. The insurance program had to be worked out in advance before the actual contributions could be known. The union thought that the company's estimate of under 1700 hours a year was far too conservative. Experience bore out the union's contention and reserves piled up. In the 1956 negotiations the fluctuation in contribution income was decreased by changing from an hourly contribution base to a monthly contribution, thereby eliminating income variation due to short time and overtime within a month and allowing a more liberal work estimate. The six cents per hour contribution was changed to $9.60 per month (this is the yield assuming 1900 working hours in the year).[10]

The second policy problem under the fixed-contribution plans was more fundamental. Before 1956 the employer's obligation was fixed regardless of any change in insurance costs. This posed difficulties, especially with the rapidly rising costs of the Blue Cross-Blue Shield coverages during 1950 to 1954. In different companies the problem was handled in different ways,[11] but in several cases an increase in employee contributions was necessary, in circumstances where many employees were already faced with short hours.[12] Hence, in the 1956 agreement the union obtained the concession that "any future increase in costs for the agreed benefits during the term of the agreement shall be equally shared by the company and the employees."[13] This lightened the employees' burden under the rising cost of service-type benefits. With the change to full company financing in 1959, basic steel wanted and got some protection from rising costs by an agreement that, for each specified increment in premiums, one cent of wages from the automatic cost of living increases would be diverted to insurance.

The Steelworkers has not insisted on a role in selecting the insurance carrier, preferring to leave that responsibility with the employer. In many cases the carrier has been the insurer for the plan which had been in effect before the union agreement; in other cases the contract has been let after competitive bidding.[14] But the union's firm policy of using Blue Cross and Blue Shield does mean direct involvement in the selection of the health insurance carrier in most cases. The union has on occasion obtained agreements from employers to discontinue insurance indemnities and to change over to Blue Cross or Blue Shield.[15] John Tomayko, Director of Insurance and Pension Activities, describes how the union argued for Blue Cross in basic steel negotiations:

We had to fight the employers, but they finally agreed to it. At one point in our negotiations they said, 'Will you take the responsibility of selecting Blue Cross and Blue Shield as a carrier?' 'Will you put it in writing to us that you demand that carrier be selected?' The union said we would. Then on second thought they said that wouldn't be necessary but they would join with us.[16]

Of the five leading companies, only Republic continued its hospital and surgical benefits with a commercial insurance carrier, Metropolitan, which, beginning in 1956, underwrote service-type coverage very similar to that provided by Blue Cross and Blue Shield.

United Steelworkers does not object so vigorously as some other unions to the practices of the insurance industry;[17] generally its leadership has been tolerant of commissions and the operations of brokers, insisting only that the union's own staff, officers, and members shall in no way personally profit from the insurance plans.[18] The union's main interest in the carrier is to see that claims are handled promptly, in accordance with the terms of the contract, and that the costs are reasonable. "In any case," says Assistant Director of Insurance Bernard Greenberg, "in which we have reason to believe that just claims are being denied or that excessive charges are being made, we will intervene as powerfully as we can for either a correction of the condition or a change in carrier."[19]

However, there have been few cases where carriers were changed, in part because such changes usually bring higher first-year premiums, and in part because mistakes and improprieties have been corrected when brought to light.

The Steelworkers Union gives two reasons for advocating company responsibility for the day-to-day handling of claims. Firstly, the union thinks it is cheaper and more efficient. The administering of claims requires much routine paperwork, such as the approval of claims forms by a foreman or a clerk in the personnel office. In large plants efficiency requires that this be handled by a going organization. Claims administration, according to the union, is as much a legitimate cost of personnel administration as administering, for example, vacation provisions or job evaluation provisions. Since 1954 the companies have been persuaded of the truth of this view and administer claims with no cost to the insurance program.

Secondly, the union argues that a fundamental element of the collective bargaining relationship is the employer's responsibility for making decisions, and the union's obligation to remain free to protest.

It very often happens that there is a difference of opinion between the employee and the company. We think that we ought not be responsible for the making of that initial personnel decision, that that is a decision that is properly a management function and that it is a function of our union to take up grievances and to pursue them until we get a satisfactory conclusion of that grievance.

We do not think it is right, for example, that our union ought to participate in the denial of sick benefits to an employee. We think that this is a management function or an insurance company function. The decision having been made, if it is correct, of course, stands. If it is incorrect, we want to preserve the right to protest and to handle it as grievance in order to protect the employee's rights.[20]

While the Steelworkers makes something of a fetish now of its "fundamental principle . . . of employer responsibility for administration"[21] the fact is that it asked for more of a role in administration than it got from the 1949 negotiations. Since then it appears to have accepted the advantages in the existing arrangements.

The Demand for Health Services

The Steelworkers, in 1949, wanted to provide the widely scattered employees of the large national steel companies with equal health services. With hospital costs varying tremendously in different parts of the country and between urban and rural areas, this could not be done by underwriting equal cash indemnity benefits. The solution lay in Blue Cross's full coverage for ward and semiprivate rooms, regardless of the cost of such accommodations. But Blue Cross then was only a patchwork of separate state and local plans showing great variations in benefits and premiums. To accommodate the union and the large companies, Blue Cross plans established, through a central co-ordinating body, an average premium for all states where steelworkers lived. Some of these plans which did not normally provide the benefits desired had to make exceptions and improve their benefits for steelworkers.[22] But the adjustment was slow.

Certain Blue Cross plans would not come up to the national Blue Cross standards, notably New Jersey, which as late as 1953 still did not offer the standard 70 days hospitalization.[23] Furthermore, there was some resistance to the union's requests that Blue Cross cover in-hospital diagnostic services, hospitalization for mental or nervous disorders, full period hospitalization for maternity complications, etc. But many of these improvements have now been adopted by Blue Cross and incorporated in the steel contract. The union continues to exert very considerable influence on Blue Cross thinking.

The union has also helped to shape the character of commercial hospitalization benefits. At Republic Steel, where management never accepted Blue Cross as the carrier, the union persuaded the company and its insurer, the Metropolitan Life Insurance Company, to work out a service-type plan that covers ward and semi-private rooms whatever their cost.[24] This arrangement is now common, but at the time was regarded as novel. At Inland Steel, the union got the underwriter to provide higher indemnity benefits in certain specified "high cost" areas.[25]

The union's experience with medical and surgical plans—primarily Blue Shield—has been very different. These plans are less adequate in their areas than the hospitalization plans, and the union has not been able to have so formative an influence toward making them more adequate. Blue Shield covered in 1960 only an estimated 52 per cent of steelworkers' physicians' bills, compared with the 95 per cent of hospital bills paid by Blue Cross.[26]

A recent study which we made in one of the largest steel companies in western Pennsylvania shows that nearly 50 percent of the bills rendered by physicians under our Blue Shield program required an additional payment by our members over and beyond the reimbursement provided through the Blue Shield schedule. Of these additional payments, one-fourth involved extra payments of over 50 percent of the amounts allowed by the Blue Shield. . . .[27]

The number and amount of charges over the benefit schedule seem to vary greatly both within any given steel area and between different steel areas.[28] The director of the union's insurance activities reported that there was "a ground swell of resentment from our members as to the effectiveness of our insurance program."[29] And he told the annual Blue Cross–Blue Shield Conference that current insurance programs in the steel industry "leave the patient exposed to overcharges by the non-cooperative physician. . . ." He warned the conference that Blue Shield must avoid deteriorating "into a collection agency for the medical profession."[30] The only place where the union has found that prepayment assures nearly complete coverage has been on the West Coast, in the Kaiser Foundation Health Plan, under which 93 per cent of physicians' services are covered.[31]

To estimate the value of its prepayment plans, the union published in 1960 the following data showing the proportion of private expenditures for various medical services actually paid by different negotiated plans in the steel industry (see Table I).[32]

These data assume that the average steelworker spends for these various kinds of medical services the same amount of money as the average person in the United States in 1957 and 1958, as estimated by the U.S. Department of Health, Education, and Welfare. The percentage of coverage in Table I would apply to families if all persons in the family were covered by insurance. Families with dependent members not

Table I: Proportion of Out-of-Pocket Expense

| | Blue Plans (standard)[a] | Commercial Contracts | | Kaiser Foundation Health Plan[d] |
		Republic Steel (standard)[b]	Inland Steel (non-standard)[c]	
All services	41+%	41+%	40+%	55+%
Hospital services	95	95	93	95
Physician services	52	50	46	93
Medicines and appliances	0	0	0	10
Dentists' services	0+	0+	0	0+
All other services	0+	0+	0+	0+

[a] Based on experience in 20 areas, July, 1957–June, 1958.
[b] Based on experience under the company-wide contract, July, 1957–June, 1958.
[c] Based on experience at the Indiana Harbor Works, January–December, 1958. Includes in-hospital medical attendance benefits, lacks most of the hospital out-patient and all the physician ancillary services, and differs in other respects from the standard (basic steel) contracts.
[d] Based on experience under contracts with the Kaiser Foundation Health Plans in California, direct type contract, July, 1957–June, 1958.

Source: United Steelworkers of America, *Special Study on the Medical Care Program for Steelworkers and their Families* (Sept., 1960), p. 96.

covered by the insurance, or with higher-than-average income and higher-than-average non-insured medical costs, would have had smaller proportions covered by prepayment than the percentage specified in the table above. Kaiser's coverage, by providing physicians' services and partial prepayment for medicines and appliances, was better.

Since some of the services in the table above are not insurable under prepayment mechanisms, the union estimated the percentage of insurable health costs covered[33] (see Table II). Thus, the report concluded by asserting the superior advantages of the "comprehensive" group practice prepayment plan such as that of the Kaiser Foundation Health Plan, which covers 71–84 per cent of insurable bills (depending on how "insurable" is defined) compared with 54–64 per cent for the standard open-panel Blue Plans.

This interest of the United Steelworkers in the advantages of prepaid group practice plans, at least in the International headquarters, marked a change from past policy. Until about 1958, the only union interest was shown at the local level in areas where direct-service plans were

Table II: Per Cent of Insurable Health Costs Covered

	Including dental charges	Excluding dental charges
Currently insurable expenditures		
Steelworker standard benefits	60	64
Kaiser Foundation Health Plan	80	84
Potentially insurable expenditures		
Steelworker standard benefits	54	56
Kaiser Foundation Health Plan	71	74

Source: United Steelworkers of America, *Special Study on the Medical Care Program for Steelworkers and their Families* (Sept., 1960), p. 97.

available, such as the West Coast and the Minnesota iron ore range. An agreement reached in 1949 with Kaiser Steel Corporation provided for coverage in the Kaiser Health Foundation group practice plan. The popularity of the group practice service is attested by the fact that at least 36,000 steelworkers have voluntarily contributed toward supplementary benefits from such plans where they are locally available.[34] These experiences however, stand as the exception. It seems clear that the Steelworkers' leadership during most of the first decade of health bargaining scorned to tamper with the organization of medical care and concentrated on more orthodox methods of prepayment. David McDonald held a far more conservative view of labor's role in health insurance than did Walter Reuther. "I firmly believe," said McDonald, "in a system which allows for freedom of choice by a patient from among different physicians."[35] In 1953, he told the Annual Conference of Blue Cross–Blue Shield Plans:

. . . It is not my desire, nor the desire of the United Steelworkers of America to change the pattern of medical practice in our country. . . . Yours is the opportunity to develop within the framework of private practice and freedom of choice for the patient, a method by which the burdensome costs of medical care may be met through privately organized prepayment plans.[36]

A short five years later, however, the union had shifted its position and McDonald was urging joint effort with the steel companies to establish a non-profit medical service plan "as an investment in the social good of the community. . . . I'd like to see something like the Kaiser hospital in Walnut Creek, California."[37] And on the question of "free choice" which he had espoused in 1953, McDonald said in 1958,

"Free choice is just a lot of conversation. . . . If you're living in a small community, how much choice have you got? . . . In Walnut Creek, a man walks into the Kaiser hospital clinic and he has a choice of eighteen physicians. . . ."[38]

Why this dramatic change in the International's approach? The union had found that it was easier to prepay doctor services under group practice, as in the Kaiser local, rather than to try to force extension of the Blue plans. A number of steel locals had good results with direct-service plans. "It is evident to us," said John Tomayko to Blue Cross, "that many health care procedures could be more effectively provided through out-patient departments of hospitals, through clinics, or even through closed panel groups."[39] Also, there was a growing interest in prepaid group practice among other unions and particularly in the auto industry, a development mirrored in AFL–CIO official statements. The basic fact that underlay a change in the Steelworkers' policy was union concern over the "skyrocketing costs of our hospitalization and medical care program"—not costs resulting from improvements in benefits or the quality of services, or even from overdue wage increases for underpaid hospital employees, but those arising from "lack of control over unnecessary and expensive in-patient hospitalization and surgery."[40] The union found a great variation in the rate of services (number of days of hospitalization or number of surgical procedures per 1000 persons) in different areas which could not be explained by the differences in age, sex, or family status among the insured population.[41] Its technical staff suspected there was too much surgery and too much hospitalization in many areas rather than too little in other areas.[42] The greatly reduced rates of hospital days and surgical services in the prepaid group practice plans suggested that substantial savings could be realized when some controls were operating.[43] In general, the Steelworkers was disenchanted with organized medicine's leadership: "Unless the medical profession changes many of its basic policy positions and practices with respect to fees, and unless it accepts greater responsibility for holding down costs and improving the comprehensiveness of benefits, we have no alternative except to explore the possibilities for achieving our goals through newer patterns."[44] And to the doctors, McDonald commented: "So far my pleas have fallen on deaf ears. . . . [Now] we ask you to join with us . . . in the development of a completely prepaid fully insured medical care system. . . . You must be prepared to accept the idea that group practice has a place in this picture.[45]

The Steelworkers' re-evaluation of its experience was completed by 1960. The 1958 Convention authorized a study of union health benefits and alternative plans. For this purpose, I. S. Falk, formerly research director of the Social Security Administration, was engaged as consultant. The study was issued at the 1960 Convention and is the most complete evaluation of its health insurance program ever issued by a union; it reviews past experience, measures accomplishment, and sets the stage. In 1965 new contract language was developed in the basic steel agreement allowing escape from the national arrangement in localities where group practice plans are available. The company and union may agree to a dual choice arrangement, or, where an employee contribution now goes for group practice services, the company's contribution may be redirected to go to the same program, on the employee's option. The union's officers have been talking in recent years about initiating a pilot plan of direct medical service in one or more steel centers. Such plans have been delayed—first they were blocked in the Big Steel negotiations of 1962 and then put on ice during a contest for the election of top officers—but meanwhile a local union in Ontario went ahead to establish steel's first medical center.

Steel's First Medical Center

Where Michigan and Ontario meet at the base of Lake Superior is the town of Sault Ste Marie. The Algoma Steel Corporation there employs 5,400 persons; it is, by far, the largest employer in the area, and is under contract to Local 2251 of the United Steelworkers of America. The local had been planning a medical center since 1958, when the United Steelworkers' Canadian National Policy Conference had recommended union-sponsored, group practice health centers. The Algoma local named a health center committee and laid its plans. Ted Goldberg, then on the union staff, has described the planning:

First a survey was conducted to determine, as precisely as possible, the family composition of the union members, as well as their patterns of utilization of medical care services, and the manner in which they were paid for. Estimates of capital and operating costs were developed which were later used in negotiating contributions from the company to the program. Contracts were made with both hospitals and assessments made of available local medical and paramedical facilities.[46]

Consultants were recommended or supplied by the international union headquarters. To carry the benefits of the planning to the membership, an educational program of two-day schools, reaching about one-fourth of the union members, was instituted.

The popularity of the project and union confidence in the planning were demonstrated by the large number of employees who gave regular contributions to the development costs. Later, when subscriptions of $135 per family were solicited for the capital costs of land, building, and equipment, 4,000 families became sponsors; in addition, half of the office employees and all the employees of a smaller Steelworkers' local also joined. With interest running so high, the Algoma Steel Corporation agreed in the 1962 negotiations to pay two-thirds of the total premium cost, leaving employee contributions as they had been under the previous insurance program.

Opposition from the local doctors had been active from the beginning. Their medical society waged a newspaper and television campaign calling the medical center, according to Goldberg, "a step backward into closed-panel medicine," and raised the question of ethics. The Ontario Medical Association was more helpful. While arguing that "closed-panel clinics" were not the best available method of providing medical care, the Association did conclude that the plan would not contravene the Code of Ethics.

One of the principles adopted in planning the center was that employees would have the choice of using the medical center or of using an indemnity insurance plan instead. The indemnity alternative would apply when any doctor not in the medical center was consulted. Under either alternative, the employee or his family would continue to derive the benefit of the employer's contribution. The Prudential Insurance Company was to be the underwriter for the alternative indemnity plan.

As time for the vote neared, the Prudential too waged a campaign to discourage health center support. "It also proposed," says Goldberg, "that should any of the union members be in doubt about the relative values of the competing plans, they ask their doctor which was better."[47]

The vote was an overwhelming 80 per cent for the medical center. The excellent early planning, the education of members in the principles of group practice, and probably some dissatisfaction with local doctors contributed to the outcome. The experience suggests that a well-administered local union receiving good technical advice can be an effective tool for reorganizing community medical facilities.

The medical center, an $800,000 establishment of attractive design, opened its doors in September, 1963. In accordance with the union policy of allotting priority of admittance to other Steelworkers' unions, central labor unions, and community groups in that order, the total number of people served has grown and exceeded 20,000 in 1966. Although data on the workings of the center have not been made available, there is every reason to think this health plan deserves much attention. If it proves to be a success, it will fan interest in other steel centers.

Through its pivotal position in manufacturing, the Steelworkers' Union has contributed much to health bargaining. In the courts it established the right to bargain; on the picket line in 1949 and 1959 it achieved full company contribution to the cost; and at the bargaining table it has solved to the mutual satisfaction of employer and union the problems of administration. The partnership of these two forces in health bargaining has brought great influence to bear on prepayment groups. Blue Cross set up its first national account for steel, and has several times extended its range of benefits to accommodate this industry. Even commercial insurance companies first wrote service-type benefits for some steel companies. But the problems in traditional open-panel arrangements led the union in 1958 to abandon such arrangements as an ultimate objective in favor of the Kaiser or Sault Ste Marie types of direct hospital-medical-service plans.

6

THE VOCAL AUTO WORKERS

The three large companies which dominate the auto industry, General Motors, Ford, and Chrysler, bargain primarily with the United Auto Workers. Other firms employing large numbers of UAW members are American Motors, Willys-Overland, Electric Auto-Lite, and Borg-Warner. While there are some 2,000 welfare plans of many different types covering UAW members, the dominant pattern in the auto industry is that set by the welfare plans of Ford, GM, and Chrysler.

Recasting the Employee Benefit Plans

Until the right of the union to bargain on welfare was clearly established, the merits of proposed liberalizations were not of primary concern to the union. When General Motors, in 1948, announced it was going to double the life insurance benefits, provide free life insurance for retirees, offer monthly payments to the totally disabled, and pay temporary disability benefits payments for 26 rather than 13 weeks, the UAW raised charges of unfair labor practice—the company was circumventing the union and dealing with the employees directly. The merits of the program were not the issue (the union actually agreed to a similar package at Ford) but unilateral determination was unacceptable.

After bargaining was established, it was clear that GM wanted to retain the lead in this area. The 1950 negotiations were concluded at Ford and Chrysler first, but the welfare plan negotiated at General Motors was more generous, and the Ford and Chrysler settlements were reopened to incorporate a comparable package.[1] The main features of the insurance settlement at these companies were:

1. Group life insurance between $2,400 and $5,000 with accidental death and dismemberment benefits at 50 per cent of these amounts.
2. In the event of permanent disability, this life insurance could be paid in 50 monthly installments of $20 per $1,000 of coverage, under the General Motors plan. Chrysler provided a similar payment, amounting to $50 per month for 72 months; Ford had no such provision.
3. Free life insurance for retirees, from $500 to $1,350, with GM giving 1½ per cent of life insurance prior to retirement times years of service.
4. Weekly accident and sickness benefits of $31.50–$45.50 at GM, $30.60–$43.60 at Ford, and $32 at Chrysler, all for up to 26 weeks.
5. Blue Cross and Blue Shield benefits, half of the premium to be paid by the company.
6. Hospital expenses up to $5 a day at GM, $4 at Ford, for a maximum of 70 days. Chrysler did not include this provision.

The cost of this insurance to the employees ranged from $2.25 to $5.75 a month, depending on the employer and the amount of coverage, which varied with a worker's wage level. Although the benefit levels under bargaining were higher than they would have been under unilateral determination—at least judging by GM's 1948 offer—there was no concession to the union's desire to participate in the administration of the plans and to be appraised of the financial and underwriting arrangements. Nor was any advance made in this area in 1955, although there were gains on other fronts. The sickness and accident benefits were further increased so that the union's objective of weekly benefits at 65 to 70 per cent of lost wages was realized.

The union persisted in its efforts to get full coverage in hospital services and full payment for surgical and inpatient medical services, but the 1955 settlement was only a step in the desired direction. The Blue Cross–Blue Shield coverage in Michigan was extended to 120 days. A surgical payments schedule with a maximum of $225 was negotiated as full payment for a family in Michigan earning $5,000 a year or less. Coverage for in-hospital expenses was added for dependents, and was improved for everyone by the inclusion of X-ray and electrocardiographic services. Although the union and the company attempted to eliminate the variations in Blue Cross–Blue Shield benefits that existed from region to region, no substantial changes came until 1961. The benefits negotiated were consequently of most value to union members in Michigan.

The problem of how to use the funds of national corporations for company- and industry-wide health plans when Blue Cross and Blue Shield benefits varied so greatly could only be solved by putting pressure on substandard plans to improve themselves, or by paying more in premiums to the less efficient plans. A related problem—the existence in some communities of excellent medical service centers with programs far better than the Blue Shield package—required some kind of escape clause in the national contracts. The union asked for and got a provision to allow local option, by which workers could elect to join comprehensive medical care plans and pay any extra cost above the amount negotiated for Blue Cross–Blue Shield coverage. In these ways, the union assumed a positive role not only in negotiating more funds for health benefits but in encouraging the more advanced forms of prepayment and medical service organization.

The 1958 settlement raised the group insurance amounts and, in health insurance, established the surgical fee schedule as full payment for Michigan families with incomes under $7,500, making it thereby a service benefit for most auto families in the state.

In 1961 the union asked for higher benefits, for uniform benefits in the different areas, and that the entire cost of the insurance program be paid by the employer. A central concern of the union throughout the 1950's was the uneven quality of the hospital, medical, and surgical benefits. The Blue plans lacked uniformity, so that many employees had to pay a substantial medical bill to supplement the insurance benefits. "Almost half of our GM membership does not have the benefits that were negotiated. Outside of Michigan, more than four out of five GM families do not have surgical-medical benefits in reasonable conformity with our negotiated standard."[2] The employers agreed to supplement the hospital-surgical benefits in areas where the Blue Cross–Blue Shield coverage was not up to the standards of the Michigan plans. This, coupled with extension of coverage to 365 days and an improved medical insurance plan, greatly reduced the out-of-pocket expenses of auto workers.

Another significant saving for union workers was the agreement reached in 1961, after a decade of wrangling in the auto and steel industries, that the companies would pay the full cost of the health insurance program. Kaiser-Frazer in 1950 had accepted a non-contributory health plan, as had American Motors in 1958. But not until after the non-contributory steel settlement of 1959 did the dominant auto companies accept this long sought union objective.

In 1964, the UAW pioneered by winning insurance of mental health services in its basic agreements. The benefits provided allow for a flexible range of services: patients confined to a hospital for mental or nervous disorders (up to 45 days for a single confinement), patients treated on an outpatient basis, and patients receiving psychiatric services in doctors' offices—all are covered. Some psychological testing is also included. Because of the absence of experience with this kind of insurance, an aggregate limit of $400 per patient per year has been set for the non-hospital benefits.

Melvin A. Glasser, the UAW's Social Security Director, has emphasized the importance of mental health benefits for industrial workers and expressed concern that even in so-called comprehensive prepayment programs there is relatively little concern with emotional illness: "Too frequently it is relegated to the list of unfulfilled plans—on the priority list somewhere between eyeglasses and artificial limbs. . . . Much of the knowledge we have about preventing and treating emotional breakdown is not being used, particularly for workers in our country."[3] The UAW will probably continue to chart new territory in mental health prepayment.

Union Participation in Administration

The UAW has repeatedly asked for voice equal to that of management in the selection of insurance carriers and in all phases of administration, including knowledge of the financial structure and review of contested claims. Most of the welfare plans in autos are single-employer plans; bargaining is on the level of benefits (rather than on the amount of the employer's contribution), and the plans are unilaterally administered and controlled by the company. Furthermore, the employer selects the insurance carrier and retains any dividend or experience rating refund paid by the carrier. Only about one-fourth of the auto welfare plans were established on a different basis, with agreement on a specified employer's contribution and joint selection of the carrier, joint determination on the use of dividends returnable to the fund, etc.[4] The prevalent situation is that at General Motors. Until a Congressional investigation lifted the shroud of secrecy in 1955, there was no way of knowing the actual cost to GM of the program for the hourly rated workers, or the division of cost between company and employees.[5] GM has kept the union helpless under a contract clause which provides that the corporation "shall receive and retain any divisible surplus, credits, or refunds or reimbursements under whatever name, made on any such contracts."[6] The union has not been able to establish an interest in the disposition of the funds even on the grounds that they involve employee contributions. In the 1955 negotiations the union made a special point of its concern with the company's closed-door administration of the funds. But the company would provide no details of its financing arrangement with Metropolitan, and even the use of grievance procedure was denied in disputes on insurance benefits. Since then, the door has been gradually opened at least to allow exchange of some financial information. The Health and Welfare Disclosure Act requires that companies file financial descriptions of their plans and that this be publicly available. Furthermore, according to Jerome Pollack, then consultant, UAW Social Security Department, "practices have arisen though not explicitly stated in the contract of joint action on choice and substitution of benefits and approval of rates."[7] The 1961 contract with GM provided that certain information shall be made available to the union, on such topics as insurance premiums, experience, and reserves on a total and per unit basis.[8] But the union did not get requested grievance machinery for health and welfare complaints.[9]

Experience with Blue Cross and Blue Shield

The union has usually preferred Blue Cross and even Blue Shield to commercial health insurance. The return in benefits relative to premiums is lower; cash indemnity benefits leave the worker "holding the bag" when hospital and doctor charges are raised. Initially, Blue Cross aided the United Auto Workers by offering better hospital coverage than was otherwise available, by offering to provide group coverage for retired workers, and by providing conversion rights.[10] For these reasons, the UAW usually negotiates a split insurance package, leaving life and weekly disability policies to insurance companies but reserving for Blue Cross and Blue Shield the medical portion.

The first shock came in the spring of 1953 when the Michigan Hospital Service announced monthly premium increases ranging from twenty to eighty cents per employee. Blue Cross in Michigan did not have any labor representation on its board of directors. As one local union officer put it "when we voted to accept Blue Cross in 1941 that was the last time the membership of our union had anything to say about the kind of protection they want."[11]

The rise in premium rates precipitated a study of its justification. The findings showed that Blue Cross prepayment was resulting in over-utilization of some kind in 36 per cent of hospital stays.[12] The Blue Cross response to over-utilization was development of co-insurance and deductible features, in part to add a financial dis-incentive; the UAW replied that professional considerations should govern the decision to hospitalize and the duration of stay. "The prepayment plans," said UAW Vice President Leonard Woodcock, "are failing to place medical controls on utilization and instead are looking for an easy way out by limiting their liability and putting economic pressures on the subscriber."[13] The union believed that the Blue Cross proposal of major medical with co-insurance and deductibles represented a reversal in direction, a movement away from the service approach. Blue Cross countered that these policies were designed to supplement and not replace the basic plans.[14] To help steer Blue Cross toward comprehensive services, the union campaigned for and won some representation on Blue Cross boards, but three years later concluded "there is very little likelihood, in Michigan or elsewhere, that consumers will win adequate representation on Blue Cross or Blue Shield boards."[15]

Even in the beginning, the UAW was more critical of Blue Shield—the medical care plan—than Blue Cross: "Blue Shield plans have tended to be dominated by the influential surgeons; they have created an entirely unjustifiable over-emphasis on surgical care."[16] Furthermore, the benefit schedules offered full coverage only for lower-income families—those with incomes under $2,000—and the 40 per cent of the union members with incomes over that had no certainty of coverage even for the listed surgical procedures.[17] The union has tried very hard to goad Blue Shield into raising the income limit but this has, however, raised the fee schedule and the premium rates.

A general problem with both Blue Cross and Blue Shield was the lack of uniformity. Michigan programs were better than those in many states covered by the Ford and GM agreements. Before 1955, GM and Ford had simply provided Blue Cross according to the benefits available in each state—which meant as low as $7 or $8 allowances for 21 or 30 days in some states, compared with the service benefits for 120 days in Michigan. The 1955 agreements provided for the "Michigan Standard"; outside of Michigan the company would pay for any comparable Blue Cross plan or make other arrangements. Full payment of surgical bills for those under $6,000 income limit was introduced in the Ford and GM contracts even before such a limit was available in Michigan and this too, it was hoped, would become a standard.

With these arrangements, the UAW expected to have some lever for improving Blue Cross–Blue Shield policies.

Under these agreements the Union in cooperation with Ford and G.M. will attempt to develop a uniform national standard of hospitalization coverage that will pay the full cost of needed hospital care in virtually all cases. . . . As soon as arrangements can be completed in Michigan and other areas, workers will be able to enroll in improved (surgical) plans.[18]

Progress was slow. The income limits slowly peeled back but at high cost. Woodcock, in November, 1956, concluded:

In most areas we are failing to get coverage conforming to this modest standard. . . . We now find that some plans are preparing to charge so much for a $6,000 income ceiling contract as to make the service principle a hollow victory. The cost of the newest Blue Shield contracts now being negotiated are so exorbitant as to exceed the value of surgical insurance by any reasonable standard.[19]

Despite all the pressures it could put on the non-profit service plans, the union stated that they were not meeting the important test of voluntary health insurance: "The extent to which the present prepayment plans are able to meet the modest but reasonable standard of protection that has been negotiated is a crucial test of their ability to serve the health security needs of the people."[20] And it concluded that "no pressure—whether collective bargaining, board representation, or publicity—is likely to be as effective as direct competition from a better program."[21] This is what led the union to organize the Community Health Association, a new and different medical care plan for Detroit.

Medical Care Plan for Detroit

At a union educational conference in 1954 a member of UAW Local 351 asked, "What can the international union do to stop the various hospital, surgical, and medical insurance programs from curtailing the benefits our members were receiving when we negotiated these insurance programs in our contracts?"

The answer was given by the Director of the UAW's Social Security Department, James Brindle:

> This question and the dilemma it poses illustrates that the purchase of a limited amount of health insurance isn't what we must strive for. The only real answer is to have available in a community the kind of comprehensive, fully prepaid, consumer-controlled medical care that will enable us to purchase at a reasonable price the full range of medical services.
>
> As we have to buy limited hospitalization and limited medical services and the price keeps inflating, the provisions become less and less satisfactory; we seem never to get away from the overcharging, and when the price begins to get high, then the carriers cut back on benefits and take it out of the worker's hide and the health security of his family.
>
> The only answer to this is for us to exert every pressure we can to cooperate with these groups in communities that are trying to set up fully prepaid, comprehensive medical services. Pushing and helping to get those plans established and bargaining for them when they are in the community is the only way we are going to get a satisfactory answer to this problem of medical care.[22]

The UAW has been giving this answer for a long time. As early as 1946, in response to a request by the convention, a thorough study of the feasibility of a comprehensive medical care program for Detroit was made by Dr. Franz Goldman.[23] He found that "there can be no doubt that the UAW is amply justified in taking the initiative and considering the establishment of a program of complete medical care exclusively for union members and their families."[24] He recommended a hospital capacity of 1800 beds, and health centers, serving as outposts for the general hospital or hospitals, which would provide preventive and treatment service for ambulatory patients and also for home care. The cost of the hospital plant would be $13,500,000 and each health center $70,000 to $80,000. He noted that the Permanente (Kaiser) Health Plan had found the annual cost per eligible person to be about $30. After discussing the legal, financial, medical, and bargaining problems involved, he concluded: "Weighing all sides of the problem one arrives at the conclusion that a program sponsored, financed, and administered by labor and management jointly is the only one to hold promise of success."[25]

The Goldman plan never got off the drafting board. Welfare bargaining was not established until 1949 and direct medical service plans were small and experimental. The Health Institute in Detroit had been established by the union in 1943 as a diagnostic center, but it never served, in any one year, more than 4 per cent of Detroit's auto workers.[26] It was closed in 1955. That same year the Willys-Overland Local 12 in Toledo opened a diagnostic clinic; it had got its start in 1953 when the local membership, on the recommendation of UAW representative Richard Gosser, voted to put a $443,280 retroactive wage increase into a health center.[27] In Baltimore at the Glenn L. Martin Local 738 union hall a small well-equipped group practice center was established in 1954 to provide medical services that supplemented insurance benefits under the Martin–UAW contract.[28] Except for these diagnostic or supplemental plans, the UAW had not ventured into the direct-service field until, in 1956, it was ready to move in Detroit.

The approach was to be different from that of the Goldman report. Instead of constructing, on the Kaiser model, new facilities which would compete with existing facilities, the new Community Health Association was to start out using existing hospitals and clinics.[29] Where group practices could be organized in these facilities, they would be brought into one overall prepayment program for union members and other Detroiters. This community emphasis followed the lead of the Health Insurance Plan of New York and marked a reaction away from other new "union-only" health centers. It was an important turning point in labor's efforts for better medical care. It fits with the increasingly integrated role labor plays in American social life, a role that carries an authority and has given the unions an acceptance unknown thirty years ago. The CHA Board of Directors broadly represents the community, the individual members being from management, labor, church, university, and hospital institutions.

The diplomacy and patience required for such a project have been continually underestimated; on the other hand, an advantage of the community approach is some saving in capitalization—about half that suggested in the Goldman report. The blueprint proposed to use available hospitals and out-patient clinics and to construct branch clinics.[30] These facilities could provide a full range of prepaid home, outpatient clinic, and in-hospital services for about 300,000 persons.

The basic principles of CHA were to be prepayment for comprehensive service benefits, emphasis on high quality of care, group practice co-ordinated by one's personal physician, and the association of each medical group with a participating hospital to assure maximum continuity of care. While CHA argued for medical control and was against lay interference in medical matters, it also demanded that the consumer be heard in non-medical matters. It was also decided that in all group enrollments the individuals should have free choice between CHA and an alternative plan.

To show the seriousness with which CHA regarded the question of quality and to deflate any hostile attacks on this score, it held a conference on the quality of medical care early in 1957. Local doctors and national medical leaders were invited; after some hesitation, officers of the Michigan State Medical Society and the Wayne County Medical Society attended and contributed to the discussions. About half of the forty-four doctors attending were from Michigan. The conference proceedings remain one of the most interesting open discussions among doctors on the effect of the economic structure of practice on the quality of the medical product.[31]

Detroit is perhaps under-supplied with doctors, and they have a relatively high average income. A greater resistance to CHA might be anticipated from the profession than that encountered by HIP in New York City, with its surplus of doctors. Among Detroit doctors in 1956 there were intense discussions about group practice and closed panels; the general practitioners especially felt threatened. But the Wayne County Medical Society restrained itself from public attacks and set to work to develop methods of improving the Michigan Medical Service (Blue Shield) as a way of heading off CHA. The *Detroit Medical News* argued that it was high time for the Michigan Medical Service to move into the field of preventive medicine.[32] Others proposed a major medical program with deductible and co-insurance features and unscheduled surgical benefits.

At the state level the air was thicker. The State Medical Society warned of the "do-gooders in the security departments of government and of unions [who] are now desperately trying to gain control of the great public trusts [hospitals] the health pioneers have built."[33] Dr. Arch Wells, its President, declared that "certain laymen have and are attempting to hire doctors so that they can make a profit on their services. . . . Certain unions have publicly announced their intention of making public utilities out of the profession. . . ."[34] The apathetic were admonished that UAW President Walter Reuther would not stop with Detroit.

At a special meeting of the House of Delegates convened in April, 1957, to discuss the crisis, the Wayne County Medical Society Committee on Prepaid Medical Care Plans introduced a resolution recommending that the Michigan Medical Service "devise a policy patterned after the General Electric Plan providing extensive care in hospital, home and office, with deductible and co-insurance features that will pay physicians without a fixed fee schedule his usual fee for a given service."[35] Another resolution proposed doing away with service benefits and substituting only an indemnity fee schedule. After a poll of its members and much planning, the Michigan Medical Service was amended by adding outpatient diagnostic services and raising the family income limit for service benefits to $7500.

Despite the opposition and counterplans, CHA began, at least on a modest basis. Dr. Fred Mott was employed as director (subsequently Dr. Caldwell Esselstyn became director). Metropolitan Hospital was purchased in 1956 with a loan from Nationwide Insurance Company, guaranteed by the union. The number served has grown steadily from 26,000 at the first option to over 70,000 and there are now (1966) three neighborhood centers in addition to the central Metropolitan Hospital. The program is described in more detail in Chapter 12.

The Detroit success has been followed by another in Baltimore. The UAW loaned $250,000 for the construction there of a medical center that could eventually accommodate 15,000 persons. This new East Point Medical Center, an outgrowth of the small center in the Local 738 union hall, was dedicated in the Spring of 1966. Subscribers will pay a flat monthly fee, with the amount depending on their Blue Cross–Blue Shield coverage plan, which East Point is designed to supplement. The bulk of the membership in the plan comes from three UAW locals in Baltimore. In Boston, the union is taking the initiative in working with other unions and medical school faculties to establish a pilot program for 6,000 members and their dependents.

More than any other American union, the United Auto Workers has provided insight into and direction on the role and aims of labor in welfare bargaining. Its able staff has carefully analyzed and vigorously asserted the limitations of traditional insurance concepts, the need for concern with medical care, and the necessity of union participation in administration of welfare plans. Health bargaining was successfully carried first into the major auto companies and then throughout the industry. The old employee benefit plans have been expanded and liberalized and priority has been won for health insurance and medical care benefits. Union participation in administration has not been made a major issue, although there has been, at least on health insurance, a transfer of cost information across the bargaining table. The union has forced some hard bargaining with Blue Cross and Blue Shield plans and has secured substantial improvements—most notably in Michigan, but in other places also. The union remains, however, highly critical of Blue Shield, and has turned to a very advanced form of private health planning, typified by the Detroit CHA, to secure prepaid comprehensive medical care.

Part II

Toward Community Health Bargaining

7

BARGAINING WITH EMPLOYERS:
BENEFITS AND COSTS

We have sketched the historical processes that brought labor and management together in welfare bargaining. Their rivalry for exclusive control of welfare plans has been replaced by joint control. Benefit plans no longer figure as one of the terrains on which management and labor fight their battles for survival; under welfare bargaining they have succeeded in accommodating each other, and now direct a welfare power that has great influence on other institutions in the community.

Within this welfare partnership, however, there are still many unresolved issues and areas of conflict. Employers and union leaders do not agree on the extent of the union's role in establishing and administering welfare plans. Management wishes to preserve traditional prerogatives associated with selection of the carrier and claims handling. There are also significant differences of opinion between labor and management about the kind of benefits, the extent of coverage, and how the cost should be shared. These issues are the subject of this and the next chapter.

The Preparation

Many unions, when they first began negotiating for health insurance, realized they were ill equipped for the new subject. Experienced negotiators, who had mastered the technical intricacies of piece rates and complex wage formulas seemed to "freeze up" on the subject of health insurance. The first task of each union was to instill in its negotiators the kind of knowledge and experience that would give them enough confidence to negotiate on this new subject.

Some of the larger unions who led the way in this field equipped themselves with experts, by either hiring or training them, and smaller unions later "borrowed" these technicians. In some unions, experts had a large role in policy decisions, but their main job was training negotiators, teaching them to separate essentials from technicalities. The important questions were: was the company willing to participate in providing health insurance coverage for workers represented by the union? for their families? would it pay the full cost of the program? Once the answers to these questions were clear, then the company and the union had at their disposal the staff or consultants to provide alternate benefit structures, cost estimates, etc. What labor leaders had initially to learn was that the same negotiating skills useful to any other important contract item were also useful for the basic questions of health insurance.

Unions prepared for health bargaining in various ways, depending on bargaining patterns in their industry and their internal administrative structure. In relatively decentralized organizations, such as the International Association of Machinists, or the Retail Clerks, or the American Newspaper Guild, initiative was taken and decisions were made at a local union level. The role of the international union headquarters was simply to give direction, advice, and, if it had a servicing staff, to provide technical help when asked. By contrast, the pattern of bargaining with big companies in steel, rubber, and autos meant that the major decisions were made at the international union level, and health insurance technicians played a direct and important part in the negotiations of the industry. But other patterns exist also: for example, although the Communications Workers of America are forced to bargain with separate telephone systems rather than with American Telephone and Telegraph Company, the structure of the union remains highly centralized and the union headquarters has a primary role in establishing bargaining demands, in the training of negotiators, and in the preparation of technical material.

More important than the mechanics of preparation was the attitude behind it, and here there were two opposed points of view, with most organizations falling somewhere between. On the one hand were those unions which negotiated prepayment plans without much investigation of alternatives; they were interested in orthodox prepayment plans similar to those other unions had obtained. On such policy questions as indemnity versus service benefits, or the range of services to be covered, they took the views of insurance companies, without involving their members or studying existing consumer experience. In short, these unions treated the subject as just another fringe benefit and showed little sophistication about the special difficulties of health bargaining.

At the other extreme were those unions which regarded the subject as a challenge, an opportunity for consumer education on medical care, and for developing the membership resources in order to strengthen the union. They discovered union members who were serving locally on Blue Cross boards or active in community health matters, and through summer schools and weekend institutes gave direction to existing interest and enlivened union deliberations. This approach refused to transfer all or even portions of health and welfare negotiations to experts, preferring to involve bargaining committees and local representatives in the policy questions. In the words of the then research director of the Communications Workers of America, Sylvia Gottlieb:

. . . the learning process, the training programs, the meeting of new challenges by full-time union representatives, as well as rank-and-file members, gives much needed vitality to a union. Becoming involved in preparations for negotiations and in actual negotiations around a new subject, can be a union-building force and this opportunity should not be lost. . . .[1]

Benefits and Compensation

The struggle to bring employee benefit plans under collective bargaining left its imprint on the union philosophy of insurance and benefit plans: negotiation of the labor contract is regarded as a transaction between parties in which equal values are exchanged, and insurance or benefit programs are part of the total compensation for labor. They are not gifts or gratuities given at the discretion of a paternalistic employer, but rather part of one's remuneration channeled to a group prepayment plan. They are an alternative form of compensation and their monetary value is an ever-present factor at the bargaining table.

In applying this philosophy, some difficult questions are raised, because the exact cost of certain benefits is frequently not known until after some experience with the program, and even then it will continue to vary with the composition of the work force, the prevalence of illness, the movement in medical prices, and the relative tightness or looseness of claims administration. The premium cost may be subject later to dividends or other retroactive rate adjustments. Is the "compensation" value then the premium cost or the eventual net cost? Do dividends and reserves belong to the company or to the employees? Can there be a predetermined compensation value as long as there are risks and variables affecting the costs?

Many debates have been waged over the relative merits of asking for specified benefits, or for the amount of money necessary to provide them. Bargaining for a certain amount of money may clarify the monetary value of the health and welfare demand, but other problems are raised. What will be the actual income to the fund from the formula proposed? If the company payments are to be made in a specified number of cents per employee-hour worked, variation in employment levels will have a substantial effect on the funds available. If other formulas are used that provide a more dependable income to the fund—such as a flat amount per week or month or each employee who has worked during that period—it will still be necessary to accumulate reserves to some estimated safe level, particularly if the plan is to be self-insured. The utility of the plan in terms of benefits can be known only after difficult estimates or accumulated experience with the income and reserves of the fund. Some funds have accumulated reserves for months, even years, before any benefits were provided. The employees knew the monetary value of the accumulation, but they didn't know what benefits they might get. Negotiating for a specified monetary contribution is the usual practice in multi-employer bargaining, not so much because of the principle of explicit compensation cited here as for the practical purpose of computing each employer's share in industries where employees change employers frequently.

The prevalent pattern for individual employer health and welfare plans is bargaining for *benefits*, in which the union specifies the insurance or medical care benefits that it wants. Unless the union can estimate the premium cost and the probable net cost of these demands, it does not know what this part of the union demand is worth and what wage or other fringe gain is being sacrificed for the health benefits. It is important that the union have the technical help necessary to make these estimates fairly closely. Then it is, in fact, bargaining on both benefits and contributions. To make the premium cost and net cost as nearly alike as possible, the union can insist that any dividend or rate credits accumulate to the plan rather than be returned to the employer. Just as the employer cannot withhold or recapture cash wage payments, he cannot under these conditions recapture premium payments, and the employee more nearly knows the amount of his compensation. Such arrangements have the further advantage that, if premiums are increased as a result of higher than expected claims, it may not be necessary to seek additional compensation to continue the same benefits.

This is the orthodox union view, but there is a school which prefers bargaining for benefits without much concern for cost estimation. The theory here is a strategic one: that employees do not finely calculate their total compensation, and that they can be most quickly motivated to act in terms of descriptive benefit changes—to protest any reduction, and to support improvement. This view has its adherents where negotiations are primarily a testing ground for tenacity.

Should Employees Contribute?

One effect of bargaining has been to raise the portion of insurance and health benefits financed by the employer and to diminish or eliminate employee contributions. This trend was noted early in welfare bargaining and has continued.[2] Full company financing has been the pattern in coal, ladies' garments, men's clothing, the building trades, and other industries where multi-employer plans predominate, including recently the fur manufacturing industry. In the single-employer plans there has been a significant shift since 1959 away from employee contributions. In steel, the union negotiated full company financing of all benefits for active workers and their dependents and of life insurance for retirees; in aluminum, the company now pays also the full cost of dependent benefits. In 1961, the United Auto Workers obtained company-financed health benefits for active workers and their dependents, and company contributions toward health benefits for retired workers were negotiated at General Motors, Ford, and elsewhere; in 1964, these companies agreed to assume the full cost of benefits for retirees.

In a group of large negotiated plans from different industries analyzed by the Bureau of Labor Statistics, the distribution according to the source of financing the health benefits is as follows.[3]

Table III: Distribution by Source of Financing Benefits

	Total plans	Full cost paid by company	Cost shared by company and worker or retiree	Full cost paid by worker or retiree
Active workers	99[a]	78	20	1[b]
Active workers' dependents	99	63	28	8
Retired workers	63	38	18	7
Retired workers' dependents	61	32	19	10

[a] All plans except those for seamen, who are entitled to complete medical care through other arrangements.

[b] The agreement in this case provided for a wage increase of 7½ cents per hour to be used solely for the purpose of financing the health and insurance programs.

Source: Bureau of Labor Statistics, *Digest of One-Hundred Selected Health and Insurance Plans under Collective Bargaining, Early 1966*, BLS Bull. No. 1502, and, for the retired workers and dependents similar survey of winter, 1961–62, BLS Bull. No. 1330.

These figures undoubtedly overstate the extent of employer financing in small companies and in the non-union sector. Data compiled under the Welfare and Pension Plans Disclosure Act show that as of July, 1963, 36.1 per cent of all health and welfare plans (excluding retirement plans) are entirely employer financed, 49.7 per cent are employer-employee financed, and only 9.7 per cent are financed by the employees only.[4] From all the available evidence it has been estimated that in 1962, about 65 to 70 per cent of all contributions to health and welfare plans (excluding retirement and supplemental unemployment benefits) were paid by employers, compared with 47 per cent in 1954.[5] Recent information suggests this trend is continuing.[6]

In appraising this trend, it is important to remember that the big, mass production unions wanted full employer financing from the beginning, but they did not get it in health and insurance benefits. Union presidents Lewis and Murray had proclaimed a principle of employer obligation, but even if a company admitted that maintaining the health of its workers was analogous to repairing its machinery, the argument could not be extended to health care for dependents. The large companies wanted employee contributions to reduce their costs and to remind employees that health and welfare plans were not "something for nothing." They felt that employee contributions would bring responsibility and restraint in future negotiations. On the union side, health benefits were altogether too important not to compromise on the principle of financing. Most unions have been willing to initiate a plan on a contributory basis if it could not be fully employer financed; and a union will not take a cut in benefit levels just to establish full employer financing; employee contributions have been adopted if that was the only way of obtaining more benefits. If employers felt strongly about the contribution principle, and unions were willing to compromise in this issue, what is the explanation for the trend to increased employer contribution?

Two recurring pressures are largely responsible. Firstly, the continuous rise in medical costs, at a rate faster than any other item on the cost-of-living index, has repeatedly made indemnity plans inadequate and raised the premium rates on the service plans: more money had to go into health and welfare if only to maintain the range of services prepaid. Secondly, the gaps and shortcomings in the existing plans became clear with experience (and with the rising costs), generating rank-and-file pressure for improvement. Many employees felt they were already making all the contribution they could afford in the form of out-of-pocket payment to the uncompensated portion of their medical bills. Why should they also have to raise their contribution? Under these pressures, the problem was how to get more money at the bargaining table in the most efficient manner, and the tax advantages of employer, as against employee, contributions became a major consideration. By foregoing some wage increases and channeling them instead to an additional employer contribution, the employee saved whatever additional income tax he would otherwise have had to pay. At the bargaining table it became apparent that for a given increase in labor costs, an additional employer contribution was the least wasteful. Some unions even changed their semantics and substituted "taxable and non-taxable" for "contributory and non-contributory."[7]

In this sense, the issue of contributory financing has been bypassed. The question does not have meaning in private benefit plans under conditions of rising wage levels. What we now call "employer financing" can also be called "employee financing" and the distinction is meaningful largely because of the Internal Revenue Code. In Canada, employee contributions to group insurance and benefit plans are tax exempt, and one might speculate on the course of history had this been the rule here.

There is another advantage besides tax savings, in employer financing. Group insurance requires participation by three-fourths of the employees. With contributory financing, employee participation is voluntary, and poorly informed or unco-operative employees can block an ambitious health program. Employer financing obviates this possibility.

What we have presented here is a view that both employers and unions take a pragmatic rather than a rigidly "principled" approach to financing, looking for simplifications and efficiencies. One such efficiency that can be realized is in the consolidation of small plans. The small company is at a disadvantage when one considers the actuarial savings that may come with big plans. A group of 100 people or fewer may require an insurance retention of 30 per cent compared with 5 per cent or less for a plan with 5,000 persons.[8] This helps explain why benefits in small plans are frequently lower, and why fewer small plans are non-contributory. One union response, in autos for example, is to try to broaden the base by combining small units into multi-employer plans.

Who Should Be Covered and When?

Some of the bitterest arguments have centered on whether employment health plans should cover dependents, laid-off workers, strikers, and whether the employer can be expected to contribute toward medical expenses of persons not on his payroll. Traditionally, the employer has thought only of his responsibility for active employees: this is the coverage provided, for example, by workmen's compensation. But unions have succeeded to some extent in establishing the broader image of the employee as an industrial "citizen"—a family man, union member, and eventually a retired man.

Family and Dependents

The number of dependents covered by health insurance plans has increased considerably, from 44 to 68 million in the 8 years prior to 1962.[9] In the study of 100 large negotiated plans cited earlier, all but 2 provide dependent benefits, and the company pays the full cost for dependents in 61 of them; in 27, the company and the employee share the cost; and in only 10 is the full cost borne by the employee. The pressure for dependent coverage comes from the fact that in the typical family 80 per cent of the medical bills are accounted for by dependents.[10] Employers have, however, shown considerably more resistance to paying for dependent coverage than for that of employees. And the unions have had to face an issue of equity—are single persons being slighted when the employer pays for dependent coverage? Both considerations help explain why in non-contributory plans the benefits for dependents are frequently less in dollar amount than those for employees, and why benefit limitations and exclusions often apply only to dependents.

Laid-Off Employees

Little progress has been made in continuing coverage for laid-off employees. Usually the policy terminates with the premium month in which the lay-off occurred, although additional months are allowed in some plans. It has been estimated that extended protection during lay-off, for longer than one month, is guaranteed to only one-tenth of the fifty million workers covered by group health insurance plans.[11]

The United Auto Workers has negotiated extended protection related to entitlement for supplemental unemployment benefits. These extended plans continue insurance up to thirteen months after the month in which the lay-off began. The United Steelworkers of America continues group hospital and surgical coverage for six months at company cost for employees with at least two years of service, and up to a year for those with ten years of service. The United Mine Workers Fund covers up to one year after lay-off. Liberal provisions are also found in some areas such as primary metals, rubber products, food products, and electrical machinery manufacturing industries.

There is some evidence, though still inconclusive, to show that utilization rates of workers on lay-off are higher than for those employed.[12] This is a deterrent to extended protection. However, the importance from the workers' viewpoint of continuing employer-paid health insurance is shown by the fact that most workers when laid off drop their coverage if they have to assume the cost, even when offered a chance to continue at group rates. Just how high the drop-out rate is under these circumstances is suggested by UAW experience in 1958: only one-third of some 3,000 laid-off Ford employees were still covered two months after they began getting individual billings.[13]

Employees on Strike

Very few union contracts explicitly provide for group insurance benefits during a strike, but the National Labor Relations Board has held that the employer is liable for benefit payments during an unfair labor practice strike.[14] There is no such liability during an economic strike, on the ground that economic pressure on the employer need not be rewarded by continuation of insurance benefits. In practice, Blue Cross and most insurance carriers will continue benefits for a month or two during a strike and then attempt to get the employees to assume the premiums; payment of back insurance premiums is frequently a minor item in the strike settlement.

In conclusion, health bargaining has established with some employers their financial obligations for dependents, and, in a limited way, for retired and laid-off workers. Some employers still insist that they have no responsibilities for such broad coverage, but with most it is a matter of cost now rather than of principle.

Bargaining for Retirees

In the 1950's employers were unwilling to contribute to coverage for retired workers in their health insurance plans, and the insurance carriers were reluctant to enter this new field. Blue Cross and Blue Shield, after some initial resistance, did agree to allow workers to continue their coverage after retirement for the same premium as that charged them while they were working, but the requirements were strict: the retiring worker had only one opportunity during his lifetime to make the decision to continue his insurance; if he later failed to make a premium payment when it fell due his policy was cancelled permanently; if the actively-employed group ceased to be enrolled (even as the result of a plant shut-down), the insurance was discontinued.

The breakthrough was achieved in rubber and autos, and continued into the steel, aluminum, meatpacking, and other industries. While Blue Cross and Blue Shield cautiously entered the new territory, the commercial carriers actively discouraged the business, demanding premiums three to four times higher than for working employees, or offering drastically reduced benefits. Since employers would not contribute to retirees' coverage, the union could only bargain for arrangements under which retirees would assume the cost of their own continued coverage. The issue became one of getting the employer and insurer to agree to a merging of the claims experience of active and retired workers before setting premium rates. Then the retired worker could continue his previous benefits at a more reasonable cost. Where the employer was contributing to coverage for active employees in these merged cases, he would now bear some of the cost of retiree protection, but only indirectly through the overall premium increase; on retirement the worker had to assume the full premium himself. It was not until 1962 that agreements were reached in major industries under which employers would pay directly half the premium for retirees.

The BLS survey of 1961–62, the last to include retirement statistics, shows the one hundred largest companies to have been at various stages in these developments. Thirty-eight provided equal benefits to active and retired workers; 25 reduced benefits for retirees; the others offered no coverage for retirees. Of the 63 plans which did provide such coverage, the employer paid full costs in 38 cases; employer and retired worker shared costs in 18 plans; the retirees paid full costs in 7 plans. Retirees' dependents were covered in 61 of the 63 plans but companies did not contribute as much for dependents as they did for retirees themselves. We emphasize that these are characteristics of the larger plans; there is evidence that there was less retiree insurance and company financing in smaller companies.[15] The UAW estimated in 1964 that an average elderly couple had to spend 15 to 20 per cent of its pension benefits for health insurance, and that for some retirees, particularly those still paying the cost, the amounts spent for health insurance were more than half the pension.[16]

During Congressional hearings on Medicare, unions testified on their difficulties with insurance carriers and employers. They estimated the number of aged persons with no health insurance; they pointed to the shortcomings in negotiated programs; they called attention to the fact that occupations filled by older persons are less likely to have health insurance plans; they cited the limitations of individual policies for those over 65.[17] George Meany argued for the AFL–CIO that the higher costs of insuring older workers and their substantially reduced financial resources put the problem outside the capacity of private insurance. He urged governmental action because other means had proved inadequate.[18]

As it emerged from Congress, the Medicare law provided for all persons over 65 eligibility to hospital insurance and also to supplementary medical insurance for those who make a voluntary contribution of $3 a month. These benefits are available whether or not one has earned entitlement to old-age and survivors' insurance. At this writing, private plans are still being adapted to Medicare benefits, and generalizations about its impact on them are therefore somewhat speculative, but the following effects are emerging.

The conflict between unions and employers about this issue is somewhat diminished. The unions clearly have public policy on their side, and the subject is removed from the bargaining table insofar as the issues are a matter of principle. However, unions will probably push for benefits to supplement Medicare in those companies that have no retiree programs. Unions will urge arrangements by which the $3 supplemental insurance contribution can be passed on to the employer. One effect of Medicare will be a larger proportion of employer-paid benefits for those over 65.

As retired workers' health insurance plans are renegotiated to adapt to Medicare and to avoid duplication of benefits, the question of what to do with the cost savings arises. (It should be noted that insurers and prepayment organizations in many cases have improved their position also; that is, the arrangements that they offer for adaptation to Medicare do not pass all the savings to the consumers.) Unions will wish to apply the freed funds in ways that improve the total package of combined benefits. Because of rising health insurance costs, managements prefer to hold freed funds to offset future premium increases.

Different methods of adapting private plans to Medicare are being tried. Insurers are taking different positions on the kinds of supplemental plans they will offer, but for large group plans they are willing to tailor programs to the union and company desires. The basic differences in adaptation are between the "building blocks" approach, in which Medicare sets the basic benefit pattern while the supplemental plan adds specific benefits to fill in Medicare gaps, and the "benefit carve-out" approach, which retains the benefit pattern of the existing group plan but allows deduction or offsetting of Medicare benefits.

Thus one question affecting the form of adaptation is whether the private plan is broader in scope than Medicare or more limited. Some forms of adaptation have the advantage of being easily understood, or easily administered, or easily adjusted to future changes in Medicare, but none seems to have all the advantages.[19]

Medicare is bringing about a restructuring of private plans on the basis of age rather than of work status. All those over 65 are eligible for Medicare whether or not they are working, and this influences the renegotiation of private plans. The issue for private plans now is the individual's age rather than whether he is actively employed or retired. This means that employees retired before age 65 are more likely to be included in the same program as working employees until they reach 65. It also means that some members of the same family may be in different plans; that is, a husband over 65 may be covered differently from his wife, who is under 65.

In addition to its effect on retirement coverage in private health plans, Medicare will affect the plans for working employees. For example, a few large plans have recently been changed from a schedule of cash allowances to payment of all "reasonable and customary" charges. Since adoption of this standard in Medicare, many more changes may be expected.[20]

The Kind and Amount of Benefits

The results of union negotiations depend on what is happening to the prices of medical services, what kind of prepayment plans are available, and how much money can be committed at the bargaining table. While looking for programs to provide comprehensive coverage, labor has helped to broaden the range of insurance available as underwriters seek to satisfy the market. In general, unions have gone beyond the early emphasis on prepayment just for daily hospital charges and surgical fees. In order to achieve a better distribution of benefits among the various kinds of medical services, unions have sought to cover the full range of in-hospital expenses and outpatient services, and doctors' charges wherever they are rendered. They are also advocating experiments in coverage for mental illness, dental services, and optical care.

Hospitalization

Negotiating daily room and board payments and allowances for "extras," or ancillary services, has been greatly complicated by the rapid rise in hospital rates. The typical indemnity plan in 1949 provided between $4 and $7 a day.[21] By 1966 the sample of one hundred large plans showed these benefits ranged from $10 to $33 with the median about $18. The only certain way to handle the problem from the employee's standpoint has been to negotiate service benefits that pay the full cost of semi-private facilities; this trend was notable before 1958, and by 1966 over half the large plans were paying for a semi-private room. Specified allowances for hospital extras or ancillary services were a median $60 in 1948 and in 1966 were around $300, but large plans were commonly providing full benefits for some or all extras.

While much of the increase in daily benefits and extra allowances has gone to offset the rising costs, the extension in duration represents a net improvement in the value of health plans. From 1948 to 1963, the typical provisions had risen from 31 days to 70 days per illness.[22] The sample of one hundred plans shows that the most common full benefit period rose from 120 days per disability in 1962 to 365 days in 1966.[23] Because of the relative infrequency of long stays, the additional cost of these long period benefits is cheaper than that of earlier extensions in duration.

Surgical Benefits

Negotiation of surgical benefits revolves around the amount allowed for each type of operation. It is always problematical whether the agreed-on amount is of any significance to doctors practicing surgery in the community, except in those plans where participating doctors agree to accept the scheduled fees as full payment. The high frequency of a few operations, however, makes possible a low-cost local survey of the level of charges. It is important to the union that such operations as tonsillectomies and appendectomies have an assigned fee close to that charged locally and that the other charges bear some recognized relationship to these benchmark fees. The benchmark fees will, because of their frequency, have the major influence on the cost and value of the schedule. It is also important that the income limits in a service plan—the income level of individuals or families for whom participating physicians will accept the scheduled benefits as full payment—be high enough to include most of the members in the bargaining unit; otherwise, the members will be subject to additional charges. Only a dozen of the Blue Shield plans around the country provide service benefits for families with incomes over $7,000; all the others set lower income limits.[24]

The typical large negotiated plan will now pay $150 for appendectomies and $300 for the most expensive operation. However, schedules with maximums of $350 or $450 are not uncommon, and a few provide full payment for any operation. Many plans specify that the surgical benefits apply whether the surgery was performed in a hospital or elsewhere. A few Blue Shield plans still do not include coverage for pathology, X ray, and anesthesia.

As with surgical benefits, payments for obstetrical care can be measured against local charges. Group policies need not have a waiting period for obstetrical coverage, although many do, and the benefit plan for a pregnancy in progress need not terminate if the plan is discontinued.

Medical Benefits

These benefits apply to doctors' charges other than surgery in the hospital, and to home and office visits. The BLS study of large plans indicates that the frequency of this coverage is somewhat less than for hospital and surgical charges (see Table IV).

Table IV: Distribution by Type of Benefits Provided

Benefit	Number of plans
Hospital	97
Surgical	97
In-hospital medical	79
Physicians' visits in the office	38
Physicians' visits in the home	35
Diagnostic X-ray outside the hospital	59
Diagnostic X-ray and laboratory outside the hospital	43

Source: Bureau of Labor Statistics, *Digest of One-Hundred Selected Health and Insurance Plans under Collective Bargaining, Early 1966*, BLS Bull. No. 1502.

The plans that provide medical benefits vary in many ways: in the amount for doctor visits, whether payments start with the first visit, whether specialists are included as well as one's "regular" doctor, the number of visits or the length of time covered, and the kinds of laboratory services included. All Blue Shield plans include some measure of in-hospital medical care, but only 35 per cent of them include home and office visits among the services covered.[25]

Limitations and Exclusions

The better (and more costly) negotiated plans contain fewer limitations and exclusions. Frequently excluded from hospital benefits are alcoholism or drug addiction, or pre-existing conditions. Surgical plans often exclude cosmetic and dental surgery. Medical plans may exclude some doctor visits for such services as diagnostic examinations, electroshock therapy, out-of-hospital drug and medication prescriptions, immunization, annual check-ups, etc.; or these may involve out-of-pocket charges to the patient.[26]

Coverage of new-born children as dependents begins immediately at birth in the best plans, but in many does not begin until ten days or two weeks after, or until discharge from the hospital, with the result that such plans may not cover expensive postnatal care for complications.

Mental Illness, Eye Care, and Dental Care

Doubts about the insurability of mental illness have delayed its availability until recently, but unions are beginning to press for such coverage. Blue Cross included mental health coverage first to accommodate the steel agreements; then in 1964 the auto agreements went to 45 days of hospitalization for mental illness, and in addition provided a broad range of diagnostic and psychotherapeutic services outside the hospital, subject to overall dollar limits. Local 770 of the Retail Clerks International Association in Los Angeles has an extensive mental health program as part of its arrangement with the Kaiser Foundation.

Dental prepayment is growing rapidly and an estimated two million persons are now included. Until 1960 dental plans were usually a part of comprehensive medical service programs, but since then dental service corporations (a kind of Blue Shield for dentists) and commercial insurance plans have been multiplying. Labor's relationship to dental service corporations and the American Dental Association is discussed in Chapter 12.

Eye or vision care is frequently integrated with other services in community and union health centers; in the best programs optometrists who give refractions are under the direction of opthalmologists.[27]

There are also specialized eye-care centers sponsored by unions and operated on a direct-service basis in several communities. Prepayment plans not associated with clinics exist, and differ widely in whether they cover lenses or lenses and frames as well as eye examinations. Lastly, some unions have made simple discount arrangements for the purchase of glasses.[28]

Among the hundred large negotiated plans six offer dental care (five since 1962) and twelve eye care (six since 1962). All of these are multi-employer plans.

Major Medical

With medical costs increasing twice and hospital costs four times as fast as the overall cost-of-living, much of the increase in funds that has been channeled into group insurance simply maintains protection already won. "We are being squeezed between the pincers of fast-rising medical costs, on the one hand, and a growing demand for broadened benefits on the other," was the typical company reaction.[29] The rapid spread of major medical insurance is best explained as a response to this problem.[30] Thirty-two of a sample of one hundred large plans in 1966 provided major medical.[31] One effect of union bargaining, however, has been to liberalize these plans by increasing the maximum benefits and reducing the deductible amounts. There is also, now, more awareness among unions of the importance of analyzing the technicalities of major medical plans.

Developed by General Electric and the Liberty Mutual Insurance Company for managerial and "white collar" employees, major medical has been extended to production workers. While the health insurance movement has been a search for more comprehensive inclusion of family medical bills, the proponents of major medical insurance would end the search by omitting prepayment for the early expenses and co-insuring the rest. This antithetical development is urged by management as a kind of terminal package to forestall successive union demands for more. Some unions retaliate that the deductibles, by relegating smaller bills to family budgeting, actually discourage justified utilization among blue collar workers where budgeting is not characteristic.[32] Co-insurance can also discourage justified as well as unjustified utilization. Union spokesmen have cited the inflationary dangers in large unscheduled benefits subject to no controls, a danger admitted by the more thoughtful insurers. This battle ebbs and flows. Most unions continue to resist efforts to replace their basic coverage with major medical or so-called "comprehensive medical insurance," but many have accepted major medical as a supplement to basic coverage.

Conversion Rights

Conversion rights are an important feature of group health insurance plans, so that the worker may continue coverage as an individual regardless of the reasons for his separation from employment, including retirement.

The Future of Health Bargaining

Health bargaining has contributed both to an increase in the portion of the consumer's disposable income going to medical care and to channeling more of those dollars through the prepayment mechanism. It is more significant to ask how much of this represents a net gain in needed medical service. An estimate has been made for the period 1954 to 1962 by using the aggregate hospital and medical payments made by all employee benefit plans (negotiated and unilateral).[33] After correcting to allow for the additional employees and dependents covered and also for the rise in hospital and medical prices, it is estimated that about one-fourth of the increase in aggregate hospital payments and two-fifths of the increase in medical payments represent net additional services to individuals that are an improvement in the scope and adequacy of the benefits. (Further refinement would be required to allow for change in utilization and over-utilization.) Although there has been net improvement, the problem of closing the gap toward comprehensive coverage is a little like racing down an upward moving escalator.

How big a gap remains? Despite what has been done, unions are finding that the negotiated plans are covering only half, one-third, or even less of family medical bills.[34] A comprehensive medical care program including prepayment for hospitalization and all doctor services in home, office, and hospital now costs about $25 a month per family covered; dental prepayment adds another $7 to $9; eye refractions still more.[35] And just to maintain the present levels of coverage will cost an additional cent per employee-hour each year. Under these circumstances the gap to be closed yawns as a chasm.

Where they can take the initiative, unions are responding to the problems of cost and quality in several ways. Firstly, they are looking for whatever efficiencies can be realized—reductions in insurance carrier retentions, methods of questioning out-of-line hospital and doctor charges, agreed fee schedules, and benefit schedules that both encourage use and discourage abuse. Secondly, they are re-examining their goals to determine what segments of medical care are most important to prepay and which should wait until sound prepayment mechanisms are available. Thirdly, they are more carefully examining the quality of medical care being purchased with the new prepayment dollars. Fourthly, they have been working to limit the area of private health insurance by taking out its most troublesome segment—health insurance for the retired. And finally, they are searching for ways to bring financing and the quality of medical services provided into a close relationship, either through controls or through direct-service arrangements that put the responsibility for both on the same shoulders.

An illustration will show how labor is drawn into the economics of medicine. An official of the United Rubber Workers has described this experience:

> In a local in Butler, Pennsylvania, we started out with an insurance program that provided fifty dollars for the maternity fee. We had found that for a number of years the maternity fee in that community was $50.
>
> Strange as it may seem, in less than a year we found that the standard charge for maternity in Butler went to $75. Then we came in with the surgical schedule we have now which provides $75 for normal delivery. We now find that the normal delivery charge in Butler is $125.[36]

This raises the question whether the union is bargaining for its members or for the medical profession. Union leaders are compelled to consider how the provision and financing of medical services can be reorganized. In this way, the search for efficiencies and responsibility in cost and quality draws labor deeply into the practices of insurers, doctors, hospitals, and medical service—a general reorientation toward "community health bargaining."

The future of health prepayment plans—at least their rate of evolution—may turn on whether labor can persuade management toward "community bargaining" on health objectives. This is a subject of intense discussion in a number of our basic industries, but it is a thorny path before which management, in this case the Ford Motor Company, hesitates:

We have in common [with the union] an interest in selecting good insurance or prepayment arrangements at good values for our employees. I think we differ, however, on the role that collective bargaining should play in shaping hospital and medical practice as such, and in solving broad community problems. The UAW quite regularly seeks, through bargaining pressure, to force our aid in implementing its social or community objectives. We, on the other hand, have a deep conviction that the collective bargaining arena, designed to resolve labor-management differences over conditions of employment, is one of the most ill-fitted places conceivable for resolving these other kinds of problems. If they were to be permitted to become entangled in the considerations for maintaining labor peace in our plants, it would be bad both for us and the community.[37]

In health and medical care questions, will labor allow management alone to define the conditions of industrial peace? If not, what will be the future impact of the industrial community on the economics of medical care?

8

BARGAINING WITH EMPLOYERS: ADMINISTRATION

In the administration of health and welfare plans, we can distinguish these patterns.

First, some of the early welfare plans financed by dues and assessments were later transformed into collectively bargained plans. Such plans, as in the needle trades for example, became financed in whole or in part by the employer, but they continued to be administered by the union. Under the Labor-Management Relations Act these plans have been allowed to continue as union-administered if established prior to 1947.

Secondly, as welfare bargaining was extended after 1947, the pattern in the service, construction, coal mining, and casual employments was the "Taft-Hartley type" plan of joint administration where the employers and the union have equal voting strength in the board of trustees. This form is adaptable to multi-employer bargaining situations and to labor markets where employment is casual or transient. It enables several employers to make a financial contribution to a central fund and spread the risk over the entire group. As a relatively new device, it has been of particular interest to students of business administration and of trust law. Congressional and state investigations uncovered serious irregularities in some of these plans. Their limitations will be discussed later.

In the third type, accounting for over 90 per cent of all plans, administration is assumed by the employer.[1] This is the usual situation in the single-employer plans that predominate in manufacturing.

Single-Employer Plans

The employer assumes the responsibility of providing the benefits that are negotiated, including selection of the carrier, financial arrangements, and claims administration. This is in the tradition of employee benefit plans where unilateral decision, undisclosed arrangements, and absence of accountability to the employees all characterized the administration of the program. Collective bargaining has modified this administrative exclusiveness in some cases. Unions hold that negotiated health and welfare plans are part of the employees' compensation and that the cost, and arrangements that affect it, should be explicit. But this touches the sore spot of management prerogative and in the typical situation the employer insists on reserving to himself the selection of the carrier and the administration of all financial and claims matters.

Selection of the Carrier

In single-employer plans there are few instances where unions participate in selecting the carrier, if the carrier is a commercial insurance company. The mass production unions have frequently insisted on the selection of Blue Cross and Blue Shield to cover health insurance, but since the premiums of these carriers involve no profit, dividends, or commissions, the employer's objections are not based on the prerogatives associated with cost disclosure. In the next chapter we discuss the extension of competitive bidding, and it is by insisting on this elementary principle of buying and selling that some unions with level-of-benefit plans have had a hand in selecting commercial carriers and in knowing something about the cost estimates on which their plan is based. But generally the employer chooses the carrier and the union rarely is informed of the basis on which the selection was made.[2]

Financial Administration

According to the Labor-Management Relations Act, the employer must provide the union with "information necessary for intelligent bargaining" and this has been interpreted to apply to at least some aspects of health and welfare financing.[3] The cost of the plan affects both the benefits that can be negotiated and the alternative wage settlement possible, subtracting greater or lesser amounts from what is available for other parts of the agreement. The employees' interests suffer when a settlement is made on the understanding that a substantial share of the cost of the plan is borne by the employer, and that share is later reduced by dividends. Transfers of funds between welfare plans for the bargaining unit and plans for those not in the union may also harm the union members' interests. Those interests also suffer, wrote an AFL–CIO spokesman, "where the employer has ties of a compromising nature with particular outside agencies or carriers whose costs might be higher and benefit services inferior to others equally available."[4]

Although there are good reasons that public policy should favor the principle of explicit financing, the fact is that in most cases of level-of-benefits bargaining the union, not being privy to the insurance arrangement, does not know the amount of employer contribution or the net cost of the benefits provided.[5] Employers regard the net costs, which vary from year to year, as not appropriately the employees' concern.[6] One large company has argued that the disposition and accounting of the employees' contribution is none of the employees' business,[7] but most employers extend the prerogative argument only to the company's contribution. Rarely will employers agree to an arrangement for disposition of any insurance dividends for fear that disclosure of dividend amounts might indicate a low net cost. Generally, management is reluctant to disclose net cost for fear that the union will make greater bargaining demands.[8] The arrangements with insurance companies are regarded as items of cost which neither management nor the insurance companies want to expose to the public or advertise to competitors.[9]

During its investigation of welfare plans, the Douglas Subcommittee unearthed an example that illustrates the need for some accountability to the union for the financial management of welfare funds. General Motors was cited as an "informed, intelligent buyer" of insurance from Metropolitan, but the company made at least one policy decision in the handling of welfare funds in which employee representatives should have participated.[10] The company separated funds for the salaried and hourly-rated employees, but assigned all the accumulated reserves to the salaried employees' fund, a decision which would certainly have been challenged by the union as spokesman for the hourly workers had it known of the matter.[11] While the Subcommittee was not concerned with the merits or rights of union participation in administration, it did conclude that:

. . . It would appear unrealistic and unfair to permit management and insurance companies to manage these reserves in secrecy without reporting to the employee beneficiaries. These reserves are a part of the costs of insurance.

Employees contribute to these costs and management's contributions are recognized by law as part of the compensation for employees' services, and are therefore exempt from taxation.[12]

Although by the terms of the Welfare and Pension Plans Disclosure Act certain information must be made available to employees and unions this is insufficient.[13] That Act was not intended to supplement the good faith bargaining provisions of the Labor Management Relations Act. There does not yet exist in the bulk of collective bargaining an "open-faced" exchange of information on the financing of health and welfare benefits, the kind of explicit discussion that experience shows to be necessary. Until regulation in this area is more actively undertaken by the government, or until unfair labor practices can be challenged with a smaller commitment of legal and financial resources than is now necessary, this issue will continue to cloud health bargaining.

Claims Administration

In level-of-benefit plans, claims are usually handled by the company as a personnel matter or by the insurance carrier. Except for some unions like the Steelworkers and Rubber Workers, which think this arrangement desirable especially if the company assumes the cost, most unions would like a larger role in claims administration. Nearly all unions preserve the right to process grievances and make appeals on benefit payments, but for a number of reasons find this authority insufficient.

The usual practice is for the employers through their personnel or employee relations departments to handle such administrative details as providing the claimant with the necessary forms, checking his eligibility, and verifying his union membership before forwarding his claim to the carrier. In some of these cases, the carrier sends the benefit checks to the employers to be forwarded to the claimant, and this is used as an opportunity to impress the employee with the company's interest in his welfare.

Many employers think that employees are likely to be more conscious and appreciative of the Company's interest in their welfare if its representatives contacted them and made disability payments directly at the time of greatest need.[14]

In addition to this bid for employee loyalty, the employer has a financial interest in keeping a large measure of control because claims adjustment has an effect on the claim rate. One study showed that the employer

might be in a more favorable position to assure equitable treatment of employees and to maintain a low claim rate by effectively policing the plan . . . [furthermore] if the employer handled claim payments, difficulties arising from contested Workmen's Compensation cases should be more readily adjusted.[15]

Another study found that carriers rarely questioned claims submitted by employers and that the forwarding of claims was tantamount to recommendation that the claims be paid.[16]

Most unions feel that without some role in claims administration the union cannot properly educate the membership about the actual part the union has had in establishing and maintaining the benefits, and that payment of claims through the company office weakens the union's hand in bargaining to improve benefits. An international representative of the CIO Textile Workers' Union said that he had been attempting

to get the local officers to seek a greater role in their plan's administration in order to impress their members with the union's role in obtaining benefits. Although the benefits may be stated in the collective bargaining contract, the members often do not read the contract and frequently do not realize that their union has secured the benefits for them.[17]

And a union officer of the Milwaukee Brewery Workers put it this way: "I think it's up to our unions to show the people that the union is responsible for these plans, not the company. The only way you're going to do that is by having a hand in the administration of the plan."[18]

Conducted at this level, the arguments about a union role in administration are only a current version of the old debates over employee benefit plans. A small but growing segment of labor is beginning to see that the more fundamental reason for union participation in administration is the need to evaluate experience, search for cost controls, and find ways of assuring that the new medical buying power actually goes to the purchase of high quality medicine. Information on insurance retentions is necessary before any better alternatives can be explored; studies are needed to see what portion of medical bills are actually covered by the benefit payments, or how the service and pricing policies of doctors and hospitals are affected by the inauguration of new and more liberal benefits. Few indeed are the unions that have conducted such inquiries or that are in a position to make a direct attack, with or despite their employers, on the problems of health pre-payment—yet this is the best justification for a larger labor role in administration.

Joint Administration Under Trustees

Two rather disparate industries—mining and music—were the focus of public interest when John L. Lewis and James Petrillo fought for union-administered welfare funds. The political reaction was the Labor-Management Relations Act, Section 302, which prescribed that employers could not give funds to union leaders for any purpose, and that welfare funds to which employers contributed would have to have employer as well as union trustees to administer them. These trusteed or "Taft-Hartley type" plans have received the lion's share of public attention although they represent less than 4 per cent of all health plans. They are usually characterized by a specified amount of employer contribution and by multi-employer bargaining. The contributions may be based on one of several systems that standardize the cost between the different employers: these are cents per hour, per cent of payroll, flat weekly amount per employee, or a royalty on the production. The trust fund may pay benefits directly or secure a policy from an insurance company, or it may employ either method for different parts of the welfare program. In an insured plan the purpose of reserves is to guarantee the payment of premiums in case business conditions greatly reduce the fund's income. In self-insured plans reserves must be larger to allow for fluctuations in both income and benefits.

Unions with trusteed welfare plans do not have to fight for the principles of explicit financing and a union role in administration, because both are inherent in the formal organization. Some unions wanted the trusteed form for this reason and won it thanks to their bargaining advantage in the industry. But other unions have had administrative responsibilities thrust upon them as a consequence of bargaining for welfare benefits because the trusteed form of welfare plan was the only one practical or even possible under the circumstances. Buying insurance in a multi-employer bargaining situation required the trust fund arrangement because most insurance companies would not bill each employer separately.[19] Where the labor force works irregularly or moves between different employers, a trusteed plan is the simplest way to provide continuity of coverage. And where the employing units are small, the risk base may be too narrow for group insurance or for any insurance at a reasonable price on the basis of separate employers.[20] For one or more of these reasons, trusteed plans predominate in the coal, building, trucking, apparel, maritime, entertainment, and service trades.

Defects in the Taft-Hartley Concept

If the public was satisfied at the time by Section 302 of the Labor-Management Relations Act, it was soon to learn that simple approaches cannot always solve complicated problems. This section was written with the idea that abuses would be automatically forestalled by requiring an employer trustee to have authority equal to the union trustee in the administration of any welfare fund to which management contributed.[21] But the belief that the trust would be observed if the employer were put in a policing role proved to be merely a pious hope. In 1953, when Tommy Lewis, a Building Service local union president in New York, was murdered, there began a series of public investigations that uncovered abuses and mismanagement in jointly administered trusteed plans.[22]

Many kinds of abuses were attributed to welfare fund trustees. Some plans were shown to lack proper administrative procedures, such as failure to record transactions, to publicize information on the fund accounting and operations, to keep minutes of trustee meetings, or to invest funds so they could earn interest. Union officials had misused funds for exorbitant salaries, purchase of unneeded automobiles, improper and unsecured loans, and for union business that had nothing to do with the welfare fund. Many of the abuses had to do with insurance, and the commissions and bonuses incident to letting a policy: high commissions; excessive administrative fees; high insurance company retentions; unequal treatment of policy holders. Unscrupulous brokers and agents, had, among other things, embezzled premiums, sometimes in collusion with union officials or management. Carriers had been "switched" to reap first-year commissions. Union and fund officials or their relatives had acted as agents or brokers of welfare funds.

Abuses of sound administration were not laid exclusively at labor's door in the trusteed plans. Some employer trustees had connived with union trustees or closed their eyes to irregularities, although in some instances they were subject to coercion.[23] Some employers had failed to make their agreed-upon contribution,[24] and in other cases had persuaded union leaders to make off-the-record settlements of delinquent contributions, in effect giving them favored treatment. This and limited evidence from other sources showing irresponsibility of employer trustees must lead to the general conclusion that moral lapses have occurred on both sides of the bargaining table.[25]

It should be noted here that the investigations concentrated on plans in a few large cities where labor-management relations are frequently plagued by racketeers who find casual urban labor a good target for their operations. Except for the Douglas Subcommittee, the investigators were more concerned in unearthing evildoing than in assessing its relative magnitude.[26] None of the investigations leaves any reason to doubt that the vast majority of welfare plans are well administered.[27]

The corrupt practices uncovered were regarded in labor as a threat to the prestige of the union movement and its venture in welfare bargaining. Responsible parties acted quickly where they had authority. In 1954, the CIO Retail, Wholesale and Department Store Union suspended local officers in six New York locals where the State Insurance Department had uncovered welfare irregularities.[28] George Meany, then AFL President, ordered annual audits to be required of the welfare funds of the 900 federal labor unions affiliated directly with the AFL.[29] The AFL–CIO and many of its affiliates passed codes of ethical practice prohibiting full-time union officers from receiving any commissions or fees incident to the placing of insurance and prohibiting them also from receiving reimbursement in addition to their regular union salary for serving as welfare fund trustees.[30] The United Association of Plumbers abolished a fraudulent sick and welfare fund uncovered by the Douglas investigation in Local 211, at Houston.[31] In 1957, as AFL–CIO President, George Meany suspended officers of two federal locals, one in Philadelphia and the other in Chicago, because of their connections with welfare fund racketeers.[32]

The AFL–CIO has no general authority to investigate the internal affairs of its affiliates, but, once wrongdoing was made public, it investigated and threatened to expel the Laundry Workers, the Distillery Workers, and the Allied Industrial Workers unless the irregularities were rectified.[33] Improper handling of welfare funds figured in the expulsion of the Teamsters in 1957. Although there are precedents for expulsion in AF of L and CIO history, this policing of ethical practice codes shows more authority by a federation over autonomous unions than has generally characterized the American labor movement.

To return to our central concern, however, it is clear that the intent of Section 302 that employers should police the trusteed plan has been shown to be fallacious. In the first place, employers are not always good policemen; labor relations is not just an exercise in morals but a process of accommodation where two power structures must live together, the ethics on either side being subject to conflicting pressures.

In the second place, the statute is not explicit about what is prohibited. The authors of the Act wanted to bring norms of conduct into the law by trying to make the words "representative" and "trustee" mean the same thing. Had they succeeded they would have brought into this federal labor relations statute all the prescriptions and norms of trust and fiduciary law; this was their intention. But trust law is in the jurisdiction of state courts, and the federal courts have refused to take jurisdiction over the wrongdoings of a "representative" acting in his capacity as a "trustee."[34] Thus the effort to graft trust law to the Labor-Management Relations Act has failed, and consequently no norms of conduct are specified for the administration of trusteed plans. The Attorney General, who is responsible for enforcement, has been quoted as finding in Section 302 "no requirement that the funds be efficiently managed, and no prohibition against exorbitant salaries and expenses, against milking of a fund by its promoters." As long as the fund is established in accordance with statutory language, he said, "there is no specific statute which makes it a federal offense for the management of the trust to ransack it."[35] The authors of Section 302 feared abuses of welfare plans but did not effectively identify what abuses should be prohibited. In 1962, however, Congress did identify one abuse it wanted to prohibit, and through amendments to the Welfare and Pension Plans Disclosure Act it made embezzlement a federal crime.

It would be over hasty to assume that the substantial body of trust law is not a deterrent to corruption, even without federal jurisdiction. The common law contains admonitions on the fiduciary responsibilities of trustees: they must be personally disinterested; administer the trust faithfully and honestly; disclose to the beneficiaries all information the trustees may have that may be necessary for the protection of the trust; preserve trust funds and take certain steps to augment them; carry out the express purposes of the trust; and refrain from waste, damage, or personal aggrandizement. The courts have applied these principles in welfare trusts.[36]

A beneficiary can bring action for the enforcement of a charitable trust. Of course, he may think twice before challenging his union leadership and the company trustee, and any legal action involves financial obstacles,[37] but beneficiaries have brought suit; and the courts have jealously guarded their right to protect the beneficiaries' interests.[38] Some states provide by statute that the Attorney General can bring action and in various ways exercise supervision over charitable trusts.[39] Where state officials have the responsibility for enforcing the law of charitable trusts, disclosure may help activate existing legal sanctions.[40]

It may well be that federal officials should be empowered to bring civil action under common law trust rules on behalf of beneficiaries. Moreover, the commission and fee practices of insurance companies were a major source of corruption in the cases investigated and have figured prominently in tarnishing both trusteed welfare plans and employer-administered plans that buy insurance. The need for better insurance regulation is discussed in the next chapter.

A review of the investigations does not lead to alarm about the capacity of union or business leaders to manage employee welfare plans in most cases, and for those tempted by wrongdoing there are deterrents in the law of trust and fiduciary responsibility as well as in the concern of higher union authorities. But the legal characteristics of welfare plans should not detour us from an understanding of their true nature. The most significant feature of these jointly administered plans is that they are an extension of collective bargaining, and the authors of the Labor-Management Relations Act erred in underestimating the importance of this. They wanted to infuse the trust idea into what was basically labor relations. "Trusteed plans" are best understood as a kind of permanent bargaining committee; only secondarily are they trusts.

Proper Use of the Two Kinds of Trusteed Plans

Much of the literature on trusteed plans draws distinctions on such matters as whether the plans are contributory, whether they are self-insured, whether they provide direct services. But it is our view here that another distinction is basic to the future success of these plans, and that is whether the plan is coterminous with an established bargaining structure, such as an employers' association. Some trusteed plans may include employers that bargain separately with the union.[41] As we shall see, where this is the case the protective safeguards may be deficient because all employers are not effectively represented by the employer trustees.

The more general situation is that where an established employers' association and the union with which it negotiates have set up a plan that includes the member companies only. It is this structure to which our earlier observation applies: such a plan functions more like a permanent bargaining committee than a trust.

This view is supported by a study of several such plans made in 1959.[42] It was noted, for example, that the employer trustees were selected not because of their knowledge of trust administration, but because of their relationship to the union negotiations.[43] Even where the trustee is a lawyer, the chances are that he speaks for the association in the bargaining.

Interviews with employer trustees suggest that they do not think primarily in terms of administering the trust for the benefit of the employees, but rather of protecting the interests of the employers, particularly with regard to avoiding situations where the union will have cause for requesting additional contributions.[44] The employer trustee has a conflict of interest—to employers as their representative, to the beneficiaries as a theoretically disinterested trustee. This raises serious questions about whether trust law is appropriate as part of labor relations. In any case, it is clear that in practice trust functions are subordinated to bargaining.

Furthermore, there appears to be considerable informality in setting up the trust. The contract may have little or nothing to say about the character of the trust, duties of the trustees, etc. Even the trust instrument itself may be silent or general on many significant points. The union and the employers are depending on the established relationships between them rather than on the formal delegation of authority and definition of responsibilities that characterize a trust.

For those who are anxious about protections and controls, there is value in understanding the plans as permanent bargaining committees. There need be no excessive concern about inadequacy of the trust instruments and procedures or a general "sloppiness" in the enterprise from a trust point of view, so long as collective bargaining controls are properly operating. The accountability of an employer trustee to the employer association and the accountability of the union trustee to his organization exist before the trust and are in many ways more real, vital, and protective of the purposes of the plan than the legal controls of a trust.

There are, however, grounds for concern where the plan includes employers not in the bargaining association or where the union bargains separately with each employer. Every such employer cannot be a trustee, and the interests of all may not be encompassed in the obligations felt by whoever is selected to be the employer trustee. This has been noted in situations where an association was represented on the board of trustees but other employers in the plan were not.[45] To provide controls and safeguards, there should be formal delineation of duties and responsibilities. The contract should specify the method of selecting trustees, and the scope or nature of the benefits. (The amount or size of benefits will have to be decided by the trustees.) The contract should also include the formula for determining the employers' contribution and procedures for terminating the trust. As for the trust instrument, it should carefully describe the responsibilities of trustees, including proper reporting to all employers concerned and to covered employees. The trust instrument should also establish a pattern of meetings and decision-making in which the trustees themselves rather than an administrator decide policy questions.

One of the conclusions of our study, to emerge more fully later, is that the basis of many health and welfare plans is not large enough to deal effectively with problems of medical economics that threaten health insurance. It is important that health plans attain a size which permits of efficient actuarial and insurance functioning. It is even more important to increase the bargaining power of consumer groups in their relations with community health facilities. Thus existing plans should when possible be combined. The joint-trustee device is a useful vehicle for this purpose so long as the distinction between "association negotiated" plans and "multiple bargaining" plans is respected. Both formal and real safeguards for adequate employer representation and participation are important, particularly in the latter.

Contributions and Claim Payments

The routine focus for administration is the collection of contributions and the payment of claims. These are more difficult in trusteed plans because of the number of employers and the turnover among employees.

The well-administered plan will have procedures that assure prompt collections and effective methods for dealing with delinquency when it occurs. In addition, periodic audit of employer payroll records may be required. Prolonged delinquency will deserve severe measures. In some states, delinquency is a misdemeanor under the law and the employer can be punished, but this is not generally true.[46] Some funds withhold employee benefits when the employer is delinquent. Even under a no-strike contract agreement, the union may reserve the right to strike a delinquent employer.

A major problem in payment of claims is determining the eligibility of the applicant. Where the pattern in the industry served by the plan is one of casual employment, with heavy turnover and frequent unemployment, eligibility determination is as important a variable in the cost of the program as are the scope of benefits and the reserve requirements. Some funds have started with loose eligibility requirements and have had to tighten them because of the cost impact, and in others the benefits provided are at the expense of the less regularly employed, owing to overly strict requirements. Various systems of eligibility verification are in use. Most common are those with a kind of "rolling eligibility" in which employment of specified duration in some previous period (such as the last three or six months) qualifies for benefits during a future period. In the building trades a system of "banking" one's excess working credits for future eligibility is developing to protect the steadier workers during long lay-offs. Record-keeping for all eligibility systems is an intricate art.[47]

Administration and Community Health Bargaining

We concluded the last chapter with the observation that the future evolution of health insurance and medical prepayment plans may depend on the development of a program of community health bargaining. Group health plans, in order to meet the consumer's concern with cost and quality, must directly confront the providers of health services. Clearly this requires a concept of administration that goes well beyond the housekeeping functions of policing contributions and paying benefits. Proper administration will develop cost controls, evaluate the services and charges of hospitals and doctors, and provide data for intelligent appraisal of the benefit structure.

These are fundamental matters in health prepayment and in some cases administrators of health plans are challenged by the responsibility. For instance, some plans keep records not only of what they pay out but of what part of the hospital or medical bill the employee himself pays. This is a significant measure of the limitations of any program. In an indemnity plan, the uncompensated portion will increase with the rise in medical costs. Evaluation at the bargaining table requires this kind of information.

If properly kept, health plan records will produce evidence with which to weigh the usefulness of adding diagnostic benefits, or extending coverage for ambulatory patients, or changing from an insured to a self-insured, or direct-service program. It is part of administration that the scope and range of any program should be examined critically in the light of its actual experience. Records should be kept so that patterns of overcharging or excessive utilization can be detected. For this purpose, some plans actually file claims records according to the doctor handling the case. If the files are kept by member-patients cross-reference tabbing by doctors and/or hospitals is required.

The lack of uniformity in hospital charges, particularly for ancillary services, makes appraisal of their billing very difficult. Plan administrators can take the initiative, as they did in Southern California, to urge some standard definitions and a code for establishing hospital charges.

In some places administrators have found it possible to talk with doctors about their charges. The profession is sensitive about this, but the use of relative-value schedules has helped. These assign co-efficients of worth to any medical service up to the most complex surgery. Each service is expressed as a multiple of some basic unit, such as a routine office visit or a simple surgical procedure. If a doctor accepts the principle of a relative-value schedule, it is possible to evaluate any one charge in the context of his other charges. Whether a health plan can get doctors in a community to agree to a fee schedule (which is a relative-value schedule expressed in dollars) is a question which we will analyze in Chapter 11. Some plan administrators, to protect their programs, have developed panels of doctors who do agree to abide by such a schedule of charges. In such cases the plan is deeply involved in community health bargaining.

These activities of imaginatively directed health plans suggest that conventional means of measuring administrative "efficiency" are inappropriate for some purposes. A simple statistical ratio of administrative cost to total benefit payments or total contributions cannot by itself alone be used as an index of performance. Farming out administration to a carrier or bank or professional administrator who guarantees low administrative costs but who also ignores the responsibilities we have described is a false economy. Administrative expenditures should be scrupulously controlled and continuously reviewed, but always in terms of the value of the functions performed.

In these important and often obscure areas where private interests and public concerns are intertwined, we must conclude that it is consistent with and even indispensable to the public interest that unions represent their members as medical care consumers. To this end, they should vigorously search for suitable and workable arrangements with others, bearing in mind the checks and balances of sound collective bargaining. In the bargaining, administering, and underwriting of these health plans, labor can perform its role as spokesman for potential patients only if it retains or obtains the freedom to plan and to act. The success of the voluntary health insurance movement depends on an effective initiative in grappling with problems of cost and quality, and this initiative, past experience shows, is more likely to come from labor than from management. It is also more likely to come from both labor and management working together than from the insurance industry.

9

BARGAINING WITH THE INSURANCE BUSINESS

The worker's conception of the proper role of insurance is as an adjunct to or extension of his group and communal living. Insurance was an integral part of the workers' benevolent associations and fraternal orders of the last century, and we have already seen how closely trade unionism and insurance were related in their origin.

Workers' loyalty to fraternal and trade union insurance was not fully rewarded by its performance, however. The financial, actuarial, and managerial problems were too great. Many plans failed during depressions and periods of long unemployment. Others were discontinued because they interfered with trade union objectives. The greatest failures were in the early 1930's; the railroad plans were taken over by the government and Social Security was enacted. During all this bad experience with trade union insurance plans, commercial insurance was steadily carving out a place in our economic life. Over the years American workers have had to admit the need for an insurance business to provide managerial and actuarial functions.

Industrial and Group Insurance

Many of the early underwriters were devoted men who thought the public should be taught the advantages of pooled risk.[1] From their modest and sometimes idealistic beginnings, insurance companies have grown into a gigantic business with assets of $140 billion, 70 per cent of which is owned by 10 companies.[2] The industry is regarded by many workers as a fortress of power, sometimes working in their interests, sometimes against them.[3]

An early chapter in insurance history was the development of "indus-

116

trial insurance." To find a mass market, insurance salesmen solicited working people. In 1879, Prudential, Metropolitan, and John Hancock began selling small life policies of $100 or more. The weekly premiums were collected by the agent at the home of the insured. The industry is proud of this industrial insurance and points to the "extremely important social role played by weekly premium insurance to thrift education."[4] But the sales techniques, which sometimes consisted of exploiting the fears, ignorance, and gullibility of immigrants and uneducated workers, were bound to fall into disfavor as soon as workers learned more about insurance.

A better invention in the search for a mass market was suggested in 1872 by an agent of the Metropolitan: "Make the bookkeeper or foreman or paymaster . . . the agent. Let him retain from the pay or collect from each insured, at the end of each month, the premium due."[5] By this invention the "boss" was brought into the picture in a significant way. It was not until 1911 that group insurance as we know it today was invented and it has evolved through many forms, but with the employer as collection agent group insurance became colored with the paternalistic overtones of welfare capitalism.

Group insurance was a mainstay of "progressive" industrial relations in the 1920's and 1930's. Insurance agents were necessarily management-oriented, since employers rather than employees decided the kind and cost of employee benefit plans. Insurance agents played their role as allies of the management market. If a feeble employee voice objected to the form or content of a proposed plan, the insurance agent provided a thorough explanation of why the suggestion was not "actuarially sound."

There is still much of the patronizing school of labor relations in the group insurance business of today, although it is more likely to have the sophisticated sound of this advice to management from an insurance consultant:

Certainly the plan will fall short of accomplishing its objectives if the representatives of the men have been ignored. . . . The maximum results are obtained where union representatives and department heads work together to "put over" this plan.[6]

Labor seeks an influential role in setting the characteristics of group insurance plans, and levels sharp criticism at the old order:

By and large, we in labor have tended to buy what was available rather than determine for ourselves what was most needed to protect the health and economic security of our people. The weakest single element in our performance has been in delegating the responsibility for programming to third parties. We who are closest to the worker's need have turned to carriers that are actually very far removed from these needs and have a different orientation.[7]

As unions have achieved a greater voice in insurance bargaining, complex relationships have developed with insurance carriers. The internal competition of the insurance business permits unions to use some carriers against their competition, inventing new types of protection and cutting insurance costs. Unions have found insurance companies useful where Blue Cross and Blue Shield plans were unresponsive to the opportunities. Some unions have uncritically accepted the maxims and limitations of commercial carriers, but more have had good reason to maintain a skeptical stance. There are several unions that have pioneered in programming of benefits, and have attempted to reform insurance sales techniques. Competitive bidding on new policies, regular reporting of claims experience, and explicit aboveboard handling of finances and commissions are lessons that many unions have had to learn—some the hard way.

The Commission System of Selling Insurance

Not understanding the character of the insurance business, labor entered welfare bargaining unprepared for exposure to the agency system by which insurance is bought and sold. The agency or commission incentive system, with its rewards for initiative and resourcefulness, has been given much credit for the expansion of insurance coverage, but it also is a potentially dangerous source of corruption.

So long as insurance education and sales techniques make the difference, the commission system rightfully rewards special effort. Even in the early days of group insurance, many employers had to be sold on the advantages of an employee benefit plan. But with the beginning of welfare bargaining, the role of the agent became more limited. His problem was not to sell the parties on the merits of insurance.[8] Management and labor knew what they wanted after hammering it out at the bargaining table, and the only decision in which the agent could participate was, who would get the business. Under this pressure, many agents became conspirators rather than salesmen, funneling part of their commissions into rewards for those who could influence the placement of the policy. In the scramble for business, the home offices began paying higher commissions, which further added to the temptations. Some agents tried to buy business by bribing union officials. Paul Bowers of the United Rubber Workers has described one such attempt:

In the very first set of negotiations with one of the big four companies, one of the local union presidents of the largest group was offered $10,000 and a new Mercury automobile, and the five members of his committee were each promised a Mercury automobile if they would divert and concentrate on negotiating one insurance company as the carrier. Happily for us, that situation was reported to me and to the general officers of our organization. We switched over and nipped it in the bud.[9]

Not all such cases were caught, however, much to the discredit of labor and its role in welfare bargaining.

Public investigations of health and welfare scandals present a catalogue of abuses which demonstrate the dangers of commission incentives when the agent's role is as diluted as it is in negotiated group insurance. In theory, commissions are a predetermined schedule of percentage rates, similar from company to company, and subject to review by the state insurance commission. In practice, the commission system has become a highly flexible and loose scale for attracting agents with the best connections.[10] Within one insurance company there may be a dozen different rate schedules in use.[11] Rivalry for welfare business bids up the commission rates offered to agents or to anyone who can bring in the business. There are many brokers who dictate what commissions the insurance company will have to pay if it wants to retain the business of the broker's client.[12] Some companies pay substantially higher rates on union business; they tailor-make specific commission rates to accommodate agents or brokers in union welfare cases.[13] Sometimes "contingent" commissions are paid: these vary in amount with the claims experience and the agent thereby has a financial incentive to discourage even legitimate claims.[14] The purpose of decremental commission schedules—designed to reduce proportionately the commission on large policies—has been widely subverted by "pyramiding," a practice of applying the scale over again to each separate item in the group insurance package.[15] Administrative and service fees,

ostensibly paid to agents or policyholders for claims processing normally handled by the insuring company, have been paid to brokers and
agents for services done by a branch office or by the policyholder; these
are in effect extra commissions paid for no service at all and may be
as high as 7.5 per cent.[16]

If all these practices are known, why have not the insurance regulatory agencies done anything about them? State laws vary widely
and state insurance departments are "small, understaffed, and underpaid and usually are no match for the industry";[17] they give more attention to company solvency and the legality and clarity of policy forms
than to commission practices. Neither by law nor by regulation are
commission rate schedules promulgated; the insurance companies are
required only to submit them for review. Even the New York Insurance Department, which stands out as a powerful setter of standards,
has admitted it is not equipped to police the practices of licensed
agents.[18] If the broker's commission is questioned by the insurance
commissioner in one state, the broker can go to an underwriter in
another state.[19]

Scarred and wiser by its experience with insurance, the AFL–CIO
has suggested the lines for reform: (1) a code of standards should
govern commissions and should be enforced by the state regulatory
body; (2) the regulatory bodies should be made more representative
of the public and consumer interest; (3) they should exercise responsibility for the integrity and character of agents and brokers and where
necessary revoke their licenses to operate; (4) when agents and brokers are not employed and render no services, no premium should be
paid or retained by the carrier.[20] In rejoinder to the last point, insurance
men argue that present law forbids discrimination between comparable buyer groups with respect to premium rates, and, further, that if
a commission is not paid and not withheld by the carrier, the carrier
would be open to the charge of price discrimination.[21] Actually, price
discrimination exists anyway, as we will show below. Probably more
fundamental to the carrier's objections is the wide reorganization that
would be caused by eliminating even some commissions:

. . . it is vital that we not provide a better price if a commission is not
paid. . . . If we were to permit a system under which a buyer could save cost,
could avoid a reasonable cost of distribution by going direct to the home
offices, we would put all home offices in competition with their field forces
and in a short time the field forces would disintegrate.[22]

This begs the question whether unearned commissions are in fact a reasonable cost of competition; it also overlooks the fact that Blue Cross has salesmen who sell insurance on salary. The fundamental question is whether public policy is best served by recognizing the new dilution and perversion of the agency system in negotiated insurance where "the availability of commissions creates a magnetic field in which the people of loose ideals and weak minds and lack of dedication to a cause, attract and create a dangerous situation."[23] While objecting to labor's proposals, the insurance business has offered no reorganization of sales methods that would be more suitable to the needs of modern industry.

To protect itself from the agency system, the AFL–CIO has enforced on staff officials the code of ethical practices described in the last chapter. In addition, affiliated unions have developed a second kind of defense—astute buying of group insurance.

The Methods of Astute Buying

Despite the fact that competitive bidding is the most elementary principle of efficient buying, it has not prevailed in group insurance. Many companies buying simply turned to the underwriter or broker handling their other casualty insurance. This emphasis on existing relationships, whether or not they were economical from the buyer's viewpoint, has not suited the unions. It seemed to them that the insurance business preferred to stress differences in product, or quality of service, or general reputation of the company rather than a lower price for an identical policy.[24] Unions, on the other hand, have been developing their own standards; and they increasingly feel that health insurance premiums should stand the test of competitive bidding. While relatively few unions (see pp. 57, 70) are directly involved in selecting a carrier, their often reiterated views on the subject have resulted in greater management use of competitive bidding to place group insurance contracts.

Competitive bidding requires that a specifications letter be prepared which outlines the desired benefits and elicits information from the competing underwriters on the following points: the initial premium cost on the proposed package; the estimated annual retention for several years; benefit provisions and limitations in the contract; claims reserve practices; administrative and claims facilities provided; and the general financial standing of the company.[25] This information helps to isolate the carrier's retentions and claims payments, the two ingredients of cost, on a comparable basis. By thus bringing underwriters into a competitive relationship with one another on cost factors, labor and management can "bargain" with the insurance business.

Without such an arrangement, unions are fair game for unscrupulous agents who can undersell because of small-print exclusions, or unbalanced surgical schedules, or oversold low-cost items in the benefit schedules.[26] An unskilled local union asking for insurance provisions may soon find itself deeply involved with insurance agents from many companies, each offering a different benefit program and without sufficient cost information so that the responsible local officers can reconcile the differences. This is a source of factionalism when insurance agents use local union politics for their purposes. Competitive bidding procedures, on the other hand, keep the agents at a distance until basic decisions have been made and a specifications letter outlining the policy is prepared.

Astute buying can influence the commission rates, which are a substantial part of the retention, if the union insists that the amount and the recipient be made known and, further, if the carrier is instructed to combine all the policies into one for calculating the commission in order to preserve the meaning of the decremental rate schedule. There should be no administrative fees under normal circumstances; if the health and welfare fund or the employer undertake administrative duties, reduced retention and premium rates should result.[27]

Continuous evaluation of claims experience can also save money. Both the company and the union should get periodic statements—either quarterly or on the anniversary date. The actual retention is then checked with the original declared estimate of retention and any variation requires justification; incurred claims reserves must be realistically based on the experience of previous years.[28]

Retentions in the group accident and health business have declined during the period of health bargaining. Some of this is attributable to more rigorous buying by labor and management. As an example, one fund covering 7,000 members achieved savings of $118,000 in annual premiums and a $20,000 reduction in retention after careful analysis of the program and elimination of unnecessary costs; careful appraising helped reduce the retention in a plan of 2,000 persons by $14,000.[29]

Insurance companies know who their astute buyers are, and contrary to the folklore of the business, do not treat all policyholders alike. While the law prohibits discrimination between comparable buyers, one insurance official reports that "this is another fallacy of this bonus or dividend system under which we operate."[30] Instances have been cited where dividends were paid, premiums reduced, and rate increases successfully challenged because of expressed interest, complaints, or pressure from the policyholders.[31] In the words of one insurance official, "the squeaking wheel gets the grease."[32]

In the typical large insurance company today, the ratio of benefits paid to net earned premiums is 89 to 90 per cent, with most companies falling between 85 and 92 per cent.[33] This is about 10 percentage points better—for the buyers—than in 1948.[34]

The procedures for astute buying—competitive bidding and continuous surveillance—have three limitations. First, technical help is required and there is no best way to get this help. An insurance agent is willing to advise "for free" but his bias is exactly what technical help is needed to overcome. A broker-consultant can have his services reimbursed by designating him the recipient of the commission, which must be paid to someone, but anyone paid by the seller suffers a conflict of interest when he advises the buyer. Hence, some unions prefer to hire a consultant paid by a fee; while this is the safest route, it is the most expensive because the commission must also be paid and will go to someone else.[35]

Second, there are definite limitations on the freedom of a policyholder to change from an unsatisfactory carrier.[36] The first years of a group premium are loaded with the higher acquisition costs from decreasing commission schedules, which have their highest rate the first year. Decremental commission schedules apply widely (although level commission rates are encouraged by some carriers) and when bidding carriers are usually asked to show their proposed retention for each year over a ten-year period. A decision to switch carriers, therefore, may mean starting over again on high first-year acquisition costs, and this must be weighed against the drawbacks of continuing the existing carrier. Policyholders often cannot effectively use countervailing force against carriers except in their initial purchase.

Community rating in health insurance is discussed in the next chapter, but we should warn here that improper competitive bidding can undermine community rated plans. To avoid this it is necessary to distinguish between retention costs and claims costs. When bidding and continuous surveillance of the policy are used primarily to isolate and evaluate the costs of retention, there can be a reduction in waste and gains in efficiency. But forcing carriers to compete on the costs of claims experience extends the use of experience rating, at first on lower than average risk groups and eventually on all groups. For several years this distinction between retention costs and claims costs was unnecessary because Blue Cross could not be underbid on its own benefits package. However, with the expansion of benefits offered by commercial carriers and rising Blue Cross premiums, the claims and retention distinction becomes important. Otherwise competitive bidding adds to the pressures on Blue Cross to use experience rating.

Union Influence in Programming Group Insurance

We now turn from the techniques of buying to the content of health insurance policies, and here too we see significant changes brought about by union policies. Labor has been a prime mover in creating the health insurance market and it has drawn the commercial insurance business deep into what the carriers regard as the insecure ground of service plans that include a wide range of contingencies and many small medical bills. These developments conflict with certain principles which have traditionally guided the thinking of carriers about the suitability of benefits, principles which define what kinds of losses can be underwritten, such as losses of "infrequent occurrence," or losses of "substantial magnitude," or losses "beyond the insured's control" or losses with "definiteness of value."[37] Life insurance, for example (if suicide is exempted), provides these characteristics, and this helps explain the note of regret in a statement by a vice president of the Equitable Life Insurance Society: "Unfortunately there seems of late to be a tendency especially under collective bargaining to de-emphasize group life insurance when developing a package of benefits."[38]

Principles of insurability serve to limit the risk of profit making institutions. They do not serve the broad goals of the health insurance movement, such as bringing medical facilities within reach of those with medical needs, and more efficiently allocating medical resources in the interest of a healthier people. For example, the carriers preferred to underwrite certain hospital and surgical bills because they meet the tests of "magnitude" and "infrequency," but this has encouraged over-use of hospital facilities when outpatient services or doctors' offices would do just as well. The efficient application of medical resources is thereby warped. The insurance industry argues that the real problem here is that the loss is not "beyond the insured's control"—the patient chooses to go to a hospital where treatment is covered rather than go to a doctor's office where it is not.[39] Can rearranging the insurance coverage help encourage a better use of facilities? The unions argue for extending coverage to outpatient services, and services in the home and in the doctor's office in order to remove any financial incentive for the insured to ask for hospitalization.[40] Here the issue is joined, because the carriers contend that these home and office bills are neither "infre-quent" nor of sufficient "magnitude" to be insurable,[41] and are more efficiently handled by family budgeting. But unions quickly point out that the incidence of small bills varies greatly and that they can add up to large expenses; that even small bills deter hard-pressed families from seeking medical care; and that budgeting is more a feature of salary-earning white collar classes than of wage earners.[42]

Nowhere is the conflict of objectives more apparent than in health insurance coverage of diagnostic and preventive services. According to the industry, ". . . diagnostic care tends to violate two of the insurance principles . . . that the loss insured against should be infrequent, and that the loss should be beyond the insured's control rather than subject to his personal desires at the time service is required."[43] However, insurance plans that do provide this coverage, such as prepaid group practice plans, make a saving in encouraging early diagnosis and pre-vention; in such plans the economic incentives run parallel with the principles of good medical care.

Despite their objections, the commercial carriers have been drawn toward comprehensive health insurance because in Blue Cross labor has had a non-profit ally interested in providing a wider range of serv-ices. And these services were available for an explicit cost unencum-bered by commissions, fees, or dividends. The more alert unions urged management to separate insurance into two packages—life, accidental death, disability, and weekly disability should go to commercial car-riers and the health insurance to Blue Cross and Blue Shield. The com-mercial carriers fought back in many ways.[44] They lowered their rates;

they argued that dividing the group insurance package would double the employer's troubles; they added "gimmicks" that Blue Cross did not provide, such as prepaid ambulance rides, which cost little but whose absence in Blue Cross could be dramatized as shortcomings. They introduced exclusions in the fine print of the policy and juggled the arithmetic in reimbursement schedules. But many unions insisted on Blue Cross, or they insisted on competitive bidding on the Blue Cross package knowing that Blue Cross could not be underbid on its own program. The carriers responded by broadening substantially their range of benefits. Some even underbid Blue Cross and made up the loss on life and disability premiums. Several began to write service-type coverage, i.e., full coverage for ward and semiprivate rooms rather than a fixed dollar indemnity.[45] (This tactic surprised many but there was no special trick in setting premiums according to customary hospital charges in a given community.) In these ways the carriers were drawn toward the unfamiliar territory of comprehensive service plans.

The invention of major medical insurance was precipitated by the insurance companies' desire to meet the demand for more protection and to do so on traditional insurance principles. The deductible features of "major medical"—$100 to $300 or more for each illness, or per individual or family each year—are designed to eliminate coverage of small, frequent bills; the co-insurance feature—20 to 25 per cent of the bill to be paid by the employee—is supposed to discourage unnecessary use of medical facilities and give the insured some incentive to "police" his own claim. The industry was lyrical over its new policy: "Gone would be the temptation of the general practitioner to hospitalize a patient because he held only a hospitalization policy. . . . Gone would be unnecessary insurance expense of insuring budgetable items. Preserved would be the patient's interest in each dollar of medical care ordered for him by the co-insurance factor of 20 per cent. Introduced would be the greatest flexibility in insurance programming yet seen. . . ."[46] Many union leaders think otherwise.[47] It is no substitute, said the AFL–CIO Executive Council, "for a comprehensive insurance protection which provides for diagnosis and treatment in the home or doctor's office as well as in the hospital, and which covers the common as well as the exceptional condition. . . ."[48] There is no evidence to show that co-insurance in major medical has prevented over-utilization of hospital facilities, and the absence of controls—such controls as exist in automobile collision insurance where bids are required and charges are checked—permits abuses such as a doctor charging a higher fee and settling for the insurance company's portion of the bill. (Usually insurers will not challenge a claim unless the fee is two, two and one-half, and sometimes even three times higher than that in a guiding fee schedule.) Whether or not the deductible is effectively bypassed, there is ample evidence of inflation of fees. A. M. Wilson, who has been called the father of major medical insurance, said that "if catastrophe coverage accomplishes nothing more than to provide more people with more money to pay higher bills for medical care, catastrophe coverage will represent an economic catastrophe."[49] Labor has discouraged substitution of major medical for existing plans (the so-called "comprehensive" major medical) and most of the group major medical policies sold to companies under collective bargaining have been supplemental to basic programs. Jerome Pollack, while with the United Auto Workers, made a study of major medical and concluded that "the attempt to insure only large and infrequent losses is a movement to make the health contingency conform to the insurance rather than make the insurance best serve the contingency."[50]

Union influence on insurance programming has been to emphasize hospital and medical benefits, to extend coverage of hospital ancillary and outpatient services, to fasten attention on the needs of dependents and retired employees, and to encourage services rather than cash indemnification. Somewhat less effective has been its demand for preventive and diagnostic services and its skepticism of major medical. The search for comprehensive coverage continues through increases in benefit periods and maximum amounts in basic contracts and the lowering of deductibles in major medical.[51]

The Limitations of Commercial Insurance, and Some Alternatives

Some of the shortcomings of commercial insurance have led the United Mine Workers, the International Ladies' Garment Workers, the Amalgamated Clothing Workers, the United Furniture Workers, and districts or locals in other internationals to carry some or all of their health and welfare programs without the help of outside underwriters. Some costs can be saved in this way:[52] the premium tax (2 per cent or less, depending on the state) does not apply to self-insured plans; commissions and fees can be saved, although technical help is required; there are savings in the handling of contingency reserves; the 2 to 4 per cent of premium that otherwise goes to the carriers' profits can be a substantial dollar saving. Another advantage of self-insured funds is their greater flexibility in benefit programming and administration, although lack of skill can be dangerous because of the sensitive and even mercurial character of the liabilities assumed, which, while not so large in amount as in life insurance or pensions, are subject to rapid change in rate of payment with only slight changes in definitions and procedures. This suggests that the union must have, in addition to good technical help, the organizational stability, and confidence in its leadership, necessary for administering the program, and a program to educate members to accept responsible administration and justified denial of claims by their own union representatives.

An important disadvantage of self-insurance is its inability to continue protection to the employee who leaves the group. Insured plans can give the terminated employee the right to convert to individual insurance with the same carrier without a physical examination, although he may pay higher individual rate. The prevalence of group health insurance assures the employee who changes jobs that he will probably be covered in his new employment, but the unemployed and the retired need conversion rights. A self-insurance group would cast a retiring employee adrift at an age when good health insurance is prohibitively expensive, unless, of course, the fund included retirees in the covered group. In general, we conclude that while there are many situations where self-insurance is not suitable, it is also true that with a large enough risk base (500 members or more) and perhaps "stop loss" insurance to cover losses in excess of the estimated volume of monthly transactions, there could be a much wider use of self-insurance for temporary disability and medical care benefits.

The real question about insurance, however, is not whether one or another form of indemnity insurance provides the best answers. By paying cash benefits under certain conditions, both commercial and self-insurance plans separate the financing of care from the services provided in a manner that may be both artificial and deleterious. In too many instances, indemnity insurance contributes to the deterioration of quality: it encourages services which are prepaid but not strictly needed from a medical standpoint; it leads to an inappropriate use of medical facilities and inflation of medical costs.[53] At the very least it finances both good and poor medicine. Furthermore, indemnity insurance leaves a continued burden of out-of-pocket medical expenses in addition to what is covered by the insurance, a gap that may in some cases prevent use of medical services by those for whom health does not, through economic necessity and cultural conditioning, rank high in the scale of values.[54] To the extent that these are the problems in prepayment, indemnity insurance is part of the problem rather than part of the solution.

The weight of informed opinion is that the problems underlying health insurance have to do with the proper and efficient use of medical facilities, the organization of professional skills, and the education of patients. If this is true, unions cannot contribute to a solution of the problems unless they think beyond "insurance" and the vehicles thereof. Some have done so. There is an accumulating body of union experience with such matters as hospital pricing policies, outpatient services, and special methods of caring for the chronically ill; and in such subjects as proper use of medical specialists, the role of the personal physician, techniques for surveillance of quality, and the impact on quality of various systems of remunerating doctors. Labor's goal of better health for more people involves social change and reform and "insurance" at best can be only one instrument. We have discussed insurance first because the labor movement has had much experience with it, but if one fact characterizes labor's health policies in recent years it is the gradual subordination of insurance to medical care considerations. The road is open to community health bargaining in which organized consumers and the providers of medical care can jointly establish the new institutional arrangements on which success ultimately depends.

It is clear that the insurance business absolves itself of responsibility in this direction. In the words of Alan Thaler of the Prudential Insurance Company:

If we could completely retrace the steps of the industry, our best approach to health insurance would undoubtedly have been through closer past cooperation with doctors and hospitals so that service type plans . . . representing a joint effort on the part of the doctors and the insurance industry, could have been made to fill the bill more generally. The further development of such plans may yet be the final answer to this whole problem, but this solution is one which unfortunately is not available at the present time. It would, therefore, seem that the insurance companies would have to run the risk of proceeding on their own if they are to provide any kind of answer now.[55]

We now inquire into labor's experience with Blue Cross which, unlike the insurance business, has attempted closer co-operation with hospitals in the development of benefits and payments.

10

BARGAINING WITH HOSPITALS AND BLUE CROSS

We have described how workers joined for self-protection in the early benefit societies and how miners formed hospital prepayment plans under the auspices of their local unions.[1] The Texas teachers who started the first Blue Cross plan were moved by the same idea.[2] They wanted a non-profit, prepayment plan to protect them against hospital bills. From its small beginnings in Dallas in 1929, Blue Cross has grown to 76 plans covering nearly 60 million people and paying for over $2 billion of hospital services annually. We have discussed commercial insurance first, but it was Blue Cross that led in developing the health insurance market. The idea of a community-service organization dedicated to providing prepayment for the bulk of hospital bills and doing it for all members of the community at the least possible cost caught on early with the unions.[3]

Unions Promote Blue Cross

The unions looking for health insurance in 1949 found a distinct advantage in Blue Cross: with all the variation in daily rates between hospitals, even those in the same area, the Blue Cross plan of guaranteeing full payment for a ward or semi-private bed was a benefit designed to fit the need. By contrast, the cash indemnity benefit of a commercial insurance company might meet the need in one area, be inadequate in another, and inflationary somewhere else. Further, Blue Cross showed more disposition to cover hospital services of various kinds than did the private companies, and offered conversion privileges for those who left the employment group at rates well below the individual rates of commercial health insurance.

Even before the war some unions showed their support. The United Auto Workers' Committee on Health gave approval at the union's 1941 convention, and CIO leaders indicated their support. Blue Cross sources report that "governmental and union support stimulated the unprecedented growth in Blue Cross plans" during the war.[4] With the rapid extension of welfare bargaining after the war, the large unions in the mass production industries insisted on Blue Cross coverage, even in level-of-benefit plans where the union otherwise had little role in placing or administering the health insurance program. Many employers had pre-existing ties to commercial insurance companies which underwrote their casualty and workmen's compensation policies. But with labor support, Blue Cross won much of the industrial market.

Effect on Organization, Program, Coverage

Health bargaining has influenced not only the rate of growth of Blue Cross but also its organizational structure, the content of its program, and the kind of groups Blue Cross will cover.

While Blue Cross is still quite decentralized in most respects,[5] techniques for handling national accounts have been developed. At the time health bargaining started Blue Cross was a crazy quilt of separate state and local plans with little co-ordination at a national level. National bargaining for Blue Cross required multi-state contracts and arrangements between local plans. The Blue Cross Association was set up for this purpose. Health Service, Incorporated, was organized in 1949 as a stock insurance company solely owned by the Blue Cross Association to offer national accounts a basic contract at a single consolidated rate. The local Blue Cross plan may take the local underwriting in full, in part, or not at all, as it chooses. A syndicate type arrangement was developed for the steel contracts: one plan—usually the one located where the company has its home offices—provides the master contract to the employer, and other plans contract with the control plan to provide services in their locality. Consolidated billings have been arranged, through an interplan agreement, for the national employers who prefer to have their branches assume the responsibility locally. The best example of interplan co-ordination is the provision of nationally uniform benefits at a uniform rate under the Federal Employees Health Benefit Plan.

The second kind of influence has been on the extent and kind of services to be prepaid by Blue Cross. Blue Cross plans have lengthened the duration of stay as required by the rubber, steel, and auto negotiations, but some Blue Cross plans adopted the extended benefits only after years of delay.

The seventy-six plans still show a wide variation in their state of development. It is estimated that 7 per cent of Blue Cross members (group and individual) are entitled to 365 days or more of full benefits, 42 per cent to 120–80 days, 23 per cent to 70–100 days, 2 per cent to 55–60 days, and 26 per cent to 40 days or less.[6] These entitlements are for semiprivate accommodations (64 per cent of members), ward accommodations (6 per cent), flat dollar allowances (24 per cent), or an arrangement requiring the patient to pay so much per day or per admission (6 per cent).

There has also been much resistance in some Blue Cross plans to the insistence, originally by the Steelworkers, that coverage be extended to in-hospital diagnostic services, hospitalization for mental or nervous disorders, full-period hospitalization for maternity complications, etc. Now most of the plans provide emergency outpatient services, including that for minor surgery; a growing number also cover diagnostic X-ray and laboratory services for outpatients. (About nine million persons are covered for these outpatient services.) Mental illness and tuberculosis are covered, but only in general hospitals and only for relatively short stays. Maternity cases are covered after a waiting period, but often not for the full amount. Supplementary "major medical" contracts similar to those sold by insurance companies have been developed.

Lastly, union demands that health insurance be made available to the aged helped bring Blue Cross toward group coverage for the old and retired as well as for the employed. Blue Cross preceded commercial insurance in this area. However, while now cited with pride by Blue Cross, this coverage, as was earlier pointed out, was first offered only after much insistence by labor, particularly in the rubber and auto industries.

Rate Increases

State legislatures passed special "enabling acts" for Blue Cross plans, which exempted them from the reserve requirements and taxes imposed on commercial insurers. In this limited sense only does Blue Cross have any special recognition or preferred position. In the setting of subscription rates, on the other hand, Blue Cross plans are more thoroughly regulated than are commercial underwriters.[7] Some large states require a public hearing and the insurance commissioner must give prior approval for rate adjustments.

The size and frequency of rate increase requests has stirred public concern. To a large extent these increases mirror higher hospital costs, particularly higher payroll costs and the expansion in range, volume, and cost of services available in hospitals.[8] Scientific and technological change now make possible a much more intensive quality of care. It is true that the duration of hospital stays has been reduced, but this saving offsets only a small portion of the rise in daily expense per patient. Labor can have no complaint with better ancillary services and higher wages for hospital employees but it has objected that Blue Cross ". . . with all its expensive machinery and considerable array of talent, seeks simply to transfer all cost problems and pressures from the effective concern of those in the hospital service field who should be looking for better solutions, to the hardpressed pocketbooks of subscribers."[9]

There are potential savings towards which labor believes Blue Cross can and should direct itself. Some of the increase in costs arises from unnecessary utilization,[10] which should be a responsibility of Blue Cross. The AFL–CIO charged Blue Cross with "inadequate policing of hospital care."[11] A UAW spokesman stated: "They [Blue Cross] are demonstrating a dangerous tendency to remove incentives for economy from participating hospitals. In a sense, they are losing control of their program because they are not masters in their own home. It is the doctor who has control."[12]

Unnecessary utilization can be understood as a kind of exploitation of Blue Cross by the medical profession, not wilful or hostile, but arising in individual cases when convenience overrides any responsibility for the prepayment mechanism. In this exploitation, the patient may be a co-conspirator, but the decision to hospitalize is a medical one and the doctor has responsibility. A Blue Cross official has admitted that "largely through failure of Blue Cross and the hospitals to fully interpret service benefits to the medical profession, the open-ended service principle of Blue Cross has been misused."[13] To allay the mounting criticism, utilization review committees composed of physicians are now widely established. They were first used in Pennsylvania after the insurance commissioner asked for them as a condition for favorable review of Blue Cross rate problems. Although little information is available on their effectiveness, their existence alone has probably had a salutary effect.

The search for savings in hospital prepayment has collided with the financial interests of doctors in certain hospital specialties. At the insistence of the medical specialists concerned, Blue Cross has been forced to exclude radiology, pathology, and anesthesia from its benefits. The doctors in these specialties insist on billing their patients themselves, whereas good hospital administration and patient convenience suggest that such charges should be included on the hospital bill. "Co-ordinating the great variety of professional and nonprofessional services in the modern hospital," said Dr. McLean for the Blue Cross Association, "would be all but impossible if each professional participant requested to be an independent entrepreneur."[14]

We shall examine later in the chapter the patterns of control by which the medical profession influences hospital and Blue Cross policies, contributing to the latter's producer rather than consumer orientation.

Adaptation to Pressures

Blue Cross has made important modifications in some of its original principles. There has, for example, been a multiplication of policies for a differentiated market, where the subscriber can find variously priced policies with different mixtures of uncovered services and special charges to match anything offered by commercial insurance. More and more plans insert co-insurance features or deductibles, and there are limits put on ancillary services and on maternity benefits. All of these changes contradict the principle of full payment and can, in the long run, only lead to dissatisfaction among the subscribers. They make Blue Cross more like commercial insurance, although many Blue Cross plans still retain full payment. Incursions into this principle are best understood as adaptation to a squeeze resulting on the one side from rising hospital prices, and on the other from competition by commercial insurance.

The Drift Away from Community Rating

There are two explanations for the drift from community rating to experience rating in establishing Blue Cross premiums. One explanation is the competitive pressure from commercial insurance; the other is the desire of Blue Cross administrators to avoid public hearings on their rate increases.

Competitive Pressure

All but one of the Blue Cross plans now have experience rating on some or all of their group policies, the only holdout being that in the Cleveland area. Having been conceived as a community-wide arrangement between hospitals and subscribers, the theory of community rating was appealing because it appeared more likely to assure participation both by the high-risk population as well as low-cost groups. In this way, those who most needed health insurance would not be priced out of the market.[15] The problem is that community rating requires a protected position to succeed, as in a government social insurance program. If commercial interest can enter and apply experience rating, they will skim off the best risks. Once the community-rating underwriter is denied the low-cost business, he can maintain a community-wide level only at a higher rate. This is part of the explanation of what has happened to Blue Cross, whose tax-exempt status does not offer enough of a protected position for community rating with impunity.[16]

Collective bargaining has both provided a mass base for Blue Cross and also contributed to the spread of experience rating in its structure, with some notable exceptions. The national Blue Cross accounts with large manufacturing companies are experience rated. Labor and industry leaders are obligated to think in terms of the best buy for the people to whom they are accountable. Community rating could have been supported only by a labor movement with an entirely different structure, where the emphasis was on community organization rather than along industry and occupational lines. But this also explains why community rating still exists in a state like Michigan: a single union, the UAW, which is so prominent in the economic life of the state, is willing to support the principle even if it costs more to their industry. In this case at least labor has been able to keep community rating alive in Blue Cross.

This discussion has oversimplified the situation to delineate the issues clearly. Actually, Blue Cross plans show shadings of compromise between their original principles and those of commercial insurance: "There are many types and degrees of experience rating," report the Somerses, "and there is a difference between differential pricing employed in a manner that results in complete exclusion of poorer risks and nongroup individuals and a scheme that continues to accept responsibility for the whole community."[17] Many of the Blue Cross plans that have abandoned community rating have increased the rate differences between classes of coverage without assigning to each its own full cost. Experience rating is alleviated when loading factors for social purposes are added to the rate. Such modified experience rating has support among some unions, for example, the Steelworkers: as beneficiaries of experience rating, the Steelworkers has indicated it is not opposed to a loading factor in Blue Cross in order to lessen premium rates paid by the aged.[18]

Avoiding Public Hearings

While competitive pressure has contributed to the extension of experience rating, another explanation is at least as significant. In his study of Blue Cross and Blue Shield regulation, Robert Eilers reports that many plans have used experience rating as a means of circumventing rate hearings: "About 60 per cent of the executives contacted in associations which use experience rating methods said that the prime motivator for the adoption of the technique was to bypass public hearings."[19] A few state insurance commissioners feel obliged to hold public hearings on community rate changes, but in the case of experience rating for group plans they are only concerned with the initial experience formula. Once it is approved, no further investigation is required in subsequent applications.

Eilers also reports that Blue-plan administrators like experience rating because it wards off pressures to pay for services not covered and because it fastens attention on "high cost elements."[20] The administrators believe that experience rating brings to subscriber groups a direct accounting of the nature of hospital costs and that this may lead to more community pressures on hospitals and regulatory officials "to rectify abuses" and "improper increases in medical care costs." However, there are certainly more direct ways of educating subscribers without at the same time raising costs for high-risk groups. Blue Cross leadership has been urged to call regional and national conferences of major subscriber groups "to establish mutual confidence and understanding" and to lead into "participation with Blue Cross and hospitals in reshaping future policies."[21]

Where the change to experience rating has been made to avoid rate hearings and to prod the public about hospital costs, then Blue Cross officials are not assuming the responsibilities inherent in a public service enterprise; they are passing on cost problems to the subscribers.

Toward a Consumer Voice

There are many, both in and out of labor, who thought that, if properly impressed with the stakes in the game, Blue Cross would take the lead in urging its member hospitals into various efficiency reforms. To this end, labor had been pursuing the double objectives of demanding more consumer representation on Blue Cross policy bodies, and also more effective public regulation.

Blue Cross Governing Boards

Unions have asked for and in some cases got more public, labor, or subscriber representation on Blue Cross governing boards, but rarely has this resulted in any dramatic policy changes. In most plans "public members" account for 20 per cent or more of the governing boards but it is sometimes difficult to say whom they represent.[22] It was estimated in the Spring of 1966 that between 50 and 60 plans had labor representation on policy-making boards, but some of these were simply appointments by the Blue Cross hierarchy rather than official representation by persons accountable to the central labor body or subscriber group.[23] Only half a dozen plans have developed a system for direct subscriber representation.[24]

In general, doctors and hospital spokesmen have dominated the governing boards: each member hospital appoints a representative, or the local hospital association elects a certain number of representatives. In 1949, hospital representatives were in the majority in about two-thirds of the plans, and the medical society in half the plans had 20 per cent or more of the board membership.[25]

There has been a response to pressures for more public representation on governing boards. During the three years from 1959 to 1962, the number of public representatives increased from 32 per cent of the total to 47 per cent, while that of hospital representatives (administrators and trustees) dropped from 50 per cent to 35 per cent; doctors remained the same at about 18 per cent.[26] In 1964 public members constituted 41 per cent of the governing boards, hospital trustees and administrators 43 per cent, and doctors 16 per cent. In these surveys plan representatives who are also board members are classed as public representatives.[27]

Consumer groups will have to constitute a majority of the governing boards in order to restore confidence that consumer interests are being respected.[28] Eilers suggests: "The most appropriate long-run solution to the entire problem of good representation is for statutory provisions to stipulate that 'less than the majority of the governing board at any official meeting will be representatives of the vendors of association services . . .'," with vendors defined to include hospital administrators, hospital trustees, and members of any segment of the medical profession.[29]

It is equally important that the public representatives not be taken on merely as decorative furniture excluded from inner councils. Even a good board can be misused and it is vital what procedures are established. The Trussel Report, made by the Columbia University School of Public Health and Administrative Medicine, found only one of the eight New York plans sending out agenda in advance of meetings, using committees to prepare specific reports for Board guidance, submitting complex issues to Board meetings, training Board members for leadership positions, etc. "This method of organization . . . broadens the community base of the Plan . . . enables the Plan to receive the advice and counsel of genuine experts for specific tasks . . . and acts as a 'farm system' for future Board members. . . ."[30]

Public Regulation

The more direct way to influence Blue Cross policies is through informed and responsible public regulation, including open hearings on rate increases. In some states the insurance commissioners have simply added another influence toward obliterating the distinguishing features of Blue Cross[31] but in other states—particularly those where the regulating authorities have some independence from the insurance business—they have demanded that Blue Cross reassess its position, and regulation has in some cases had dramatic results. In New York, a valuable study of Blue Cross plans, following public hearings, resulted in a new emphasis on hospital planning in the state.[32] In Pennsylvania, following directives by the Pennsylvania Insurance Commissioner, physician review committees were established to sift cases of unnecessary hospital admission and confront the offending physician. In Philadelphia, a hospital administrators' board also reviews cases where the duration of the stay may be excessive.

Aside from such occasional windfalls, the prospects for change through regulation are not bright. There are serious weaknesses in state regulatory agencies, including domination by the insurance business and shortage of staff and funds.[33] Nevertheless, unions continue to appear at public hearings as spokesmen for hardpressed Blue Cross subscribers and continue to work behind the scenes where they have political influence to put muscle into regulation.[34]

When Blue Cross attempts to introduce efficiencies in hospital administration it encounters a morass of problems that has foundered even the most vigorous Blue Cross organizations. In some cases Blue Cross has attempted to negotiate reimbursement formulas that would control costs by rewarding the more efficient hospitals.[35] But hospitals have insisted on reimbursement on the basis of the individual hospital according to its own unique cost structure. It is even argued by the hospitals that there are always good reasons why they are structured the way they are.[36] There is no need, they say, to question the cost of such an institution because it is non-profit in character and the trustees will guard the public interest. This principle of reimbursement according to the costs has become a fundamental idea of equity with the hospitals. But, in the words of one scholar, "there is no escaping the fact that the usual incentives for efficient operation, are lacking when a major purchaser of services pays each hospital at its own cost."[37]

Blue Cross's inability to serve as a reform agency in the whirlwind of rising costs suggests that the center of power lies with the hospitals. In any case it is probably true that even with more consumer representation on its boards and with effective public regulation Blue Cross could not do the job of rationalizing hospital financing. A more powerful sanction is required.

Hospital Planning

A form of direct bargaining with hospitals has been undertaken by some union health and welfare funds. In Southern California, for example, union health and welfare plan administrators found that no two hospitals had similar methods of billing and that there was a wide variation in charges for ancillary services. Under these conditions, it was almost impossible to evaluate the claims experience and responsibly to administer the funds. A group of the health and welfare plan officials working together urged on the Hospital Council of Southern California a code of hospital charges with standard definitions of services. This "bargaining" terminated successfully. By rationalizing hospital billing to some degree, it helped bring savings to the health and welfare funds.

This only suggests the possibilities, because the rapid growth of hospitals and their soaring costs require consumer attention to more than just billing procedures. The basic questions are: how many hospitals? what kind should there be? and how should they work? In the words of the Trussel Report, there should be "regional action by the professions, the public and the government for continuing review of utilization and costs, for promotion of standards and for long-range community action in developing necessary and good health services, while preventing unnecessary construction and correcting substandard performance."[38]

Several kinds of planning councils, usually on a voluntary or non-statutory basis, have been established in several states and major cities. There is much interest in their work—in their effectiveness, the use and nature of the sanctions, and in whether the councils can succeed without some governmental authority.[39]

An outstanding example of hospital planning was the ten hospitals built by the United Mine Workers in the medically deprived coal fields of Appalachia. Miners' Memorial Hospital Association achieved high quality and cost savings by centralizing the rarer specialties and treatments, and by central purchasing, laundering, etc.[40]

By contrast, the main problems of hospitals in most places is that they are established and they operate as separate, self-contained units. The accumulation of funds for hospital construction may bear little relationship to the needs of the community.[41] All advantages of scale are lost, if at each hospital the staff doctors want the latest equipment in their specialty, or if excessive hospital beds are provided. Peak loads may be determined and the number of beds decided without any reference to the fact that utilization rates at all hospitals in a community do not peak at the same time, permitting inter-hospital arrangements for overflow.[42] The result of over-construction must be either higher per-patient charges or over-utilization. The per-patient cost of hospitalization is directly affected by fixed costs including that of unoccupied beds.[43] Rather than raising charges, individual hospitals may try to meet their higher costs by encouraging occupancy.[44] Either way, the result is an increase in the prepayment premium.

Some labor organizations other than the United Mine Workers have been directly involved in hospital problems. In Detroit, when the United Automobile Workers was hard pressed by the increase in Blue Cross rates, it engaged in "bargaining" with hospitals and Blue Cross; the union reported the greatest success only when it actually began to develop plans for a competitive alternative—the Community Health Association. In New York City, a cost crisis stimulated the New York City Central Labor Council to establish a Hospital Committee under the chairmanship of an official of the Hotel Trades Council, which has had considerable experience in direct hospital care planning. In lower Bucks County, Pennsylvania, the unions spearheaded a hospital construction fund drive, and in Philadelphia, the AFL–CIO Medical Health Plan recently built a modern hospital. In general, however, unions have not played much of a role in hospital construction or maintenance.

The economics of hospitals suggests that no group should go it alone in hospital planning. The miners' hospitals were an exception because they were built in an area that was a medical vacuum, but even there the problems created when the UMW unloaded these hospitals from their welfare fund assets raise the question whether it would have been better originally to have had more community involvement in the project. Labor's temptation on occasion is to work independently of the community for better medical care at reasonable costs. But unless the unions are part of regional planning for hospital expansion, they will add to the problem rather than to its solution.

In a "Statement on Hospitals" the AFL–CIO emphasizes that hospitals should be built and enlarged only in accord with a systematic plan prepared by a "Hospital Planning Council."[45] The plan should be based on estimates of present and future needs. The Council can consist of private or public persons, or both, and should be widely representative of the community, not just of the health resources. Furthermore, the planning should not be in terms of beds for the acutely ill only. "Progressive care" and differentiated facilities are an important key to more efficient use of health resources because not all chronic illness and convalescing cases require concentrated attention. Planning them must also encompass facilities for long-term patients, nursing homes, outpatient services, and home care. The "Statement" also recommends that no existing hospital should receive a Hill-Burton grant unless it meets the requirements of state and regional planning. The weight of the AFL–CIO view is to warn against the dangers of "unbridled individual autonomy" in hospital construction and use, and it urges local unions to unify their policies and pool their efforts in dealing with hospitals, physicians, and Blue Cross.

Labor has played an important role in the development of Blue Cross, and disappointments have been more intense because expectations were so high. It is still true that some Blue Cross administrators have retained their original consumer orientation, but most have adopted features of their private insurance competitors. It is also true, however, that commercial insurance has had to accept innovations in health insurance pioneered by Blue Cross with labor encouragement. Some labor leaders feel Blue Cross now is only a collection agency for the hospitals rather than an independent purchaser of hospital services. The gap between promise and performance has made Blue Cross much talked at and talked about, but it is not clear that expectations have been realistic. In any case, the problems that Blue Cross has been unable to solve persist, and will have to be solved in other ways. There is an increasing role for both government and consumers in hospital planning, and there is an opportunity for private capital to organize hospital service programs.

11

BARGAINING WITH DOCTORS:
FEES AND QUALITY

Organized labor and organized medicine have grappled for generations over a wide range of subjects. When the fights are about health legislation, they are well publicized. But what escapes public notice is the hand-to-hand combat in local communities over the organization and economics of medical practice.

The character of this practice is changing under many pressures. The higher costs of medical care have given great incentive to prepayment. The increase in medical knowledge and new techniques have created specialties and heightened interdependence among doctors, and in order to establish an easy consultative relationship more and more specialists and general practitioners have joined in group practice arrangements. The need for expensive equipment makes individual entrepreneurship difficult so that hospitals, groups of doctors, and consumer organizations able to supply the needed capital have hired doctors, sometimes on a salaried basis. The traditional practice where a doctor works alone and charges a fee for each service rendered is being challenged by all these developments—prepayment, group practice, lay sponsorship, and salaried reimbursement. By encouraging and promoting such changes, labor comes into conflict with the officials of organized medicine whose recognition of the new order is reluctant, even begrudging.[1]

The Pricing Problem

At the end of the 1940's, when health insurance rose high on labor's bargaining agenda, there were usually only two alternative methods of prepaying medical services—commercial insurance and Blue

Shield. Commercial insurance offered cash indemnification at specified amounts for surgical procedures, and occasionally for other in-
or out-of-hospital doctor services; doctor bills went directly to the
subscriber who in turn collected from the insurer. The Blue Shield
plans sponsored by state and local medical societies provided cash
indemnity benefits also, but for subscribers below specified incomes
the participating doctors agreed to accept the surgical schedule as full
reimbursement. Only for lower-income subscribers could these be
called "service plans" in which medical services where offered rather
than partial indemnification. In general, then, both the available alternatives left a great deal wanting from labor's point of view.

Labor wanted programs where it could be certain the prepayment
plan would cover medical bills. It became a source of frustration to the
unions that they could not obtain service benefits for all members
regardless of their income. A victory in collective bargaining that
established hospital and surgical prepayment benefits often bred dissatisfaction when the members found that doctors charged more than
the plan provided; and it was only one step to a real or fancied conclusion that doctors regarded the negotiated gains as evidence of ability
to pay higher fees.[2] There developed within the unions an internal
dynamic of pressures from the members to do something about this,
and the steady rise in fees simply added to the pressure for service-type
plans.

Looking into the problem, union technicians soon realized there was
a more subtle aspect to the rise in prices. The upward movement in
fees was a general testing of the market by even the physician who
did not charge his patients sliding scale fees. Doctors may move up-
wards all their fees for all patients following improvements in group
health plans in the community. The United Rubber Workers made a
study in twenty-seven areas of what it would take to constitute a full
payment schedule, and then negotiated cash indemnity benefits at that
level. Four years later another survey showed that fees had risen and
the original indemnity schedules covered only a portion of the bills,
averaging as low as 63 per cent in one area.[3] Other unions have
reported similar experiences.[4] Since the difference in an indemnity
prepayment plan has to be paid out of the pockets of the members,
the situation inevitably stimulates union efforts to close the gap.

The gap between benefits and fees could be closed in a period of stable fees by increasing the premium contributions and raising the dollar value of the benefits. Toward this end higher employer contributions have been negotiated, with or without higher employee contributions. In a period of rising fees, however, the union negotiators were bound to be disappointed. A survey by one firm of insurance consultants illustrates the futility from the union viewpoint of negotiating higher fee schedules:

Our company analyzed over 10,000 surgical claims where benefits were paid under a $150.00 surgical schedule. We found that this surgical schedule paid only 55% of the surgeon's total charges. And an analysis of claims paid under a $300.00 surgical schedule showed that such a schedule paid only 69% of the surgeon's total charges. As you can see, a 100% increase in the surgical indemnity schedule served to reduce the patients' share of the bills by only 14%.[5]

Doctors have argued that increasing costs and rising price levels are justification for the upward movement in fees, arguments the unions wanted to study more closely. The subject of rising fees thus brought labor and medicine into direct discussions in twenty or more large cities in the United States. The character and objectives of these meetings have varied considerably. In Milwaukee, labor and doctors had a few casual meetings—"we want them to see we don't have horns" said the union spokesman.[6] But other meetings drew the parties into the fundamental question of medical economics: how can organized consumers and organized doctors with their opposing interests in medical fees establish some mechanism for setting fees to their mutual satisfaction? Can institutional adjustments be made to rationalize medical pricing?

Labor's objectives in these discussions have been to obtain predetermined prices for medical services in order to have a basis for negotiating full coverage fee schedules, or to extend the service benefits so that no union members, regardless of their incomes, will have additional out-of-pocket expenses. In general, these efforts have failed, either because medical societies have been unwilling to bargain on these issues or unable to obtain the commitments from member doctors to observe a predetermined price schedule. For example, the United Rubber Workers in Akron attempted to get the Summit County Medical Society to agree to a schedule or to discuss any needed upward revisions, but met with no success.[7] The same union had more success elsewhere in getting commitments from a medical society "to follow closely a schedule of payments" but soon found that many doctors were violating the agreement.[8] In Los Angeles, unions formed a Health Plan Consultants Committee and negotiated for over a year with the president and responsible officers of the Los Angeles County Medical Society.[9] Although the Society's president strongly favored agreement on a fee schedule and a committee of the Society worked out such a schedule, it was not adopted by the required two-thirds of the Society. In San Francisco, the California Metal Trades Association and the San Francisco Labor Council met over several years with representatives of the San Francisco Medical Society. Fee schedules "for the guidance" of union negotiators were developed but never officially sanctioned by the Medical Society which stated that "there must be no set or frozen fee schedule," that the "doctor's right to establish with his patient the fee to be paid must be respected," and that "there can be no 'third party' placed in the middle of the all-important and confidential doctor-patient relationship."[10] In general, medical societies would not accept the principle of negotiation and claimed to be unable to provide a medical bargaining representative with power to reach a binding agreement. Labor remained suspicious of "recommended schedules" or schedules for "general guidance," fearing that their effect would only be to set a new, higher floor of charges for such services. These are not fee schedules at all "but merely a guess as to what the fee may be unless the County Medical Society is willing to support and stand behind such a schedule."[11] When the San Francisco Medical Society in 1953 finally brought forth a proposed fee schedule, its cost was regarded by the Labor Council as far beyond the possibilities of prepayment.[12] The charges for house calls varied from $7.50 to $12.50, depending on the time of day. The Society further recommended this schedule be applicable only where the wage earner was earning under $5,000, and stated: "No member of the Society is obligated or compelled to work by this schedule."[13]

A flock of disturbing questions are raised by such experiences. Will doctors really discuss their prices in an objective setting? Can they give up the unilateral determination of fees? Will they reach agreements with healthy people and spokesmen for groups? Are they willing to recognize any authority on fee questions within their own ranks? The doctors' reply to these pressing questions has been that they are officially committed to their own plans, the Blue Shield organizations.

Negotiating with Blue Shield

Although linked with Blue Cross in the public mind, the Blue Shield plans had an entirely separate origin. Dissatisfaction with contract arrangements in logging and other industries in California and Oregon had led some of the county medical societies in those states to establish "medical bureaus." These "medical bureaus" offered prepayment opportunities more acceptable to the profession. When a state health insurance plan was urged by the Governor of California in 1938, the California Medical Association hastened to establish the California Physician's Service, the first Blue Shield program. A similar step was taken by the Michigan State Medical Society. In both states, leaders in the profession felt that the public was asking for medical care on a prepayment basis. Admittedly, their purpose was to keep prepayment voluntary rather than governmental, and to assure the profession a hand in shaping it. Real growth came during the war years: in 1946 there were 44 Blue Shield plans with over 4 million subscribers.[14]

The rapid growth in Blue Shield came long after that in Blue Cross (which had spread rapidly in the middle thirties) in part because of deep-seated reluctance in the medical profession, which displayed little interest in prepayment as a service to the public, even in the case of low income groups. The "Ten Principles" adopted by the American Medical Association in 1934–35 declared medical prepayment plans to be "systems for the relief of low income classes,"[15] and further prescribed that such systems should be controlled by physicians, should include all physicians in the community, and should allow no third-party intervention. An amendment in 1935 permitted prepayment if fees were "paid for by the patient in accordance with his income status." Hospital services were removed from these limitations by the House of Delegates in 1937, but they were applied to all doctors' services until 1941; at that time the "Principles" were altered to allow service-type benefits for low income groups. By setting the income limits sufficiently low, the doctors retained freedom to set fees for each service and each patient with no control nor even any element of predetermination. Many doctors still regard the service feature below the income limitation as a subsidy, a kind of physician-sponsored relief.[16] They believe they are justified in providing medical services to indigents or near-indigents who could not otherwise pay for care, as long as there are enough over the income limit who can be charged more.

By contrast, labor's interest in prepayment was as insurance against medical bills. They wanted to negotiate benefits in order to be able to budget the cost of medical care and thereby be able to avoid any kind of charity, including private charity. There was then inherent in Blue Shield a conflict between the consumer and producer over its fundamental objectives.

In addition, the practical problem of administering Blue Shield led to subtle but profound changes in pricing. To distinguish between classes of patients according to income puts the doctor in a difficult position, unless he knows the income levels of all his patients. He either has to determine these incomes to his satisfaction or to develop a kind of two-price system. For instance, an obstetrician may explain to his patient that his fee is $150, but that the Blue Shield payment of $75 will cover the bill if her husband's income is under $4,200, as specified by the Blue Shield contract. The patient, therefore, must pay twice the fee in the Blue Shield contract if her husband's income is over the limit, and even if it is barely over the limit. Few and far between are the patients able to argue that their income is not enough higher than the Blue Shield limit to justify doubling the fee. Some doctors do not leave it to the patient to decide their obligation, but prefer by indirect means to obtain clues to the patient's income. A surgeon once asked me about my place of work, pretending to have a brother who was interested in employment there: the whole purpose of the exercise (never acknowledged) was to determine whether the Blue Shield income level applied.

Dissatisfaction with income limits in Blue Shield plans is not confined to unions or covered persons. Pollack and Bloch, on the basis of their New York City investigation, report that many physicians admit they have "as little and perhaps less chance of making accurate determination of family income as anyone else" and that they prefer "to set fixed charges with procedures which apply to all patients, but make adjustments downward when hardship is demonstrated." They conclude that "many doctors would welcome arrangements for payment that relieve them from awkward, deceptive and frequently inequitable determinations of family income."[17]

To the extent that the income limits can be raised, the character of the Blue Shield program shifts from an indemnity to a service plan, and with fewer persons over the income limits the administrative confusions are minimized. We have already described the United Auto Workers' and the United Steelworkers' efforts in this direction (Chapters 5 and 6). After each upward adjustment in the Michigan income limit, the UAW would then attempt to get Blue Shield plans in other cities with organized plants to raise their limit,[18] but this rarely succeeded and then only after much delay.[19] Similarly, the Steelworkers, with some 700,000 members in Blue Cross-Blue Shield, warned the national Blue Shield organization of mounting resentment among its members.[20] These labor pressures were both for extended services and for higher income levels, and are to some extent a cause of the newly-evolving patterns in Blue Shield.

Thirteen plans in 1965 were entirely on an indemnity basis in which there is no commitment by the participating physicians that the fees scheduled are full payment to any subscriber. Fifty-five plans provide full payment under specified income levels—typically $4,000 for a single person and $6,000 for a family—and indemnity benefits for those with higher incomes. (Thirty-four of these are "omni-level" plans with two or more sets of income ceilings and corresponding fee schedules for the service subscribers.) Only six of the smaller plans provide service benefits to all subscribers regardless of income.[21] Blue Shield sources claim that two-thirds of Blue Shield payments to physicians are accepted in full payment, but it is difficult to estimate this accurately.[22]

The National Association of Blue Shield Plans is encouraging its constituent plans to dispense with a formal fee schedule. It is urging an arrangement whereby each physician files his customary or regular charges. If these fall within the ninth decile of the charges of all physicians in the area, he is paid his regular fee and accepts this as full payment.[23]

Although there are tremendous differences in Blue Shield plans, even in the same state, the good plans from labor's point of view are rare. The reason for this probably lies in the cost of such plans, and the absence of centralized responsibility for pricing medical services in the medical profession itself. Unlike the medical society plan in Windsor, Ontario,[24] where strict control of doctors' services and charges is maintained by medical society action, in the United States there is usually little authority exercised over doctors' fees. (A notable exception to that rule in this country is the San Joaquin Foundation in California, described below.) The board of trustees of a Blue Shield plan negotiates the fee schedule with representatives of the medical society in the area. But since the plan's board of trustees is designated by the same society, in effect only one party is on both sides of the bargaining.

The way a medical society or a Blue Shield governing board avoids the prospect of having to do any "whipcracking" in its own ranks is to propose a fee schedule so inflated that all doctors are satisfied with it. Thus, while many doctors themselves recognize that the "charity" concept used to justify the income differentiation is inappropriate for modern prepayment plans, and while they may be willing to establish service or full payment plans, these doctors may also insist that their reimbursement from Blue Shield must be comparable with their income from other sources.[25] The effect of such considerations may be to put an impossibly high selling price on a good proposal. We come back to the same issues we started with in discussing the San Francisco negotiations: under what conditions can fees be a subject for bargaining between doctors and consumers?

The general conclusion from labor's experience is this: in open-panel plans under typical conditions, bargaining with medicine cannot succeed because there is no discipline, no compelling reasons for the medical society to take an authoritative stance with member doctors on fees.[26] Only when alternatives to the open-panel arrangement are available to the unions is the situation different. Then doctors do feel the need of organizational discipline and only then can direct negotiations for predetermined fee schedules have any hope of success.

The positive side of this lesson was borne out in California.[27] At Santa Monica, for example, the unions had never been able to get any co-operation from any substantial segment of the medical profession until a Kaiser Plan was considered for the Douglas Aircraft plant; it was never consummated, but some of the favorable relationships established at that time linger on. "We have noticed that our relationships [with doctors and hospitals] improve and our problems become alleviated sharply by the operation of a closed panel plan in the area."[28] The doctors themselves gauge their strategy by these considerations, as, for example, when the president of the Medical Society in Los Angeles urged support of his colleagues for an agreed fee schedule:

It should be clear at the outset that the medical profession has but two choices. It can accept a leading role in determining the shape of health pro-

grams . . . and cooperative fee setting . . . or it can run away from consideration of such proposals. . . . If the first choice is not made, there is a large
monopolistic closed panel system which is perfectly willing and anxious to
cooperate and to thereby supplant the medical association and its members.[29]

It has been largely due to the expanding Kaiser Plan and to union
interest in independent labor health centers in San Francisco and elsewhere that efforts to improve on cash indemnity prepayment have
met with some success in California. Several medical societies, led
by the Alameda-Contra Costa Medical Association, broke with tradition and unilaterally promulgated "median fee lists" which they are
committed to support as maximum payments under certain circumstances. The California Physician's Service (Blue Shield) has adopted
a $6,000 income ceiling ($8,000 for family) and most of the state has
accepted it. These are not "solutions" from the labor point of view,
most notably because their acceptability to the medical profession has
depended in part on a generous fee structure, but they show the medical profession feeling its way toward a program. The existence of the
Kaiser and labor health center alternatives has cast a long shadow over
traditional solo practice and fee-for-service arrangements, and restored
to some extent the climate for experimentation that existed in California at the end of the thirties, when a state health insurance plan was
imminent.

Doctor-Administered Price Controls

There is one particular innovation by Californian medical societies that
has seriously interested some unions—the San Joaquin Foundation for
Medical Care.[30] Through the Foundation, the doctors in San Joaquin
County offer service benefits at all income levels; and they have taken
on the responsibility for policing claims while leaving to outside
insurers the underwriting and sales functions.

The Foundation is a corporation established by the County Medical
Society to sell medical services at predetermined fees. It is completely
controlled by the Society, the Foundation's Board of Directors being
selected by the Board of the Medical Society and serving also as the
Society's Medical Services Committee. Three successively higher fee
and premium levels have been established for subscribers. For the
group policies, all subscribers are assigned to the same income level,
somewhere near the group average. Since the individual's income is

determined when the policy is issued, the doctor does not have to inquire about or guess his patient's income when the bill is rendered.

The Foundation sets the fees and approves the policies and the premiums; the promoting, selling, and actuarial risk-assessing are left to the insurance carriers. Nine commercial underwriters and the California Physician's Service (the state-wide Blue Shield plan) offer policies approved by the Foundation; these policies can be of different kinds with scheduled or unscheduled limitations and varying maximums, depending on the market response to differing premium levels. However, all have deductibles or co-insurance because the Foundation feels that full prepayment of the established fees would require too high a premium. Thus there are out-of-pocket payments involved, but at least the amount is known because fees and benefits are predetermined. All policies, whatever their differences, have in common the same assumptions on the fees to be charged and Foundation commitment to keep fees within the specified limits.

How is this done? The unique feature of this plan, and the one which distinguishes it from other medical service corporations, is the sanction it holds. A committee of doctors reviews the claims, working individually about one hour a week and without pay; difficult or contested claims are reviewed by the whole committee. Each year the doctors participating in the plan must apply again for admission, and, if the reviewing committee is dissatisfied with a participating doctor, he can be denied readmission. Obviously, the plan could not work at all if there were not widespread participation and acceptance of this supervision and sanction. In short, the Foundation is a kind of "open-ended, closed panel" under medical society auspices.

Union people evaluate the San Joaquin Foundation in various ways. Some see in it the prior fee agreement on a county-wide basis that has been unattainable in so many labor negotiations with medical societies. They also see here the makings of a meaningful relationship between insurers and the providers of services—a framework for the responsible financing of prepaid benefits. They see the unique contribution of the Foundation in its ability to introduce controls and thereby provide a sound basis for underwriting service benefits.

On the other hand, it is argued that the Foundation's fee schedules inflated customary fees and that this is inevitably the price for support from most doctors. It is significant that a package of services comparable to that provided by Kaiser (e.g., the Longshoremen's Fund discussed below) costs a lot more through the San Joaquin Foundation.

Foundation-approved policies enrolled over 20,000 persons—about 10 per cent of the area's population—in the first 5 years of operation. The plan was a response to growing labor interest in closed panels; in 1952 and 1953, the unions in San Joaquin were talking with Kaiser about expanding into their area, and they were also exploring the union health center possibilities. "We felt we needed to answer the complaint of labor unions that they could not get certainty coverage," said the organizer and later president of the Foundation, Dr. Donald Harrington.[31] The first group to participate were the Lathers', Plasterers', and Hod Carriers' union. There are now over forty groups enrolled, eight of which came through union agreements.

The International Longshoremen's and Warehousemen's Union saw in the self-policing feature of the Foundation an opportunity to obtain comprehensive services even under an open-panel arrangement. The union-industry welfare fund negotiated with the Foundation for a comprehensive package of benefits, fully prepaid, including some preventive services for 700 longshoremen and their families. Unlike other Foundation policies, this one involves no outside insurance carrier. Negotiations were concluded in 1955. Later the monthly premium per employee (which includes the hospitalization and major medical benefits not provided by the Foundation) had to be increased, in part due to underestimates in the early years. Former fund secretary, Goldie Krantz, has reported that the program enhances quality in three ways: (1) by encouraging the utilization and providing the continuity of medical care possible only under full prepayment for comprehensive benefits; (2) by eliminating benefit definitions and restrictions which, in many health insurance plans, encourage the substitution of economic for medical considerations in providing care; and (3) by the claims review by doctors themselves which has stimulated their interest in the quality of medicine practiced by their colleagues. She concludes, "The millenium has not arrived in California insofar as the organization and provision of medical care are concerned, notwithstanding the existence of the largest prepaid group plan, Kaiser, and the Foundation plans. . . . As a consumer we think the Foundation program is a step forward within the variegated 'trial and error' method of our voluntary system of prepaid medical care."[32]

The medical profession has shown some interest in the San Joaquin Foundation,[33] as have insurance industry officials.[34] There are fifteen similar programs in California and two elsewhere at various stages of development. Whether this experiment will be applicable elsewhere remains to be seen. It is argued that claims review by doctors can be effective only in medical societies small enough so that personal, face-to-face relationships exist among the doctors. (San Joaquin has a few more than 300 doctors.) San Joaquin had the advantage of effective local leadership, which was able to involve nearly all county doctors in the Foundation. It may also be true that the incentive exists only where alternative closed-panel plans are under active consideration.

In their dealings with doctors, union leaders have learned a great deal about medicine and its economic characteristics. They can be more tolerant of the conservative outlook of the physician, seeing in it one characteristic of a profession that requires scientific detachment. The doctors on their side have been pressed to clarify and distinguish between their professional concerns as doctors and their economic interests as business men. These meetings have not always been in the recommended climate of "calm understanding, with dignity, and without rancor"[35] but to realistic men some heat is necessary for understanding. It would be naive, however, to rest with an appraisal of the educational values of these negotiations. We are interested in their results and the conclusion is inescapable that the results have been a function of the pressures felt by the parties and the alternatives open to them.

The Surveillance of Quality and Cost

It was inevitable, with the spread of negotiated prepayment plans and their continued improvement in successive contracts, that labor leaders would raise questions about the quality of the medical care actually being purchased. Were the new medical funds really bringing better health? Al Hayes, then President of the Machinists, argued in 1955: "It is high time we stopped emphasizing insurance against the high cost of neglected health and devoted more of our efforts to developing a system of prepayment which will give the American people greater access to the kind of health care which prevents illness or nips it in the bud."[36] Similarly, George Meany: "A medical care program that begins to operate only when the patient is flat on his back in a hospital is a program of poor quality."[37] Speaking before the Michigan State Medical Society in 1957, Walter Reuther argued the limitations of orthodox health insurance: "I really don't believe the average doctor, with his deep interest in medical services, is ready to adopt the insurance industry's concepts of losses rather than benefits, indemnity rather than service, financial devices to inhibit use . . . rather than preventive care, early diagnosis, and easy access to health services."[38] These concerns have carried influential elements in the labor movement far beyond a simple search for predetermined prices and toward surveillance of quality as well as cost.

Since organized medicine has firmly stood by a rule that consumer groups have no role in setting quality standards, unions wanting advice and guidance have had to bypass medical societies and appeal to sympathetic doctors enlisted on a consultant and advisory basis. In its more elementary form, this consultation has sometimes produced improvements: (1) better fee schedules by weighting fees according to relative value; (2) medical review to determine proper payment for unusual cases; (3) different methods for including early diagnosis without prohibitive prepayment costs; (4) liberalization of prepayment benefits to include services without which the quality of care may be warped for financial reasons.[39] Medical consulting committees have been used for these purposes by union negotiators and fund administrators on either an *ad hoc* or a permanent basis. In this way unions procured the "know-how" which is not available either from insurance companies that claim they have nothing to do with quality of care, nor from medical societies alarmed about "outside controls." In its more advanced forms, medical advice is employed by unions to give guidance on alternative ways to organize medical practice for higher quality. Outstanding private practitioners, authorities in public health, and medical school staffs have been sought out by unions both for their technical help, and, in battles with organized medicine, in order to have both the guidance and the prestige of the profession on the union's side.

The United Mine Workers' welfare fund experience is notable as the most ambitious attempt at continuous surveillance of both quality and cost.[40] We are not concerned here just with the hospital chain, which was a small part of the whole program. The bulk of medical services are bought from local facilities and doctors engaged in fee-for-service solo practice. The significant point is that even under these conditions the fund practices quality surveillance.

The fund buys the miners in-hospital medical and surgical benefits, outpatient care by specialists, and some drugs. Any physician selected by a miner could be reimbursed by the fund so long as he was in good professional repute, his charge was reasonable, and he was willing to submit certain clinical records (pathological reports, X-rays, etc.) required for payment of services. The fund, through its own staff of doctors, challenged unnecessary hospitalization, undue length of stay, failure of physicians to make specialist referral, surgery by general practitioners, and unnecessary surgery. There was grumbling in local medical societies over some of these decisions. In cases of flagrant misconduct, Dr. Draper reported his findings to grievance committees of local medical societies for action. The standards of quality desired by the fund were higher than local medical societies could or would enforce, and the only recourse available to the fund was to drop doctors from the approved list.[41]

The reaction at the local level was instantaneous. Not infrequently in small mining communities, it was the oldest and best known doctors who were removed from the approved list. The AMA was more cautious, being itself committed to the quality standards sought, and did not attack the fund until the medical societies of three states spoke for the disappointed practitioners. Dr. Draper had to drop his newly imposed requirement that there had to be consultation with a UMW approved specialist when any miner was committed to a hospital. But he made no other concessions, and in 1957, when he issued a list of approved hospitals and doctors, another storm was loosed. In Ohio and Colorado, doctors were expelled from their medical societies for participating in the fund; such pressures have caused some doctors on the approved list to withdraw.[42]

In conclusion, there are here pointed lessons for the rest of labor. First, the surveillance of cost and quality where fee-for-service solo practice prevails is not a stable situation. It may begin as an open-panel plan but cannot remain so. Both the San Joaquin and UMW program became "open-ended closed panels" as non-co-operating doctors were dropped.

Second, solo practitioners will object to quality surveillance even under the best of conditions. In the physicians' own San Joaquin plan, surveillance is directed more to anomalies in fees rather than in quality. When an outside group attempts quality surveillance there is even less tolerance, and this is true even when competently done, as by other doctors in the UMW fund.

Third, it is nevertheless true, as the UMW experience suggests, that cost and quality surveillance can be made to stick if the union and fund can "stand the heat." The plan must be centrally administered and the union a stable institution capable of withstanding local pressures generated in the community and among the union membership by an antagonistic medical society.

While these lessons are clear, and in part because they are so clear, other unions have chosen different routes to quality with reasonable cost. The special conditions of centralized control necessary for success have not existed in them, nor has it been felt worthwhile in itself to centralize the union and bargaining structure for this purpose.

Rather than attempt surveillance of the quality of medical care under open-panel or near open-panel conditions, most other unions have moved directly to the closed-panel approach. Prepaid group practice permits the attainment of quality and cost objectives through a system of internal controls and is easier to administer once it is established.

12

BARGAINING WITH DOCTORS: PREPAID GROUP PRACTICE

Within both organized labor and organized medicine there are differences of opinion about group practice, but labor leaders and policy makers in the unions have generally emphasized the better quality that group practice can give the patient, whereas until recently the AMA leadership has disparaged group practice.[1] The AMA has cited group practice as an infringement of the patient's free choice of physician and, therefore, unethical; has denied either the necessity for or the success of groups; and has emphasized negative aspects of group practice, such as the causes for dissolution and legal snarls of partnership agreements. The expansion of group practice,[2] especially in recent years, has toned down this negativism.[3] A group practice doctor (Dr. Gunner Gunderson) even acceded to the AMA presidency in 1957 and was outspoken in his opinion that group practice provided better medicine because of the "free referrals to physicians in the group who are most qualified . . . it is the most efficient way of using a doctor's services."[4] While there are many in official labor and official medicine who now agree about group practice,[5] there remains a chasm between them on the issue of whether prepayment may be combined with group practice.

Combining prepayment with group practice ties the subscriber to one group or panel of doctors, it is argued by the AMA. It forecloses his free choice of physician, i.e., any physician in the community, and this free choice is essential to a good doctor-patient relationship. The AMA, as will become clear, has consistently regarded any limitation of free choice as "unethical." Prepaid group practice is adapted to sponsorship by lay groups and thus becomes a kind of contract medi-

159

cine, which, it is officially charged, necessarily means deterioration in the quality of care. Prepaid group practice, with its ease of referral and consultation, threatens the fee-for-service principle by complicating reimbursement according to value rendered and ability to pay, and may even introduce other bases for allotting income among the medical group.

Negotiating with the AMA

Labor has negotiated with the AMA on these questions at a national level. In 1948 and 1949, several labor, co-operative, and consumer groups met with AMA representatives to work out a suitable program to make available on the widest possible basis medical services under health insurance. There was no progress at the first meeting, except that the AMA delegates promised to prepare a set of standards applicable to consumer-sponsored, direct-service plans. At the second meeting, ten months later, this had not yet been done, and Fred Umhey, the AFL representative, and other labor delegates threatened to walk out and issue a press statement charging the AMA with bad faith unless some action were taken. As a result, a subcommittee was appointed to frame a set of principles applicable to consumer plans for submission to the AMA House of Delegates in June, 1949. Twenty principles were formulated and, according to Dr. Leo Price of the ILGWU, the AMA members of the committee actively promoted them for adoption, but finally were compelled to yield to an amendment from the floor to the effect that the principles as adopted were to be merely a guide for the consideration of local and state medical societies.[6]

Since then the negotiations have been conducted unofficially through a few doctors in their dual capacity as labor health plan directors and members of the AMA Committee on Medical Care for Industrial Workers. Some "Standards of Acceptance for Medical Care Plans" were promulgated in 1953. In 1955, "Guiding Principles for Evaluating Management and Union Health Centers" were drawn up by the Committee, which then included Dr. W. A. Sawyer of the International Association of Machinists, Dr. Leo Price of the International Ladies' Garment Workers' Union, and Dr. Warren Draper of the United Mine Workers' welfare fund. These were amended in 1957. While some of these "guides" have an air of unreality—such as the requirement that physicians not in the plan should be entitled to use the facilities of a health center—it is even more significant that the Committee accepted the existence of health centers and discussed the specifics of their internal organization.

Policies of the AMA show some evolution. Prior to 1957, "free-choice-of-doctor" and "fee-for-service" were so deeply imbedded as "ethical principles" that the AMA Judicial Council frequently found itself trapped between the logic of the AMA's policies and its knowledge that courts would not support these "ethical principles" against prepaid group practice plans. As a matter of practice, the Judicial Council was willing to recognize that "free choice" may properly be limited if a "third party" has a "valid interest" and no financial profit is involved. In 1957, "free choice" was taken out of the "Principles of Ethics," but still the doctor's fee "should be commensurate with the services rendered and the patient's ability to pay. . . ."[7] Neither this nor subsequent action in 1959 has really cleared up AMA policy toward prepaid group practice. In June of 1959, the House of Delegates held that the individual should be able to select his physician "or to select his preferred system of medical care"; this was hailed by the press as opening the door to prepaid group practice, but in December the House said, "Lest there be no misinterpretation, we . . . firmly subscribe to freedom of choice of physician and free competition among physicians as being prerequisites to optimal medical care. The benefits of any system which provides medical care must be judged on the degree to which it allows of, or abridges, such freedom of choice and such competition." Adding still more uncertainty, the *Journal of the American Medical Association* explained that the December amendment "was intended to strengthen the position stated last June, not to modify or retract such position."[8]

The semantic problems besetting the AMA are no different from those besetting any organization with members of diverse and conflicting interest. The resolutions offer little comfort or restraint to either side of the controversy. Labor is faced with the fact that there remains an intense hostility in wide areas of the profession to prepaid group practice plans. At the risk of slandering their colleagues in the armed forces, in the public health service, in veterans hospitals, and wherever else they are paid a salary, many delegates argued before the

1957 House of Delegates that unless the physician was paid a fee for each service rendered, his services deteriorated. One delegate called the employer contribution to union health and welfare plans "charity."[9] Behind this rhetoric is an unpleasant economic fact: the kind of prepaid group practice plan labor wants would provide comprehensive care at home, doctors' offices, medical group center, and hospital; this takes the insured completely out of the general medical market and there is no more money to be made out of this part of the population. As Dr. George Baehr states it: "When a doctor loses a patient to a medical group, [he is] injured financially . . . [and] is resentful toward the group because he knows it possesses many advantages over him."[10] These motives are covered by the battle cry of "free choice of physician" although the disaffected physicians themselves would deny free choice of the "only form of prepaid medical care that can provide comprehensive coverage to insured persons, with all its advantages of economy, preventive services and facilities for early detection of disease."[11]

It is at the local level where individual doctors are threatened with specific loss that medicine and labor have their most significant conflicts over prepaid group practice. A brief summary of two of these situations—one involving the Health Insurance Plan of Greater New York and the other the Kaiser Foundation Health Plan—will give the tone of these skirmishes.

Labor's Role in the Struggles of HIP

The Health Insurance Plan (HIP) of Greater New York was organized by Mayor Fiorello La Guardia to provide medical care to city employees and people in middle- and low-income groups.

The rapid growth of HIP, beginning in 1947, caused panic in the medical societies which contended that HIP was dominated by lay personnel, that there was no effective free choice of doctor, that HIP engaged in unethical advertising, that HIP's group structure did not permit a proper relationship between physician and patient, and that HIP was a trial balloon for national health insurance. In the words of the past president of the Medical Society of the County of New York:

In my opinion, this health insurance plan is undemocratic and unfair in that it receives a monopolistic subsidy from the City of New York. Furthermore, it is not only subsidized by the City of New York to the exclusion of plans that allow free choice of physician but it is also by private foundations, by trade unions. . . . Comprehensive medical care plans, at least in New York City, can operate in only one of three ways or their combination: (a) by subsidy that comes from philanthropy or from participating physicians by their willingness to render medical care at substandard fees; (b) without subsidy, by giving low grade medical care; (c) by "sweatshop" labor of the participating physicians. The advertising used by the Health Insurance Plan of Greater New York may be legal, but is also unethical.[12]

In 1952, when residents of large, low-rent New York housing projects were allowed to come in without any employer being required to pay half of the premium, physicians who had signed leases for offices in the housing developments stimulated more opposition. The New York County Medical Society, which had informed HIP in 1948 that it could not advertise, rescinded its decision in 1952.[13] A bill was sponsored but not passed to destroy panel practice.[14] Group Health Insurance, Inc., a competing indemnity plan, capitalized on the disturbance by signing up 8,000 doctors who would agree to provide prepaid home and office calls.[15] The Kings County Society demanded that HIP make basic changes in its program, and further proposed "clarifications" to the written code of ethics of the New York State Medical Society that would destroy the plan by limiting panel practice to charity patients.[16] The House of Delegates of the New York Medical Society adopted these changes in the code of ethics, and also supported an action by the Queens County Medical Society finding Dr. Ben E. Landess, director of an HIP medical group, guilty of "unethical practices" because his name appeared on a brochure advertising HIP.

The AFL and the CIO in New York made this fight their own. The Central Trades and Labor Council passed on August 20, 1953, a resolution condemning the action of the Kings County Medical Society as "typical [of] the reactionary and obstructive attitude of organized medicine."[17] The resolution pointed out that some 275,000 city employees and dependents had elected to join HIP, and 60,000 additional union members and dependents were insured under HIP through union welfare programs.

The proposals and objectives of the Kings County Medical Society would also curtail the operation of union health centers and medical programs such as those conducted by the International Ladies' Garment Workers Union, the New York Hotel Trades Council, the International Brotherhood of Electrical

Workers Local 3, the Meatcutters' Union and a number of others. The action of the Kings County Medical Society would deny to organized labor and to the consumer the right to choose the type of medical insurance program which most nearly met their needs.[18]

The CIO Council wrote the Kings County Society that:

At least 75% of the 400,000 subscribers of H.I.P. belong to organized labor and your attack on H.I.P. is a direct attack on attempts of organized labor to mitigate prohibitive medical costs . . . you are unable to offer a decent substitute for H.I.P. . . . We challenge you to convince the subscribers of H.I.P. that they do not have free choice of doctors.[19]

The battle was resolved, not by a court test but by a decision of the AMA. The five-man Judicial Council of the AMA first absolved Dr. Landess of personal responsibility for having his name used on HIP advertising. Far more significant was its finding to the effect that the case against HIP would not stand up in court, that HIP operates in accordance with the law, and that it may lawfully advertise. And when organized medicine's "supreme court" concluded that "no further action is called for at this time," it in effect denied *certiorari* on all the other charges that had been raised against HIP.[20]

The Judicial Council's awareness of legal limits was a cold bath for the Kings County Society, some of whose leaders accepted HIP as inevitable.[21] Nevertheless, there was subsequent harassment in the form of attempts to deny HIP doctors admitting privileges.[22] And it has been said that attempts to establish similar plans in other cities can expect combat conditions.[23]

The Battle of Pittsburg, California

Joseph Garbarino has reported in detail the conflict between the United Steelworkers Local Union 1440 at the Columbia Plant of United States Steel in Pittsburg, California, and the doctors of that city.[24] A summary of events will illustrate the extremes to which an embattled medical society will go to prevent union enrollment in a prepaid group practice plan.

In 1948, the local had approached physicians in Pittsburg and two adjoining communities to discuss a hospital plan and other subjects related to the local's health insurance program. The local had a fully contributory plan first established in 1941 and was hard pressed by increases in fees and medical costs generally. The doctors in Pittsburg failed to respond. The next year, when the United Steelworkers negotiated its national Blue Cross-Blue Shield program with United States Steel, the basic agreement applied in Pittsburg but the local continued a supplemental program with its previous underwriter. As the basic Blue Cross-Blue Shield plan was altered in national negotiations, the supplemental program in Pittsburg was adjusted to pay bills above those covered by the national agreement. The continued rise in fees thus pressed the supplemental program and intensified local dissatisfaction with the community doctors.

In 1953, Kaiser built a hospital within 20 miles of Pittsburg, opening up for the first time the possibility of outpatient services for the Pittsburg area. Local 1440's insurance committee began discussions with Kaiser, hoping to replace their supplemental plan with Kaiser benefits. Since half of the 13,000 people in Pittsburg were in steelworker families, the Pittsburg doctors reacted immediately to this emergency and proposed their own plan, which, in effect, would be an agreement to accept as full payment the fee schedules in the national steel Blue Shield contract; they further agreed to "enforce the performance of the plan by the doctors, and prevent overuse and abuse by patients." In other words, for a supplemental premium, the local could obtain certainty of coverage.

Up to this point, the "Pittsburg Story" could be cited as just another illustration of how a local medical society cannot or will not "negotiate" with a consumer group until that group has alternatives available.

What is interesting about the Pittsburg situation, however, is the character of the ensuing battle, in which the doctors attempted to bypass the local union's insurance committee and appeal directly to the union members for support of their plan, a tactic sometimes occurring in labor-management negotiations. The medical society used newspaper advertisements, direct mailings, handbills, speeches, and even sound trucks to argue that the insurance committee did not represent the rank and file, that it was a "clique" of thirty or forty members, and that ". . . the steelworkers should be allowed to decide on a democratic basis what medical plan they want." They warned the union insurance committee of the "terrible responsibility" of recommending a break in the traditional doctor-patient relationship. They broadened the doctors' plan to include additional services to meet the objection that it was not a complete health plan. Finally, they challenged Local 1440 to hold a membership referendum by secret ballot so that democratic decision-making would prevail.

The union agreed that a referendum would be held, and a final flurry of pre-election activity began. The number of participating physicians in the doctor plan was increased from the original 40 to 115, in order to include a wide variety of specialists in an expanded geographical area. Benefits were further extended until the plan was probably better than most open-panel plans in the area, and for a supplementary premium of less than $5.00 per month for family coverage. Had such a program been available a year earlier, there is little doubt the union would have been favorably impressed, but with the additional advantages of Kaiser's group practice and with the prestige of the union itself at stake, the local officers campaigned vigorously against the Doctors' Plan. The climax to the drama is vividly described by Garbarino:

> "Election day" was marked by developments that must be almost unique in the record of public relations of the medical profession. As the working shifts changed in the steel plant, incoming workers were met in the company parking lot by a number of doctors, their wives, and members of the hospital auxiliary who were distributing campaign literature for the Doctors Plan. For part of the day a sound truck was stationed at one strategic location exhorting the workers to "Retain your family doctor," or warning them, "Don't be a captive patient." So intent were the backers on getting their message across that, at one point when it appeared they might be denied access to the parking lot, plans were made to drop the leaflets from an airplane. Representatives of the sheriff's office appeared on the scene, summoned by a telephone call warning of possible trouble, but no incidents occurred.
>
> During the day reports on the progress of the election were issued and Pittsburg experienced some of the traditional excitement of the election process. When the polls were closed, almost two-thirds of the eligible workers had voted. The Kaiser Plan won by a margin of 2,182 to 440.[25]

Following the referendum, the Kaiser supplement was made available to all employees; those requesting it could have the premium deducted from their pay by the company. The Doctors' Plan was dropped, but a year later the doctors of Pittsburg offered a similar plan through California Physician's Service (Blue Shield) at a higher cost ($7.00) for individual subscribers. Steelworkers who did not enroll in the Kaiser Plan could send their premium themselves to California

Physician's Service. But only 400 subscribed in 2 years, compared with 3,000 in the Kaiser supplement. The doctors of Pittsburg have attempted unsuccessfully to get check-off privileges for the California Physician's Service to make subscription as simple as for the Kaiser supplement. This check-off privilege has not been granted both because the company has been unwilling to allow the check-off for a plan in which only a small proportion of the employees are interested, and because the union also feels it has more of a role in the policies and administration of the Kaiser program than it would in the California Physician's Service alternative. There is also some lingering resentment among the union leadership over the 1953 fight with the medical society.

Other Experiences and Some Lessons

In 1948, Frederick Umhey, the Executive Secretary of the Ladies' Garment Workers' Union, told the AMA, "if the medical societies of certain areas had been a little more cooperative and a little more alert and aware of changing conceptions in this field, a greater number of I.L.G.W.U. health centers could have been established."[26]

Rarely can labor reach an agreement with a medical society on any but a restricted services center. In Philadelphia, in 1945, an agreement was reached between the ILGWU and the medical society permitting the union's center to provide "diagnostic and curative treatment and services if requested" but differences of interpretation soon developed and the doctors objected that the center was providing too much therapy. In Milwaukee, labor efforts in 1955 to establish a Cooperative Health Insurance Plan did not succeed, in large part because the medical society there destroyed a group practice prepayment plan in the thirties and continued to prevail against the idea. In 1957, the Lehigh County (Pennsylvania) Medical Society wrote all its doctors that they should not provide services to any members of the new Amalgamated Clothing Workers' Health Plan unless it mended its ways and became an open-panel, fee-for-service program.[27]

It would be a mistake to conclude that medical society opposition in itself determines the outcome. Sometimes there is not effective leadership and determined strategy in labor's ranks, with the result that labor does not muster its full community bargaining power. In San

Francisco, the opposition of the Teamsters to the Central Labor Council's health plan probably tipped the balance to failure.[28] In Denver, the direct-service idea has been nursed along for years by a small group of devoted people who never succeeded in involving other unions, employers, and community leaders in their plans. The Milwaukee effort of 1951–53 might have had a better chance had there not been too much propaganda and mass promotion before the ground work was laid. The Upholsterers' International Union was willing to put up medical centers in Chicago, Philadelphia, and one other urban center, if the members would contribute $2.00 a month; but a justified lack of confidence in the administration of the health and welfare funds plus inadequate preparation and education on the issue combined to defeat the proposal in a referendum.

There are ingredients for success that can be encouraged by an effective union leadership. The simplest of these is that one victory can breed another. In Philadelphia, after the ILGWU center came the Clothing Workers' Sidney Hillman Center, and then the AFL Medical Services Plan, both of which added to organized medicine's regrets over its original commitment to the ILGWU. In St. Louis, too, one success has encouraged other unions. Following Local 688's Labor Health Institute, the ILGWU was able to establish a health center with more extensive services than most other plans of that size elsewhere. The Amalgamated Meat Cutters Local 88 started a diagnostic center and expanded it to include therapy at the center, home, and hospital. It is easier to start new plans in a city where some success has been achieved than it is to begin elsewhere. When the ILGWU tried to extend its St. Louis-type center to Kansas City, it was blocked by the medical society there and had to agree to a less ambitious undertaking.

There may be sources of support in a community to offset the medical society. The faculty of a medical school, for example, can encourage good medicine and group practice, which is the method used in medical schools. The St. Louis Labor Health Institute received much encouragement from the excellent medical schools in that city. The newly established Community Health Foundation in Cleveland, composed of locals of the Amalgamated Meat Cutters, the Retail Clerks, and others, received help from the faculty at Western Reserve Medical School. Labor leaders in Boston are working with faculty at Tufts Medical College and the New England Medical Center to develop a pilot program. In New Haven, Connecticut, the Central Labor Union has been receiving help from some of the faculty of the Yale School of Medicine.

A city administration, looking for good medical care for its employees, may also be a source of support. The solid backbone of HIP in New York is city employees. The Ross-Loos group in Los Angeles began with employees of the Water and Sewer Department. The American Federation of State, County and Municipal Employees in Philadelphia negotiated coverage in the AFL Medical Center for all city employees who were members of their union.

As medical society opposition can be overcome by astute labor planning, so can legal opposition—although this too is formidable enough to deserve our attention.

How Public Policy Has Favored Organized Medicine

The future of consumer-sponsored, prepaid group practice plans will test the organizing skill of the contending private organization, but public policy is also involved. Organized medicine has enlisted the support of a number of states on its side, in the form of statutes and attorney generals' decisions supporting medical society control of prepaid service plans.

Since the first public interest in government health insurance, about 1910, the AMA has opposed any government intervention, claiming that any incursion would lead to "socialism" and the eclipse of independence in the profession. But the AMA is not opposed to governmental intervention if that intervention bolsters the position of state and local medical societies. Since 1939, organized medicine has been lobbying at the state level for laws to fortify medical society control of prepayment plans. Three states acted in 1939, and by 1950 there were twenty-six such statutes. These laws insured professional control in a variety of ways.[29] Either the incorporators had to be doctors (four states), or a majority of the directors had to be doctors, or the plan required approval by the medical society (sixteen states). The number of doctors in the plan was specified in ten states, usually as 50 or 51 per cent of the doctors in the state or area of the plan. In seventeen states, free choice of doctor had to be allowed in the medical care plan; since a service plan embodying free choice of doctor was actuarially feasible only if the physicians agreed to a special fee schedule and since this could only be effected through a state medical society, such a free-choice requirement maintained ultimate authority with the society. Thus, by one or more devices, twenty-six states attempted to buttress organized medicine's control over medical prepayment. The objective was to give the organized profession a state-enforced business privilege or monopoly comparable to that of the public utilities, with the important difference that there was no price regulation. These efforts did not fully succeed.

The fight against these restrictive laws by doctors and consumer groups interested in group practice has met with some success in the courts. In 1954, the California Supreme Court held that the state enabling act could only be "permissive," and that plans not sponsored by doctors would not necessarily have to conform. Otherwise Blue Shield "might exercise a monopoly in that field and thus raise other legal problems."[30] Where a state law is explicitly "mandatory" and has the effect of granting a monopoly to doctor-sponsored plans, the law has been challenged on constitutional grounds. Thus, the New Jersey Supreme Court declared that the power to restrict or prohibit "competition in a field so vitally connected with the public welfare may not constitutionally be placed in the hands of a private organization such as the Medical Society" and declared the law void for lack of due process protections against "unfairness, arbitrariness, or favoritism."[31]

Medical societies have tried to use other law to discourage consumer groups interested in prepaid group practice. The common law prohibition against corporate practice has not successfully served this purpose, however. "No sharper rebukes appear in any anti-trust decision," says Horace Hansen, "than in those cases where organized medicine is taken to task for using ethics as an economic weapon."[32]

In states with "permissive" statutes, it has been possible in some cases to avoid them by incorporating the plan under general, non-profit corporation law. Medical societies have attempted to stop this by citing licensing laws, originally designed to prohibit quackery and commercialization. Some of these licensing laws prohibit doctors from being employed by corporations.[33] There are state insurance statutes which declare their purposes so broadly that they have been construed to include group health plans, but the majority of court decisions in these cases distinguish between "indemnity" provided by insurance companies and "service" by group health plans.[34] The unwillingness of the courts to help medical societies establish a monopoly situation has been recognized by the AMA. It has warned that a medical society is on dangerous grounds "if it denies membership to physicians, disciplines members, or threatens to do so because they render services for prepaid plans, including closed panel plans."[35]

A more direct method of discouraging doctors interested in prepaid group practice is to deny them hospital privileges. While this is prohibited by law in tax-supported hospitals, it is much more difficult to prevent in private or charity hospitals. According to Hansen, "the right of a private hospital to choose its staff is not absolute, and must yield in some instances to considerations of the public interest."[36] Discrimination has been held to be against the public interest where no other hospital was available. The difficulty in these cases is to prove that the discrimination by a private hospital against a doctor is solely because of his participation in a group health plan. New York (as a result of the fight over HIP in Nassau County) enacted in 1963 a law prohibiting denial to licensed doctors of hospital privileges "solely because of participation in any medical practice or authorized nonprofit health insurance plan." Louisiana also passed such a law in 1964. The only other state with a similar statute is Montana.[37]

What are the lessons from all this legal experience? First, it is clear that unionists wishing to establish a health center need not be discouraged by formal prohibitions of group health plans. Legal obstacles have proven surmountable. Co-operatives in Minnesota have organized medical plans even though the legislature has not passed a bill that permits these plans to incorporate.[38] Any orthodox method of setting up the AFL Medical Plan in Philadelphia would have brought all kinds of legal problems, and a simple non-profit charter was procured. The able organizer of this plan has drawn an appropriate lesson from the earlier day when "all legal machinery was against us, however, it didn't stop us: we just went ahead and organized unions."[39] In some cases the law has been changed to permit a group health center. Officers of the Chicago Building Service Employees Local 25 were instrumental in initiating the Illinois Voluntary Health Services Plan Act, which was enacted in 1951 and paved the way for that union's health center in Chicago (see Chapter 13).[40] Separate enabling acts for consumer plans have also been adopted in Ohio and Wis-

consin. On a defensive front, labor has helped block in the Colorado
and Kentucky legislatures bills that would make it illegal for any doctor
to aid or participate in a program which did not guarantee free choice
of any licensed physician. The Group Health Association of America
has established a "medical rights fund" to combat discrimination
against physicians associated with prepaid group practice plans.

The second lesson of labor's experience is that each state presents a
different problem and must be approached appropriately. "We have
seen," says Hansen, "a group health plan in full operation fail simply
because the corporate structure was improperly designed. On the other
hand, we have seen some plans achieve tremendous success in the face
of seemingly unsurmountable obstacles by the use of well-devised legal
expedients."[41] Decisions about the legal design, about court tests, about
new enabling legislation—all these must be based on study of each
state's law early in the planning stage.

Bargaining with Dentists

Dental prepayment plans have grown rapidly in recent years—more
than doubled between 1960 and 1966—and now cover over two million
persons. Labor's experience with these plans shows some parallels
with experience under medical care plans. However, the dental societies have not been quite so hard to bargain with, in part because
they do not play so authoritative a role in their profession as the medical societies do in theirs, but also because labor has been somewhat
more sophisticated about applying the lessons of health bargaining.

Before 1960 a number of unions had established direct service plans
which employed dentists or contracted with a dental group for services.
Some of these plans were part of wider services provided by a health
center, in the Labor Health Institute at St. Louis, for example. The
Amalgamated Clothing Workers Union, the Laborers, and the Amalgamated Meat Cutters have such integrated programs in some places.
More than three out of four people covered by prepaid dental plans
in 1960 received these benefits under medical care plans.[42]

In 1961 the American Dental Association passed a resolution urging
that such direct-service or closed-panel plans should be discouraged.
As alternatives the dental societies, first in Washington State, began
to encourage dental service corporations, a dental version of Blue

Shield. Enabling legislation was sought in state legislatures. In addition, about a dozen commercial insurance companies entered the field to provide coverage for dental care. In the last five years most of the expansion in dental prepayment has been underwritten through these open-panel arrangements, either dental service corporations or commercial insurance. The largest group contract with a dental service corporation was negotiated by the International Association of Machinists with the Aerojet-General Corporation in 1963 covering 35,000 employees and their 81,000 dependents. This plan covers dental expenses except for orthodontics, with a lifetime $25 deductible per patient and with 20 per cent co-insurance.

Despite these developments, the AFL–CIO pressed the advantages of direct-service programs. Although officially opposed to them, the American Dental Association seemed somewhat more disposed to work with consumer groups than was the American Medical Association. The AFL–CIO undertook discussions with representatives of the dental profession in 1963 and by August of the following year a statement of principles had been worked out. This document, though a compromise on some matters, nevertheless recognizes principles labor had unsuccessfully urged on organized medicine. It was issued as a joint statement of the AFL–CIO and the American Dental Association and consists of the following ten principles:[43]

1. Dental prepayment programs should make provision for ensuring high quality comprehensive dental care.

2. Where dental prepayment programs are organized, preference should be given to programs organized to serve groups within the entire community.

3. Regardless of the organizational structure of a prepaid dental care program, the practice of dentistry is, of course, the exclusive prerogative of the dental profession; however, the provision of dental health services must also be the concern of the consumer and the public.

4. Freedom of choice for individuals under group programs should include not only free choice of dentists but free choice of plan or program as well.

5. Remuneration for professional services may be on a fee-for-service, per capita, salary or other basis, depending upon the plan or

program. Such remuneration should meet standards of adequacy in relation to the training and experience of the dentist and to the standards established by the dental profession.

6. Dental prepayment programs should provide for an effective mechanism to insure that the fee procedures stipulated in the contract between the subscribers and the providers of professional services are maintained.

7. Where funding limitations prevent consideration of a comprehensive prepayment program, deductibles and co-insurance should be considered but the minimization of such features should be given high priority in future developments of the plan or program. High priority should be placed on comprehensive coverage for all patients, particularly children.

8. Any contract between an organization offering dental prepayment plans and a group of consumers should provide a means by which participants may receive the benefit of impartial review of grievances which may arise out of services provided by the plan or its administration.

9. Provision should be made for public, consumer, and professional representation on the governing boards of dental prepayment and direct-service organizations.

10. Dental health education should be a part of dental prepayment programs and should be jointly planned and conducted by the dental profession and the consumer organizations involved.

Just how much this agreement on principles has actually shaped the growth of dental prepayment is not known. It is known that most, though not all, of the dental service corporations are exercising surveillance over the quality of care. This is done through a system of spot audits where the charts, X-rays, and dental records are reviewed by a committee of dentists for adequacy and quality of the work performed. Review of quality is of course easier in dental than in medical care, but dental corporations could have developed otherwise. In this respect the dental service corporations are a higher form of evolution than the Blue Shield plans of the doctors. On the other hand, dentists have been quite reluctant to admit consumer representation on their boards, despite the statement of principles. There has been little sensitivity to the consumers' interest when fees and premium structures were established.

It may be that dental plans would have developed about as they have with or without the "Ten Principles." For this reason, there has been some reluctance in labor to enter into a similar arrangement with optometrists. Dental plans and other prepayment arrangements will develop as the providers of service wish unless there are alternatives for the consumers. Far more important than any declarations by national bodies is the actual health bargaining that goes on locally, and here, as in bargaining with doctors, labor's voice is felt in direct proportion to the availability of direct-service programs.

Summary and Implications

Labor's role in the evolution and improvement of health care is to speed the rate of change by giving consumer encouragement to the positive and progressive forces. This has taken three forms: (a) attempting to obtain doctors' commitment to an explicit fee schedule which then serves as the goal for constructing the prepayment plans; (b) surveillance of cost and quality through the administration of the plans; and (c) supporting or establishing prepaid group practice plans.

The first approach seems, in general, to work only when opportunities in the third are available: the medical society is in a bargaining mood only if a competing direct service plan is available as an alternative. For this reason, union policy increasingly tends to work directly toward the last alternative. Only the United Mine Workers, with a strong centralized fund and overwhelming bargaining power relative to medical societies in coal communities, has succeeded in making the second approach workable.

The AMA's opposition to prepaid group practice has weakened, partly under the impact of labor bargaining, but also because the more progressive forces in organized medicine, operating at the national level, are not directly confronted by the implied threat to orthodox methods of practicing and pricing. It is at the local level that bargaining is hardest and there the big battles have been fought.

The record of the AMA shows its purpose as the double one of strengthening the scientific basis of medicine and encouraging the technical competence of doctors, but also of raising the profession's economic and social status and protecting its business interests. A confusion between these two functions, as in the use of "medical ethics" to resist economic change, has led local medical societies to act as a medical monopoly of the economic organization of medical care in the community. Justice Hanley of the Washington Supreme Court put the issue clearly in 1951: "If respondents are successful in this effort [to pre-empt and control all contract practice of medicine], there will be no competition in the contract medicine field. Members of the public will have no opportunity to choose between two or more plans offering this type of service. The result will be a complete monopoly of this product throughout the county."[44] There is of course competition between doctors, but when it comes to the means by which medical care shall be dispensed, the medical society usually speaks as a monopoly.

Labor's efforts on a multi-faceted bargaining front are best understood as the application of countervailing power in medical economics. The phrase "countervailing power" has been used in business to describe the strategy of buyers merging together to overcome the advantage of big sellers, as when retailers combine to force down the prices of wholesalers. As long as the lower price or better product is passed on to the consumer, the process is economically healthy and efficient. Traditionally, consumers have been unorganized individual buyers of medical services dispensed in a manner determined by a medical monopoly. Welfare bargaining has changed this by organizing consumers into group buyers of medical services, in effect pitting organized buyers against organized sellers. The essence of labor "bargaining" with medical societies is finding alternative forms of medical practice and pricing which work to the advantage of the medical consumer.

Before carrying these implications any further, it is necessary to inquire into the experience of unions with group practice prepayment plans, to establish whether in fact the medical consumer is the ultimate beneficiary of the conflicts described in this chapter. Our argument so far has taken at face value the contentions of those who argue the merits of prepaid group practice, whether from the ranks of labor or medicine. But are the claims for prepaid group practice being realized? What are the components of high quality medical care and what does union experience suggest about their attainability? Does union experience with medical service plans justify the travail involved in their establishment, and is there good reason for accelerating the reorganization of medical care?

13

BARGAINING FOR AND WITH
MEDICAL SERVICE CENTERS

Seventy-seven new medical care plans combining prepayment and group practice have been established since 1946. Some originated through capital advanced by employers.[1] Some were established by physicians who wanted to combine modern practice with a satisfactory business arrangement.[2] Organizational backing has also come from co-operatives, from city governments concerned with the health problems of their employees, and from unions.

In this chapter we look at union experience with the quality and structure of these plans—first, several of the better union-sponsored plans; then, a co-operative plan in Washington, D.C.; and finally, the two biggest plans in the country, the Health Insurance Plan of Greater New York, and the Kaiser Foundation on the West Coast. This union experience under programs sponsored by others will further develop the picture of community health bargaining.

Union-Sponsored Plans

There are now about fifty union-sponsored medical service plans, nearly all established since World War II, and serving about one million persons. The better known include the United Mine Workers' program, the eighteen plans initiated by the International Ladies' Garment Workers' Union, four by the Amalgamated Clothing Workers (and another by the affiliated Laundry Workers Local 169), and four by the Hotel and Restaurant Workers. There are also medical service centers sponsored by the Seafarers and the Amalgamated Meat Cutters. One of the oldest and best plans is the Teamsters' Labor Health Institute in St. Louis; one of the newest is the United Steelworkers' center in Sault Ste Marie. Several plans started by a single union or local have become multi-union community programs: the Union Health Service in Chicago, the Community Health Association in Detroit, and the recently organized Community Health Foundation in Cleveland. These plans originated through the efforts of the Building Service Employees' Union, the United Auto Workers, and the Amalgamated Meat Cutters and the Retail Clerks, respectively.

Union-sponsored or union-originated plans show a wide range in scope and quality. About twenty-five are probably too small in membership.[3] Health centers under ten or fifteen thousand members have to make sacrifices in equipment and in the specialties that are included. Also, staff turnover in a small health center interrupts the flow of services. Some plans have been disappointing[4] either because they were not well conceived or because they have not yet been able to obtain funds for an adequate scope of services. When the funds needed cannot be negotiated, compromises are made: diagnostic services only may be provided; doctors' care may be limited to the center; dependents may be excluded; fees may be charged for home calls or for certain services; utilization may not be encouraged. Preventive as well as diagnostic services are offered in only a dozen of these health centers, and only half of these provide nearly comprehensive care for the worker and his family.

The important role of cost in limiting the scope of these plans can be seen by a glance at annual reports. At one extreme are plans that have compromised in all respects and cost only a few dollars a year per enrollee. At the other extreme, the cost of a plan offering hospital service and comprehensive medical care through group practice ranged from $300 to $400 a year per family in 1966, depending on variation in medical and hospital prices.[5] This estimate takes cognizance of two important factors. First, it assumes a high rate of utilization, which will characterize a plan that is popular with the union members and their families.[6] Second, it assumes that the group practice care is of high quality and is continuous—that is, that the group practice doctors can care for their patients in the clinics when they are ambulatory, and at home or in a hospital when they are not.

Although the cost of the comprehensive program is close to a dollar a day for each family there are definite savings realized by a medical service approach that combines responsibility for hospital, office, and home care in one medical group. There is, first, an economic incentive to practice preventive care. Second, a more efficient use of resources is practiced as, whenever possible, diagnosis and treatment are done on an ambulatory basis; there is no economic incentive for hospitalization and in good plans unnecessary surgery is discouraged through formal and informal methods of case review.[7]

The over-all record of union-sponsored plans is not encouraging, but the few good plans do demonstrate the possibilities. Some of them are worthy of examination as models for further effort. (There is not yet sufficient information to enable me to comment on two other interesting plans—the Community Health Foundation in Cleveland and the Sault Ste Marie and District Group Health Association.)

Labor Health Institute, St. Louis

This program started in 1945 and is still in the forefront. Over 26,000 people (1965)—employees in warehousing, merchandising, and distributive trades, and their families in the St. Louis area—receive complete medical and dental care through modern group practice at home, medical center, and hospital.[8] Though originally in the Retail, Wholesale, and Department Store Union, Local 688 and its Labor Health Institute are now affiliated with the Teamsters; the health center occupied two floors of the Teamsters' office building, but a new building has been constructed in downtown St. Louis.

The group practice doctors, who are on a part-time basis except for the medical director, can care for their patients wherever it is best to do so from a medical standpoint without weighing financial considerations. The Institute has given a lot of attention to the quality of care, and has enlisted advice and assistance from the excellent medical schools in St. Louis. There are few exclusions or limitations in the coverage. The dental coverage is unique among union medical centers. Dental plates and eyeglasses are provided at nominal cost; the Institute has its own pharmacy which dispenses prescriptions at a price to cover overhead costs only. It has been estimated that for $37 out-of-pocket expenditure a "typical" Labor Health Institute family obtains in one year what would ordinarily cost $337. The plan is financed by 5 per cent of payroll (a few companies still contribute only 3½ per cent for the employee only) which is about $250 per employee, per year.

From the beginning the rank-and-file of the union was involved in studying health and medical problems and in the planning of the center. Along with the comprehensive benefits and dependents' coverage, this dynamic union atmosphere produces a relatively high rate of utilization, even if dental care is not counted, when compared with other union health centers. With this program, which costs the union members almost nothing out-of-pocket, Harold Gibbons and Local 688 captured the imagination of a wide public both in and outside labor. Trade unionists from all over the United States and many foreign countries visit the Labor Health Institute, and its institutional standards have been favorably reviewed by outstanding authorities.

Union Health Service, Inc., Chicago

Started in 1955, Union Health Service is a medical group practice serving sixteen different organizations, including four Chicago locals of the Building Service Employees (among them is Local 25, which was the founding group), the Chicago Typographical Workers Union, a small group of United Auto Workers, the staff of the Chicago Federation of Labor–CIO, and others. The United Auto Workers have negotiated a dual choice arrangement with the International Harvester Company allowing employees to choose between the Union Health Service and insurance company indemnity benefits. The total covered membership of Union Health Service is now about 20,000.[9]

The program provides comprehensive medical care. The group practice doctors serve their patients at a medical center, at the hospitals in which they have privileges, and at the patient's home. There is a charge to patients for home visits.

The Medical Center is a fully equipped ambulatory clinic. It was relocated in 1965 and brought together in the same building with the Union Eye Care Center. It is hoped that a dental plan can be developed. The medical staff consists of a full-time director and thirty-five part-time physicians, equivalent to about eight full-time doctors. Fifteen are internists who serve as personal physicians; the rest represent eleven other specialties.

The health and welfare funds covering the union members contribute $54 a year per member or $150 for a family. Some of the larger component unions do not yet have dependents' coverage. However, through employer payment and voluntary enrollment, about 25 per cent of the 20,000 members are dependents. In addition, the welfare funds must provide hospitalization insurance.

The Union Health Service enjoys an excellent reputation for several reasons. The standards for group practice are high. A detailed review of selected cases is made by a rotating medical audit committee of the staff. The patient has a personal physician who co-ordinates the specialties needed. There is complete freedom of referral within the group and to outside consultants. A Medical Advisory Committee of distinguished physicians meets monthly with the Medical Director. Frequent staff meetings review cases and administrative problems. Preventive medicine is emphasized and tailored to the high age group of the enrollees. Continuity of care is provided through home, center, and hospital.

The Center supplements existing community facilities—such as the Union Eye Care Center—rather than competes with them. The organizational structure of Union Health Service properly relates the interests of professional staff, and labor and management representation. The main shortcomings of the program lie in the part-time commitment of most of the doctors. Another limitation is the absence for most of the employees of dependent coverage, which would probably serve to increase utilization by the present union members.

Philadelphia AFL–CIO Hospital Association

Unlike the plans we have discussed above, the Philadelphia AFL Hospital Association originated as a multi-union enterprise.[10] Its forerunner, which continues a separate existence, was the AFL Medical Services Plan, which began in 1951 as a very modest clinic in a wing of St. Luke's and Children's Hospital, and grew to become a modern, four-story health center serving over 50,000 people. It was officially sponsored by the Philadelphia Central Labor Union, and the early participants were Luggage Workers, Painters District Council, and the Amalgamated Meat Cutters; these were later joined by nearly thirty other local unions. The Philadelphia AFL–CIO Hospital Association is a separate enterprise but has developed under the same leadership, partly because of the limited purposes of the AFL Medical Services Plan, which does not attempt to give complete and continuous medical service through group practice. No home care is given directly by the medical staff. Its main contribution is in providing diagnostic and supplemental therapeutic care for ambulatory patients, and in this way it supplements the medical and hospital benefits of the participating health and welfare funds.

The limited scope of the Medical Services Plan was sufficient for some of the welfare funds participating, but it is obvious that others wanted to go further. Plans were laid for a 200-bed hospital, and although it appears that no effort was made to consult with the Philadelphia medical schools, and the hospital was not planned in the light of overall community needs, the confidence of the leadership has since been justified. The hospital has been approved by the Joint Commission of Accreditation. It is one of the showplaces of multi-union participation and also, since it is open to the community, serves more than union membership. The largest group served is District 33 of the American Federation of State, County, and Municipal Employees. Thirty thousand municipal employees and their families receive comprehensive care both in and out of the hospital.

Community Health Association, Detroit

In Chapter 6 we described the origins of the Community Health Association and the battles undertaken to establish it. It is the only labor program with a combination of ambulatory medical centers and hospital facilities, all integrated into a comprehensive medical care system. Another feature of this program is that, while the United Auto Workers were the initiators and moving spirit, they insisted on multi-union participation and joint planning and participation with non-union community groups. The range of services and facilities, the use of full-time physicians, and the community orientation make CHA unique.

A modern downtown hospital and three neighborhood clinics are all located and equipped to offer the highest standards of service to about 75,000 persons who have individually chosen this arrangement over Blue-plan or commercial alternatives. Under the union contracts, the individual worker chooses annually whether he wants to participate in or discontinue this group practice arrangement. Complete ambulatory diagnostic and therapeutic care is provided in the clinic. Hospitalization is provided up to 365 days for each illness; there are no exclusions for pre-existing conditions. Doctors' house calls are included for extra charges within a defined area of Detroit. Conversion to individual memberships for retiring workers and for dependents who become of age and marry is permitted at higher rates. As with the Union Health Service, Inc., in Chicago, the standards for quality and comprehensive care are carefully observed, with the additional advantages that the hospital care is integrated into the program, and that the medical staff, except for certain specialties, is on a full-time basis.

Co-operative-Sponsored Plans

Pioneering by the Co-ops

The single-minded determination of co-operatives has, more than any other effort, cleared the way for medical service plans.[11] Their legal battles[12] with organized medicine are established landmarks. The co-operative work shop of the last century left no lasting imprint on labor; the co-op medical center of this century has.

There are at least four co-operative medical service plans to which labor groups are now subscribing. The largest, Group Health Co-operative of Puget Sound, covering 85,000 persons in Seattle, began with several physicians in the Medical Security Clinic and with group support that expanded to include the Washington State Grange, the Pacific Supply Cooperative, Boeing District Lodge No. 751 of the International Association of Machinists, and the Student Cooperative at the University of Washington. In Washington, D.C., Group Health Association, Inc., has realized the possibilities inherent in a merger of co-operative and labor efforts by bringing in union transit employees; the federal employees' health program added another spurt in growth to this old veteran of battles with organized medicine. In St. Paul, Minnesota, the Group Health Mutual opened in the fall of 1957 a medical center that admits labor groups. The San Diego Health Association in San Diego, California, has about 25,000 members and contracts with at least three labor unions. Most other co-operative centers are in small towns and rural communities, such as the community hospital and clinic in Elk City, Oklahoma,[13] and the community health centers in Two Harbors, Minnesota, and do not have occasion to deal with unions, although the latter does have many railroad employees and ore dock workers as members.

There are obstacles to understanding between unions and co-operatives that derive from different operational methods of implementing democratic principles. The co-operatives operate on principles of farm-bred individualism, individual membership, use of referenda for policy decisions, "one member, one vote," etc. Unions, on the other hand, show urban group-mindedness and the local meeting is the major vehicle of group decision. The spirit of these meetings is not always understood by co-operatives, because union meetings perform a variety of functions in addition to being a forum for policy decision: they are also rallies for group spirit, informal clearing houses for exchanging information among the elected and natural leaders, and a place where the dissatisfied member comes to vent his feelings about the boss and the union.[14] Union members are more accustomed to rely on leadership, less interested in the niceties of parliamentary forms, generally more political and less individualistic than co-operative members.

In negotiations between a co-operative and a union, practical problems arise: if the union cannot command the resources needed to buy the standard coverage provided co-operative members, what can be done; should there be various stages of more limited participation at lower premium rates; is it fair to original co-operative members if group rates provide different benefit arrangements for the union members; what arrangements can be made for the purchase of membership shares that is customarily required of co-operative members; will the co-operative group lose control of its own policies; will the union be able to handle the double problem of negotiating with the employer on the one hand and the co-operative on the other?[15]

Resolutions of these recurrent questions[16] was the striking feature of negotiations in 1958 between the Group Health Association, Inc., of Washington, D.C., and Local 689 Transit Employees Health and Welfare Plan.[17]

Group Health Association, Washington, D.C.

Group Health Association was founded in the late thirties by a group of federal employees. There ensued a classic battle with the District Medical Society and a favorable decision from the Supreme Court.[18] Growth at first consisted of individual and family rather than group enrollments. Several District of Columbia unions studied labor health centers, but none joined GHA. In a referendum, GHA members turned down one union group; another—the Hod Carriers' and Laborers' Union—established its own health center. Then in rapid succession came the transit employees and their families, a group that added almost 10,000 members, and the new government employees' health plan, which added another 10,000 (most of the original members were also government employees). GHA has 60,000 enrollees (December, 1966): about 66 per cent are federal government workers, 17 per cent D.C. Transit employees, and 17 per cent general membership and small groups. There are 100 full- or part-time physicians (equivalent to 57 full-time) and 17 dentists and dental consultants (equivalent to 9 full-time). A new central ambulatory clinic in downtown Washington, D.C., is supplemented by three branch clinics—one in Maryland, one in Virginia, and one under contract with Allied Medical Services (the latter for "premium" members only). Comprehensive medical care and hospitalization is provided for $14.50 (single) and $36.90 (family). Cheaper plans are offered, but require extra charges for certain services. Dental services can be prepaid for an additional amount or paid on a fee-for-service basis. In a recent study of prepaid group practice plans, GHA was particularly noted for offering "an impressive array of extra services," including dental, psychiatric, podiatric, and nutritional care, prescription drugs, eye glasses, and social work services. "In addition, it was the only plan studied which had instituted a special adolescent clinic and regularly scheduled night clinics."[19]

Our particular interest here is in the period of GHA's history when it took in the D.C. Transit employees, and how a co-operative–sponsored clinic and a labor union resolved their differences.

The Transit Employees Health and Welfare Fund began preparing for a health center in 1955. Accumulated surplus and an increased employer contribution in 1958 provided the resources,[20] and the union investigated on three fronts: purchasing a hospital, building its own medical center, and contracting for coverage under GHA. This last alternative resulted in an agreement.

During the negotiations, there was soul searching in GHA. It was argued that the facilities could not take a 40 per cent increase in membership and that Group Health did not have the funds with which to expand. Some argued forcefully that the existing membership of 22,000 was the most efficient size. Spokesmen for the administrative staff wanted only a minor expansion from which GHA could retreat easily. Longtime members of GHA and some of the medical staff expressed the fear that the quality of service would deteriorate because the efforts of the existing medical staff would be diluted, and newer, less experienced doctors would be added. In some cases the medical staff members were concerned over the possibility of needing to take Maryland or Virginia Board exams in order to continue with GHA.

The union, on its side, objected to what it called the "deterrent fee" concept in the GHA program—extra charges for X-rays, electrocardiograms, physical therapy, basal metabolism, injections, transfusions, etc. Walter Bierwagen, President of the transit local, has stated, "throughout our negotiations with G.H.A. our Fund trustees sought constantly to keep to an absolute minimum the cost burden placed upon the worker. . . . It was our firm belief that when the worker or a member of his family is ill, the question of whether good medical care is supplied should not be determined by whether he then has the money to pay for such care."[21] The Transit Fund also wanted to keep its Blue Cross coverage rather than substitute the hospitalization program then offered at GHA. The key factors in the negotiation lay in the financing of additional facilities and in the provision of full prepayment for the range of services desired by the Transit Employees Fund within the limits of what it was able to pay.

The final agreement provided that the Transit Fund would spend $200,000 for the establishment of a new branch center, and up to $25,000 for expansion of the main GHA center. This capital expenditure relieved the transit employees of the customary $50 membership fee. The subject of transferring title of the new branch center from the Transit Fund to GHA would be discussed at a later date. Transit workers and regular GHA members would be free to use whichever center was most convenient. GHA assumed full responsibility for staffing and servicing the new branch center.

Transit workers were to enjoy substantially the same services now enjoyed by GHA members, at a price of $4.15 per covered person to be experience rated at six-month intervals (now $8.50 in December, 1966). This rate was set in anticipation of somewhat lower utilization by the transit group and the elimination of extra charges borne by regular GHA members.[22] The Transit Employees had to give up their Blue Cross and accept the combined ambulatory, house call, and hospitalization program provided regular GHA members. Transit union members who preferred non-GHA doctors were to be rebated their $2 a month contribution. GHA agreed that the Transit Fund could designate three trustees to the GHA Board, but they would not be allowed to vote on the negotiation, amendment, or extension of the contract.

Success of the negotiations, which proceeded over a year and a half, can be attributed to four factors. (1) Earlier efforts to bring in a union group had foundered on too quick a use of the referendum. This time the trustees assumed more authority: they directed the staff to make the necessary studies for a basic expansion, and they conducted negotiations in a quiet atmosphere subject only to eventual membership approval of a change in by-laws. (2) GHA's Board of Trustees included people cognizant of and sympathetic to labor unions and their health aims, and this offset the negative viewpoint of some of the staff and membership. (3) The union leadership, particularly Walter Bierwagen, was both skillful and patient and genuinely desired the best possible medical care plan. And (4) the employer (O. Roy Chalk of the D.C. Transit System, Inc.) co-operated by allowing the union to take the leadership in negotiations with GHA and by extending the time limit for a decision.

A review of experience after the first few years of the Transit Fund merger with GHA showed that union members had some difficulty learning to use the unique advantages of GHA—its outpatient services. While the transit workers and their dependents at first comprised 30 per cent of the total membership of GHA, the union group utilized only 15 per cent of the doctor visits, but more than 30 per cent of the hospitalization. This suggested in part the existence of hitherto untreated illnesses, but it also suggested that transit members needed to learn the preventive features of their plan. More educational work and special efforts by the medical staff to help the transit workers have greatly improved use of the facilities in recent years.

Those transit workers using their new plan found they enjoyed better care with more continuity and follow up than they experienced before.[23] Out-of-pocket costs under the previous Blue Shield plan deterred some patients from submitting to prescribed procedures.[24] These are absent under GHA comprehensive coverage, which permits decisions to be made on medical rather than financial grounds. GHA's superiority to open-panel practice has been shown even though there were some deficiencies in its operation of group practice. Some members felt there was poor coordination in the use of specialists. This shortcoming had been aggravated by the tremendous increase in the size of GHA, a growth which proceeded more rapidly than the necessary staffing. Nevertheless, the superiority of GHA medicine to the solo practice experienced by the transit workers under their previous prepayment plan was clear. Serious cases of undiagnosed or misdiagnosed illness and improper treatment were discovered by GHA staff.[25]

The union believes it has gone in the "right direction" and that there will be a reduction in "the incidence of complex and costly surgery and hospitalization. . . . We subscribe," says Walter Bierwagen, "to the view that the medical care consumer has the same interest whether he is a union member or a subscriber to a co-op health plan. . . ."[26] When genuine alternative choice was offered individual transit workers in 1965, 6 per cent decided to go to Blue Cross–Blue Shield while 94 per cent voted to stay with GHA.

The Kaiser Foundation Health Plan

The Kaiser Foundation Health Plan on the West Coast, by providing a group practice prepayment plan, gave organized labor a lever for bargaining with local medical societies, and thereby greatly speeded up experimentation in medical economics. What about union experience with the Kaiser Plan itself?

Description of Kaiser Plan

The main features of the Kaiser Plan have evolved from the experiences of Dr. Sidney Garfield, who has provided medical care for a succession of Kaiser enterprises—first on the Colorado River–Los Angeles aqueduct in the early 1930's, later at the Grand Coulee Dam, and finally at the wartime shipyards.[27] He started out with a fee-for-service clinic, but many construction workers were unable to pay for their non-industrial illnesses. It appeared that prepayment was the only way that employees could finance the services of the medical staff, and a prepaid health plan was established. In addition, the insurance companies, which had been sending serious industrial injury cases to Los Angeles for treatment, were persuaded to prepay for industrial medical care in Dr. Garfield's clinic.

At Grand Coulee Dam, the service approach was extended to the employee's dependents. Dr. Garfield also found that the cost of building a hospital could be amortized out of prepayment income—a controversial subject in the growth of the Kaiser Plan. With the coming of the war, Kaiser asked Dr. Garfield to organize a voluntary prepaid medical care program at the shipyards in Richmond, California, and Vancouver, Washington, and at the steel mill in Fontana, California. At the end of the war the remaining shipyard workers and others in the San Francisco Bay area asked for continuation of the health plan, which was opened to other Bay area residents at the end of 1945.

Today, Kaiser is the largest direct-service plan in the United States, both in membership and in capitalization. Any statement of its size that appears in print is already outdated. On September 30, 1966, 716,069 people were covered in the San Francisco Bay area; 599,822 in the Los Angeles-Fontana region; 86,604 in the Portland-Vancouver area; and 58,936 in Hawaii; this made a total membership of 1,461,431. There are 15 hospitals with a capacity of 2,913 beds, 47 outpatient medical centers, and approximately 1,300 full-time physicians who are in medical partnerships which contract with the Kaiser Plan, and over 9,500 non-physician personnel.

The plan provides most essential preventive, diagnostic, and therapeutic services which, in a typical case, will cover about 75 per cent of all medical bills for those using its services. The most commonly negotiated group contract in northern California includes: 111 days of hospital care; physician's care in the office, home, and hospital; all surgery; full maternity care for a flat charge of $60; X-rays and laboratory tests; preventive care, including periodic health examinations, immunizations, and refractions; private nurses as required; physical therapy; home nursing care; ambulance service; drugs and medicines furnished outside the hospital at reasonable cost. Excluded are tuberculosis; custodial, or convalescent care; care for intentionally self-inflicted injuries, or for drug addiction; cosmetic surgery, corrective appliances, and artificial aids; and service-connected conditions. To the extent possible in Kaiser hospitals and outpatient offices, members will be provided medical services in a major disaster or epidemic. For contagious diseases and diseases requiring isolation for which Kaiser hospitals are not equipped, a $300 indemnity is provided when the patient is referred by a Kaiser physician. Mental disease is also excluded from coverage, but at the Kaiser medical centers in Oakland, Vallejo, Richmond, and San Francisco, there are psychiatric clinics where mild mental disorders are treated on an out-patient basis at the relatively moderate fee of $7.50 for each visit. In addition to the dues, there are some extra charges and incidental fees, such as the $1.00 charge for an office visit, and doctor home calls at $3.50 and $5.00, for day and night service respectively. In most labor group contracts the dependents have the same benefits as the employee. It is this broad spectrum of benefits coupled with a minimum amount of red tape (no claim forms) and a reasonable dues structure that accounts for much of Kaiser's wide appeal.

Union Participation and Influence

When the plan was first opened to groups in the Bay area, it immediately attracted the attention and support of some labor organizations. County labor councils endorsed it and recommended it to the local unions. The initial subscribers were largely groups—labor organizations, teachers, and civil service employees.[28] This was before welfare bargaining, and some of the unions collected premiums directly while others arranged for payroll deductions. In some cases, employers contributed part of the dues.

The advantages of the Kaiser approach were not apparent to all unions. In the elementary stages of health bargaining (see Chapter 15), some union leaders negotiated indemnity benefits as the easiest course. Only after several years of negotiations in a medical inflationary spiral did they come to realize they were not obtaining significantly greater benefits. Even where the Kaiser program was desired, a bargaining problem presented itself. Unions wanted health insurance for all employees, many of whom did not live in an area served by Kaiser. They were, therefore, obliged both because of the spread of union membership and the difficulties of negotiating employer contributions to prepayment plans to seek the more generally applicable Blue plans and commercial insurance. The bargaining problems were too difficult in themselves and could not be complicated by demanding Kaiser benefits for some and indemnity insurance for others outside the Kaiser area. Where labor preferred to buy services rather than insurance, company-, area-, and industry-wide bargaining was not yet flexible enough to buy the best program available in each community.

This diversion from Kaiser was temporary, however. The United Automobile Workers quickly recognized the importance of providing local option in areas where direct service plans were available. On union insistence, the General Motors contract and then the Ford and Chrysler contracts were amended to provide local option subject to company discretion where the local Blue plans were inferior. These local option clauses allowed auto locals to come into Kaiser. Local unions in the United Steelworkers were held by standard contract clauses that allowed no escape, but they subscribed to supplementary benefits from Kaiser, paid for by employee contributions. As the Kaiser program expanded geographically, unions concentrated in the San Francisco Bay area and the Los Angeles metropolitan area could more easily negotiate Kaiser coverage for all their members.

The efforts of San Francisco unions, beginning about 1951, to establish their own health center also diverted attention from Kaiser, but the failure of those efforts and of negotiations with the medical society finally left Kaiser as the only direct-service prospect. In 1954, four Culinary Workers' welfare funds entered a dual choice arrangement with Kaiser. Union membership is about one-fifth of all Kaiser enrollments, the largest union groups being the Culinary Workers, the Retail Clerks, and Longshoremen.

Unions have found that Kaiser is flexible in some matters. Adjustments in the benefits structure have been worked out to satisfy the group buyer, especially if he is a big buyer. In adjusting to market demand, Kaiser maintains much local variation and flexibility and there are many deviations from the standard contract. This flexibility in group contracts is reflected in different provisions available in the same area at slightly varying rates. The main differences among the contracts are in the liberality of benefits for dependents and the number and amount of extra charges. Special arrangements to supplement commercial insurance and Blue plans have been worked out with Kaiser by several unions.

The unions have no direct role in forming Kaiser policies. While the Kaiser Plan is non-profit, there is no community or consumer representation in its policy-making. On the contrary, it is directed with all the centralization and businesslike efficiency of a profit-making corporation. The governing board is controlled by Kaiser Industries. The Plan in this respect is still an overgrown company medical care program. The Kaiser Plan sells medical care the way a company sells its product and decisions are made with a competitive medical market in mind.

Union influence on Kaiser policies flows through the market mechanism and is roughly in proportion to the union's membership as a group buyer. This influence is significant, more so than that figurehead representation of labor which is not uncommon on the boards of some health plans. Probably unions have not realized the full potential of their influence that could come through co-ordinating their relationships with the Kaiser Plan;[29] now it is simply the larger subscribers that carry the most weight. By whatever means it is achieved, a greater sensitivity to subscribers would probably improve Kaiser policies.

Since 1954 Kaiser has insisted that all group subscribers must provide an alternative plan in addition to Kaiser benefits, leaving to the individual member the choice of plans and allowing him to make a change at stated intervals. The alternative may be either a commercial insurance indemnity plan or Blue plan. There are now in northern California over 140 negotiated agreements that offer the union member an alternative between Kaiser and an open-panel plan.

Alternative choice at Kaiser has been lauded as consistent with the democratic principles of a free society, but it is also true that practical considerations were involved in this decision. Both Kaiser and labor had emphasized, in their battles with the local medical societies, that "free choice of doctor" should also mean the freedom to choose a closed-panel plan. There was a reverse side to this logic: why not also allow individuals in the Kaiser Plan to go "outside" if they wished? Kaiser needed an answer to this. It became increasingly clear that, if Kaiser were going to have a meaningful part of the health and welfare market, some way must be found to give an individual choice between Kaiser, a closed-panel plan, and an indemnity program, with freedom of choice of physician and hospital. There was another very practical reason Kaiser favored the dual choice arrangement. It did not want members unable to establish a satisfactory doctor-patient relationship within the medical group to be in any sense a "captive" of the program. Put simply: "if you don't like it, you should be able to leave it." We shall see in Chapter 14 that there is serious question about this rationale for dual choice.

The merits of alternative choice arrangements are discussed later; here the question is, why Kaiser made such an arrangement compulsory for group enrollments? Their public explanation—that collective bargaining should not be used to force unwilling employees into a plan they don't want—was both insufficient and destructive of some of the good will they had with labor. The authority of union and management to allocate group business was one of the major influences enlarging the Kaiser Plan. When some union groups, because of divided opinion in their ranks, would not join Kaiser without an alternative choice arrangement, Kaiser could have offered such an arrangement without also deciding on a policy requiring alternative choice in every union group in the future. At least, they need not have explained their policy in terms which had some negative repercussions in labor and which suggested that collective bargaining as an institution limited rather than expanded opportunities for employees.[30]

A more accurate explanation for the insistence on compulsory dual choice lies in the relations of Kaiser with the larger medical community. As union after union negotiated Kaiser coverage, there was widespread concern that solo practitioners were being cut off from a practice. To Kaiser it became clear that the price of peace with the rest of the medical profession was some arrangement for decentralizing the decision in order that the individual might have a "free choice"; Kaiser felt well enough established by 1954 to face the risks of actuarial uncertainty and competitive comparison entailed in alternative choice plans.[31] Some unions, not wholly convinced of the advantages of Kaiser over solo practice, or having members outside the Kaiser area, liked the alternative choice idea; but, had Kaiser been interested merely in making the choice plan available to groups who wanted it for one reason or another, they would not have made it a compulsory condition for participation in the Kaiser program. By making it a requirement for group subscription, Kaiser announced a truce with the medical profession and tempered the most threatening feature of its success.[32] This may well be a necessary step in the evolution of a large direct-service plan—a device to prevent monopoly on its side.

There is one feature of collective bargaining that several unions have worked into their relations with the Kaiser plan—a "grievance proceddure" by which enrolled members can effectively raise complaints exists in the Longshoremen, Culinary Workers, and Retail Clerks groups. When a member is unable to solve his problem at the point of service, he may contact a Kaiser service representative or bring it to the attention of the union who may take it up with the Kaiser Plan. Regular meetings are held between representatives of the welfare funds and the Kaiser Plan to consider unsettled complaints. Under an alternative choice arrangement, the dissatisfied member might switch to the indemnity plan without ever facing his problems. Complaint machinery, however, provides an educational opportunity for the patient as well as a test of responsibility for the Kaiser organization.

Quality of Care

There is no doubt about the superiority of the Kaiser medical organization. The completeness of its services, the well-paid and full-time medical staff (of which 75 per cent are Board certified), and its reasonable prepayment charges make it an outstanding program.[33] This does not mean, however, that union leadership in California has found it without faults, and at one time or another shortcomings have been cited.[34] Most serious is criticism to the effect that continuity of care has not been observed: student doctors have been used for initial work-ups; on weekends too many doctors are off and those on duty are overworked (according to one welfare fund executive, at one point no one was ever discharged from a Kaiser hospital on a Sunday); extra doctors are hired for home calls; in general, the Kaiser Plan does not put much emphasis on the personal or family physician method for coordinating group practice.[35] Most recently complaints about the excessive waiting time in the outpatient departments have become intense, and there is now a widespread feeling that the facilities are not adequate for the size of the enrollment. The situation is serious enough that it is one factor bringing into existence the California Council for Health Plan Alternatives, a committee of about a dozen California unions under Teamsters leadership, to reappraise all medical care resources available in the state.

Kaiser can be criticized for failing to employ some of the imagination shown, for example, by the Health Insurance Plan of New York in research and educational efforts that must accompany any reorganization of medical care. It is not that Kaiser is devoid of any such efforts: to some extent they use university consultants and outside evaluation teams to improve the quality of their services; they also have Plan representatives working full time on "service" complaints and a doctor working part of the time in each area on medical complaints. But they have discouraged research even on the quality of their program, arguing that it leads to bureaucratic growth, detracts from the practice of medicine and diverts attention from patient needs. There is some truth here, just as there is in their contention that quality comes primarily from good medical leadership and good staff, but there is also an element of rationalization.

One highly regarded labor consultant has probably summed up the view of many that "the Kaiser plan meets some of the requisites at least on paper: relatively low cost, relatively complete services, nominally a group practice, but, and there are many 'buts,' there is no consumer control and there is much dissatisfaction arising from policies of the administration."[36] If the union subscribers could have had more of a voice in Kaiser policies, they might have been able to correct some of the shortcomings, but nonetheless they still find Kaiser the best program available to them.

Health Insurance Plan of Greater New York

In the last chapter we recounted how unions supported the struggle for existence of the Health Insurance Plan of Greater New York (HIP). Like the Kaiser Foundation, HIP is a mechanism for procuring medical services through group practice under a system of prepayment.[37] However, HIP's organizational principles differ in significant ways from the Kaiser Plan.

Description of HIP

With a membership of 700,000, HIP proper is a central prepayment and quality control body for 32 groups of doctors practicing around the urban area in separate medical centers. The central organization administers a single prepayment plan,[38] sets the conditions for participation of the medical group centers, and works to raise the quality of care of the medical groups. Each medical group is paid an annual per capita sum for each HIP subscriber who uses that group's center, but it is the doctors in that medical group and not HIP who both own the center and its equipment and decide how to divide up the center's income. Nor does HIP prohibit doctors from having an "outside" practice, which many of them do.

HIP does not own any hospitals, although as a condition for enrollment in HIP the subscriber must have hospital insurance; continuity of care thus depends on the participating doctors' hospital privileges. This weakness has in the past made it possible for doctors in some hospitals, most recently those in Staten Island, to harass HIP by denying to doctors in HIP medical groups the privilege of admitting patients.

There are, however, partially compensating features to the HIP organization. It is a flexible method of starting and expanding, drawing into its orbit existing medical facilities as well as new ones that develop, without being dependent on a central source for capital accumulation. The crucial question here is whether the decentralization of authority in the separate medical group encourages resistance to the supervision of quality by the central body, so that what is gained in flexibility can be lost in the quality of medical care. As we shall see, HIP has been working to assert quality standards and establish more authority for this purpose in the central prepayment organization.

Union Participation and Influence

The first persons enrolled in HIP in 1947 were members of the Chefs' and Cooks' Union, Local 89, and they were followed by increasing numbers of New York City employees. Today, about 55 per cent of the total enrollment is composed of municipal employees; 45 per cent are workers in private industry. Some of the unions that have negotiated HIP coverage are the luggage workers; the painters' union; motion picture projectionists; District 15 of the International Association of Machinists; the Dress Joint Board of the International Ladies' Garment Workers Union; the New York Newspaper Guild; District 65 of the Retail, Wholesale, and Department Store Union; and others.

One clearly superior feature in the HIP organization from a labor viewpoint is that the Board of Directors, unlike that at Kaiser, does represent the community in a broad sense. The original committee appointed by Mayor La Guardia to recommend a program was composed of representatives of the medical profession, industry, labor, and the community in general. The medical representatives were adamant that the majority of HIP's Board should be physicians, but the community interest won out. The Board of Directors is now composed of 29 members, 10 of whom are physicians and 6 labor representatives. In general, the policy leadership in HIP has been sensitive to social needs, a quality that brought La Guardia's active support. Furthermore, there has been a candid and articulate public discussion of problems and goals by HIP spokesmen, which contrasts with the rather icy public relations of Kaiser. HIP has genuinely attempted to educate its subscribers and the public.

Since HIP was organized in large part because of La Guardia's concern with the medical care problems of low- and middle-income people and particularly of city employees, union subscribers have found HIP striving for most of the same goals as the unions themselves.

Because HIP regarded itself as an embattled advocate for reform in medical care, there were at first no alternative or multiple choice arrangements. Some union leaders wanted to move their membership into HIP but the "free choice of doctor" campaign by medical societies and open-panel plans was providing stiff competition for HIP. By 1955 it was clear that the internal pressures in some unions made it impossible to transfer the whole union group out of its existing commitments. To accommodate this situation, HIP agreed to accept groups under multiple choice arrangements.

We note here that the introduction of multiple choice into HIP was motivated by competitive pressures. In this respect the experience was similar to that at Kaiser, but there was an important difference between the attitudes of these two plans toward multiple choice. HIP did not make multiple choice a requirement for group subscription; it indicated its readiness to work out multiple choice where a group desired it, but was not prepared to pay the price of peace with non-HIP doctors in New York—that price being compulsory multiple choice for all group subscribers, including the city employees for whom HIP was originally organized. However, as time has passed, even the city employee groups have come to prefer multiple choice arrangements and today almost all of the subscribers have multiple choice even though HIP has never insisted on it.

Quality of Care

Research at HIP has produced convincing evidence of the generally superior organization and quality of HIP medicine. It is established that there are fewer prenatal deaths in the HIP population than among the patients of other physicians in the city.[39] An early study also showed that HIP enrollees have more contacts with physicians, use more pediatric care and dental care, and even use family doctors more than the general population of New York City.[40] A lower hospital admissions rate has been observed for HIP than for other plans in the city and this is a gain in both quality and cost.[41] The quality is achieved by the emphasis on an extensive range of outpatient services including diagnostic services (without limitations inherent in fee-for-service compensation) and by the fact that group practice brings the full range of specialties to bear in diagnosis and treatment.[42] High quality is encouraged by the standards HIP has set for the affiliated medical group centers. In general, even allowing for the effect of the slightly higher socio-economic bias of the HIP sample in these surveys, there is sufficient evidence to support union confidence in HIP quality.

Before being admitted to HIP a medical center must meet minimum standards for its physical facilities and its staff; these standards are administered by a medical control board composed of eighteen physicians, the majority of whom are not affiliated with the medical centers. Further, HIP has gone to the heart of the quality problem by studying the clinical records themselves. In an early study, the medical center groups were rated into four successive ranks according to criteria available in the clinical records: accurate recording of medical information; how patient was "handled" at each stage in the diagnosis, therapy, and follow-up; whether preventive medicine was practiced; whether the laboratory was properly used and special procedures required when indicated; and, in general, the extent to which judgment and skill were employed in meeting the medical problems.[43] It was found that two-thirds of the membership were cared for by the 17 groups falling in the 2 highest ratings; and 7 per cent of the enrollees were in the 5 groups that fell in the lowest. The majority of HIP members are getting good medical service, probably much better than average, but there is a great variation in quality between the centers. While the low-rated centers have taken steps to improve themselves, the central HIP organization does not have all the authority necessary to assure this. A kind of seesawing between the medical control board and the medical groups has developed on some fundamental questions. Underlying these difficulties is a lack of commitment toward HIP that derives from doctors being allowed to have outside practice; there is a temptation here to regard HIP patients as a source of supplementary income that is guaranteed regardless of how they are treated. This conflict of interest, according to Dr. George Baehr, is "a serious defect which H.I.P. must eventually eliminate," by requiring every medical group to pool the professional income earned outside the plan with the capitation income derived from the premium of HIP subscribers.[44] This is now true in only one of the thirty-one medical groups.

As important as pooling income is the need for proximity of doctors in group practice. Consultation and co-ordination of specialist services is more difficult for the patient when doctors practice out of their own private offices rather than in the medical group centers—a not unfamiliar situation in some HIP groups.

These problems would disappear if the doctors were employed full-time attending HIP patients, and this has been actively encouraged by the central organization, which contributes $6,000 annually for each full-time physician that a medical group adds to its staff. There were (in 1966) nearly 200 doctors under this arrangement, and they accounted for about 20 per cent of the physicians and 30 per cent of the professional services rendered. Recent negotiations with the medical groups have evolved another plan whereby the central organization will purchase the facilities and rent them to the medical group on favorable terms provided the group elects to move toward more full-time group practice. The real key to staffing with full-time physicians probably lies in HIP's obtaining its own hospital facilities, a development which requires permissive legislation that HIP is seeking in Albany.

The medical groups have co-operated with the central HIP organization in a thorough evaluation of the performance of each HIP doctor.[45] A committee of outside specialists completed a three-year study of all doctors in each medical group in six specialties. The Woodruff Committee consisted of specialists who were leaders in their profession but were outside HIP. They studied a sufficient number of clinical records completely to evaluate the competence of each doctor; each case was also discussed with the physician involved so that he was properly credited if he had acted on additional information not in the records. After the study was completed, the medical groups terminated the services of several physicians with low scores, but an even more important effect of the study was the way it stimulated the staff. Rechecks have shown much improvement in clinical records. It is reported that there is improved use of consultation and diagnostic services, and that "a better understanding of the potentialities of teamwork in group practice is evident in many of the physicians." Now the chiefs of departments, "often for the first time, assume full responsibility for directing and supervising the work of their associates and integrating their work with other departments."[46]

The imaginative and educational approach that has characterized HIP's research and quality improvement program also characterizes its relations with its subscribers. Underlying these is the assumption that subscribers and physicians are equals in a health improvement enterprise, that both have something to learn about each other's role. Complaints are handled systematically at both the HIP office and the medical group centers: if in writing, they must be answered in writing; the medical administrative staff of HIP may find it necessary to interview the persons concerned, and to make recommendations for appropriate handling of the complaints. Complaints are received by the HIP medical staff, and by the staff of the medical group concerned. A health education staff provides guidance in the preparation of a bulletin that gives health information and also information on group practice, appointment systems, doctor-patient relations, etc. Most important of all, there are meetings between subscribers and doctors on these subjects, and also for airing criticism and soliciting suggestions.[47] These meetings have allayed the apprehensions of some of the doctors who were fearful of unwarranted and intemperate criticism.

From the Kaiser and HIP experiences there are several conclusions that may help point the way for future community-wide plans. There are clear advantages in the central prepayment organization's providing the capital for the ambulatory clinics and the hospital services. The commitment of the staff doctors is best assured by full-time medical staff. Consistent with a non-profit purpose, there should be a governing structure that is sensitive to the membership of the plan and to the general community. A program of continuous evaluation and testing of all the dimensions of quality should be an inherent part of the administration. There should be encouragement of the family or personal physician in order that specialist and other services can be properly co-ordinated in the interest of the patient. Alternative choice should be optional for enrolling groups but should not be regarded as a substitute for either educational efforts or mechanisms of subscriber participation. Educational work can be directed both toward increasing the medical sophistication of members and toward developing positive attitudes among both staff and patients. We shall have more to say about some of these points in the next chapter. Here we note that while union members have many justified criticisms of both Kaiser and HIP, these plans are giving two million people medical care which falls short of the ideal but is generally superior to any available alternative.

Some Lessons for Health Planning

We closed the last chapter by asking whether the quality of medical service plans justifies the travail of their establishment. Our conclusion is that they can do so, but the experience is mixed and there is confusion on objectives. Several guiding principles seem to be emerging:

1. *In health center planning, union security objectives should not be confused with medical care objectives.* The union-sponsored diagnostic clinic can no longer be a model for labor health centers. In its time, it did fill a vacuum in the usual practice of medicine, but it also represented a search for union security in lower-paid industries of small units and much turnover. At its worst, the health center can become a mere edifice or monument to show the members how far their union has come. By the standards of modern medicine, clinics limited to diagnosis add to the fragmentation and discontinuity of medical attention. Medical care suffers in quality if the health center physician cannot supervise the entire range of service from diagnosis to treatment and recovery whether in his office, hospital, or the patient's home. Supply him also with accessible specialists through group practice and the ingredients for high quality care are at hand. This objective is attainable, as some labor medical service plans have demonstrated.

2. *In labor-sponsored medical service plans, the efficient use of resources requires multi-union planning.* The multiplicity of small union health centers in large cities, duplicating services for different union constituencies, represents a waste in labor health planning. In Chicago, there are four union health centers all within three miles of each other, while the membership of the separate unions involved spreads over the entire urban area. Members of each union must go to their own center. In New York, fifteen local unions have their own health centers, many of which are quite limited in scope, and all of which are unrelated to each other; at one time there were two different health centers on different floors of the same building, duplicating equipment and personnel. If the unions in metropolitan centers pool their resources, they could have one plan with clinics spaced so as to be geographically accessible to all their people.

3. *Labor should not sponsor its own plan where a good medical service plan is already in operation and the conditions of group enrollment can be negotiated.* Although the union will not have the primary

role in administering the plan, neither will it be without responsibility. The union as a large group buyer of services will have opportunities through negotiations to influence the administration and improve the program. In the case of co-operative medical centers, which are usually in need of a broader membership base, it has been demonstrated that differences can be overcome—at least where the co-op leadership is not basically hostile, where the union leadership genuinely wants the best medical care possible, and where the employer is willing to give the union some freedom in working out the arrangements.

4. *The highest standards of service probably cannot be achieved when the medical staff is also engaged in outside private practice.* Except at Kaiser and a few of the HIP groups, and except for medical directors and staff with medical school connections, many health center doctors have an outside practice. This may yet prove to be the Achilles heel of group practice centers. When a physician has private patients in addition to those in the medical service plan, he may be tempted to favor the former, or even to recruit private patients from dissatisfied enrollees. This financial incentive exists so long as outside patients supply income in addition to his income from the health center. It follows that there will be strains in the discipline of group practice. A conflict of interest can develop in the mind of the doctor and diminish his sense of responsibility toward the health center patients. Unless he is fully committed to the program, the doctor may not want, above all other considerations, to make the medical group practice a high quality performance.[48]

5. *These four principles—clarity of objectives, multi-union planning, integration of community facilities, and full-time medical staff—are fundamental and should be embodied in the early planning.* Most medical service plans continue to show their early defects. There are some respects in which a plan can be tailored down without permanent damage: for example, if the worker's family is excluded from coverage, or if substantial out-of-pocket charges are required, utilization will be adversely affected; but these shortcomings can be remedied when more operating funds are available. It is also possible at a later date to build a hospital to accompany the medical clinic. But single-union plans seem to stay that way; plans which duplicate service have not merged; part-time staff rarely evolves into full-time staff; and medical services, once confined to the medical clinic, face resistance to later extension.

6. *Multi-union planning of a medical service program requires new organizational vehicles or refurbishment of existing ones.* The structural features of the labor movement itself encourage the single union health center, which is more easily established within the existing bargaining pattern of one union and one employer or an employer association. Outside or beyond this bargaining structure, union discipline grows rapidly weaker; the new problems of authority and responsibility posed by a multi-union health center become exceedingly difficult to solve. The natural vehicle of inter-union co-operation at a local level is the city central body but its function has atrophied over the years as the international unions have become the power centers. City central bodies do important work and can co-ordinate international union efforts in some projects, such as building a labor temple or engaging in political elections, but they rarely provide the leadership required for promoting a health center that involves the bargaining policies of different unions.[49] Unless some way can be found to revitalize the role of the city central bodies or to provide them with help from the national level, multi-union health centers will remain the exception. Plans large enough to provide wide ranging health services will probably be realized first in Detroit, Pittsburgh, waterfront towns, coal centers, etc., where one industry and a single international union dominate the community's economic life. In economically diverse cities, the hope for health center development lies in co-ordinated union planning with a community focus.

14

ADMINISTERING MEDICAL SERVICE CENTERS

When the objectives of a medical center are clarified, a basis exists for solving the problems of administration. These involve the relationships of policy groups and the processes of decision-making. They deal with the roles of professional staff, lay staff, and patients. In short, administration is the assigning of functions and the ordering of authority. The issues are complex, and they can be analyzed intelligently only in relation to the high standards of quality at which the entire enterprise must aim.

The important concerns of administration can be grouped around several main questions. How should the administration and policy-making be organized so as to leave medical decisions in the hands of doctors, and other decisions in the hands of the sponsors? How should the patients, their personal physicians, and the specialists work together to garner the advantages inherent in group practice? What can the administrators of the plan do to raise the medical sophistication of its members? How far should collective bargaining go in keeping the union member in such a plan, particularly if he doesn't like it?

These are all sensitive, even controversial questions. They involve fundamental values of responsibility and freedom, the use and abuse of controls, the checks and balances needed in productive institutions.

Policy Roles for Laymen and Doctors

The relationship between lay or union leaders and professional medical staff remains one of the most delicate questions in prepaid group practice plans. It is generally accepted that there should be no lay interference in medical decisions, but what is meant by "medical deci-

204

sions?" Obviously, these include examination, treatment, and referral of the patient. Do they also include selection of doctors, the need for extra fees, the technical equipment to be installed, and the range of services to be provided? The AMA leans toward the all-inclusive view that "all phases of medical work should be under medical control."[1] A typical doctor's point of view is given by Dr. Russell V. Lee of Palo Alto:

Even in those areas that concern the economics of such a system, the doctors are going to insist that they be consulted as to what fees shall be and what portion of those fees the doctor gets. The doctors, being the kind of people they are, are going to insist on having a say on all those matters . . . the doctors will have to be permitted to choose the people that deliver the goods, the methods by which they shall be delivered, and participate in the operation of this system, if they are going to be kept happy. They are not going to stand still for you, a lay board, to tell them that patients are going to pay $2.00 a month and the doctor is going to get $500.00 a month salary.[2]

But unions and co-operatives argue that the doctor's responsibility is diagnosis, treatment, and the actual practice of medicine. It is the author's impression that union leaders with responsibilities to administer a direct-service plan feel that they cannot give over to the local medical society or to the medical staff of a health plan such basic economic decisions. If the local medical society can control the scope of the program, that program will be severely limited, as is shown by the UAW health center in Toledo, or the Amalgamated Clothing Workers' plan in Rochester, New York, or many of the ILGWU health centers. If the medical staff of the health center itself makes such decisions, they are performing as both physicians and business men, defining unilaterally not only how they will practice medicine but the terms of their remuneration.

The Health Insurance Plan of Greater New York has in recent years had difficulty resolving problems of authority between the medical group clinics and the central prepayment organization, problems which arise in part because the medical groups are owned by the medical staff itself. The AFL–CIO Social Security Committee recommends against capitalizing medical centers through participating physicians, "as evidence accumulates that relationship between the plan and the participating physicians is detrimentally affected by such a financial arrangement."[3]

If there are problems about properly defining the professional's role, there are also problems about defining and limiting the layman's role. Doctors in some cases have had grounds for complaint and there are at least two instances of alleged lay interference in medical practice.[4] Fortunately, there are devices that have worked in practice for resolving the conflicts. The structure of good plans can be drawn on for guidance, as can the opinions of doctors who have had experience in health plan administration. The following organizational principles are recommended.[5]

1. There should be a governing body composed primarily of union or lay leaders from the internationals or locals sponsoring the program or from community interests co-operating with the plan. The duties of the governing body are to determine coverage and scope of services provided, appoint the medical director, and appoint a medical advisory board.

2. The medical director may be responsible to the governing body for both medical and administrative functions (if he has an administrative assistant), or these functions can be divided between two persons whose respective duties must be carefully defined and co-ordinated.

3. In order to promote effective and democratic relations between the medical and lay groups of the center, there should be a conference committee representing both the professional staff and the governing body. The conference committee is a common practice at many hospitals.

4. The device by which the governing body gets the medical opinion it needs for making policy decisions is the medical advisory board, which is distinct from the medical staff. It should consist of physicians of standing. They advise the governing body on qualification standards for the staff, assist the medical director and staff concerning professional standards, and help them in their relations with hospitals and the local medical society.

With this kind of governing organization, medical policies and medical practice are in the hands of the director and his staff; the medical staff has direct access to the governing board and a mechanism for resolving differences; and medical opinion can be brought to bear on policy decisions before the governing board without creating conflicts of interest for the medical staff.

Securing the Fruits of Group Practice

What is good quality medicine and what conditions of practice make it possible? Official medicine has not been of much help to labor and lay groups interested in the answers,[6] but unions have conferred with doctors about standards before embarking on their programs.[7] And labor health center medical directors have frequent opportunities to discuss among themselves and with union leaders the conditions conducive to good group practice.[8]

Though we have little authoritative measure of their effectiveness, techniques of quality control are widely used in labor health centers. Doctors are chosen for their competence and required to practice within the limits of their specialty. Group consultations are frequent, following the practice in medical schools. The co-ordinated services of specialists with adequate laboratory facilities can bring to bear on a problem many minds all scientifically attuned. Doctors have testified to the stimulating effect of competent criticism from their colleagues. All this contrasts with the free-wheeling attitudes sometimes found in solo practice where physicians may regard their patients as personal property.[9] Dr. Allen Gregg suggests the stimulus provided by group practice:

Whether we realize it or not, the presence of merely a competent nurse tends to raise the doctor's level of performance. Reluctant as an anxious patient may be to think that his doctor, above all people, might ever need the stimulus of competent critics, the fact remains that doctors sometimes do need, and usually respond well, to the realization that their work is observable and observed.[10]

The patient's records, in the better plans, are kept in files subject to the official review of other professional eyes. Records may be pulled at random for spot checks on the adequacy of record-keeping (an important test of quality) and on the accuracy of diagnosis and proper use of laboratory or specialist facilities. At the St. Louis Labor Health Institute all cases are reviewed in staff conference before a patient is hospitalized; in several instances a doctor has been overruled by his colleagues and unnecessary surgery prevented.[11]

Procedures for attaining excellence are, however, no substitute for objectively measuring the quality achieved.[12] The usual definition of excellent medical care is adequate therapy based on correct diagnosis rather than on symptomatology. Putting this definition into practice requires *evaluation* of the degree to which such adequate therapy is available, acceptable, comprehensive, and documented.[13] Very few labor health centers have made this evaluation and published the results.[14] Outside experts studied the Labor Health Institute, using criteria such as the qualifications of the professional and non-professional staffs, the facilities, the record-keeping, the controls imposed on medical staff, etc. These results were compared with the minimum standards for hospitals of the American College of Surgeons, with much credit to the Labor Health Institute. No labor health center has published results of any investigations of quality that proceeded directly by study of patient records, a method used by the Health Insurance Plan of Greater New York.[15] Such an evaluation would be preferable to the usual labor health center annual report that glorifies the volume of services rendered. "There ought to be some machinery by which, periodically, somebody on the outside looks at the thing," suggests Walter Reuther, who has applied a variation of this principle in union administration. "Then their evaluation gets to the level of the organization in terms of its administrative procedures, so that there will be an impact of their outside objective evaluation upon the structure."[16] Plans sponsored by co-operatives and physicians are as deficient as most labor plans in methods for evaluating the quality of medical care.[17]

The system for remunerating doctors can have an important influence on the quality of group practice. Experience suggests there are divisive effects on the group when the individual doctor's income is set according to the volume of patients he handles. Such systems as fee-for-service, or percentage of earnings, or a point system are all inappropriate for a medical group.[18] They set up a conflict between the doctor's financial concerns and the interests of group practice. It has been recommended that the health center's income should be pooled and the individual doctors paid a salary to achieve the cohesive effect necessary for good group practice.[19] Men of equal training and equal length of service should be paid equally and there should be seniority increments.[20] In short, it is not enough that the staff have professional competence and good attitudes toward people; in the words of Dr. Abrams, "their conditions of work must encourage the full employment of these qualities."[21]

Dr. William A. MacColl, in his recent review of prepaid group practice plans, suggests that some consensus has developed around the following principles of reimbursement:

1. As a member of the medical team each physician is generally to be considered of equal value to the group.
2. Physicians' incomes should be high enough to attract and hold well-trained and competent doctors.
3. In determining initial salary the length of training should be recognized and rewarded, as long as that training increased the competence of the physician.
4. Certification and special competence may be the basis of increased pay. Length of service with the organization should be the major basis of increasing income.
5. Admission to the partnership, where applicable, should bring increased income.
6. The physician has a long-term interest in the health of the member rather than in sporadic episodes of illness. Hence, just as the patients pay a monthly premium whether ill or well, the physician receives his compensation regardless of fluctuations in load.[22]

High competence and morale in a medical service center achieves little in itself if the patients do not understand group practice or do not like it. Attitudes toward the patient-doctor relationship have been formed by traditional solo practice, but they constitute only one part of a general view of medicine which is marked by widespread ignorance of what constitutes good medical care.

It has been shown that the patient-physician relationship under solo practice is built on insecure foundations in many cases, especially for the less privileged members of the community.[23] People may choose their doctor, remain with him, or leave him for good reasons based on information and experience, but the reasons can also be frivolous and based on misconceptions about medicine. The problem in group practice is to teach patients some sophistication about medical care, including the use of consultants and specialists. The medical service plan is uniquely equipped to provide easy consultive arrangements that bring together specialized knowledge and technique, and to do so by encouraging the use of a personal physician within the medical group.

Patients rightly object to being "shuttled around" among doctors without the co-ordination and explanation that could be provided by a personal physician. Dr. E. Richard Weinerman has warned against the "fragmentation of the patient among an array of specialists and technicians" in some labor health centers.[24] Labor health programs cannot all cite a personal physician experience as good as that in solo practice. More attention must be given to the concept of general or "managing physician," the personal doctor who is closest to the patient and who assumes responsibility for co-ordinating the specialist and technical services, helping the patient see the need for them.[25] Effective and continuous education is required; so is a high staff morale in order that doctors will assume the responsibilities that go with a close relationship to the patient.

At the Labor Health Institute, a survey showed that many patients found a family doctor. Sixty per cent of the membership had a family doctor before coming to LHI; of those who used the center's services, 65 per cent said an LHI doctor was now their family physician. "It appears that once a member begins using the services of the plan, the chances that he will establish a stable relationship with a physician are just as good as they would be in private practice."[26] People can find a family doctor in prepaid group practice as well as in solo practice, but there is nothing certain or automatic about the selection just because the individual is committed to a particular group of doctors. "The accolade of family doctor is not easily won," concluded the LHI study, "there must be a trial by fire in which the physician shows certain qualities that win for him that added measure of confidence embodied in that title."[27]

Obtaining acceptance of group practice through proper use of personal physicians, is, we repeat, part of the larger problem of getting patients to accept the implications of good medical care. This is a very difficult assignment for a medical service plan, especially where the previous experience of the patient has not taught him anything about good medicine. A medical staff—or any doctor—has to counteract the quick remedy advertising of drug companies and cultists of all kinds; the Union Eye Care Center in Chicago, for example, has the perennial problem of explaining to its members the superiority of high quality ophthalmological care over the commercial vendors of eyeglasses.[28] Even more to the point is the experience reported by Dr. Langbord of the Sidney Hillman Medical Center in Philadelphia. He found some patients who wanted treatment on the spot. They were impatient not only with long, drawn-out laboratory examinations but even with routine studies for simple treatments. They were used to simple prescriptions and that is what they wanted.[29]

We conclude that the importance of forming the right attitudes among both patients and physicians has been underestimated in health center administration, and is especially important in a program for wage earners. Medical service centers have a unique opportunity to improve attitudes and encourage proper utilization of medical facilities through health education.

Education, Attitudes, and Utilization

The union cannot too early begin involving union members in the success of the health center, from the initial surveys of members' needs and existing facilities through the planning of the establishment.[30] No union has started its health plan with as much rank-and-file involvement at all stages of development as the Labor Health Institute.[31] There were hundreds of small group meetings where a union representative could explain the program, answer questions, and take back suggestions. Even with this conscientious leadership, two-fifths of the members when surveyed said they had never received a detailed explanation of the benefits and services.[32] But the special efforts at LHI have contributed to making the utilization rate higher than in other health centers.[33]

Too modest or ascetic an establishment runs the risk of simply recalling to the workers their past experience with charity clinics and hospital wards, "hard benches, long waiting periods, rushed and impersonal doctors."[34] To have the appearance of being a step forward, the union center will be "something our members don't have to apologize to their neighbors for."[35]

Union members' willingness to use an available health center is affected by their general attitudes toward health. Health center doctors are learning what sociologists have discovered, that health care generally holds a lower valuation—because of economic necessity, group conditioning, and fear—among the less fortunate people in a community. Koos has reported a close correlation between one's ability to recognize symptoms as needing medical attention and his socio-economic position in the community.[36] Only one-third or one-half as many working class people would seek medical attention as would members of the most prestigious class, even given the same symptoms. Some respondents gave economic explanations for not seeking medical attention: "If something was wrong with my husband, we would get it fixed right away. He earns the money and we can't let him stop work. I can drag around with my housework, but he can't drag around and still earn a living."[37] For some wage earners, their responsibilities may actually be a negative factor: "How do I know, if I have something wrong with me, what it's going to cost? Maybe if I started being treated, it will take me away from my job and my family won't be able to live."[38] Such economic factors have conditioned this group to believe that one should put up with things. This folk lore of suffering and endurance is expressed in the words:

There's a lot of things I know you are supposed to do something about but there's a lot of reasons why you don't. . . . I would look silly, wouldn't I, going to see a doctor for a backache. My mother had a backache, as long as I can remember, and didn't do anything about it. It didn't kill her, either. . . . If I went to the doctor for that, my friends would hoot me out of town. That's just something you have, I guess. Why let it get you down?[39]

A study of households of members of the Amalgamated Clothing Workers in New York City showed that about 63 per cent of those with disabling chronic illness had no desire for any help, although a number of these could have profited in some way from rehabilitation.[40]

When health falls so low in the worker's value structure, it is probably because other needs—prestige, education, economic security—are unsatisfied and pressing. And the low valuation of health may persist even when its economic source is removed; the result is low utilization of new medical facilities.

It is clear that the labor health center must play a positive role in raising the level of health education. Some of the factors that affect utilization are decided by where the medical center is built, how it is built, what services are provided, and whether the whole family is included. But utilization is also affected by the membership's and patients' attitudes, by the attitudes of the doctors, by the processes of education and communication at all levels of the health center operation.

A study of the attitudes of group practice physicians toward their prepaid patients is revealing: "These physicians indicated the beliefs that their patients were worse off economically than the population average, that the prepaid members were much more abusive of their medical services than were private patients, and that prepayment itself was perceived as a constraining influence upon the doctor. The views pertaining to patients were held despite the facts statistically demonstrated in the same study that the group health patients had, on the average, higher incomes than the general population and requested physicians' services at about the same rate."[41] It may well be that there is a conflict of expectation between doctor and patient, in part based on class attitudes, in part based on different ideas of the way the health center should function, in part based on the physician's desire to be the analytic and detached scientist when the patient needs reassurance, warmth, personal understanding, and emotional support. And Weinerman poses this question to group health administrators: "Has the preconditioned conflict in doctor-patient relationships been recognized in the design and function of the group health team?"[42]

Several labor health centers have used common-sense techniques for informing members of their opportunities: weekly orientation courses for new members; printed notices urging a physical examination; informal meetings about health center policies.[43] More effective and personal are the opportunities present in each consultation, which can be in spirit a teaching process. As Dr. William A. Sawyer has suggested, "every service rendered can be looked upon and handled as health education."[44] Here some of the deep-seated difficulties in doctor-patient relationships are operating—the barriers to understanding between professionally trained staff, confident in their surroundings, and the insecure patient who is awed and uncertain about what is relevant and sometimes prevented by fright from using his own native critical faculties.

Awareness of this led one medical director to emphasize the importance of selecting doctors whose "basic convictions recognize and support the center's guiding principles."[45] Dr. Herbert Abrams argues that the health center should be administered so that the patient as well as the doctor gets understanding and respect. The staff must teach and be willing to learn from their patients. "There has to be time for the patient to ask questions and the doctor to explain."[46] One critic suggests that "the values have not been fully appreciated of regular, small, informal round-table, get-togethers among members, doctors and administrators."[47] This may build a climate where the physicians are interested in how their actions look from the patient's side in order that the patient-physician relationship can be built less on the priesthood of superior knowledge and more on mutual respect between people equally interested in making the plan work. In labor relations, a similar concern for dignity in the employer-employee relationship is behind the steward structure and grievance procedure. Some unions are experimenting with a system of "health stewards" who communicate workers' attitudes to the health center administration and inform workers about the health center's facilities and policies.[48]

A study of co-operative plans shows great variation in the extent of membership participation, and the same is undoubtedly true of union plans.[49] Some plans will show little despite their consumer sponsorship. Consumer sponsorship of itself does not insure participation or the formation of positive attitudes. The attitudes and education of both staff and patient-members must be an essential concern of the enterprise from the first stages of planning to the final routine administration.

Alternative Choice Arrangements

One of the significant developments in the competition between new forms of providing medical care was the invention of alternative choice plans. These are arrangements whereby the individual members in a group such as a union may choose between a prepaid group practice plan and some alternative, such as indemnity insurance or Blue Cross-Blue Shield. The negotiated employer contribution pays the premium for either choice. There is, therefore, no monetary influence nor financial penalty working on the member's acceptance or rejection of group practice.

The union member must make a choice—he cannot be in both plans at once. He can make this choice not only at the beginning of the program but also at stated intervals thereafter. He can later reverse himself. While he can go back and forth between the alternatives, he can do so only at specified times; this is usually once each year on a predetermined date. In this way the individual member has a free choice of doctor in the broadest sense, including choice between a medical group on the one hand and an open-panel arrangement on the other.

Alternative choice arrangements have become a common feature of the larger prepaid group practice plans. The Kaiser Foundation Plan requires alternative choice for any group seeking coverage. The Health Insurance Plan of Greater New York permits enrolled groups to provide alternatives but does not require it. Most union-sponsored medical centers do not include alternative choice arrangements, except for local unions or individuals residing outside the area of medical service facilities. A notable exception is the Community Health Association in Detroit, which included alternative choice as one of its original features.

A strong argument has been made for the alternate choice arrangement. Kaiser officials see it as an opportunity for "an exchange of views, for discussion of experience, and for critical evaluation of the two methods [direct service and cash indemnity] through which medical care is being obtained by the members of the group."[50] And Garbarino justifies the individual's right to make a decision "that may be against his best interest as these interests are interpreted by someone else (e.g. his employer, his union officials, their consultants, or the medical profession)."[51]

The opportunity to make decisions undoubtedly encourages many persons critically to examine their experience, but it is not certain that sound and rational decision-making—as emphasized in the Kaiser statement—always occurs in alternative choice decisions. There is too much evidence that employees and their families often do not understand good medical care and may prefer unscientific medicine because they are accustomed to it. We have seen that health "intelligence" varies with education and socio-economic status.[52] It may be that even the choice of a medical plan is a function of education.[53] A union member who stays away from doctors as long as possible regardless of his symptoms, or who chooses his doctor by looking for the cheeriest extrovert, or who wants pills rather than diagnosis—such a person needs more than the freedom to make a decision. He needs medical education.

We have noted in the last chapter that the Kaiser Foundation decision to require alternative choice in participating groups came in part as a consequence of its growing monopoly position and the need to reach some kind of truce with economically hard pressed solo practitioners and their medical societies. This is one of the real uses and indisputable values of alternative choice. The United Auto Workers

Union in Detroit decided to include alternative choice in the Community Health Association although it had no doubt that the program it was offering was far superior in quality to what its members could buy in the open medical market. But alternative choice blunted some of the criticism of the medical society, and, after a slow beginning, CHA's popularity is growing. On the other hand HIP in New York allows indemnity alternatives for union groups that want it, but has resisted it for the bulk of city employees who make up the backbone of the program. Under pressure HIP has had to modify its stand which has been that of an embattled reformer of medical care organization.[54] Similarly, there are union programs that would not have come into existence at all if the entire group could not be committed.

It has been noted that members of a prepaid group practice plan are less likely to go "outside" for care if their families as well as themselves are covered by the plan.[55] In a close family, the doctor is usually the same for all members. It may be that medical service centers are most appropriate for family units; it follows that a plan which covers employees only should seriously consider an alternative choice system.

Obviously, a plan must have alternative choice if it is not accessible to all members, and accessible as they themselves see it—that is, either geographically close or "near" through available transportation, and open when people are free to use it. Otherwise, there must be an indemnity alternative so the worker is not at a financial disadvantage compared with those who can use the medical service center.

These specific advantages of alternative choice in certain situations are clear. Much less clear is any argument from a fundamental principle of freedom to choose. Freedom is involved, but so is responsibility—the responsibility for making good medical care available to and desired by more people. It is this responsibility that underlies union bargaining for health. The employee who has to make decisions under the usual conditions of solo practice is frequently overwhelmed by the problems: he has to decide who the good doctors are; he must evaluate their advice when it is conflicting; he has to search out specialist help when needed; he has to buy the necessary drugs or special treatment. The system of independent and separate practitioners makes every patient his own contractor. Administering one's health today is a demanding enterprise, even for persons with business or professional experience. The conditions of working-class life where "a thousand influences press a working man down into a passive role"[56] do not develop the entrepreneurial talents needed to manage one's medical care. The frequency of poor medical practice,[57] unnecessary surgery,[58] and questionable drugs[59] dogs the worker's every decision. The open medical market includes the best of services and also the worst in exploitation. If a union has the means for establishing a good medical care program, it cannot waive the responsibility.

Our knowledge of the reasons for which members choose one plan rather than another in an alternative choice situation is quite limited. The experiences of "cross-overs" and their motives for changing between group practice and indemnity insurance have important implications for the popularity and utility of group practice, and may some-day shed light on difficult questions.[60] There is already, however, enough evidence to suggest that people's past experience weighs against change—that there is a kind of inertia, and that this operates in both directions.[61] Groups previously in indemnity plans will split with the larger number and choose to continue with the indemnity plan. The majority of a group enrolled in a prepaid group practice plan will, when offered an indemnity alternative, stick with group practice. Where there has been no plan before, the group will most likely divide equally, although in some cases the point of view of the union leadership and the amount of discussion or education among the membership can affect the results. Whether a union can succeed through educational processes in preparing its membership for change in their existing relationship to doctors depends on a great many factors, including the amount of outside pressure from the medical societies or others who oppose any change. It may well be that if members can elect out of a new medical service plan even before they have experience of it, half or fewer than half of the group may choose it, whereas if the choice were offered at a later date a much larger number would voluntarily stay with group practice.[62]

It is difficult to know when group responsibility reinforces and when it interferes with the individual's desire for better medical care. The value of getting the plan started may have to take priority over the value of allowing individual decisions about participating. Without a medical service plan, there is no option possible. There are then, it appears, four important considerations which lead to an operational as opposed to a doctrinaire view of free choice.

Firstly, it should be clear that popularity alone is no final test of a medical program. Popularity is important, but it cannot replace continuity of care, accessibility of facilities, comprehensiveness of services, and other features of high quality medicine. The objective is to make scientific diagnosis and treatment widely desired, and one of the best ways to do this is through education and experience with good group practice plans.

Secondly, alternative choice is a useful device for several purposes, but can be misused. Where plans have obvious shortcomings, alternative choice permits the union member to adjust to these deficiencies in a way that suits him best, and as the plan improves he can reassess its value to him. In this way the annual voluntary choices will be a measure of relative popularity and the development of attitudes toward group practice. Alternative choice can be used to blunt medical society propaganda about free choice of physician and to reach an accommodation with individual practitioners when the monopoly is on the side of the group medical service plan. Alternative choice should not be used by the staff of a group practice plan as a safety valve for malcontents. Nor should it be a substitute for education by the group health program to help patients understand medicine and work constructively with the staff.

Thirdly, tradition and past experience with the medical market conditions workers' attitudes and results in a built-in bias for the status quo, which is usually the solo, fee-for-service practice that is the most difficult for workers to manage in their own interest. Where the union becomes a force for reform in the medical market, it has to decide whether the losses in community bargaining power that will follow if alternative choice is instituted at the beginning may founder the entire venture.

Lastly, as collective bargaining lends its weight to reform in medical economics, the place unions can give to individual decision as opposed to group decision may depend on how tightly the line is drawn by organized medicine. If the medical society leaders remain unwilling to give lay organizations any power of decision in the economics (as opposed to the practice) of medicine, unions will for strategic reasons have to diminish the role of options, free choice, and individual determination in the administration of health plans. As consumers, union members who want a choice between orthodox practice and prepaid group practice may have to fight for it. So long as the atmosphere in the medical market is one of war, the use of countervailing force is the only possible expression of democratic values.

We conclude that there is no overriding principle involved but rather that the decision of whether to include an indemnity alternative to a group practice medical service plan is a matter of particular contingencies, of community tone and accommodation, of tactics and strategy. In each situation it will be a vital question in community health bargaining.

Part III

Implications

15

RATIONALIZING THE MEDICAL MARKET

In this chapter we discuss several problem areas in order to show the role community health bargaining can play in the evolution of medical institutions.

The Problem of Price

The characteristics of the medical market are beginning to get more attention, particularly from economists.[1] Until recently there has always been considerable doubt whether economics had anything to offer. It is clear that the rise in the cost of medical care has outstripped that of other major components of the consumer price index, and also that a larger portion of family expenditures is flowing in the direction of health insurance and medical care. The explanation of this trend is controversial because no one has succeeded in assigning to all the supply and all the demand factors their particular responsibility for the rise in medical prices. To some extent this rise is attributable to a growing consumer preference for health and medical care services. It is also attributable to broader based financing from employer contributions and the regularity of payments through insurance and prepayment. Both consumer preference and broader financing are responsible for the increasing use of doctors and hospitals.

Various supply factors are also cited as operating on prices. A shortage and mal-distribution of physicians and medical personnel is frequently mentioned. Although there is little agreement about the reasons for shortage or for the best remedial action, one of the most impressive studies cites enforced limitation of access to the profession as a significant influence on the level of doctor's incomes.[2] The rise in hospital bills has been attributed to wage movements, to ancillary services, and to better accommodations, but none of these is a complete explanation. There appears to be a lag in productivity gains behind the rest of the economy, even behind comparable service industries, and according to Herbert Klarman this is "accepted as an important factor by most economists who have thought [sic] or dealt with hospital cost."[3]

This brings us to an important feature of medical economics—the persistence of traditional pricing attitudes among the suppliers of care. Doctors are accustomed to think in terms of the patient's ability to pay. Surgeons' fees, for example, have increased as the schedule of insurance allowances for various operations increases. And hospitals have long justified their bills on the grounds that they simply reflect their costs. Blue Cross has been unable to establish reimbursement formulas that might encourage hospital efficiencies. The situation created by the level of demand and the traditional pricing by suppliers seems to make possible what John Dunlop has called "pass-through" pricing:

I think that in the medical care area the tendency to institutionalize the cost-pass-through, without regard to ideology and without regard to public or private administration, is one of the fundamental problems that needs attention. It is a swinging door. You push on costs and prices go up. But the purpose of price, the purpose of financial constraints, in our society is to force efficiency, to force reorganization, to force changes in technology and change in method. When we institutionalize the cost-pass-through, we tend to take away from this sector much of the stimulus that is essential to structural change, and we are in trouble. Medical care should not be insulated from the beneficial effects and reorganization that develop from severe cost pressures.[4]

Community health bargaining can attack some of the factors on both the demand side—such as improper utilization—and the supply side that needlessly inflate prices. By developing market pressures to encourage reorganization and more efficient use of resources, community health bargaining can help rationalize the medical market.

The Problem of Quality

In less than two generations we have witnessed the conquest of infectious diseases; the isolation of bacterial infections and discovery of antidotes; the breakthrough in attack on polio and other viruses. We have seen miracles of brain and heart surgery with unheard-of human and mechanical skills. X-ray and pathology and a host of laboratory services are standard orders of procedure. We ought to be able to take good medical care for granted.

But can we? The president of the Federation of State Medical Boards has forcibly called attention to the extent of incompetence among practicing physicians. "Despite the large number of medical regulatory bodies with varying degrees of authority and improvements in medical education, incompetent physicians still present a problem. Although they constitute a small minority of the profession, their potential dangers are disproportionate to their numbers."[5] Incompetence however is not just an individual failing. The scientific and technological revolution that has transformed medicine in the past fifty years has led to great disparities in medical practice.

Two studies (1959 and 1962) of the medical records of hospitalized members of the International Brotherhood of Teamsters in New York City showed that one-fifth of the patients had received poor care and another fifth only fair care; the quality of surgery was labeled "poor" in 20 per cent of the cases. Only 57 per cent of the hospital admissions received "optimal" care. "Essentially, there were two causes for care that was judged to be inferior," the first report stated: "One was related to surgery performed on essentially normal organs, where the grave suspicion of patient exploitation could be raised. The other factor, equally discouraging in a city that has such a large number of fine hospitals and high proportion of well-trained physicians, was inferior care resulting from poor clinical judgment on the part of a certain number of physicians without either adequate training or supervision."[6]

These findings from an urban center have put to rest doubts expressed about the North Carolina investigation sponsored by the Rockefeller Foundation in which 88 physicians picked at random were subject to intensive observation by teams of specialists.[7] The study showed tremendous variations in the quality of medical care, and stated that half the doctors were inadequate. There was a shortage of case histories, many perfunctory examinations, extensive use of unsterilized instruments, neglect of essential laboratory procedures, indiscriminate use of antibiotics, and a high proportion of hasty and wrong diagnoses. There has been no controversy about these findings, but

rather about whether the physicians whose work was studied represented an adverse selection. The report itself stated that the sample
physicians appeared to be typical of the run of general practitioners.

In any case, we have in the New York and North Carolina studies
and in experience already cited in preceding chapters enough evidence
for concern about the quality of care that Americans receive. And this
is only when they use doctors. If we add the evidence of untreated
disease among the poor generally; and the longevity and mortality statistics which show shocking differences between whites and Negroes,
we then begin to see that the "best medical care in the world" is a
rare commodity.[8]

The Problems of Organization

In part, some of the very developments that have made medical care
of the highest quality possible have also made it more difficult to obtain
for the average person. Advanced technology has changed the character of medical practice from that of an individual profession into an
institutionalized industry. It has forced specialization as the only means
of coping with the multiplication of knowledge, and 60 per cent of the
private practitioners in the United States today are specialists, compared with only 16 per cent in 1931.[9] Technology also makes expensive equipment necessary as aids to diagnosis and treatment, with the
result that only through pooled arrangements can individual doctors
meet the capital costs required. Of necessity much less medicine is
now practiced in the home and much more in the office. Both the specialization and the high capital costs bring doctors together into pooled
arrangements and group practice as the most feasible ways to practice.
Thus, as Anne Somers told the Pennsylvania Medical Society, "the
spectacular advances in medical science and technology, which have
so vastly increased the capacity of medicine as a whole, have also
brought a relative decline in the capacity of the individual doctor."[10]
In another paper[11] she has described the difficulties of the general
practitioner whose heavy patient load and lack of contact with medical centers, teaching hospitals, or other sources of intellectual inspiration have made him obsolete long before his working life is over.

As doctors have trouble keeping up with changes in their profession,
the potential patients have difficulty knowing what is expected of

them. A study of doctor-patient relationships in an economically mixed suburb of the type in which Americans are living in increasing numbers found that the family doctor who delivered the baby, set the bone, removed the tonsils, and gave comfort where he could do no more had ceased to exist in the experience of much of the population: "Working-class families still have a 'family doctor' in the sense that they secure most of their medical care from general practitioners. The remainder of the population seek in their own way to obtain the best of modern medicine by employing specialists in internal medicine, pediatricians, obstetricians, orthopedists and others—each to treat a pain or problem the patient believes to be in his field."[12] In part because of the difficulties of dealing with separate specialists, workers have a high stake in seeking to update and reorganize medicine along modern lines.

The Problem of Change

The economist sees in medicine a personal service industry disrupted by a revolutionary technology, with the forms of practice now showing widest diversity. As in any such period of rapid economic change, there are groups who ally themselves with the forces of change, and those who are threatened by them. Spokesmen for progress at one stage of development may become spokesmen for reaction at a later date. The American Medical Association pioneered in establishing the scientific basis of medicine, and in enforcing standards of education and practice, but now allies itself politically with the very elements most resistant to change. Today it is becoming the spokesman for the independent general practitioner who is being passed by, and it uses its powerful sanctions as an economic weapon to inhibit change. If the spread of understanding about medical economics could alone produce the desired results, there would be no need for organized consumer pressures. But this is not the case. In the words of Reinhold Niebuhr, "since reason is always, to some degree, the servant of interest in a social situation, social injustice cannot be resolved by moral and rational suasion alone. . . . Conflict is inevitable, and in this conflict, power must be challenged by power."[13] It is my view that our egalitarian ideals impose a moral urgency for organized consumer pressure wherever the medical profession itself is fighting the requirements of progress.

It is here that we can take guidance from the "bargaining power" theory of John R. Commons and the "countervailing power" idea of John Kenneth Galbraith.[14] They provide a kind of general theory to guide the organized consumer of medical services. Both men see the social value of accumulations of economic power that offset other accumulations. Commons applied the idea to labor-management relations where he saw the union as the vehicle to offset certain forces in the product and financial markets that would otherwise force down wages. Galbraith was interested in the seryice offered consumers by large supermarkets (or other buyers) who bargain down wholesalers or go around them to alternative sources of supply.

In medicine there is need for organizers to pull specialists and paramedical personnel and capital equipment together into new enterprises. This is an entrepreneurial function that need not be preserved exclusively for doctors, because there is nothing about practicing medicine that equips one to perform the "business" functions of organization, search for efficiency, and new relationships with potential patients. Increasingly, this entrepreneurial role is being played by consumer groups such as unions and co-operatives, and by business acting either through welfare plans or directly (as at Kaiser), as well as by doctors.

Galbraith's formulation of the process is particularly interesting when applied to medicine because of his distinction between "original market power" and "countervailing market power." Original market power, he says, is held by any firm with a strategic hold on the market. When others attempt to unseat this hold by building up alternatives and competitors, they are developing a countervailing power which is socially useful. This distinction he felt was essential to successful anti-trust policy, since it is not bigness as such that is undesirable.

If the organized doctors in a community, the medical society, insist that the only way medicine can be practiced is by independent physicians charging on a fee-for-service basis, or that prepayment and group practice cannot be combined, they are acting as an original market power. Competition may occur only among the authorized forms of practice, and there is no competition between alternative kinds of medical organization. When organized consumers search for alternatives, either by establishing a prepaid health center or inviting others to do so, they are using countervailing power. They are attempting to establish effective leverage on behalf of potential patients so that competition may take place between older and newer forms of financing and organization.

This is why there has been so much experimentation in California, where the Kaiser Foundation is in effective competition with other forms of financing and organization and the consumer has real choices to make.

Rationalizing the Medical Market

There are some important cautions to be observed by any union or combination of unions that want to use countervailing power in the medical market. Firstly, they must be absolutely uncompromising that their objective is the best in medical care; there should be no confusion between the objectives of medical care and those of union security. Every decision must emphasize high quality medicine in the broadest sense with all its implications. And planning for high quality does have direct implications for the location, staffing, and coverage of the health center; for the division of responsibilities between lay and professional administrators; for the proper functioning of group practice; and for forming the attitudes of both doctors and patients. Secondly, it should be clear that the objective is not to replace one monopoly with another nor to set apart one group in the population from the health facilities of the community. The effort should be to improve the quality and availability of community health facilities. The greatest possible range of free choice should be given to the participants in any health plan so that there will be no sense of entrapment to prevent patients learning the ingredients of good medical care.

The pattern of health facilities in any community shows disparity and contrast in the stages of technical development. The nature and number of hospitals depend on historical factors some of which are only remotely related to modern health needs. The character of the public health facilities also has evolved over a long time and has been affected by changing political and social currents. Doctors themselves, their attitudes, points-of-view, and position in the community all reflect complicated social growth patterns. It can be misleading to talk of the organization of health facilities, because there rarely is any rationalized overall planning of community health activities. A tugging and hauling of different health interests takes place with the hospital, public health authorities, and medical society each feeling it is the logical center around which all health services in a community should be structured. Dr. Roemer has concluded that "the obvious and pressing need for coordination of health services in American communities has not yet been found."[15] Public and private forces that urge this co-ordination are however slowly developing. Organized consumers working through their labor organization are one such private force performing this needed public service.

16

COMMUNITY HEALTH BARGAINING

Because of the kinds of evidence selected for this study, the reader
has quite possibly been left with an impression that the entire labor
movement is headed with determination and sense of purpose toward
community health bargaining, and yet this is far from the truth. The
routine and the unimaginative have been omitted simply because
they are less relevant to the processes of social change that have been
our central concern. I have not tried to paint an idealistic picture of
what labor ought to do, but to highlight the evolution of health bargaining of the last decade and a half, and to describe what the more
innovating and experimental leaders have accomplished. The ideals
of the labor movement in health bargaining can come only from its
own experience, and one task of this book has been to see how labor
leadership has interpreted the lessons of that experience. The future,
like the past, will be a mixture of bumbling and brilliance, of opportunities missed and opportunities seized.

Stages Leading Up to Community Health Bargaining

Labor leaders did not suddenly wake up to their members' anxieties
over illness and health during the wage stabilization period of World
War II. One thread of labor history has been a search for ways of solving the problems associated with injury, illness, and death. The need
to find a balance between these problems of personal security on the
one hand and employment problems on the other has occupied union
policy for well over a hundred years. War Labor Board policies did
create an opportunity to return to the fundamental concern of insurance and medical care. The innovation of the nineteen forties was in

negotiating employer contributions to health and welfare plans rather than financing them through dues and assessments. Legal and bargaining obstacles were overcome to make employer financing an adequate and dependable source of funds for workers' health security.

Union efforts since World War II have been directed to expanding the management's view of the objectives and range of health bargaining. When employers agreed, in order to encourage employee morale and efficiency, to add health insurance to the more traditional provisions of employee benefit plans, they made it clear they were primarily interested in benefits for their active employees. They resisted adding dependents and retirees to the programs, in part because of the greater cost of these types of coverage. To assure employee responsibility and to restrain excessive demands, management generally wanted some degree of contributory financing, whereas more and more unions, preoccupied with the limitations of existing plans, pressed for additional employer contributions. Except in the multi-employer trusteed plans, management wanted to negotiate on specific benefits rather than on premiums, dividends, reserves, or net cost, and for this reason resisted incursion of the union into its relations with the insurer. In general, management has sought to assist employees in meeting some of the costs of health services without impairing what it believes to be the employee's personal obligation to budget for "normal" expenses. The unions emphasized the plight of their members who were squeezed between rising medical costs and limited benefits; in such circumstances, they argued, there are no "normal" expenses, and prepayment appears to be the only realistic kind of budgeting. More and more unions pressed for the savings and efficiencies to be gained through employer contributions and tax deductions, through group insurance and sophisticated surveillance of insurance carriers, and through the introduction of cost and quality controls in the provision of medical services. With management, however, the upward movement in medical pricing induced a cautious attitude, including doubts about innovation in the insurance and medical markets.

The burdens imposed by health bargaining on the time and energy of union leaders were considerable. Several years ago the author was talking with a grand lodge representative of the International Association of Machinists and his complaints went something like this:

I'm having one hell of a time. I negotiate thirteen contracts. These group insurance problems have tripled the amount of work. There is always something going wrong. A premium increase the employer doesn't want to pay, or a worker who thinks some item on his hospital bill should have been covered; a lodge where some insurance agent has convinced the officers they ought to have his kind of policy; doctors in town deciding to up their rates; employers falling behind in their premium payments. I don't see how I can keep handling all these things myself.[1]

It was out of bargaining experiences like this one that union leaders developed more sophistication about the organization and economics of insurance and of medicine. Their perception expanded as the implications of health bargaining were clarified by experience. The stages of development are not clearly distinguishable, but rather describe a continuous evolution that is characterized by less and less dependence on the commercial insurance industry, and more and more concern with comprehensive health care and the work of doctors and hospitals.

Elementary Health Bargaining

The first stage in union thinking was a simple adaptation to pressures from the rank-and-file, who wanted insurance because more people were buying it, and from the insurance industry, which wanted to sell it. At this level nothing was very complicated because employers wanted their personnel policies to be up to date. Nobody thought about the kind of benefits desired, and a kind of follow-the-leader mentality ensued, as is suggested by the words of one union president in 1951: "No doubt we shall make a study of our plans in comparison with those in other industries and if we find that we are lagging behind we shall undoubtedly then ask for improvement in our plans."[2] With no clear union objectives there was free play for the employer and his insurance agent, whose opinion on what was good for the employees and the company probably prevailed; who knew any better than he the mystery of limited liability and the principles of profitable insurance? Details of financing were left entirely to the company and the underwriter, with the union knowing little about the amount of premium, retention, dividend, reserve, etc. Patterns in doctors' fees or hospital billing were still more obscure.

Advanced Health Bargaining

At this stage, union leaders were learning about health insurance from rank-and-file complaints that members were not getting the expected coverage of their medical bills. Technicians were consulted. At the next negotiations, more careful phrasing of benefit demands would follow a thorough study of the shortcomings of the insurance policy in effect. New doubts about the underwriter's role and company resistance to the higher costs would bring the issues of explicit financing onto the bargaining table: what are the dividends; who gets the commission and how much is it; what total was paid out in benefits; is a better arrangement possible by getting other underwriters to bid on this policy?

The insurance and welfare investigations contributed to this stage of education for many union leaders. At one of many meetings on health and welfare problems during the fifties, a delegate tried to calm his agitated colleagues with these words:

> . . . the things that are ailing us today are precisely the result of the American labor movement entering into a field of which we knew nothing. As long as the free enterprise system exists in the sale of insurance you are going to have gripes, and corruption, and some weak sisters. But we have extended collective bargaining from its traditional field into this field where we had no experience. We stumbled into this thing. . . . We are now having children's diseases and we are emotionally upset because we cannot get cured of them in 24 hours.[3]

Also at this stage there occurred the beginning of a profound shift in thinking. "How can we get our people covered by benefit plans to recognize a fully qualified physician, and to patronize him?" asked the president of the International Association of Machinists.[4] Insurance was now seen as both a vehicle and an obstruction to obtaining quality medical care. Union leadership recognized that basically it was buying medical services rather than insurance, and the insurance industry lost its grip on the union's thinking.

Community Health Bargaining

Finally, the union may become fully engaged with the basic problems that have plagued the voluntary health insurance movement. It realizes that insurance and prepayment systems affect and are affected by the organization and pricing of medical care services. It understands that prepayment divorced from the provision of services can inflate the cost, and even encourage the poor practice of medicine. The union leadership now knows it must work directly to shape the institutional relationships through which medical services are provided. The union has to get in a position to use its economic strength, not only with the employer, but also with organized doctors and hospitals for reform in prevailing practice. The union sees itself as a mass purchaser of medical services and wants to behave as an intelligent buyer. It sees the need for mechanisms to institute some kind of surveillance on both the cost and quality of services. The search for alternatives begins: How best to encourage the development of high grade medical organization? How can the membership learn the importance of this? What can be done to establish group practice and get the best results from it?

These stages—elementary, advanced, and community bargaining— can be understood as a kind of educational model to which unions in varying degrees have approximated. Some union leaders have travelled swiftly towards community health bargaining, others slowly; some have gotten stalled along the way—there are many union leaders today who still depend on the insurance industry for their ideas and for the administration of their welfare plans.

One by product of health bargaining, however, has been further professionalization of union staff. Even union leaders of the old school who distrust "intellectuals" (technicians) realized they were out of their depth in health bargaining. Several courses were open: either they worked with universities on the problems of insurance and medical economics they encountered, or they trained their staff in the negotiation and administration of health plans, or they depended on consultants. Some of the larger organizations added to their permanent staffs—actuaries, economists, doctors, and medical directors.

Not infrequently the feeling of union leadership is like that expressed by the then director of the AFL–CIO Social Security Department, Nelson Cruikshank: "I find myself wishing that this venture into mass purchasing might have started with some common commodity where the standards were simple and objective. But no, it had to be medical care where criteria are even less objective than those available for ladies' hats."[5]

To understand a particular union's role in health bargaining one must look to its experiences with the medical market rather than to its social or political history. A union's general stance or ideology does not necessarily provide clues as to how it will behave in the medical market. For example, the International Ladies' Garment Workers' Union has a strong social democratic tradition, and, while it is true that it pioneered in limited medical services, it has not achieved by itself the bargaining power needed for effectiveness in the medical market. On the other hand, the United Mine Workers under conservative leadership established a radical health program with a central fund strong enough to supervise cost and quality—a revolutionary development. Sometimes a union may start in one direction and then change, as its gets experience. For example, the leaders of the United Steelworkers of America felt at first that the union's responsibility was to negotiate health insurance with employers, leaving the manner of providing care entirely to physicians. But as experience with the medical market accumulated, the union began to chafe at the costliness and poor quality of traditional practice, and finally switched to open advocacy of prepaid group practice.

Unions are labor market institutions, but health bargaining has brought them into the medical market, and as purchasers rather than producers. This is a new dimension to union history and carries with it a new set of rules.

The Strategy of Community Health Bargaining

Leadership that perceives the character of community health bargaining and wants to act will be able to figure out the strategy appropriate to the community concerned, but our review of experience suggests some general implications for union-management relations, for union structure, and for community action. The question here is: what are the ways to augment bargaining power in the medical market?

Bargaining Power and Freedom of Action

Bargaining power in a labor market is a necessary condition for bargaining power in a medical market. It is no accident that much of the innovation in health bargaining has been in multi-employer bargaining where the union played a central co-ordinating role. The Warehouse and Distribution Workers' Union in St. Louis, Building Service Employees in Chicago, Hotel Workers in New York, Retail Clerks and Longshoremen in California, Amalgamated Clothing Workers in New York and Philadelphia, and the United Mine Workers have had general bargaining advantages with their employers which permitted innovation in their health efforts.

Bargaining power in the industry is a necessary condition but it is not a sufficient one. In fact, it can detract from success in the medical market under circumstances where most of the collective bargaining is national in character and conducted with large, national companies. The United Steelworkers of America, for example, has great power with the steel industry and its national bargaining has had great influence in shaping the structure and policies of Blue Cross and Blue Shield and commercial insurance. But this very success has drawn attention away from medical markets which are local in character. The UAW pioneered in getting local option in its contracts so that employees could take advantage of medical service plans where they are available. The Steelworkers is moving in this direction. Even where a union is convinced that such "deviation" from standard contracts is desirable, national companies may be reluctant to decentralize authority in such matters. It may be difficult for national organizations on both sides of the table actively to encourage local initiative; the whole history of bargaining may be against it, but it is indispensable for success in medical markets. The Community Health Association in Detroit, however, initiated by the UAW, indicates the possibilities when a union with national wage bargains makes a determined effort to establish a local prepaid health program. But its long period of incubation is testimony to the elaborate social engineering required.

National Support with a Local Focus

It is clear that the structure of collective bargaining in most manufacturing unions is not appropriate for effective confrontation of the purveyors of medical services. Large sectors of the labor movement are built on economic lines of occupations and industrial sectors, and a relatively small part of the financial and organizational resources go toward community-level activity. This has not always been so, but the once powerful "city centrals" have little authority left in matters of union contracts or negotiations, subjects that are almost exclusively the jurisdiction of national unions. And yet direct-service health planning brings certain economies of scale that cannot be realized by most unions "going it alone." Furthermore, the opposition of a medical society in a community can be offset only with considerable community support. The elaborate planning and community organization required puts more responsibility on central labor unions or joint committees than they can usually sustain.

If the further growth of small, one-union clinics is to be averted, channels must be created that are sensitive to local aspirations but by which the headquarters of international unions can co-operate for sustained community health bargaining in any promising locality. Inter-union co-operation at many levels has produced results in some political elections and is being developed in union organizing campaigns. Lessons from these experiences may help in the necessary restructuring. The same kind of advance planning, assessment of resources, and selection of target areas used in political action and organizing may be able to build more "muscle" into community health bargaining.

A Community-wide Perspective

So long as a union does not confuse its security needs with the medical needs of its membership, it will find that the health interests of its members are best served in terms of the health resources of the entire community. "Exclusivist" thinking, on the other hand, while it can build edifices, does not solve health problems, and makes others. Herein lies the importance of multi-union planning directed to community needs, and leaving the door open to other groups. The interests of co-operatives, public employees, hospitals, and many doctors frequently lie in the same direction.

The legal climate should be expertly canvassed in advance. Medical society regulation or legal provisions buttressing medical society control should be regarded as formal only. There has been enough litigation to show that the rhetoric of medical society control has little to do with ethics and much to do with business advantages. If a genuine desire can be created for closed-panel plans as a better approach to practicing medicine, the formal strictures can be eliminated through legislative action or court decision.

Support from within the medical community must be sought locally and nationally because the success of any medical plan rests heavily on its staff. Medical school faculties, physicians associated with pre-paid group practice centers, and the Group Health Association of America can aid in the planning and can help offset objections of local doctors who feel threatened. The United Auto Workers' Conference on Quality was an important part of the early planning for the Community Health Association. The proper role for medical authority in the policy-making and administration of a health center must be worked out in the early stages.

The potential population to be covered have many existing relationships that must be recognized and respected in health center planning. They are employees, union members, citizens with a stake in public opinion, and patients of doctors with a stake in the status quo. Success in planning and administering a health center requires continuous involvement of the membership. Initial surveys of community resources and the extent of prepayment coverage will stimulate critical evaluation of existing arrangements. Opportunities to visit successful programs and to talk with informed people must be encouraged. The educational effort should include basic information about health values, about the economics of medicine, about the role of professionals, and about the place for consumer participation. The effort to encourage a positive attitude on the part of both enrollees and professional staff must carry through the planning stages and into the administrative arrangements and day-to-day operation of the health center.

Whether individual choice of alternative plans can be incorporated from the beginning will depend on several considerations. There always is a built-in bias for the existing arrangements, and nobody will select new medical service arrangements simply because they are new. It is difficult to appreciate fully the possibilities of group practice without some experience with it. On the other hand, initial inclusion of an alternative choice arrangement may serve to diminish the fear of being forced into something unknown; if combined with an effective educational campaign, initial alternative choice may not threaten the number of enrollees necessary for success. The stance of doctors themselves has to be taken into account: if physicians decide to fight the introduction of a prepaid group practice plan, they could create such an atmosphere of hostility that alternative choice becomes a luxury that cannot be afforded in the initial stages. Under a better climate, alternative choice does serve a positive purpose in helping to raise the general level of understanding of the practice of modern medicine. It can be an annual opportunity for evaluation and decision. In no case should it be used by the staff of a group practice plan simply as a safety valve for malcontents who probably have trouble relating to physicians under any conditions of practice.

The Political Dimension

Labor has become more of an integrated part of American social life, and health bargaining is part of this process. Being close to the sensitive junctures of community organization means that alliances are made and enemies are identified. Any effort to change the medical institutions of a community has immediate and dramatic political implications. The hand of government is apparent in at least three different ways in community health bargaining—as umpire, as buyer and investor, and as equalizer.[6]

Government as Umpire

Government has a key role in mapping the terrain and establishing the ground rules for the struggle of private interest. We have noted at least five points at which governmental intervention can have beneficial results:

1. Regulatory commissions can encourage Blue Cross to emphasize certain of its originating principles that relate to the public interest, and help it to assume the mantle of chosen instrument for certain public purposes.

2. State insurance laws can be amended to provide for the codification and regulation of the commission policies of commercial insurance carriers. Where brokers and agents operate across state lines there should be some degree of federal regulation. Unjustifiable legal obstacles to self-insurance should be eliminated.

3. Public regulatory and investigative bodies can acknowledge the responsibility of health and welfare funds to be intelligent buyers of medical services. The criteria of efficient administration that might be applied to an insurance company are inappropriate to health and welfare funds which are engaged in surveys, surveillance, and developing alternative medical care resources.

4. By its regulation of collective bargaining, the government can improve union performance in the medical market. Administration of Section 8 of the Labor-Management Relations Act, which deals with good faith bargaining, has impeded access to data on health and welfare financing.

5. Tax exemption of employee contributions to group health plans, as in Canada, would diminish bargaining conflicts on the contributory issue, since employer contributions are tax exempt.

6. Repeal of state laws that allow only doctors to incorporate pre-paid service plans, or that give medical societies policy control or veto power over such plans would go far to restoring equality in health bargaining. In these cases, government is in effect supporting a medical society monopoly over the organization of the medical market. Medical societies' support of these laws, more than anything else, shows that their basic concern is not with government intervention, as such, but with any and all ways of enhancing their power to resist experimentation and economic change.

Changes in the medical market place are of direct concern to the public, and government has an obligation through its regulatory powers to tip the balance so that more rapid social change can take place through health bargaining.

Government as Buyer and Investor

Among the buyers in the medical market are federal, state, and local governments. Each year they buy about one-fourth of the more than $30 billion in medical services and supplies sold in the United States. Government expenditures for these purposes in 1966 reached an estimated $8.5 to $9 billion (another $2 billion was spent for medical research and construction).[7] As big buyers and big investors, governments have a profound effect on the kind and quality of services provided. The day when workmen's compensation or welfare vendor payments for medical care were made without any concern about the quality or price of those services is rapidly disappearing, and we may hope for increasingly sophisticated surveillance and careful evaluation of performance.

As an investor in health facilities, government will have an important role in shaping the medicine of the future. Hospital development under the Hill-Burton Act can alter the nature of private practice. Government is increasingly involved in state-wide and regional planning of medical facilities, in hospital utilization procedures and in hospital cost accounting, and in providing support to increase the supply of doctors and other medical personnel. The Community Health Planning and Public Health Services Amendments of 1966 may be the beginning of a new effort to rationalize the organization of health care facilities.

Also enacted in 1966 was a law providing government guarantee of 90 per cent of mortgage loans to direct-service medical plans. This may help in attracting capital, but government should in addition make its own direct contribution through the loan of public monies to aid in the development of hospital outpatient facilities, ambulatory clinics, and hospitals built by consumer groups, and by permitting tax exemptions for contributions to direct-service prepayment plans. Prepaid group-practice plans are an important demonstration area for testing ways in which medical care can be organized more efficiently.

Many of the vital questions of the day lie in the administration of the hospital and physicians' payments by the Social Security Administration. Will the funds be administered in such a way as to encourage efficient use of hospital facilities? Will standards for hospitals and nursing homes be established and enforced? Can Blue Cross, as an agent in the administration of the program, exercise more surveillance than it has so far done over its own work? It remains to be seen whether the performance will meet the test suggested by Dr. Frank Furstenberg, medical director of Sinai Hospital's outpatient department in Baltimore: "The fund itself should not become a vendor-paying agency, as indeed, in many instances, the Blue Cross has been. . . . Federal funds should be used in such a fashion that sensitive service will be given, that there will be standards for services, and that this should be kept under a public agency's authority."[8]

Both public and private efforts will lose much by separating the financing of care from planning and institutional reshaping. The controller of the purse must exercise some surveillance over the production of the services he is buying—whether that controller is a consumer group, a Blue Cross organization, or a government agency. The most satisfactory direction in which medical care institutions can evolve is towards the development of necessary controls; if this evolution is to be a rational process, discipline is necessary. The objective is the extension of high quality medicine, and two corollaries are efficient use of resources, and education of consumer-patients about modern medicine. To attain these ends, various kinds of checks and balances are necessary, whether self-imposed, or built into the inter-relationships of medical care institutions, or superimposed by government.

Government as Equalizer

Behind both health bargaining and Medicare has been a drive to make modern medical care financially accessible within the framework of democratic values, that is, without demeaning tests of need and dependency. Because it included a means test, the Kerr-Mills Act was an unacceptable substitute for Medicare, which offered health benefits as social insurance and as a claim of right. Our democratic and affluent society is in the process of arriving at a fundamental principle, namely, that medical need alone should determine eligibility for medical service. Tests of economic means, or skin color, or educational sophistication are gradually being taken out of the picture by private and public health planning. The New York Academy of Medicine may have sounded a note for the future: "The availability of health services, as a matter of right, should be based on health needs alone, not on a test of ability to pay. The attainment of this goal requires the broadest possible participation in the systems of financing health services, if individual dignity and self-dependency are to be enhanced."[9]

The real significance of the Social Security Amendments of 1965 lies in the fact that there is no longer an indigent-aid category of medical care for anyone over 65; the historical rule that a means test is required for tax-supported care is thus broken. There are still great gaps to be filled for the disadvantaged, for the unemployed, for migrants, and also for many others of modest means. In some cases the approach can be that of social insurance, in others the direct building and staffing of medical care facilities, for example, those recently contracted by the Office of Economic Opportunity. The problems of quality and utilization and cost are thorny ones that must get further attention from health bargaining and government. If the labor movement is to make one special contribution, it probably will be through emphasizing that services for the protection of health must be attractive to be considered available. There must be dignity for both providers of service and for patients. The programs of the future must conform to the principles of a self-respecting society.

Reference Matter

NOTES

Chapter 1: Wages, Health, and History

1 These plans paid cash benefits for burial expenses and general aid; later they provided benefits in the event of prolonged sickness. They were a kind of group budgeting when individual budgeting was impossible. English medieval craft guilds had programs of mutual assistance and the English friendly societies, on which were patterned the American benevolent societies, began as early as the sixteenth century.

2 James B. Kennedy, *Beneficiary Features of American Trade Unions* (Baltimore: Johns Hopkins University Studies in Historical and Political Science, 1908), p. 9.

3 *Ibid.*

4 The discussions were in terms of both death benefit plans and cash sickness plans. The latter were more difficult to administer but they tided the union man over his illness or unemployment and diminished the temptations to work below the union rate.

5 According to Perlman, the only unions that survived after the Napoleonic Wars were those which had turned to mutual insurance, such as the printers' societies, whereas the shoemakers, which had remained a purely trade organization, "went to the wall." Selig Perlman, *History of Trade Unionism in the United States* (New York: Macmillan, 1923), p. 7.

6 Kennedy, *Beneficiary Features of American Trade Unions,* p. 11.

7 Nathaniel Minkoff, *Union Health and Welfare Plans,* U.S. Dept. of Labor, Bureau of Labor Statistics Bull. No. 900 (Washington, D.C.: Government Printing Office, 1947), p. 22.

8 Matthew Woll, "Why Take Union Group Insurance Rather Than a Benefit Plan?" *The American Photo Engraver,* XXII, No. 5 (April, 1930), 451.

9 *International Teamster* (April, 1944), p. 21. Many of the AF of L plans have continued, however, covering over a million members and paying out over $60 million a year in death, sick, unemployment, old-age, disability, and strike benefits. In recent years they have not been improved substantially, usually being supplemented by negotiated benefit plans.

10 The credit union, however, serves some of the same purposes.

11 Pierce Williams, *The Purchase of Medical Care Through Fixed Periodic Prepayment* (New York: National Bureau of Economic Research, 1932), pp. 292–98.

12 Jerome L. Schwartz, "Early History of Prepaid Medical Care Plans," *Bulletin of the History of Medicine,* XXXIX (1965), 455.

13 Michael M. Davis, *America Organizes Medicine* (New York: Harper, 1941), pp. 147–48.

14 Williams, *Purchase of Medical Care* . . . , pp. 3–4.

15 Ten states in this period had commissions studying the need for government health insurance but "the selfish and highly organized oppposition of commercial insurance companies and medical societies succeeded in so misleading the public mind as to the true purposes and merits of health insurance, that legislative work in this field became totally impossible in the period immediately following."—John R. Commons and John B. Andrews, *Principles of Labor Legislation* (New York: Harper, 1927), p. 465.

16 Jay V. Strong, *Employee Benefit Plans in Operation* (Washington, D.C.: Bureau of National Affairs, 1951), pp. 125–26.

17 The National Labor Relations Act ban on company unions required that steps be taken to divorce the mutual aid association from management. But the Board also noted that nothing in its order should be taken to require the company to vary or abandon the substantive features of any existing contract on rates of pay or other conditions of employment. The practical effect of the ruling was that a welfare plan could be kept intact even though a company-dominated labor organization was ordered dissolved. See Kresge Department Store, 77 NLRB 212 (1948).

18 Minkoff, *Union Health and Welfare Plans,* p. 13.

19 Where employers still maintain control over the benefit program, the union is apt to be either weak or nonexistent. There are exceptions, however; some very good plans combining medical services and liberal insurance benefits exist side by side with effective unions, e.g., Cutler-Hammer (International Association of Machinists) and Allen-Bradley Co. (International Brotherhood of Electrical Workers) in Milwaukee.

20 Collective bargaining on health and welfare first occurred in 1917 when the International Ladies' Garment Workers' Union and the New York Dress Industry jointly supported the Union Health Center, but after a short time the union and its membership assumed full financial responsibility. Not until 1943 were employer contributions negotiated for this program. In 1923 an employee benefit fund providing unemployment insurance was negotiated by the Amalgamated Clothing Workers and the Hart, Schaffner and Marx plant in Chicago, jointly supported by employer and employee contributions. After the enactment of unemployment compensation, this fund was converted in 1938 to provide weekly disability and death benefits. The first collective bargaining agreement to provide

for non-occupational sickness and accident benefits was negotiated in 1926 by the Public Service Corporation of Newburgh, New York, and the Amalgamated Association of Street and Electric Railway Employees. The contract included life insurance as well as weekly sick benefits.

21 *Daily Proceedings of the Eighth Constitution Convention of the C.I.O. November 20, 1946*, Resolution No. 34 (Washington, D.C.; CIO, 1964).

22 The unions were the Amalgamated Clothing Workers of America, CIO; Federation of Dyers, Finishers, Printers, and Bleachers of America, CIO; United Furniture Workers of America, CIO; United Hatters, Cap and Millinery Workers' International Union, AFL; Upholsterers' International Union of North America, AFL; Hotel and Restaurant Employees, AFL (in its New York Hotel Trades Council, and also in its Chain Service Restaurant Employees' Union); International Jewelry Workers' Union, AFL; International Union of Mine, Mill and Smelter Workers, CIO; and the International Printing Pressmen and Assistants' Union, AFL.

23 The United Auto Workers and Steelworkers were able to lay some advance groundwork for welfare bargaining, nevertheless. The Steelworkers had reached an agreement in May, 1947, with the Allegheny-Ludlum Steel Corporation, replacing a company-established, non-contractual, contributory insurance plan with a bargained program. They also signed a contract with the Aluminum Company of America providing health, sickness, accident, and hospitalization benefits. More significant, the United States Steel Corporation had agreed to study insurance coverage. In June, 1948, the United Auto Workers obtained its first major employee welfare plan under collective bargaining when the Kaiser-Frazer Corporation agreed to put five cents for each hour worked by its employees into a jointly administered social security fund. In both the auto and steel industries, an assault on the main targets waited, however, for a legal determination of whether employers had to bargain on welfare issues.

24 Congressman Hartley's Education and Labor Committee, as quoted in National Labor Relations Board, *Legislative History of the Labor Management Relations Act, 1947*, 2 vols. (Washington, D.C.: Government Printing Office, 1948), I, 320.

25 *Ibid.*, p. 313.

26 The decision turned on a broad interpretation of "wages" as "emoluments of value" as well as a general interpretation of "other conditions of employment": Inland Steel Company, 77 NLRB 1 (1948), aff'd, 170 F.2d 247 (7th Cir. 1949). Also see Black-Clawson Company, 103 NLRB 928 (1953); Anchor Rome Mills, Inc., 86 NLRB 1120 (1949); Allied Mills, Inc., 82 NLRB 854 (1949). Other related issues were soon clarified also. The union's right to negotiate changes in a company-initiated plan was recognized: W. W. Cross & Company, 77 NLRB 1162 (1948), aff'd, 174 F.2d 875 (1st Cir. 1949). Once a union expressed an interest in an established plan, the Board required the employer to consult the

union before modifying his plan: Inland Steel Company. When no plan was in existence and a union indicated its desire to bargain on the subject, it was held that an employer was not free to institute a welfare plan by unilateral action: General Motors Corp., 81 NLRB 779 (1949). The complexity of bargaining on pension plans or other benefits has not excused a refusal to bargain on them, even when there were several unions and different plans involved: Tide Water Associated Oil Company, 85 NLRB 1096 (1949).

27 *Report to the President of the United States on the Labor Dispute in the Basic Steel Industry,* submitted by the Steel Industry Board appointed by the President, July 15, 1949 (Washington, D.C.: Government Printing Office, Sept. 10, 1949), p. 8.

28 In steel there were 236 contracts providing for group insurance and pensions within three months after the Big Steel settlement. The auto pattern was set by Ford in September and by the next summer all major auto companies had negotiated insurance and pensions.

Chapter 2: Health Experiments in the Needle Trades

1 Benjamin Stolberg, *Tailor's Progress* (New York: Doubleday, 1944), p. 14.

2 Adolph Held, "Health and Welfare Funds in the Needle Trades," *Industrial and Labor Relations Review,* V, No. 2 (Jan., 1948), 248.

3 While many locals established these funds despite the difficulties involved, others were satisfied with the illness and death benefits of the Workmen's Circle, a Jewish fraternal organization.

4 Data on the funds are available in the ILGWU annual *Financial Report of the Health, Welfare, and Retirement Funds.* This source is used here unless otherwise indicated.

5 The contribution desired by the union includes vacations, but in some areas vacation payments are made directly by the employers, and payments to the fund are at a lower rate.

6 David Dubinsky did not hesitate to turn over to a local district attorney two union accountants who had conspired with some employers and accepted bribes to certify underpayments to a health and welfare fund. *Monthly Labor Review,* LXXVII, No. 6 (June, 1954), 620.

7 *New York Times,* May 11, 1958, p. 46.

8 Held, "Health and Welfare Funds in the Needle Trades," p. 253.

9 Fred Slavick, *The Operation of Sickness Benefit Plans in Collective Bargaining,* Dept. of Economics and Social Institutions, Industrial Relations Section, Research Report Series No. 84 (Princeton: Princeton University, 1951), p. 79.

10 Health Center activities are summarized in convention reports every four years: ILGWU, *Report of the General Executive Board to the Convention,* 1952, 1956, 1960, 1964.

11 Another factor that permits a better health center in St. Louis is the success of the Teamsters' Labor Health Institute there, which fought out
some of the issues dividing labor and medical authorities, and in this way,
helped pave the way for a more advanced program than the ILGWU
has been able to achieve in most of its Health Centers.

12 E. Richard Weinerman, M.D., "An Appraisal of Medical Care in Group
Health Centers," *American Journal of Public Health*, XLVI (March,
1956), 301.

13 Frederick F. Umhey, "Health and Welfare in the Ladies' Garment Industry," presented before the Eighth Annual Congress on Industrial Health,
printed in *Occupational Medicine*, V, No. 3 (March, 1948), 265.

14 Held, "Health and Welfare Funds in the Needle Trades," p. 256.

15 Dr. Leo Price, former director of the New York Union Health Center,
never joined with other health plan doctors and unions in the American
Labor Health Association or its successor, the Group Health Association
of America. This association promotes prepaid group practice and other
advanced developments in medical economics that are irritating to official medicine.

16 For an excellent study of the Dress Joint Board's health and welfare administration, see Morris Sackman, *Welfare Bargaining in Action*, New
York State School of Industrial and Labor Relations Research Bull. No.
3 (Ithaca: Cornell University Press, July, 1949).

17 This background is developed in detail in U. S. Congress, Senate Committee on Labor and Public Welfare, *Welfare and Pension Plan Investigation, Final Report*, 84 Cong., 2 sess. (April 16, 1956), pp. 115–22.

18 David J. Faber, *The Administration Under Collective Bargaining of Welfare Plans Based on Employer Contributions* (Washington, D.C.: National Wage Stabilization Board, Sept. 18, 1956), p. 7.

19 Adolph Held has put it this way: "The plan of the Amalgamated, it will
be noted, is highly centralized; the relation of the insured is mainly with
the office of the insurance company; the plan requires little contact by the
members with the office of the Union." "Health and Welfare Funds in the
Needle Trades," p. 252.

20 ACWA Research Dept., "Memorandum on Medical Care and Hospital
Insurance Benefits Provided Under the Social Insurance Program of the
Amalgamated Clothing Workers of America" (mimeo., Jan. 3, 1951), p. 2.

21 For further information on the conditions of these programs, see ACWA,
General Executive Board Reports to the Biennial Conventions, 1954–
1966.

22 See the *Annual Reports of the Sidney Hillman Health Center of New
York;* also, American Medical Association, *A Survey of Union Health
Centers* (Chicago: AMA, 1958); Margaret C. Klem and Margaret F.
McKiever, *Management and Union Health and Medical Programs*, U.S.
Dept. of Health, Education, and Welfare, Public Health Service Pub. No.
329 (Washington, D.C.: Government Printing Office, 1953), pp. 116–

34; Morris Brand, M.D., "The Medical Service Plan of the Sidney Hill-
man Health Center of New York," presented at the Medical Care Section,
American Public Health Association, Oct. 24, 1952; Abe Bluestein, "New
Horizons for Medical Care," presented at the National Conference on
Social Welfare, Sec. III, May 14, 1958; and the following papers by Dr.
Joseph A. Langbord, Medical Director of the Philadelphia Center: (with
George Shucker, M.D.) "Problems Encountered in the Operation of the
Health and Welfare Plan of the Philadelphia Male Apparel Industry,"
Pennsylvania Medical Journal, LIX (April, 1956), 457–61; "A New
Concept of Voluntary Prepaid Medical Care," presented before the Presi-
dent's Commission on the Health Needs of the Nation, Aug. 11, 1952;
"Evolution of a Comprehensive Industrial Health Plan," presented before
the Annual Congress on Industrial Health, Pittsburgh, Pa., Jan. 18, 1952.
23 This program, the only one of its kind in a union health plan, is under the
direction of Dr. Hyman J. Weiner. A mental health team including psy-
chiatrists, psychologists, social workers, and nurses is working with a
labor-management committee established for that purpose.

Chapter 3: Miners and Their Powerful Fund

1 H. L. Morris, *The Plight of the Bituminous Coal Miner* (Philadelphia:
University of Pennsylvania Press, 1934), p. 92.
2 1916 Constitution of the United Mine Workers of America, Art. XXI,
Sec. 9.
3 *United Mine Workers' Journal* (Aug. 10, 1916), p. 91.
4 *Ibid.* (March 12, 1903), p. 5.
5 *Ibid.* (Dec. 30, 1915), p. 9.
6 Local Union 1855 operated a co-operative hospital. Each miner paid
$1.60 a month and received free ward facilities or a 37.5 per cent reduc-
tion on a private-room charge. *1946 Convention Proceedings,* United
Mine Workers of America (Washington, D.C.: UMWA, 1946), p. 340.
7 By 1946 about half the miners had some such arrangement. *Report of the
Coal Mines Administration, A Medical Survey of the Bituminous Industry,* survey conducted by Joel T. Boone, Rear Admiral (M.C.), U.S.
Navy (Washington, D.C.: Government Printing Office, 1947), p. 6.
8 Dr. Warren Draper, Medical Director of the Fund, as quoted in Ira Wolfert, "The Miners' Fund—A Tribute to Good Management," *Reader's
Digest* (Sept., 1956), p. 173.
9 *United Mine Workers of America Welfare and Retirement Fund. Report
for Year Ending June 30, 1966* (Washington, D.C.: UMW, 1966).
Annual reports in recent years have shown some slight decline in fund
revenues going to hospital and medical care, down to $48,816,359 in
1965, until the jump in the 1966 fiscal year. It is anticipated that there
will be substantial savings to the fund as a result of enactment of Medicare, but increasing medical care costs are expected to reduce some of
this gain.

10 Reported by Wolfert, "The Miners' Fund—A Tribute to Good Management," p. 178.

11 *1918, 1919 Convention Proceedings*, United Mine Workers of America (n.p.: n.d.).

12 *United Mine Workers' Journal* (March 15, 1946), p. 3.

13 *U. S. News and World Report* (Nov. 19, 1948), p. 35.

14 *Ibid.*

15 For a more detailed account of the early years of the Welfare and Retirement Fund, see U.S. Congress, Senate Committee on Labor and Public Welfare, *Welfare and Pension Plan Investigation, Final Report*, 84 Cong., 2 sess. (April 16, 1956), pp. 166–91 [cited hereafter as *Douglas Report*].

16 The preceding three quotations come from the *Report of the Coal Mines Administration . . . .*, pp. 122–27, 191–93, 192, respectively.

17 *New York Times*, May 15, 1946, p. 14.

18 *Ibid.*, p. 1.

19 See "Pension and Insurance Bargaining," speech by Joseph E. Moody, President, Southern Coal Producers' Association, in *Collective Bargaining Negotiations and Contracts* (Washington, D.C.: BNA, Oct. 23, 1953), p. 2 of UMW notes.

20 *National Bituminous Wage Agreement* (July, 1947)

21 See Robert J. Myers, "Experience of the U.M.W.A. Welfare and Retirement Fund," *Industrial and Labor Relations Review*, X (Oct., 1956), 93–100.

22 Van Horn *v.* Lewis, 79 F.Supp. 541 (D.C., D.C., 1948).

23 *1948 Constitutional Convention Proceedings*, United Mine Workers of America (n.p.: n.d.).

24 The eligibility conditions for pensions have been changed a number of times. An important change was made in 1953 when the conditions for eligibility were changed to require that the twenty years of service must have been within the thirty years preceding retirement, and that the applicant must have been regularly employed immediately prior to May 29, 1946. These changes have caused a considerable number of persons to be denied pensions who would have been eligible under the former requirements. Experience showed that many individuals who had retired or who had left the industry prior to May 29, 1946, were obtaining temporary employment as miners only to qualify for pensions, and the mounting costs of the pension program required tightening eligibility conditions.

25 *Douglas Report*, p. 190.

26 Louis S. Reed, "Impact of Union Welfare Funds on the Practice of Medicine," *Journal of the National Medical Association*, XLVIII, No. 6 (Nov., 1956), 394.

27 As quoted by John Pemberton, "The Coal Miner and His Doctor," *New England Journal of Medicine*, CCLIII, No. 6 (Aug., 1955), 244.

28 Dr. Warren Draper in a talk to physicians in Charleston, West Virginia, reported in the *United Mine Workers' Journal* (Oct. 1, 1952), pp. 5–6.

29 *Ibid.*
30 *Ibid.*
31 In December, 1954, the *Journal of the American Medical Association* carried the following editorial: "The relationship between the medical profession and the United Mine Workers of America provides a heartening example of how labor and medicine, when each side is represented by medical leaders sincerely devoted to high standards and imbued with a desire for mutual understanding, can work together amicably and effectively in a program to improve medical care for workers. . . . The American Medical Association is more than happy to tell the world about it, for the story reflects credit on all concerned. Labor leaders, labor union medical administrators, and physicians everywhere can learn valuable lessons from the way in which organized medicine and the United Mine Workers have sat down together to iron out a host of difficult problems." —*Journal of the American Medical Association,* CLVI, No. 15 (Dec. 11, 1954), 1405–06.
32 These are conclusions reached after interviews with some doctors in the coal fields, reported by John R. Lindsey, "Medicine by the Ton," *Medical Economics* (Oct., 1955), p. 117.
33 *Ibid.*
34 *Ibid.*
35 Dr. Edgar W. Meiser of the state society admitted at the meeting that the broader issue was simply one of reimbursement: "Let us be absolutely honest about the whole thing; every problem that has arisen between labor and medicine in the operation of these funds—when stripped to their barest essentials—is based on one simple, single thing . . . the dollar." As quoted in the *United Mine Workers' Journal* (Nov. 1, 1955), p. 10.
36 For the UMW version of these disputes, see Warren F. Draper, M.D., "The Quest of the U.M.W.A. Welfare and Retirement Fund for the Best Medical Care Obtainable for its Beneficiaries," presented in Hot Springs, Va. (Nov., 1957) [reprinted]; "The Medical Care Program of the United Mine Workers of America Welfare and Retirement Fund," presented in Boston, Mass. (March, 1958) [reprinted]; and "Facts Pertaining to the Medical and Hospital Care Program of the U.M.W.A. Welfare and Retirement Fund," *Pennsylvania Medical Journal,* LXI (Sept., 1958), 1185–89.
37 As quoted by Wallace Croatman, "Is Labor Through with Private Medicine," *Medical Economics* (Oct., 1957), p. 187.
38 *Ibid.,* p. 194.
39 Statement to author by staff members of Welfare and Retirement Fund, Jan., 1957.
40 Warren F. Draper, M.D., "Medical Program of Welfare and Retirement Fund of the United Mine Workers of America," *Journal of the American Medical Association,* CLXXII, No. 1 (Jan. 2, 1960), 33–36.

41 This policy developed gradually over a period of time and without any fanfare. The fund staff was convinced of this line of development as a way to reduce hospital costs before the fund trustees were. Lewis himself has never disavowed the principle he established, that the industry should bear the full cost of health and medical care, whereas clinics permit supplemental financing from alternative sources such as local unions or members themselves. Although some of these clinics have existed for almost fourteen years, there has been little about them in UMW or fund literature. The 1966 annual report, however, does have this to say:

"Through arrangements with physicians carefully selected by the Fund's Medical, Health, and Hospital Service beneficiaries are assured of receiving the highest quality of medical care obtainable including the benefit of new techniques and improved methods of diagnosis and treatment constantly being developed. Important features of the Hospital and Medical Care Program include services of managing physicians who become responsible for personally supervising the entire range of medical care considered to be in the best interest of the beneficiary, utilization of group practice clinics providing a wide range of preventive and corrective out-patient services by medical specialists, and arrangements with universities, and other medical centers." *United Mine Workers . . . Report for Year Ending June 30, 1966,* p. 13.

42 According to Pemberton ("The Coal Miner and His Doctor," p. 245), the Russelton Clinic, in Pennsylvania, reduced hospital admissions by half.

43 *American Journal of Public Health,* XLVI (Dec., 1956), 1604.

Chapter 4: *The Mainstream: Beginnings in Autos and Steel*

1 For background on General Motors' and United States Steel's welfare programs, see U.S. Congress, Senate Committee on Labor and Public Welfare, *Welfare and Pension Plan Investigation, Final Report,* 84 Cong., 2 sess. (April 16, 1956).

2 U.S. Congress, Senate, *Welfare and Pension Plans Investigation, Hearings Before a Subcommittee of the Committee on Labor and Public Welfare,* 84 Cong., 1 sess. (1955), 3 parts, Part I, p. 111.

3 Inland Steel Company, 77 NLRB 1 (1948), aff'd, 170 F.2d 247 (7th Cir. 1949); W. W. Cross & Company, 77 NLRB 1162 (1948), aff'd, 174 F.2d 875 (1st Cir. 1949).

4 Eighty-seven per cent of the auto workers interviewed found medical costs difficult to meet; 59 per cent thought the government should develop a program to ease the burden of medical costs. When asked specifically if unions should attempt to meet the problem, 80 per cent replied that they should. "The average wage of the auto workers is around $200 a year less than the minimum budget for health and decency. Of the auto workers interviewed in the poll, 41 per cent of those feeling the need for

medical care had not seen a doctor at all. . . . Auto workers are not receiving and at present wage levels cannot afford the health services they and their families need. This need is immediate and pressing." Harry Becker, speech before National Health Assembly, Washington, D.C., May 2, 1948.

5 See *U.A.W.–C.I.O. Collective Bargaining Handbook for Workers' Security Program* (Detroit: UAW, n.d.), p. 17.

6 *Ibid.*

7 Kaiser-Frazer served as a trial balloon preparatory to "big three" negotiations. See Jerome Pollack, "Kaiser-Frazer U.A.W. Social Security Program," *Industrial and Labor Relations Review*, I (Oct., 1952), 94–109.

8 Report of Walter Reuther in *Proceedings, Ninth Constitutional Convention, United Automobile, Aircraft, and Agricultural Implement Workers Union of America (U.A.W.–C.I.O.), 1949* (Detroit: UAW, 1949), p. 9.

9 On March 1, 1950, the insurance program went into effect, providing life insurance in amounts ranging from $2,000 to $4,500; retired life insurance after age 65 of $1,250; weekly disability benefit of $26 per week for 26 weeks payable the first day for accident, 8th day for sickness; and 70 days Blue Cross hospitalization coverage. In September, 1951, a $200 Blue Shield surgical schedule was added. The Blue Cross and Blue Shield covered dependents. The original agreement had specified that the union would abstain from demands on the insurance program until 1954, but a favorable experience and the accrual of funds made the company agreeable to adding the surgical benefits. For detail on these and subsequent collective bargaining developments in the steel industry, see the regular reporting and year-end summaries featured in the *Monthly Labor Review*, published by the U.S. Dept. of Labor.

10 See Evan Keith Rowe, "Health and Welfare Plans in the Automobile Industry," *Monthly Labor Review*, Vol. LXXIII, No. 3 (Sept., 1951).

Chapter 5:   The Partnership in Steel

1 Press Release, United Steelworkers of America, Aug. 5, 1949.

2 A Bureau of Labor Statistics' survey in 1951 shows the application of variations from the pattern in the basic steel industry. Of 46 plans covering 434,000 workers, the benefits varied as follows:

Life Insurance: Nine plans covering 75 per cent of the workers had benefits graduated according to earnings: for a worker making $1.50 an hour ($3,000 a year), insurance varied from $2,500 to $5,000, but over half were at the lower end of this range. The remaining 36 plans, covering 25 per cent of the workers, provided flat payments ranging from $1,000 to $4,000, with most in the lower half of this range.

Accidental Death and Dismemberment: Only 12 plans covering 12 per cent of the workers had this benefit, which was usually a flat benefit varying from $1,000 to $4,000. (This type of coverage has been discouraged by the union.)

Temporary Disability: This protection was provided by all plans. Two-thirds of the workers were in 38 plans, which provided uniform or flat benefits of from $18 to $30, depending on the plan; the other 7 plans graduated benefits according to income. In both the flat and graduated plans, the great majority of workers were entitled to $26 a week for 26 weeks following a waiting week, except in case of accident.

Hospitalization: Sixteen plans, covering 60 per cent of the workers, included Blue Cross for up to 70 days. This covered semi-private rooms and meals, general nursing care, operating and delivery rooms, anesthetics administered by a hospital employee, casts and splints, surgical dressing, laboratory examinations, basal metabolism tests, X-ray examinations, electrocardiograms, physiotherapy and hydrotherapy, oxygen, drugs and medicines and administration of blood and plasma (but not the blood or plasma itself). Thirty plans provided cash indemnity benefits, usually $8 to $10 daily, with extras at 10 or 20 times the daily benefits, running for 30 to 70 days, the majority being at 70 days.

Surgical: Forty plans covering 54 per cent of the workers had surgical coverage, the majority being the Blue Shield. The maximum allowances for specified operations ranged from $150 to $240, depending on the plan, with over half of the plans at $200.

Medical: Only 6 plans covering 4 per cent of the workers included this, 2 including home and office calls and the others providing in-hospital medical benefits only.

Dependent coverage: Provided in 41 plans covering 99 per cent of the workers. Under all the Blue Cross–Blue Shield plans and 11 of the 14 indemnity plans the dependent coverage was the same as for the employee.

By far the most frequent method of financing was 5¢ per hour, 2½¢ each from the companies and the employees as in the large steel companies. *See Monthly Labor Review,* LXXIII, No. 4 (Oct., 1951), 447–51.

3 For details of benefit levels see United Steelworkers of America, *Special Officers' Report on 1954 Insurance and Pension Negotiations, Convention Proceedings* (Sept., 1954) [Cited hereafter as *Special Officers' Report. . . .*]. These benefits, which were subsequently extended elsewhere, were refinements of the basic coverage and included: (1) inpatient hospitalization for mental or nervous disorders or for tuberculosis for 30 days; (2) radiation therapy for a hospital inpatient or outpatient or in a physician's office; (3) hospitalization for physiotherapy and hydrotherapy; (4) administration of anesthesia, whether billed by the hospital or by a physician; (5) outpatient surgery performed at a hospital; (6) hospitalization for the extraction of impacted teeth; (7) up to 120 days of maternity coverage in complicated cases; (8) non-occupational accident (emergency) cases if treatment begins within 48 hours after accident and care is rendered in a hospital; and (9) oxygen, regardless of source of supply,

if administered in a hospital. United Steelworkers of America, *Insurance, Pension and Unemployment Benefits* (Sept., 1956) [cited hereafter as *Insurance . . . Benefits*]. For developments in subsequent negotiations, see the regular reporting in *Monthly Labor Review*.

4 United Steelworkers of America, *Special Study on the Medical Care Program for Steelworkers and their Families* (Sept., 1960), p. 2 [cited hereafter as *Special Study . . .*].

5 In 1960 the union argued that its smaller units with 150 to 350 employees had medical care benefits that compared favorably with those of much larger units in other industries. *Ibid.*, p. 3.

6 In preparing for 1954 negotiations the union requested considerable information and material for joint studies. Some of the basic steel companies "restricted the fields they were willing to investigate, so that not as much useful data was obtained as had been anticipated." Of companies other than basic steel, "many failed to respond or failed to respond adequately. . . ." *Special Officers' Report . . .* , p. 78.

7 The financial information that the companies are willing to supply is analyzed by the Joint Committees on Insurance and Pensions (study and review committees) set up in each major company and by the union consultant, Murray Latimer. To that extent, the administration of every insurance plan is reviewed to see that all contributions and expenditures are in accordance with the provisions of the agreements. The union has been trying to extend the use of these committees to all plants where it has contracts. See *Statement of Policy of the United Steelworkers of America as to Health and Welfare Funds* adopted March 4, 1955 (Pittsburgh: United Steelworkers of America, 1955).

8 See U.S. Congress, Senate Committee on Labor and Public Welfare, *Welfare and Pension Plan Investigation, Final Report*, 84 Cong., 2 sess. (April 16, 1956), pp. 133–34 [cited hereafter as *Douglas Report*].

9 This generalization is suggested by a survey of 26 companies of widely varying sizes made by the Douglas Subcommittee. *Douglas Report*, pp. 94–96.

10 See *Insurance . . . Benefits*, pp. 10 ff.

11 These different ways included: (a) drawing on funds accumulated during the period of high employment following the Korean crisis; (b) by company advances in anticipation of dividends; (c) at Bethlehem, by a special company contribution of $2,500,000 over and above the company's 2½¢ per hour contribution for life insurance for employees who retired before 1950.

12 At Republic, Youngstown, and Inland Steel, where the rising costs were not a problem because the insurance provided cash indemnity benefits, the employees also in effect increased their contribution by having to pay the higher hospital and doctor charges.

13 *Memorandum of Agreement Between United Steelworkers of America and United States Steel Corporation, Bethlehem Steel Company, Repub-*

*lic Steel Corporation, Jones & Laughlin Steel Corporation, The Youngs-
town Sheet and Tube Company, Inland Steel Company, Armco Steel
Corporation, Great Lakes Steel Corporation, Wheeling Steel Corporation,
Pittsburgh Steel Company, Allegheny Ludlum Steel Corporation, Colorado Fuel and Iron Corporation* (July 27, 1956), p. 5.

14 In response to a survey conducted by the Douglas Subcommittee, eight
companies reported that the union had no voice in selecting the carrier.
Eighteen companies reported that selection of the carrier was through
bidding. *Douglas Report*, p. 94.

15 Bernard Greenberg, Steelworkers' insurance specialist, reports that there
are exceptions. "Largely, we urge Blue Cross. We don't do it all of the
time and I have been able to hand them a couple of surprises from time
to time when we have not pushed the Blue Cross, when we have felt
Blue Cross was not the proper arrangement." Remarks in Proceedings,
Conference on Negotiation and Administration of Health and Welfare
Plans of the Industrial Union Department, AFL–CIO, Washington, D.C.,
March 27–28, 1957 (typewritten copy at AFL–CIO headquarters) [cited
hereafter as IUD Health and Welfare Conference].

16 Tomayko, remarks before *ibid.*

17 Remarks of Tomayko and Greenberg, before *ibid.*

18 Greenberg recalls an amusing case that illustrates the problems faced by
a responsible union officer: "The local union wanted to have a local union
member, who was a broker, named as the broker of record, so I asked for
the man who was pushing him to stand up and explain why it should be
him, why it wasn't somebody else. 'Well, this guy is a real friend of ours.'
He had promised that a part of his brokerage fee would go to P.A.C.
[Political Action Committee]. I said, 'Is that the basis on which we will
determine who the broker will be? I am quite sure that if we announce
the percentage you give to P.A.C. will be the basis on which the broker
is chosen, we can have some fine competition and get it on that basis.'"
Remarks before *ibid.*

In the *Statement of Policy of the United Steelworkers of America as
to Health and Welfare Funds*, adopted March 4, 1955, Sec. 4 states that
no officer, member employee or representative or other person connected
with the union shall personally profit in any way from any union insurance or pension program.

19 U.S. Congress, Senate, *Welfare and Pension Plans Investigation, Hearings Before a Subcommittee of the Committee on Labor and Public Welfare*, 84 Cong., 1 sess. (1955), 3 parts, Part 1, p. 127 [cited hereafter as
Welfare and Pension Plans Investigation, Hearings . . .].

20 *Ibid.*, p. 121.

21 *Ibid.*, p. 119.

22 See *Insurance . . . Benefits*, p. 6, and *Welfare and Pension Plans Investigation, Hearings . . .* , p. 127.

23 David J. McDonald, "Health Care Objectives," speech before the Annual

Conference of Blue Cross and Blue Shield Plans, Hollywood, Fla., April, 1953 (United Steelworkers of America, 1953), p. 7.

24 *Welfare and Pension Plans Investigation, Hearings . . .* , p. 134.

25 *Employee Benefit Plan Review* (Sept., 1956), pp. 7–10.

26 *Special Study . . .* , p. 96.

27 John Tomayko, remarks before the Pennsylvania State Medical Society, as quoted by Louis S. Reed, "Impact of Union Welfare Funds on the Practice of Medicine," *Journal of the National Medical Association,* XLVIII, No. 6 (Nov., 1956), 392.

28 *Special Study . . .* , p. 75.

29 John Tomayko, remarks before the IUD Health and Welfare Conference.

30 *Health and Welfare Newsletter,* Cooperative Health Federation of America, VI, No. 6 (May, 1957), 1.

31 *Special Study . . .* , p. 96.

32 *Ibid.*

33 *Ibid.,* p. 97.

34 *Ibid.,* p. 28.

35 McDonald, "Health Care Objectives," p. 10.

36 *Ibid.*

37 From David McDonald's talk to the Pennsylvania Medical Society in December, 1958, as quoted by John R. Lindsey, "What the Steelworkers Want from Medicine," *Medical Economics* (Jan. 5, 1959), p. 126.

38 *Ibid.,* p. 128.

39 In this speech in 1957, Tomayko also gave the first intimation that changes were brewing in the union's policy. *Health and Welfare Newsletter,* CHFA, VI, No. 6 (May, 1957), 1.

40 *Special Study . . .* , p. 8.

41 *Ibid.,* p. 52.

42 *Ibid.,* p. 7.

43 *Ibid.,* pp. 86–93.

44 *Ibid.,* p. 9.

45 As quoted in Lindsey, "What the Steelworkers Want from Medicine," p. 126.

46 Ted Goldberg, "Breakthrough in Canada," *I.U.D. Digest* (Winter, 1962), p. 6.

47 *Ibid.,* p. 10.

Chapter 6: *The Vocal Auto Workers*

1 For the successive settlements referred to here, see the reporting in the U.S. Department of Labor's *Monthly Labor Review.* The earlier years are summarized in U.S. Congress, Senate Committee on Labor and Public Welfare, *Welfare and Pension Plan Investigation, Final Report,* 84 Cong., 2 sess. (April 16, 1956) [cited hereafter as *Douglas Report*]. Special attention is given the health and welfare provisions in "Historic Summary: Auto Workers Contracts, 1939–1963," *Employee Benefit Plan*

Review, Research Reports 450,008 (Chicago: Spencer Associates, 1963).

2 From UAW "Statement to G.M." in opening round of 1961 negotiations.

3 Melvin A. Glasser, "Mental Health and Negotiated Health and Welfare Plans," presented at the AFL–CIO Community Services meeting on Mental Health, New York, May 21, 1964 (mimeo.).

4 Estimated from replies to questionnaires sent to 115 companies by the Douglas Subcommittee in 1955; usable answers were received from 48.

5 *Douglas Report.*

6 Art. I, Sec. 3(a), Exhibit A-1, "The General Motors Hourly-Rated Employees' Pension Plan, *Supplementary Agreements Covering Pension Plan and Insurance Program, G.M.–U.A.W., 1955.* This clause was also in the 1950–55 contract.

7 Letter to the author, dated Nov. 4, 1963.

8 Sec. 4, Exhibit B, *Supplementary Agreements, G.M.–U.A.W. Agreement, 1961.*

9 The union argued that "a well defined and well understood mechanism for processing complaints is necessary if claimants are to receive justice expeditiously" but Sec. 5 of the *Supplementary Agreements, G.M.–U.A.W. Agreement, 1961,* retains the old language that, "No matter respecting the Program . . . shall be subject to the grievance procedure. . . ."

10 See Jerome Pollack, speech in Proceedings, Conference on Negotiation and Administration of Health and Welfare Plans of the Industrial Union Department, AFL–CIO, Washington, D.C., March 27–28, 1957 (typewriter copy at AFL–CIO headquarters) [cited hereafter as IUD Health and Welfare Conference].

11 Quoted in *Health and Welfare Newsletter,* Cooperative Health Federation of America, Vol. II, No. 3 (March, 1953).

12 Reported by Harry Becker before the American Hospital Association. Becker also reported that commercially insured patients misused their hospital stays nearly 30 per cent of the time, but patients paying their own bills showed faulty use in less than 14 per cent of admissions. The overall result was that 20 per cent of all hospital admissions contained some faulty element. *New York Times,* Sept. 17, 1954.

13 Speech by Woodcock before the Association of Labor Health Administrators, Nov. 14, 1956, Atlantic City, N. J.

14 See "Major Illness Benefits Plan Approved," *Journal of Commerce* (April 14, 1955), for the Blue Cross argument.

15 Memo from James Brindle, Director, Social Security Department, to UAW International Executive Board, May 3, 1956. Located in Files, Social Security Dept., UAW, 8000 Jefferson Ave., Detroit, Mich.

16 Jerome Pollack, speech before IUD Health and Welfare Conference.

17 From material furnished by Harry Becker, appearing in U.S. Congress, Senate Welfare and Pension Plans Investigation, *Report of a Subcommittee on Health of the Committee on Labor and Public Welfare,* 82 Cong., 1 sess. (March 10, 1951), Confidential Committee Print, p. 56.

18 UAW–CIO Social Security Department, *Social Security Reporter* (Aug., 1955).
19 Speech before the Association of American Labor Health Administrators.
20 *Social Security Reporter* (Nov., 1955).
21 Memo from James Brindle to UAW International Executive Board.
22 As reported in *Health and Welfare Newsletter*, CHFA, Vol. III, No. 5 (May, 1954).
23 Franz Goldman, M.D., *The Problem of Establishing a Medical Care Program for Members of the U.A.W.–C.I.O. in Detroit* (Detroit: UAW, n.d.).
24 *Ibid.*, p. 3.
25 *Ibid.*, p. 18.
26 For a complete description of the Health Institute, see Margaret C. Klem and Margaret F. McKiever, *Management and Union Health and Medical Programs*, U.S. Dept. of Health, Education, and Welfare, Public Health Service Pub. No. 329 (Washington, D.C.: Government Printing Office, 1953), pp. 77–82.
27 See "Better Health in Toledo," *Ammunition* (July, 1955), pp. 8–12; "New Local 12 Diagnostic Clinic Sets Precedent, Lets Patients Choose Own Doctor," *Toledo Blade*, Feb. 27, 1955.
28 *Health and Welfare Newsletter*, CHFA, Vol. IV, No. 5 (May, 1955); *Labor Health Plan, Inc., of Maryland* (n.d.).
29 See UAW "Community Health Association, Program and Development," March 1, 1957 (mimeo.). See also *Detroit Free Press*, Oct. 12, 1956; *The Detroit News*, Oct. 12, 1956.
30 Memo from James Brindle to UAW International Union Executive Board.
31 "Proceedings, Conference on Quality of Medical Care," Community Health Association, Detroit, Mich., Jan. 11–12, 1957 (mimeo.). Located in files, Social Security Dept., UAW, 8000 Jefferson Ave., Detroit.
32 William Bromme, *Detroit Medical News*, XLVIII (Feb. 11, 1957), 6.
33 Editorial, *Journal of the State Medical Society* (Michigan), LV, No. 6 (June, 1956), 706.
34 In speech before the Economic Club of Detroit, March 4, 1957 (mimeo.), p. 5.
35 *Detroit Medical News*, XLVIII (May 6, 1957), 5.

Chapter 7: Bargaining with Employers: Benefits and Costs

1 Proceedings, Conference on Negotiation and Administration of Health and Welfare Plans of the Industrial Union Department, AFL–CIO, March 27–28, 1957 (typescript at AFL–CIO headquarters) [cited hereater as IUD Health and Welfare Conference].
2 In 1949, the President's Steel Fact-finding Board drew on the fact that most of the three million workers covered by health and welfare plans were in non-contributory plans, but most of these were of the multi-em-

ployer type. To make its case for non-contributory financing, the Board cited BLS Bull. No. 946 to the effect that most of the plans were financed entirely by the employer, and concluded that the trend was in the direction of non-contributory financing. The evidence for a trend at that time has been disputed on the ground that before 1940 a majority of plans were non-contributory; and during the immediate war and postwar years, the trend, if any, was toward more contributory plans. See, for example, the editorial in *Employee Benefit Plan Review* (Fall, 1949), pp. 2–4.

3 Here, as in the rest of this chapter, the basic source of data is three successive studies of a hundred large plans under collective bargaining conducted by the Bureau of Labor Statistics of the U.S. Dept. of Labor: *Digest of One-Hundred Selected Health and Insurance Plans under Collective Bargaining, 1954,* BLS Bull. No. 1180; *Digest . . . , Winter, 1961–62,* BLS Bull. No. 1330; *Digest . . . ,Early 1966,* BLS Bull. No. 1502 (all published Washington, D.C.: Government Printing Office, 1954, 1962, and 1966, respectively). The last of these studies does not include data on retired workers. Unless otherwise indicated, these three studies are used as the basis for conclusions in the text. Several articles comparing these studies or relating them to other data have been made: Louis S. Reed and Betty S. Rasmussen, "Research and Statistics Note No. 1, 1964," U.S. Dept. of Health, Education, and Welfare, Social Security Administration, Division of Research and Statistics (mimeo.); Dorothy R. Kittner, "Recent Changes in Negotiated Health and Insurance Plans," *Monthly Labor Review,* LXXXV, No. 9 (Sept., 1962), 1015–18; Robert C. Joiner, "Changes in Negotiated Health and Insurance Plans, 1962–1966," *Monthly Labor Review,* LXXXIX, No. 9 (Nov., 1966) 1246–49.

4 *Characteristics of 161,750 Plans Filed as of July 1, 1963,* U.S. Dept. of Labor, Office of Labor-Management and Welfare-Pension Reports (Washington, D.C.: Government Printing Office, 1963).

5 Joseph Krislov, "Employee-Benefit Plans, 1954–62," *Social Security Bulletin,* XXVII, No. 4 (April, 1964), 16.

6 Robert Joiner notes, "The trend toward the elimination of employee contributions gained momentum during the past four years. With one exception, all major plans negotiated by the Automobile Workers in the automobile and machinery and manufacturing industries became complete employer financed. . . . Other plans modified their financing arrangements to eliminate or reduce employee contributions for certain benefits. . . ." "Changes in Negotiated Health and Insurance Plans, 1962–1966," p. 1246.

7 IUD Health and Welfare Conference.

8 Foundation on Employee Health, Medical Care, and Welfare, Inc., *Problems and Solutions of Health and Welfare Programs, Study No. 1, Part A, Improving Value and Reducing Costs* (New York: FEH, MC, and W, 1958), p. 31.

9 Krislov, "Employee-Benefit Plans, 1954–62," p. 6.

10 From surveys conducted by the Health Information Foundation.

11 Walter W. Kolodrubetz, "Health Insurance Coverage for Workers on Lay-off," *Monthly Labor Review*, LXXXIX, No. 8 (Aug., 1966), 851.

12 *Ibid.*, p. 854.

13 Jerome Pollack as quoted by Herman M. Somers and Anne R. Somers, *Doctors, Patients, and Health Insurance* (Washington, D.C.: Brookings Institution, 1961), p. 370. See also Walter J. McNerney and Study Staff, University of Michigan, *Hospital and Medical Economics* (Chicago: Hospital Research and Editorial Trust, 1962), II, 1121.

14 See David E. Vollmer, "Effect of the National Labor Relations Act Upon Welfare Plans," *Proceedings of New York University Fifth Annual Conference on Labor, 1952* (Albany: Matthew Bender, 1952), pp. 199–228.

15 Governor's Commission on Aging, *Industrial Pension and Insurance Plans for Ohio Senior Citizens*, as quoted in U.S. Senate, *Blue Cross and Other Private Health Insurance for the Elderly, Hearings before the Subcommittee on Health of the Elderly of the Special Committee on Aging*, 88 Cong., 2 sess., April 27–29, 1964, 3 parts, Part 1, p. 49 [cited hereafter as *Blue Cross and Other Private Health Insurance for the Elderly, Hearings . . .*].

16 "U.A.W. Experience with Retiree Health Insurance," memorandum from UAW to AFL–CIO Social Security Department, April 17, 1964. Located in files, AFL–CIO, 815 16th St., N.W., Washington, D.C.

17 The interpretation and conclusions in this section on the problems of coverage for retirees are based on answers to mail inquiries from the AFL–CIO to constituent unions in 1964. The answers are on file at the AFL–CIO headquarters, Washington, D.C. See also the statement of Nelson Cruikshank, then director of the AFL–CIO Department of Social Security, in *Blue Cross and Other Private Health Insurance for the Elderly, Hearings . . .* , pp. 47–59.

18 George Meany, President, AFL–CIO, before U.S. House of Representatives, *Medical Care for the Aged, Hearing Before the Committee on Ways and Means*, 85 Cong., 1 and 2 sess., Nov. 18, 1963–Jan. 24, 1964, 5 parts, Part III, pp. 1206–7.

19 See Emerson H. Beier, "Adapting Group Health Insurance to Medicare," *Monthly Labor Review*, LXXXVII, No. 5 (May, 1966), pp. 49–95.

20 Joiner, "Changes in Negotiated Health and Insurance Plans, 1962–1966," p. 1249.

21 Reed and Rasmussen, "Research and Statistics Note 1, 1964," p. 5.

22 *Ibid.*, p. 6.

23 Joiner, "Changes in Negotiated Health and Insurance Plans, 1962–1966," p. 1248.

24 Arthur J. Offerman, "Accomplishments of Yesterday—Blue Shield," *Proceedings, 3rd National Congress on Voluntary Health Insurance and Prepayment* (Chicago: AMA, 1963).

25 Krislov, "Employee-Benefit Plans, 1954–62," p. 14.

26 For a useful checklist of these features of health insurance plans, see Foundation on Employee Health, Medical Care, and Welfare, Inc., *Problems and Solutions of Health and Welfare Programs, Study No. 1, Parts B and C, Service Benefits—and How to Compare Service vs. Indemnity Benefits* (New York: FEH, MC and W, 1958), pp. 56–78.

27 Richard Shoemaker, "New Directions in Health Benefits," AFL–CIO *American Federationist* (Sept., 1965), p. 11.

28 Raymond Munts, "Labor Looks at Eye Care Prepayment," address to the American Optometry Society, June, 1958.

29 Benson Ford in a speech before the 56th Annual Meeting of the American Hospital Association, printed in Bureau of National Affairs, *Collective Bargaining News and Comment* (Sept. 24, 1954).

30 See *Health and Insurance Plans Under Collective Bargaining: Main Medical Expense Benefits, Fall 1960,* Bull. No. 1293 (Washington, D.C.: Government Printing Office, 1961).

31 Joiner, "Changes in Negotiated Health and Insurance Plans, 1962–1966," p. 1249.

32 Only the International Union of Electrical, Radio and Machine Workers and the National Federation of Postal Clerks took a positive view of the development of major medical insurance. For the predominant view, see Jerome Pollack, "Major Medical Expense Insurance: An Evaluation speech before the Medical Care Section of the American Public Health Association, Atlantic City, N.J., Nov. 15, 1956; R. Munts, *Catastrophic Illness Insurance,* AFL–CIO Pub. No. 51 (May, 1957). For the other side, see E. C. Hallbeck, *Advantages of Major Medical Group Insurance,* statement before the House Committee on Post Office and Civil Service in support of H.R. 11630–11633, June 29, 1956 (reprinted by the Union Labor Life Insurance Company).

33 Krislov, "Employee-Benefit Plans, 1954–62," pp. 11–14.

34 Even a good plan, like that in basic steel, has been estimated to cover on the average only a portion of each family's medical bills: 60 per cent of "currently insurable expenditure," 54 per cent of "potentially insurable expenditure," and 41 per cent of all medical care expenditure. United Steelworkers, *Special Study on the Medical Care Program for Steelworkers and their Families* (Sept., 1960), pp. 96–97. See also Fred Slavick, *Distribution of Medical Care Costs and Benefits Under Four Collectively Bargained Insurance Plans,* New York State School of Industrial and Labor Relations, Research Bull. No. 37 (Ithaca: Cornell University Press, 1956), pp. 32–39.

35 Estimated from rates of comprehensive group practice plans; providing comprehensive benefits through open-panel programs would run even higher, unless preventive services were excluded.

36 Paul E. Bowers, Director of the United Rubber Workers Pension and Insurance Department, at the I.U.D. Health and Welfare Conference.

37 Malcolm L. Denise, Vice-President, Labor Relations, Ford Motor Com-

pany, remarks before the Annual Conference of Blue Shield Plans at Los Angeles, April 5, 1960.

Chapter 8:   Bargaining with Employers: Administration

1 From data filed under the requirements of the Health and Welfare Disclosure Act, there are 116,910 employer-administered welfare plans, 4,280 joint employer-employee trusteed plans, and 2,970 "employee organization" plans. These do not include pension plans or combination welfare-pension plans, nor do they include plans unclassifiable according to administration. The figures apply to both bargained and non-bargained plans. *Characteristics of 161,750 Plans Filed as of July 1, 1963,* U.S. Dept. of Labor, Office of Labor-Management and Welfare-Pension Reports (Washington, D.C.: Government Printing Office, 1963).

2 The available evidence on carrier selection is, at this writing, about ten years old, but there does not seem to be any reason to think that the situation has changed. See the *Report of the Committee on Ethical Practices,* Proceedings, Sixteenth Constitutional Convention, CIO, Los Angeles, Calif., Dec. 6–10, 1954, pp. 434–57. See also U.S. Congress, Senate Committee on Labor and Public Welfare, *Welfare and Pension Plan Investigation, Final Report,* 84 Cong., 2 sess. (April 16, 1956), p. 203 [cited hereafter as *Douglas Report*].

3 Jacobs Manufacturing Co., 94 NLRB 1214 (1951), *aff'd,* 196 F.2nd 680 (2nd Cir. 1952); Aluminum Ore Co., v. NRLB, 131 F.2d, 485 (7th Cir. 1952); Phelps Dodge Copper Products Corp., 101 NLRB 360 (1952); Reed & Prince Manufacturing Co., 96 NLRB 850 (1951). The clearest recent case is Sylvania Electric Products Co., Inc., 127 NLRB 117 (1960).

4 Lane Kirkland, "Negotiation and Administration of Health and Welfare Programs," *Monthly Labor Review,* LXXX, No. 5 (May, 1957), 577.

5 Not all employers with level-of-benefit agreements refuse to disclose their financial arrangements, but most do, and these include such prominent companies as General Motors, Westinghouse, and General Electric. Some of the larger steel companies, on the other hand, bargain on both benefit and cost and admit the union into some policy decisions involving financing (see Chapter 5).

6 *Douglas Report,* p. 19.

7 General Electric. For George Meany's comments on this, see *New York Times,* June 12, 1957, p. 21.

8 *Douglas Report,* p. 19.

9 *Ibid.*

10 General Motors had secured a full and complete breakdown of the costs of its insurance. While the insurance reserves established by Metropolitan from General Motors premiums were large, this was for entirely understandable cost and tax reasons, according to the Subcommittee.

(*Ibid.*, p. 148.) Whether these "understandable" reasons are a justifiable use of funds that are part of employee compensation was beyond the scope of the Subcommittee's evaluation.

11 Before September 1, 1950, salaried and hourly-rated employees had been covered by the same policy, but on that date separate policies were instituted. The accumulated reserves were all assigned to the salaried employee policy, with the result that premium payments were higher per dollar of benefit received by the hourly-paid workers. The salaried employee policy with its reserves well in hand paid a dividend so great ($3,641,672) that it "exceeded the corporation's contribution, converting General Motors' 1952 contribution (a debit) into an actual gain (a credit) of $233,585." (*Ibid.*, p. 151.) To argue that this is merely a transaction involving the left and right hands of the company, and that it is the company which stands to lose by inefficient management is to miss the point that the UAW was bargaining in 1950 for the hourly-rated employees. The shuffling of welfare funds by unilateral company decision between a plan affected by bargaining and one not affected by bargaining even raises a legal question of good faith in bargaining under the Labor-Management Relations Act.

12 *Ibid.*

13 The Act does not require employers with fewer than 25 persons to file even a plan description, and employers with fewer than 100 employees need not file an annual report. Furthermore, employer-administered plans are not required to provide as much information in the annual report they must file as are jointly administered trusteed plans, which must furnish a statement of receipts and disbursements for the reporting year, including a breakdown of all administrative expenses and a detailed report on the operation of each insurance carrier, including commissions.

14 Jay V. Strong, *Employee Benefit Plans in Operation* (Washington, D.C.: Bureau of National Affairs, 1951), p. 171.

15 *Ibid.*

16 Fred Slavick, *The Operation of Sickness Benefit Plans in Collective Bargaining*, Dept. of Economics and Social Institutions, Industrial Relations Section, Research Report Series No. 84 (Princeton: Princeton University, 1951), p. 64.

17 *Ibid.*, p. 65.

18 John Schmidt, then Secretary-Treasurer of Local 9, Brewery Workers, remarks before Health and Welfare Conference, sponsored by University of Wisconsin, May 14, 1955, Milwaukee, Wis.

19 Blue Cross will accept a small number of multiple billings under one policy and commercial carriers may also relax their general rule on occasion.

20 See Robert Tilove, "Welfare and Pension Funds in Multi-employer Bargaining," *Proceedings of New York University Ninth Annual Conference on Labor* (Albany: Mathew Bender, 1956).

21 Congress feared unions would become powerful with such funds. Despite the creditable record of the Ladies' Garment Workers in welfare administration, many Congressmen felt that union leaders—such as Lewis and Petrillo—were not competent to administer these funds. See National Labor Relations Board, *Legislative History of the Labor Management Relations Act, 1947*, 2 vols. (Washington, D.C.: Government Printing Office, 1948).

22 Investigations by the New York Insurance Department in 1953 and 1954 concentrated on the jointly administered plans, of which there are an estimated 500 in the state. The 162 plans selected for investigation were chosen in most cases because of some suspicion of mismanagement. Glaring abuses were unearthed in 34, some 37 others were subject to irregularities of varying degrees, and 91 were found on the whole to be honestly administered. In 1954, the Ives' Subcommittee of the Senate Committee on Labor and Public Welfare investigated 29 funds in Philadelphia, Chicago, and San Francisco, selected for reasons that have never been made explicit by the Subcommittee's Chief Counsel. The Subcommittee concluded that 6 were grossly mismanaged, 14 were marred by questionable practices, and 6 or 7 were well managed. Neither of these investigations were concerned with employer-administered plans and the New York investigation was somewhat overprotective of the insurance industry. The Douglas Subcommittee, which succeeded Ives' Subcommittee when the Democrats took over the Eighty-Fifth Congress, attempted to correct these biases and also to look into a few employer-administered plans. See Adelbert G. Straub, Jr., *Whose Welfare? A Report on Union and Employer Welfare Plans in New York* (n.p: State of New York Insurance Dept., 1954); also, U.S. Congress, Senate, *Interim Report, Submitted to the Committee on Labor and Public Welfare by its Subcommittee on Welfare and Pension Funds*, 84 Cong., 1 sess. (Jan. 10, 1955) [cited hereafter as the *Ives Report*]. See also *Douglas Report, passim.*

23 *Douglas Report*, p. 29.

24 "Employer delinquency on contributions in certain industries [has] been widespread. . . ." Slavick, *Operation of Sickness Benefit Plans in Collective Bargaining*, p. 64. The United Mine Workers usually had about 30 suits going to collect delinquent payments. *Douglas Report*, p. 25.

25 Several illustrations of lapses can be cited in welfare plans administered solely by employers. The author had personal experience as one of a negotiating team attempting to get reconsideration of the group insurance program of a small throwing mill in Pennsylvania, where the owner's brother-in-law was receiving the commission. For other examples where undue influence is exercised by agent or broker, see George Meany's testimony in U.S. Congress, Senate, *Welfare and Pension Plans Legislation, Hearings Before a Subcommittee of the Committee on Labor and Public Welfare*, 85 Cong., 1 sess. (1957), pp. 179–215. The same statement refers to absence of reports to employees on how their funds are

being handled, violations of the "prudent-man rule" in investment of welfare funds, including investment of welfare funds in the company's own business. On this latter, also see *Douglas Report,* pp. 515–54, 359–63. There has been overcharging of employees for benefits toward which the employer is neither contributing nor reporting dividends or overcharges. (Reported by Robert Tilove, before IAM Health and Welfare Conference, Madison, Wisc., 1953; and Paul Bowers in Proceedings, Conference on Negotiation and Adminstration of Health and Welfare Plans of the Industrial Union Department, AFL–CIO, Washington, D.C., March 27–28, 1957 [typescript at AFL–CIO headquarters], cited hereafter as IUD Health and Welfare Conference.) And high salaries have been paid corporation officers by the corporation's self-insurance fund in addition to their regular salaries. (Meany, in *Welfare and Pension Plans Legislation, Hearings . . .,* pp. 193–94.)

26 In the New York investigation, plans were selected, according to the report, "in some instances . . . at random, others were chosen because the Department had received specific complaints or had reason to believe that irregularities existed. Consequently, it would be most unfortunate if the disclosures contained herein were construed as being representative of most union welfare plans." (Straub, *Whose Welfare?*, p. 109). The Ives' Subcommittee misunderstood the scope of its subject—"welfare and pension plans subject to collective bargaining": its Report implies that there were in existence throughout the nation 1,596 insured health and welfare plans, an absurdly low figure. The Subcommittee actually investigated only jointly administered plans. This and other mistakes prompted Martin E. Segal, President, Martin E. Segal Co., insurance consultants, to say "the committee's staff is at least to date still somewhat inexperienced in the many actuarial and administrative and other technical ramifications of welfare funds, to have come to some of the broad generalizations that they have in the report." U.S. Congress, Senate, *Welfare and Pension Plans Investigation, Hearings Before a Subcommittee of the Committee on Labor and Public Welfare,* 84 Cong., 1 sess. (1955), 3 parts, Part I, p. 48.

27 The New York report went further to comment on a widely held misunderstanding: "The thesis that union and welfare fund officials are, ipso facto, persons of questionable moral fiber is one that cannot be seriously maintained. The conviction of those who have been engaged in the Department's investigation and who have thus been in close contact with many such officials is quite to the contrary. Corruption in this field is probably no more prevalent than in any other activity where similar opportunities for illicit gains exist." Straub, *Whose Welfare?*, p. 109.

28 *New York Times,* Sept. 17, 1954, p. 1.

29 See "Policing Union Funds," editorial, *New York Times,* Oct. 14, 1954.

30 *Resolutions,* AFL–CIO Convention, Dec. 7, 1955.

31 *Douglas Report,* p. 292.

32 AFL–CIO News Release, Dec. 28, 1956.

33 Executive Council Reports, Supplemental Report I, *Proceedings, A.F.L.–
C.I.O. Constitutional Convention,* II (Washington, D.C.: AFL–CIO,
1957), 405–68.

34 In Van Horn v. Lewis, 79 F.Supp. 541 (D.C., D.C. 1948), the Court emphasized the independent character of the trust. The distinction between
"representative" and "trustee" was made in Rice-Stix Co. v. St. Louis Labor Health Institute, 22 LRRM 2528, and in Marine Division, ILA v. Essex Trans. Co. 35 LRRM 2049. When the indictment against Sol Cilento
of the Distillery Workers Union was dismissed on the ground that Cilento
was not acting as an official of the union but solely as a trustee of the
fund, the *New York Times* (May 24, 1955) editorialized: "Amazing as
it may seem to the layman, the law makes it a crime for a union official to
accept a bribe, but no such law applies to a welfare fund trustee."

35 *Ibid.,* July 2, 1955, p. 1.

36 For example, a Pennsylvania District Court in 1949 said: "The burdening
of the fund with undue administrative expenses or lush salaries for union
officials will not be tolerated; excessive restriction, either in the insurance
policies or the by-laws and regulations, or the providing of small benefits
to the employee-members in proportion to the amount contributed by the
employee-parties or the premiums paid, taking into consideration the
risk involved, will cause more than a lifting of the eyebrows." Upholsterers' International Union v. Leathercraft Furniture Co., 82 F.Supp.
570, 575 or 23 LRRM 2315.

37 A miner who filed suit in Tennessee was told by the Tennessee Supreme
Court that where the trustee and the property of the welfare and retirement trust all are located in the District of Columbia, a Tennessee Court
does not have jurisdiction. See *Ives Report,* p. 39.

38 In two UMW cases, the courts have decided for the beneficiary even
though his rights to benefits were not vested. In one of the cases, the
miner was ruled ineligible for benefits because he had failed to work on
the last two days before the eligibility date through no fault of his own
(Bednar v. United Mine Workers Welfare and Retirement Fund, *et al.*
[D.C., D.C., 1953], 34 LRRM 2163). In the other, the issue was whether
the man was a union member in good standing. The court upheld both
claimants. The purposes of the trust, it said, cannot be frustrated at the
whim and caprice of the trustees, and courts of equity can always intervene to control such unreasonable exercise of discretion (Forrish v. Kennedy, 105 A.2d 67 [Pa. 1954], 25 CCH Labor Cases, 68:434). In another case, the court refused to be denied its proper role as a tribunal for
aggrieved beneficiaries. The court "considers such funds as rather sacred,
and it is the purpose of the law that they be available when due under
the contract. Therefore, whenever the trustees use, or attempt to use,
directly or indirectly, the fund for a purpose other than for the sole and
exclusive benefit of the employee members, this Court, when called upon,

will enjoin the trustees from making the improper expenditures. . . . A provision in the by-laws or regulations denying the employee members the right to resort to courts to protect their beneficial interest in the fund is of no legal effect." (United Garment Workers of America v. Jacob Reed's Sons, *et al.* [D.C., Pa., 1949], 23 LRRM 2291.)

39 This may be on his own information or upon the complaint of an interested party. In Wisconsin if the Attorney General refuses to act, a specific number of "interested parties" may bring an action in the name of the state on their own complaint (*Wisconsin Laws,* 1945, Chapter 458, p. 822). Three states (New Hampshire, Rhode Island, Massachusetts) have statutes giving the Attorney General or other state agencies the authority to require financial data and otherwise exercise supervision over charitable trusts. In these states, too, the power is not exclusively vested in the Attorney General: a person with a special interest in the performance of a charitable trust can bring an action for its enforcement. Austin W. Scott, *Law of Trusts* (Boston: Little, 1952), p. 2054.

40 Under their insurance or banking laws, the states of New York, Connecticut, Massachusetts, Washington, and Wisconsin require registration, filing of annual reports and financial statements, or periodic examination of each fund, or some combination of these. On state legislative considerations at the time of the investigations, see George G. Bogert, "Proposed Legislation Regarding State Supervision of Charities," *Michigan Law Review,* LIII (March, 1954), 6333.

41 Some unions are building national funds to include companies that do not bargain on an industry-wide basis: the Upholsterers, the Brotherhood of Electrical Workers, and the American Bakery and Confectionery Workers have such funds on a national basis while the Machinists, Allied Industrial Workers, and other unions have them on a regional basis. These plans may extend beyond one labor market area, and may allow for variable employer contributions. Thus, the usual justifications for trusteed plans—such as continuity of coverage and uniformity of cost—do not apply. But they are being urged from some quarters on the grounds that they "focus the management" of the plan: "The whole technical problem of creating, managing, developing, and improving these plans can be brought into manageable proportions through containing it within an industry-wide fund." (Tilove, "Welfare and Pension Funds in Multi-employer Bargaining," p. 103.) By their nature, they also obtain the advantage of explicit financing. The problems in such funds are representation of employer interests and flexibility to allow participation in local health service plans.

42 Paul L. Poston, "The Administration of Joint Union-Employer Health and Welfare Plans" (unpub. Ph.D. thesis, Harvard University, 1959).

43 "Employer trustees are usually personnel of participating companies engaged in labor relations work and union trustees are invariably officers of the union. Frequently, the adverse points of view that may exist

at the bargaining table spill over into the trustee meetings." *Ibid*, pp. 262–63.

44 *Ibid.*, p. 264.

45 *Ibid.*, p. 262.

46 In addition, California law provides that the state labor commissioner's office can help in collection of delinquent assessments. In New York and New Jersey, a delinquent employer commits a violation of the disability insurance law because the law allows contribution to an approved private welfare fund only as an alternative to paying the state disability tax.

47 For details of record-keeping and the more significant features of administration discussed in the next section, see Anne Ramsey Somers (in association with the Martin E. Segal Company), *Health Plan Administration, A Guide to the Management of Negotiated Hospital, Surgical, and Medical Care Benefits* (New York: Foundation on Employee Health, Medical Care and Welfare, 1961), 64 pp.

Chapter 9: Bargaining with the Insurance Business

1 For background on the insurance business, see Edmund L. Zalinski, "Observations on the Development of American Life Insurance," *Journal of the American Society of Chartered Life Underwriters*, Vol. X (Winter, 1955); and N. E. Horelick, "The Development of Group Life Insurance," *Journal of the American Society of Chartered Life Underwriters*, Vol. VI (June, 1952).

2 Estimated from *Life Insurance Fact Book* (New York: Statistical Division of the Institute of Life Insurance, 1966) and *1966 Argus Chart of Accident, Sickness and Hospital Insurance* (Cincinnati: National Underwriter Co., 1966).

3 The insurance company retention in workmen's compensation—which runs about 37 per cent for stock companies and 25 per cent for mutuals—has long been a sore point with labor. So has insurance company opposition to including Medicare under social security.

4 Zalinski, "Observations on the Development of American Life Insurance," p. 72.

5 Marquis James, *The Metropolitan Life* (New York: Viking, 1947), p. 72.

6 A. S. Carstens, an independent group insurance specialist, in *Employee Benefit Plan Review* (Winter, 1947), p. 41.

7 Jerome Pollack, UAW, statement in Proceedings, Conference on Negotiation and Administration of Health and Welfare Plans of the Industrial Union Department, AFL–CIO, Washington, D.C., March 27–28, 1957 (typescript at AFL–CIO headquarters) [cited hereafter as IUD Health and Welfare Conference].

8 Nor is there much for him to do in the way of actuarial work. With the extension of group insurance, staff actuaries were added to backstop the

agents. It is frequently true that the policyholder has more contact with the branch office actuarial staff, who are paid by salary rather than commission on the theory they play no role in sales, than with the agent or broker. U.S. Congress, Senate Committee on Labor and Public Welfare, *Welfare and Pension Plan Investigation, Final Report*, 84 Cong., 2 sess. (April 16, 1956), pp. 222, 254 [cited hereafter as *Douglas Report*].

9 Remarks before IUD Health and Welfare Conference.

10 *Douglas Report*, p. 219.

11 *Ibid.*, p. 221.

12 *Ibid.*, pp. 226, 228, 229, 240.

13 Adelbert G. Straub, Jr., *Whose Welfare? A Report on Union and Employer Welfare Plans in New York* (n.p.: State of New York Insurance Dept., 1954), p. 95.

14 *Douglas Report*, p. 30.

15 *Ibid.*, p. 222.

16 *Ibid.*, p. 32.

17 Herman M. Somers and Anne R. Somers, *Doctors, Patients, and Health Insurance* (Washington, D.C.: Brookings Institution, 1961), p. 267.

18 "The existence of improper practices, such as 'kickbacks,' is not readily susceptible for proof because of the clandestine nature of such acts . . . the law does not require that the Department anticipate improper conduct on the part of its licensees. . . . The law does not contemplate a day-to-day surveillance of the more than 70,000 licenses of this Department. . . ." Straub, *Whose Welfare?*, pp. 60–61.

19 See, for example, the testimony of Louis P. Saperstein, in U.S. Senate, *Welfare and Pension Plans Investigation, Hearings Before a Subcommittee of the Committee on Labor and Public Welfare*, 84 Cong., 1 sess. (1955), 3 parts, Part II, pp. 501–70 [cited hereafter as *Welfare and Pension Plans Investigation, Hearings*].

20 See *Resolutions*, AFL–CIO Convention, Dec. 7, 1955.

21 *Welfare and Pension Plans Investigation, Hearings . . .* , Part I, pp. 86–89.

22 C. Manton Eddy, *Ibid.*, Part I, p. 89.

23 Jack Barbash, *Ibid.*, Part I, p. 85.

24 To help buyers of health insurance find their way in the maze of alternative policies, Leroy K. Young, M.D., has prepared *A Study of Health Insurance Policies Available in New York State for the Purpose of Developing a Procedure for their Evaluation and Grading* (Ithaca: Sloan Institute of Hospital Administration, Cornell University, Feb. 7, 1964). This document is prepared with the individual rather than the group buyer in mind, but it is also useful for the latter. See also the studies of the Foundation on Employee Health, Medical Care, and Welfare, Inc., cited in n. 25 below, prepared specifically for group buyers.

25 Foundation on Employee Health, Medical Care, and Welfare, Inc., *Problems and Solutions of Health and Welfare Programs, Study No. 1,*

Part A, Improving Value and Reducing Costs (New York: FEH, MC, and W, 1958), pp. 26–28 [cited hereafter as *Problems and Solutions . . . Study No. 1*].

26 Ted Ellsworth, Administrator of the Motion Picture Health and Welfare Plan, has illustrated the selling practices of some carriers: "Some insurance companies have a number of devices for making their bids appear favorable. In one case, for supposedly equal medical coverage, most of the companies bid around $1.40 per month, while one bid $1.10. It underbid the others merely by excluding treatment for chronic diseases, treatment by injection, physiotherapy, treatment for allergies, and a few others. Its bid, in light of its exclusions, was high. Another cute trick of cut-rate companies is to underbid, on say a $300 surgical schedule, by cutting down on the more frequent operations. For example, about 16 per cent of all surgical procedures in some programs are for tonsillectomies and one or two other common operations. In a legitimate $300 schedule the plan will pay $45 to $52.50, and perhaps more, for a tonsillectomy, but the cut-rate plan may pay, say $32.50. There are many other ways to defeat true competitive bidding, if the proposals are not thoroughly analyzed." From "Methods of Evaluating Health and Welfare Plans," address delivered to Eighth Annual AFL Education Conference, April 26, 1955, Santa Barbara, California (mimeo.), p. 2.

27 The New York Insurance Department recommends that "Any savings to an insurer resulting from the assumption by the policyholder of certain accounting functions that might otherwise be handled by the insurer can more logically be reflected by adjustment in the premium rate or through the dividend or experience rating formula. . . ." Straub, *Whose Welfare?*, p. 107.

28 While there is no legal obligation that the retention be observed, there is cause for concern by the insured if it is not.

29 *Problems and Solutions . . . Study No. 1*, p. 38.

30 *Douglas Report*, p. 38.

31 ". . . insurance companies sometimes pursue variable policies with respect to dividends or rate credit refunds . . . the subcommittee found case after case in which insurance carriers after an exchange of correspondence with policyholders or their representatives have paid dividends that otherwise would not have been paid, or paid more because of pressure. . . . Premium rates have been lowered in cases in which the policyholder or his agent has exerted some pressure on the carrier." (*Douglas Report*, pp. 37–38.) Even more common than discrimination in procuring policies, is discrimination when policies are renewable on their anniversary dates. "Since the life insurance premium for a given group may be expected to rise simply because the group, as a whole, has become older, companies commonly recalculate the rates periodically. The subcommittee developed instances in which policyholders, or their agents, challenged the announced increases and the companies reduced

the increases or eliminated them altogether. If no questions were raised, the rates stood. With respect to renewal rates for accident and health insurance, many cases were found in which the rates were reduced, not because of favorable experience, but simply because the policyholders or their agents, complained to the companies." (*Ibid.*, p. 38.)

32 *Ibid.*, p. 38.

33 This data is for the 21 companies doing more than $30 million of group health business in 1962. See *1966 Argus Chart of Health Insurance*.

34 In 1948, the benefits paid were typically about 79 per cent of earned premiums, less dividends. U.S. Congress, Senate Committee on Labor and Public Welfare, *Health Insurance Plans in the United States*, S. Doc. 359, 82 Cong., 1 sess. (1951), Part II, pp. 110–11.

35 See the discussions between David Kaplan, David Feller, and others on this question in *Benefit Plans in Collective Bargaining* (New Brunswick, N.J.: Institute of Management and Labor Relations, Rutgers University, April 26, 1955), pp. 57–61.

36 "Switching"—the term for such a change—has become a bad word because it has been used by unscrupulous people to keep commissions and kickbacks high. But switching, when done for an honest and intelligent purpose, is both a legitimate and a competent way of using countervailing power to improve health and welfare programs.

37 These principles were originally stated in this form by Ray D. Murphy, now president of the Equitable Life Assurance Society, in 1949. Two years later, John H. Miller, Vice-President and Actuary of the Monarch Life Insurance Company, restated these principles before the United States Senate Committee on Labor and Public Welfare. They are frequently quoted in the insurance literature. See James Andrews, Jr., "How Changing Medical Care Affects the Public's Need for Accident and Health Insurance," *Journal of the American Society of Chartered Life Underwriters*, IX (Spring, 1955), 257–58, and also Emil E. Brill, "Group Major Medical Expense Insurance," *Journal of the American Society of Chartered Life Underwriters*, X (Fall, 1956), 312.

38 Horclick, "The Development of Group Life Insurance," p. 357.

39 "The pressure on a doctor's time may cause him to hospitalize patients for types of attention which could be as satisfactorily performed on an outpatient basis; many patients may choose to go to a hospital for a few days if it will not be anything directly out of their pocket, when they might better remain at home." Brill, "Group Major Medical Expense Insurance," p. 312.

40 Lane Kirkland, "What Kind of Prepaid Medical Care?" address before the California State Chamber of Commerce, Insurance Section, San Francisco, Calif., Nov. 29, 1956 (mimeo.), p. 6.

41 "The use of insurance to pay these relatively small and easily budgetable bills is an economic waste; it is believed that about 30 per cent of the claims being presented to insurance companies today are for less than

$25." Brill, "Group Major Medical Expense Insurance," pp. 312–13.

42 See R. Munts, *Catastrophic Illness Insurance,* AFL–CIO Pub. No. 51 (May, 1957).

43 Brill, "Group Major Medical Expense Insurance," p. 312.

44 The author was directly involved in the controversies described here in his capacity as health and welfare consultant to unions during the years 1953–56.

45 Metropolitan and Aetna paved the way, the former in part because the United Steelworkers desired to have Republic Steel employees covered, with benefits similar to the Blue Cross benefits in other basic steel plants.

46 Andrews, "Changing Medical Care . . . ," p. 260.

47 With the notable exception of the International Union of Electrical Workers and the National Federation of Post Office Clerks.

48 Resolution released by the Executive Council at the quarterly meeting, February, 1956.

49 Quoted by Jerome Pollack in "Major Medical Expense Insurance: An Evaluation," presented before the Medical Care Section, American Public Health Association, Atlantic City, N. J., Nov. 15, 1956, p. 17 of reprint.

50 *Ibid.,* p. 21.

51 O. D. Dickerson, *Health Insurance* (Homewood, Ill.: Richard D. Irwin, 1963), p. 216.

52 See Martin E. Segal, "Self-Insuranced v. Insured Pension and Welfare Programs," *Proceedings of New York University Ninth Annual Conference on Labor* (Albany: Mathew Bender, 1956); and John Liner, "Proposed: Self-Insurance of Group Welfare Plans," *Harvard Business Review,* Vol. XXXIII (Jan.-Feb., 1956).

53 See Herbert E. Klarman, *The Economics of Health* (New York and London, Columbia University Press, 1965), pp. 33–36.

54 This sentence anticipates dimensions of quality discussed in Ch. 14.

55 A. M. Thaler, "Group Major-Medical Expense Insurance," *Transactions, Society of Actuaries,* I (1952), 429–66.

Chapter 10: Bargaining with Hospitals and Blue Cross

1 See Chapter 3 above. For other examples of hospital prepayment before 1929, see Paul R. Hawley, M.D., *Nonprofit Health Service Plan* (Chicago: Blue Cross Commission, 1949), p. 12.

2 These Dallas teachers were able to persuade Baylor University Hospital to agree, for $3 per teacher each school semester, to provide up to 21 days of hospital care to any one of them who needed it. The idea quickly spread because in the early thirties the financial plight of the hospitals and the difficulty people had paying their hospital bills were serious community problems all over the country. It soon became clear, however, that for the plan to work more than one hospital in a community would

have to participate. So, the early plans in Sacramento (California), Essex County (New Jersey), St. Paul (Minnesota), and Durham (North Carolina) were city-wide plans. For background information on Blue Cross, see Robert D. Eilers, *Regulation of Blue Cross and Blue Shield Plans* (Homewood, Ill.: Richard D. Irwin for the S. S. Huebner Foundation, 1963); Louis H. Pink, *The Story of the Blue Cross,* Public Affairs Pamphlet No. 101 (New York: Public Affairs Committee, 1950); Hawley, *Nonprofit Health Service Plan;* Blue Cross Commission, *The History of Blue Cross,* and *Chronological Listing of Outstanding Dates in Early Blue Cross History* (mimeo.), 1955; U.S. Congress, Senate Committee on Labor and Public Welfare, *Health Insurance Plans in the United States,* Report No. 359, 82 Cong., 1 sess. (May 28, 1951), Part II, Appendix A, pp. 1–31.

3 Blue Cross plans began on three operating principles which contrast with those of commercial insurance:

Comprehensive service-type benefits: Blue Cross has reimbursement contracts with hospitals and makes payments directly to the hospitals for services rendered rather than paying limited cash indemnities to the policyholder as in commercial insurance. Blue Cross has a preferred position with the hospital, which the insurance companies do not like, but which is necessary to the purpose of providing services rather than compensation benefits. The national Blue Cross Commission does not insist on full observance of this principle but requires that an affiliated group must have contracts with hospitals to provide service and that they must cover for most of their subscribers an average of not less than 75 per cent of the charges for hospital care in ward or semi-private accommodations during the period for which the patient is eligible for benefits.

Non-profit public purpose: Blue Cross, like community hospitals, operates as a non-profit, community-service organization. While mutual companies are technically non-profit, the distinguishing feature of Blue Cross is its assumption of underlying responsibility for providing hospital service. Sales agents do not receive commissions and commercial insurance principles are not applied so vigorously in the determination of liability. Some Blue Cross plans have public or subscriber representation on their policy-making boards or advisory councils.

Standard community rates and benefits: Blue Cross is interested in the health problem of all members of the community. At the outset, the entire community was given the opportunity to enroll for equal benefits at a premium rate based on community-wide experience. This is called "community rating," and contrasts with commercial insurance "experience rating." An early feature of Blue Cross was equal benefits for all members of the family—not partial benefits for the wife and children. And people were to be allowed in the plan regardless of changes in employment, age, or deteriorating health. For further description of these principles, see James E. Stuart, "How Is Blue Cross Meeting the Demands," *Hospitals,*

XXX (Jan. 16, 1956), 43–46; see also the testimony of Dr. Madison B. Brown before the Metcalf Committee in State of New York, *Report of the Joint Legislative Committee on Health Insurance Plans* (Legislative Doc. No. 64, 1956), pp. 15–18.

4 Blue Cross Commission, *The History of Blue Cross,* p. 22.

5 For example, Blue Cross was unable to develop one national policy to cover the aged in 1960.

6 Blue Cross Association, Statistical Bull. No. 28, *Special Blue Cross Enrollment Report, March 5, 1964,* Table 1.

7 See Eilers, *Regulation of Blue Cross and Blue Shield Plans.*

8 Eugenia Sullivan and Earl E. Huyck, "Hospital Costs, 1946–1962," *Health, Education and Welfare Indicators* (Feb., 1964).

9 Lane Kirkland, *Statement before New York State Insurance Department,* Nov. 19, 1957 (mimeo.), p. 2.

10 The definition of under- and over-utilization and the measuring of the amount has been a problem for considerable research, some of which is summarized in Herman M. Somers and Anne R. Somers, *Doctors, Patients, and Health Insurance* (Washington, D.C.: Brookings Institution, 1961), pp. 174–81. Dr. Matthew Marshall of Pittsburgh has reported that out of 800,000 charts reviewed by a Western Pennsylvania hospital utilization committee, there was unnecessary hospitalization in one-fifth of the cases. (*Employee Benefit Plan Review, Research Reports* 312.–1 [Chicago: Spencer Associates, Sept., 1962].) In a study of a sample of Teamster families in New York, "hospitalization was judged by the surveyors to be unnecessary in one-fifth of the admissions." (School of Public Health and Administrative Medicine, *The Quantity, Quality and Costs of Medical and Hospital Care Secured by a Sample of Teamster Families in the New York Area* [New York: Columbia University Press, 1962], p. 5.) By contrast, a recent study of all Maryland hospital admissions on a single day showed agreement that only .6 per cent could be medically questioned, although one or another of the reviewing doctors questioned 4.8 per cent more admissions, and elements of doubt existed in another 5.5 per cent of the admissions. Needlessly prolonged stay was found for 14 per cent, unnecessary laboratory tests for 6 per cent, and unnecessary procedures for 4 per cent. *Report of the State of Maryland Commission to Study Hospital Costs* (Annapolis, June 25, 1964), pp. 10–11.

11 Kirkland, *Statement before New York State Insurance Department,* p. 7.

12 Jerome Pollack, statement in Proceedings, Conference on Negotiation and Administration of Health and Welfare Plans of the Industrial Union Department, AFL–CIO, Washington, D.C., March 27–28, 1957 (typescript at AFL–CIO headquarters).

13 Stuart, "How Is Blue Cross Meeting the Demands," p. 45.

14 Basil C. McLean, M.D., Blue Cross Association Release, April 22, 1958, p. 7.

15 For a sophisticated probing of the issues of community rating versus

experience rating, see Duncan M. MacIntyre, *Voluntary Health Insurance and Rate Making* (Ithaca: Cornell University Press, 1962). MacIntyre argues that "Experience rating is first and foremost a device . . . to increase sales in a competitive market. Through its strong appeal to buyer self-interest it serves a developing public interest—maximizing health insurance coverage . . ." (p. 285). He also argues that experience rating does not leave all heavy risk groups high and dry: ". . . a number of developments—the growth of multi-employer welfare funds, increased risk pooling by private insurance companies, and the growth of employer contributions—are combining to mitigate, but not eliminate, the cost impact" of experience rating for high risk groups (p. 274). But he is conceding here that some groups are not eliminated from adverse effect. The question then boils down to who is left out and to what groups can afford only minimal benefits because of their risk position. MacIntyre has given a strong rationale to Blue Cross capitulation to experience rating, but he has not answered this question of the limits of health insurance coverage under experience rating. The enactment of Medicare and Medicaid to assist high risk groups suggests that qualifications are needed to his assesssment that ". . . ours is still a business society in which self-interest is a motivational mainspring" (p. 285).

16 For a defense of experience rating, see J. F. Follman, Jr., *The Role of Insurance Companies in Financing Hospital Care* (New York: Health Insurance Council, 1962).

17 Somers and Somers, *Doctors, Patients, and Health Insurance*, p. 314.

18 At Blue Cross hearing before Insurance Commissioner of Pennsylvania, in 1958. In his decision, the Insurance Commissioner commended the United Steelworkers for its views. See Francis R. Smith, *General Discussion and Orders, Filing of Three Blue Cross Plans* (Harrisburg, Pa., April, 1958).

19 Eilers, *Regulation of Blue Cross and Blue Shield Plans*, p. 216.

20 *Ibid.*, p. 217.

21 Michael M. Davis, "What Blue Cross Must Do to Survive," *Modern Hospital* (Feb., 1960) [Reprint].

22 Thus Kirkland, *Statement before New York State Insurance Department:* "without implying any disrespect for the character and good intentions of the individuals involved, we submit that as 'subscriber representatives,' an executive of *Time, Inc.*, an executive of the New York Telephone Co., and the President of the Empire Trust Co., who is also President of the United Hospital Fund, do not represent the point of view of those who depend upon prepayment as the means of gaining full access to hospital services" (p. 11).

23 Estimate by staff of AFL–CIO Community Services Committee.

24 In Massachusetts, a number not to exceed 46 subscriber groups have 1 vote each as members of the corporation which elects the board. In Philadelphia, the subscribers may elect 6 of the board members. In Cincin-

nati, councils of subscriber respresentatives elect regional subscriber committees which, in turn, elect a subscriber committee for the plan as a whole, and the chairman of this committee is automatically a member of the board; a similar arrangement exists in Kansas.

25 See Hawley, *Nonprofit Health Service Plan,* p. 20.

26 Louis S. Reed, "Private Health Insurance in the United States: An Overview," *Social Security Bulletin,* XXVIII, No. 12 (Dec., 1965), 8.

27 From statistics collected by the Blue Cross Commission in 1959 and the Blue Cross Association in 1962, as reported by Eilers, *Regulation of Blue Cross and Blue Shield Plans,* p. 142.

28 As President of the Blue Cross Association in 1958, Dr. Basil C. McLean argued: ". . . it is frequently charged that Blue Cross Boards are silk-stockinged, self-perpetuating hierarchies. That's not generally true, but it is true that most Boards have far too little representation of important consumer groups. We can't continue to ignore what management and organized labor contribute to Blue Cross enrollment and support. Hospitals, I would say, should not have more than one-third of the membership on Blue Cross governing Boards. . . . That would mean a more reasonable balance between the buyers and the sellers of our product. . . ." McLean, Blue Cross Association Release, p. 10.

29 Eilers, *Regulation of Blue Cross and Blue Shield Plans,* p. 155. State statutes range widely in the matter of board composition, as a partial list indicates. Ten states require public representation; 4 states require that hospital representatives be in the majority; 2 states specify the proportion of the board (⅔ and ½) that must be made up of doctors and hospital representatives combined; 3 states require an equal representation for medical, hospitals, and the public; 2 do not mention board composition (*ibid.,* p. 140). The approval program of the American Hospital Association requires that governing boards be composed of one-third hospital representatives, one-third representatives of the general public.

30 School of Public Health and Administrative Medicine, *Prepayment for Hospital Care in New York City* (New York: Columbia University, 1961), p. 29.

31 Many insurance commissioners, particularly in the western states, have treated Blue Cross and its problems as though it were an insurance company. Even the New York Insurance Commission, in 1963, when it ruled on the Rochester Hospital Service request for general rate and benefit increases, insisted that the additional benefits be offered as "riders." This requires segregating the commmunity into different risks for the sale of a variegated product and puts on higher risk groups the full cost of the additional coverage.

32 School of Public Health . . ., *Prepayment for Hospital Care in New York City.*

33 In his letter of resignation to Governor Romney, the Insurance Commissioner of Michigan indicated what he thought was necessary for proper

regulation: (1) immediate enactment of a law requiring a clear majority of public members appointed by the Governor on the boards of both Blue Cross and Blue Shield; (2) addition of four competent staff people in the Insurance Department to work full time in the area of prepaid hospital, medical, and dental care programs; (3) creation of a single state agency to set standards, perform planning, and make necessary decisions regarding construction of hospital facilities; and (4) immediate establishment of a State Hospital Commission to both license and regulate hospitals and nursing homes in the state. *Ann Arbor News* (Oct. 28, 1963), as reported in *Public Health Economics*, XX, No. 11 (Dec., 1963), 546.

34 Most recently, the state AFL–CIO bodies in New York, New Jersey, and Rhode Island appeared during 1964 Blue Cross hearings.

35 Somers and Somers, *Doctors, Patients, and Health Insurance*, pp. 416–21.

36 See Mark Berke, "No Defense Needed," *Hospitals*, XXXII (Aug. 16, 1958), 37.

37 Herbert E. Klarman, "The Increased Cost of Hospital Care," *The Economics of Health and Medical Care, Proceedings of the Conference on the Economics of Health and Medical Care, May 10–12, 1962* (Ann Arbor: University of Michigan, 1964), pp. 244–45.

38 School of Public Health . . . , *Prepayment for Hospital Care in New York City*, p. 3.

39 For a short review of the present status of hospital planning, see Kenneth W. Wisowaty, Charles C. Edwards, M.D., and Raymond L. White, M.D., Health Facilities Planning," *Journal of the American Medical Association*, CXC, No. 8 (Nov. 23, 1964), 752–56.

40 See Chapter 3.

41 "Unlike thoughtful government planning or an efficient market mechanism, this process (of obtaining capital funds for hospital construction) does not involve a careful balancing of costs against benefits for the community . . . I do not intend to suggest that the process is either selfish or irrational, only that the independent hospital behaves as though capital had a zero price and invests funds regardless of the rate of return to the community. . . ." Millard F. Long, "Efficient Use of Hospitals," in *The Economics of Health and Medical Care*, p. 213.

42 *Ibid.*, p. 214.

43 Maintaining an empty hospital bed costs about 75 per cent of its cost in use. John Mannix of Blue Cross of Northeast Ohio reported in 1962 that empty beds there are costing $8,250 a year compared with $11,000 for a bed in full use during the year. *Employee Benefit Plan Review, Research Reports* 312.–1.

44 The important thing here is to realize that utilization as defined by the hospital administrator means ratio to total beds, whereas to the prepayment agency it means days of hospitalization per 1,000 prepayment subscribers. Cost control to the hospital administrator depends on high utilization in his terms; cost control for the prepayment plan depends on

low utilization in its terms. Cost controls for both are possible, by limiting the total number of hospital beds in the community.
45 Adopted by the AFL–CIO Executive Council, February, 1963.

Chapter 11: Bargaining with Doctors: Fees and Quality

1 For the record of opposition by the AMA to these changes, see David R. Hyde *et al.*, "The American Medical Association: Power, Purpose, and Politics in Organized Medicine," *Yale Law Journal*, LXIII, No. 7 (May, 1954), 938–1022.
2 The "Robin Hood" method of charging fees according to the patient's economic potential persists as an anachronism in an age of health insurance. Although not the primary factor in fee determination, it persists "apparently . . . primarily as a device for raising fees above the standard, as increasingly established by health insurance practices, rather than for lowering them for the poor, their major historical justification." Herman M. Somers and Anne R. Somers, *Doctors, Patients, and Health Insurance* (Washington, D.C.: Brookings Institution, 1961), p. 54. See also Herbert E. Klarman, *The Economics of Health* (New York and London: Columbia University Press, 1965), pp. 21–23.
3 Reported by Paul Bowers, United Rubber Workers, in Proceedings, Conference on Negotiation and Administration of Health and Welfare Plans of the Industrial Union Department, AFL–CIO, Washington, D.C., March 27–28, 1957 (typescript at AFL–CIO headquarters) [cited hereafter as IUD Health and Welfare Conference].
4 See IUD Health and Welfare Conference.
5 Quoted by Lane Kirkland in "What Kind of Prepaid Medical Care?" address delivered to California State Chamber of Commerce Insurance Section, San Francisco, Nov. 29, 1956.
6 George Haberman, Wisconsin State AFL–CIO President, in conversation with author, 1954.
7 Bowers, to IUD Health and Welfare Conference.
8 Letter from Woodrow L. Ginsburg, United Rubber Workers Research Director, to George Guernsey, Asst. Dir., AFL–CIO Education Dept., June 8, 1956. Located in files, UAW Research Dept., 8000 Jefferson Ave., Detroit, Mich.
9 See Paul D. Foster, M.D., "Labor Relations Report, Article No. 1," *Minutes and Materials of the Health Plan Consultants Committee, 1953–55*, University of California at Los Angeles (mimeo.).
10 San Francisco Medical Society *Bulletin* (May, 1950), p. 18.
11 San Francisco Labor Council *Official Bulletin* (Dec. 5, 1951).
12 See *ibid.* (Nov. 18, 1953; March 3, 10, 1954).
13 Quoted in *ibid.* (Nov. 18, 1953).
14 Louis S. Reed, "Private Health Insurance in the United States: An Overview," *Social Security Bulletin*, XXVIII, No. 12 (Dec., 1965), 4–5.

15 American Medical Association, *Digest of Official Actions 1946–1958* ([Chicago]: AMA, 1959), pp. 315 ff.

16 A study of the medical service corporations in the state of Washington included a survey of physicians' attitudes from which the authors conclude as follows:

"The answers . . . suggest strongly that physicians as a group do not think in terms of health insurance principles. Many conceive of the plan as a means of handling charity cases. In this view, the physicians are making special arrangements for those unable to pay standard rates. These arrangements appropriately call for some sacrifice by physicians in the form of lower rates and a certain amount of 'red tape.' But according to this view, such a plan should not be allowed to grow to cover any substantial part of the population, nor should the utilization of care by low-income people be encouraged so that it takes a larger than normal share of the physician's time and energy. . . .

"Only a minority of the physicians hold what might be called an 'insurance view' of the plan, seeing it as an alternative to private insurance companies. These physicians view the plan as selling the services of a group of physicians in a competitive market, with the many buyers spreading the risk. In this view, the insurance reserve exists in the willingness of the physicians to supply services beyond some 'normal' amount during the contract period. If the physicians don't get their full price after allowance for overhead, they have simply made a bad bargain . . . though they may have retained more control of the situation than they might otherwise have done, and this should be reckoned as a part of their equity return.

"A careful reading of the questionnaires shows that most physicians do not think in these terms. Rather they think of individual cases and the alternative ways in which they might be compensated for them. They express little appreciation of the subscriber's view of the expense (and uncertainty of such expense) and insurance against it. Similarly, few physicians think in terms of discounts from a standard fee for quantity purchase and prepayment (and hence certain payment) that might be justified in the minds of the buyers of services. Nor is there any general feeling that greater utilization may keep down total medical costs for the whole subscriber population by avoiding some serious illnesses and conditions.

"How do these attitudes bear upon the potential of the program? To the outsider, the inference is unavoidable that there is little dynamic for expansion among participating physicians, even though these physicians feel a moral and professional obligation to serve low-income people and are aware of increasing public interest in prepayment of medical expenses. The evidence strongly suggests that the program will grow only as growth is forced by external pressures and as physicians become convinced that, unless they provide care under plans like this one, the need will be filled by other plans, not sponsored by physicians themselves, that are more likely to change traditional patterns of medical practice." George A. Shipman, Robert J. Lampman, and S. Frank Miyamoto, *Medical Service Corporations in the State of Washington* (Cambridge, Mass.: Harvard University Press, 1962), pp. 116–17.

17 Jerome Pollack and Irvin Bloch, *Blue Shield in New York City* (New York: New York Labor-Management Council of Health and Welfare Plans, n.d.).

18 In 1955, following the UAW's negotiations with the "big three" in auto, Michigan Blue Shield agreed to accept scheduled benefits as full payment for those families with incomes under $5,000. Later this was raised to $7,500. After each such adjustment of the Michigan "standard," the UAW initiated discussions with Blue Shield plans in Colorado, Minnesota, Pennsylvania, Indiana, Delaware, Florida, Cleveland, Kansas City, Cincinnati, Columbus, Toledo, Milwaukee, Chicago, Des Moines, Dallas, Los Angeles, Oakland, Canton, St. Louis, and Janesville (Wisconsin) where auto plants were under contract.

19 As reported by Jerome Pollack, IUD Health and Welfare Conference.

20 Bernard Greenberg, to IUD Health and Welfare Conference.

21 *Blue Shield Manual* (Chicago, 1965).

22 U.S. Congress, Senate, *Social Security, Hearings Before the Committee on Finance*, 89 Cong., 2 sess., on H.R. 6675 (April 29–May 5, 1965), Part II, p. 405.

23 Reed, "Private Health Insurance in the United States: An Overview," p. 9, n. 9.

24 Benjamin J. Darsky, Nathan Sinai, and Solomon J. Axelrod, *Comprehensive Medical Services Under Voluntary Health Insurance* (Cambridge, Mass.: Harvard University Press, 1958), pp. 210–13, 220–22, 231–33.

25 Even in the United Mine Workers, where sanctions are available because the fund can and will drop a doctor from the approved list of physicians if his fees are out of line, the union is doubtful about any attempt to negotiate a schedule of fees. Fund officials think that instead of being a maximum or average schedule, such agreements tend to become the minimum, both because lower charging doctors have new justification for raising their fees, and because higher charging doctors claim independence from the schedule. The fund prefers to deal with doctors individually and simply question fees that it regards as excessive.

26 It is interesting to compare the experience of the federal government's Medicare program for the dependents of servicemen, as described by Paul I. Robinson, M.D., Coordinator, Medical Relations, Metropolitan Life Insurance Company, formerly Executive Director, Office for Dependents' Medical Care, Office of the Surgeon General, U.S. Army, Washington, D.C.: ". . . . At the inception of the program, the Office of Dependents' Medical Care depended a great deal on the experience and

wisdom of the state medical associations in many aspects of the program. Notable in this regard was the determination as to whether or not the schedules of allowances would or would not be published to the physicians of the state. There was, and still is, a great difference in [the] philosophy of state medical associations as to physicians' charges. Some, our experience would indicate, believe that physicians should be entitled to a fixed fee, regardless of type of practice or state of training. These states published their schedules of allowances, and, with few exceptions, physicians' charges conform therewith. Others were of the opinion that every physician should know the maximum negotiated allowance but that he could charge his usual fee. These states also published their schedules but encouraged physicians to charge their usual charges. Our experience in these areas indicates that there are a considerable number of physicians who do charge below the maximum of the schedule but by far the greater majority charge the amount published in the schedule. A third group of states feels that physicians should determine their charges in each individual case, considering all factors. They have not published their schedules but have assured their physicians that a fair and equitable amount has been negotiated and have instructed them to charge an amount equal to their ordinary charge for patients in like circumstances. Our experience in this group of states indicates that the physicians' charges conform, in general, to normal civilian practice, a considerably greater number being below the modal amount and a few being higher than the schedule." "Experience with Medicare," *Journal of the American Medical Association,* CLXVIII, No. 12 (Nov. 22, 1958), 1630–33.

27 See Joseph W. Garbarino, *Health Plans and Collective Bargaining* (Berkeley: University of California Press, 1960).

28 Ted Ellsworth, "Relations with Doctors and Hospitals," paper presented at the IUD Health and Welfare Conference (mimeo.), p. 1.

29 Foster, "Labor Relations Report, Article No. 1."

30 For information on San Joaquin and union attitudes to it, see Garbarino, *Health Plans and Collective Bargaining,* pp. 232–41; Donald C. Harrington, M.D., "Foundation for Medical Care," *Journal of the American Medical Association,* CLXX, No. 8 (June 20, 1959), 969–72; "San Joaquin's Medical Foundation," *California GP* (March, 1959); Goldie Krantz, "The San Joaquin Foundation for Medical Care," presented before the Medical Care Section of the Group Health Association of America, Oct. 21, 1959 (mimeo.).

31 "San Joaquin's Medical Foundation."

32 Krantz, "The San Joaquin Foundation for Medical Care," p. 8.

33 *Journal of the American Medical Association,* CLXX, No. 8 (June 20, 1959), 969–72.

34 Conversations with author, June, 1966.

35 George Baker, M.D., "The Need for Medical Care," *Proceedings of New York University Ninth Annual Conference on Labor* (Albany: Matthew Bender, 1956), p. 189.
36 A. J. Hayes, "A New Look at Health Insurance," address before the 1955 Convention of the American Hospital Association, printed in *The Machinist* (Sept., 1955).
37 George Meany, address delivered at the dedication of the AFL Medical Service Center, Philadelphia, Feb., 1957 (mimeo.).
38 Walter Reuther, W. Biddle Lecture, Annual Convention of the Michigan State Medical Society, Sept., 1957.
39 See Ellsworth, "Relations with Doctors and Hospitals," p. 7.
40 For details, see Chapter 3.
41 According to Dr. Draper, "The difficulties which we have with individual physicians are seldom of a character to warrant the filing of specific charges. Unnecessary hospitalization, unnecessary surgery, and the other procedures mentioned all deal with various facets of medical treatment of patients and do not in themselves constitute unethical or dishonest conduct and, therefore do not afford grounds for charges against individual physicians." Warren F. Draper, M.D., "Problems Encountered in the Operation of the United Mine Workers of America Welfare and Retirement Fund," *Pennsylvania Medical Journal*, LVIII (Dec., 1955), 1336.
42 See "Report of Subcommittee on Ways and Means of Meeting the Restrictive Practices of Organized Medicine as they affect the Policies of the AFL–CIO," AFL–CIO Committee on Social Security, Washington, D.C., May 16, 1957.

Chapter 12: Bargaining with Doctors: Prepaid Group Practice

1 See David R. Hyde *et al.*, "The American Medical Association: Power, Purpose and Politics in Organized Medicine," *Yale Law Journal*, LXIII, No. 7 (May, 1954), 977–78.
2 The number of group practice units tripled from 1946 to 1959, according to a survey reported in *Medical Groups in the United States, 1959*, Public Health Service Pub. No. 1063 (Washington, D.C.: Government Printing Office, 1963), pp. 11–12.
3 In 1962 the AMA joined with others in publishing a book (since revised) on group practice. AMA, the American Association of Medical Clinics, and the Medical Group Management Association, *Group Practice: Guidelines to Forming or Joining a Medical Group* (Chicago, 1965), 40 pp.
4 *Wall Street Journal*, Dec. 24, 1959, p. 1.
5 In a poll by *Medical Tribune*, 85 per cent of the 1,130 doctors responding indicated that they were favorably impressed at least in part by group practice. Reported in *Group Health and Welfare News*, Group Health Association of America, Vol. V, No. 3 (April, 1964).

6 These events are summarized in a letter from Frederick F. Umhey, Executive Secretary, ILGWU, to William Green, AFL President, July 12, 1949. Located in files, AFL–CIO, 815 16th Street, N.W., Washington, D.C.

7 See American Medical Association, *Digest of Official Actions 1946–1958* ([Chicago]: AMA, 1959), pp. 235–36.

8 *Journal of the American Medical Association,* CLXXI, No. 17 (Dec. 26, 1959), 2334.

9 As reported by Dr. Morris Brand in *AFL–CIO News* (Aug. 15, 1957).

10 George Baehr, M.D., "The Attitude of Medical Societies to Prepaid Group Practice," *New England Journal of Medicine,* CCXLVII, No. 17 (Oct. 23, 1952), 628.

11 *Ibid.,* p. 4.

12 Arthur M. Master, M.D., "Impact of Medical Care Plans on the Medical Profession," *Journal of the American Medical Association,* CL, No. 8 (Oct. 25, 1952), 766.

13 *New York Times,* Jan. 15, 1954, p. 21.

14 "In 1952, the medical societies supported the Panken Bill which would prohibit the operation of plans like the H.I.P. The bill died in committee. In the 1954 legislature, a similar measure was introduced in both houses." Hyde *et al.,* "The American Medical Association . . . ," p. 996, *n.* 471.

15 *New York Times,* April 26, 1955, p. 31.

16 These proposed changes in the code of ethics specified four points. (1) Advertising should be understood to be unethical if it is aimed at getting patients for a panel of physicians of a medical care plan, company, or other organization. (2) The practice of medicine by physicians on a salary should be restricted to institutions where patients are "public charges." (3) Free choice of physician, one of the requirements of the present code, must be understood to be initiated if the patient is required to choose a physician from a panel or group of practitioners. (4) Proration of fees is not unethical if both physicians or surgeons actively participate in providing medical care and if the fee is paid by an insurance company.

17 Press Release, Committee of the Nation's Health, Washington, D.C., Aug. 25, 1953.

18 *Ibid.*

19 *New York Times,* Aug. 10, 1953, p. 19.

20 *New York Times,* Feb. 16, 1955, p. 23.

21 The conflicting opinions within the Medical Society of the County of New York about labor and health plans are seen in these two statements by successive presidents: "The physician must realize that for his protection our medical society is essential. If in the inevitable struggle around the conference table we are not to be conquered by division in our ranks, we must have a strong, united organization comparable to the ones with which we must deal, [otherwise] the practitioner as an indi-

vidual is at the mercy of any group which decides to provide medical care through a closed panel system. . . ." (Dr. Samuel Z. Freedman as quoted in *New York Times,* Oct. 23, 1956, p. 35.) "While I am president of this society, I will welcome their [union's] cooperation in solving what I consider to be a mutual problem. . . . Whether we like it or not, it is a well-established fact that in large metropolitan areas such as ours, the labor unions are playing a big role in the dispensing of health services. . . ." (Dr. Philip D. Allen as quoted in *New York Times,* Oct. 29, 1957, p. 32.)

22 At Staten Island where HIP has 24,000 subscribers, the HIP doctors have had considerable trouble getting hospital privileges. Dr. N. Joseph Garabedian, an obstetrician, allegedly died from overwork because the three Staten Island hospitals would not give privileges to another HIP obstetrician. Thomas Carey, business manager of District 15 of the International Association of Machinists, which has one thousand union members on the Island, stated: "The doctors who control the hospital appointments on Staten Island have never before so clearly demonstrated that they will stop at nothing to protect what amounts to an economic monopoly for themselves and their colleagues." *Health and Welfare Newsletter,* Cooperative Health Federation of America, Vol. IX, No. 7 (July–Aug., 1960).

23 Master, "Impact of Medical Care Plans . . . ," p. 770.

24 Joseph W. Garbarino, *Health Plans and Collective Bargaining* (Berkeley: University of California Press, 1960), pp. 178–203. The quotations following appear on pp. 189, 193 resp.

25 *Ibid.,* pp. 195–96.

26 Frederick F. Umhey, "Health and Welfare in the Ladies' Garment Industry," panel discussion before the Eighth Annual Congress on Industrial Health, sponsored by the Council on Industrial Health, AMA, Jan. 5, 1948, at Cleveland, Ohio (mimeo.).

27 See Ray Taylor, "A.M.A. Opposition to Medical Centers," Ch. VIII of *The Decline of the Medical Profession in Public Esteem* (Milwaukee: The Milwaukee Labor Press, n.d.). For the Lehigh County reference, see "Report of Subcommittee on Ways and Means of Meeting the Restrictive Practices of Organized Medicine as They Affect the Policies of the AFL–CIO," AFL–CIO Committee on Social Security, Washington, D.C., May 16, 1957.

28 For a multi-causal explanation of the failure of the San Francisco plan, see Garbarino, *Health Plans and Collective Bargaining,* pp. 154–57.

29 See Horace R. Hansen, "Laws Affecting Group Health Plans," *Iowa Law Review,* XXXV (Winter, 1950), 209–36; and Hansen, "Group Health Plans—A Twenty-Year Legal Review," *Minnesota Law Review,* XXIV, No. 4 (March, 1958), 531–32.

30 Complete Service Bureau v. San Diego County Medical Society, 272 P.2d 497 (Cal. 1954).

31 As quoted in *Group Health and Welfare News,* Group Health Association of America, Vol. IV, No. 5 (June-July, 1963).

32 Hansen, "Group Health Plans . . . ," pp. 547–48.

33 In Texas, the Harris County Medical Society succeeded in closing a hospital operated for Humble Oil Company's Baytown plant of 10,000 employees; it also threatened the Southern Pacific Hospital and the Houston Belt Terminal Railway's Clinic. *Labor* (June 28, 1958).

34 For cases in various states, see Horace R. Hansen, *Legal Rights of Group Health Plans* (Washington, D.C.: Group Health Association of America, May, 1964).

35 "Report of the Commission on Medical Care Plans," *Journal of the American Medical Association,* CLXIX, Special Edition (Jan. 17, 1959), 51.

36 Hansen, *Legal Rights of Group Health Plans,* p. 8.

37 Enacted in 1947, the Montana statute forbids discrimination by any tax-exempt hospital against any licensed doctor, whether or not a member of the staff, and requires compliance as a condition for maintaining a license.

38 To get around the limitations of the law, the Community Health Center, Inc., owns and operates the hospital in Two Harbors, Minnesota, and the Community Health Association, not incorporated, operates the prepaid medical and hospital care plan. Jerry Voorhis and Robert E. Van Goor, eds., *The Cooperative Health Federation of America and Its Member Plans* (Chicago: CHFA, March, 1955), p. 6.

39 Isadore Melamed in Proceedings, Conference on Negotiation and Administration of Health and Welfare Plans of the Industrial Union Department of the AFL–CIO, Washington, D.C., March 27–28, 1957 (typescript at AFL–CIO headquarters).

40 *Health and Welfare Newsletter,* Cooperative Health Federation of America, Vol. IV, No. 5 (May, 1955).

41 Hansen, *Legal Rights of Group Health Plans,* p. 10.

42 This section draws upon an excellent study by Richard Shoemaker, "New Directions in Health Benefits," AFL–CIO *American Federationist* (Sept., 1965), p. 8.

43 "Prepayment Dental Health Program," statement by AFL–CIO Executive Council, Aug. 5, 1964.

44 Group Health Cooperative of Puget Sound v. King County Medical Society, 39 Wash.2d 586, 237 Pac.2d 737 (1951).

Chapter 13:   Bargaining For and With Medical Service Centers

1 The most notable example, the Kaiser Foundation, is discussed later in this chapter. Industry-sponsored plans have long existed in railroads, some mining centers, public utilities, etc. Two of these in New York, the medical care program at Consolidated-Edison and that at Endicott-Johnson, are outstanding; for a description, see *Medical Care Programs in*

290 Notes to Pages 177–178

Industry, Federal Security Agency, Public Health Service (Washington, D.C.: Government Printing Office, 1949), reprinted from Division of Industrial Hygiene, *Industrial Hygiene Newsletter* (May and Dec., 1948). For a complete listing of all independent health plans (other than Blue Cross-Blue Shield) providing medical services and with designation of sponsorship, see *Independent Health Insurance Plans,* U.S. Dept. of Health, Education, and Welfare, Social Security Administration (Washington, D.C.: Government Printing Office, 1962).

2 For example, the Ross-Loos program in Los Angeles. For a comparison of doctor-sponsored and consumer plans, see Jerome L. Schwartz, "Consumer Sponsorship and Physician Sponsorship of Prepaid Group Practice Health Plans: Some Similarities and Differences," *American Journal of Public Health,* LV (Jan., 1965), 94–99.

3 Minimum and optimal size determination involves several factors. There is a pre-existing minimum of specialties that must be included before the requirements of group practice are met: a medical group must include at least a general physician and surgeon, an internist, and part-time specialists in obstetrics and gynecology, pediatrics, ear, eye and throat, and dermatology. This full- and part-time practice will add up to the equivalent of three or four full-time doctors. With the necessary auxiliary help, this minimum-size medical group could provide diagnosis and medical treatment in the health center and home (not including dental work or eye refraction) for 3,000 persons, assuming a utilization of between four and five clinical visits each year per person covered. This can be characterized as a "bare-bones" approach and actually is costly because it achieves none of the savings of scale that are possible. Although operating costs vary proportionately with size, capital costs do not; equipment and furniture costs for a group of 20,000 are only 2 or 3 times that for a group of 3,000. Lastly, there are the dangers of large size. With a coverage of 40,000 a health center begins to suffer from impersonal services, overdepartmentalization, and a loss of informal consultation and personal responsibility. Taking all things into account, the optimal size range probably begins around 10,000 or 15,000 and extends to 40,000, this in terms of a single facility which provides all ambulatory services under one roof. The analysis would differ where a central facility is fully equipped and staffed with specialist services but related to medical service clinics dispersed into suburban areas to provide general medical care. Still another pattern exists where the hospital is an integral part of the program, with clinic and hospital in the same building or adjacent to one another. For a general discussion of facilities see William A. Mac-Coll, M.D., *Group Practice and Prepayment of Medical Care* (Washington, D.C.: Public Affairs Press, 1966), pp. 116–30. See also Emil Sekerak, *Minimum Staff, Facilities, and Costs for a Group Health Clinic* (San Jose, Calif.: People's Hospital, mimeo., n.d.); Y. S. Yerby and B. Yurchenco, "Guide to Organization of Group Practice," *Modern Hospital,*

Vol. LXXXIII (Nov., 1952); Michael M. Davis, "Setting Up Union Health Centers," AFL–CIO *American Federationist* (Nov., 1956); Dean A. Clark, M.D., and Katherine G. Clark, *Organization and Administration of Group Medical Practice* (Boston: Twentieth Century Fund and Good Will Fund, 1941); and Robert E. Rothenberg, M.D., and Karl Pickard, M.D., *Group Practice and Health Insurance in Action* (New York: Crown Publishers, 1949).

4 For an excellent critical evaluation, see E. Richard Weinerman, M.D., "An Appraisal of Medical Care in Group Health Centers," *American Journal of Public Health*, XLVI (March, 1956), 300–309.

5 The Kaiser Foundation has various plans ranging in price up to $25.90 a month ($311 per year). Community Health Association, Detroit, has a group rate of $27.85 for 3 persons. Medical Centers affiliated with hospital or Blue Cross arrangements show similar costs when premiums are combined: Union Health Services, Inc., Chicago—$29.86; Group Health Association, Inc., Washington, D.C.—$29.95; Health Insurance Plan of Greater New York—$27.50. These rates are not comparable for many reasons, including variations in regional costs, different benefit packages, and occasional supplemental or out-of-pocket fee arrangements.

6 See note 33, Chapter 14.

7 Records of the United Steelworkers of America show that under Blue Cross the annual average for a period of five years was 1,032 hospital days per 1,000 insured, while under the Kaiser plan there were only 570 hospital days per 1,000 insured. Furthermore, there were twice as many operations under Blue Shield as under the Kaiser plan. See United Steelworkers of America, *Special Study on the Medical Care Program for Steelworkers and their Families* (Sept., 1960).

A study of three New York locals in International Ladies' Garment Workers' Union offers further evidence. Blue Cross records show that the hospital admission rate is about 25 per cent higher for those who chose a cash indemnity prepayment plan with solo practicing physicians than for those under a prepaid group practice plan. Paul Densen, Ellen Jones, Eve Balamuth, and Sam Shapiro, "Prepaid Medical Care and Hospital Utilization in a Dual Choice Situation," *American Journal of Public Health*, L (Nov., 1960), 1710–26.

The annual reports of the Federal Employees Health Benefits Program show similar hospitalization savings for enrollees in group practice plans. These enrollees use from only one-half to two-thirds as many days of hospitalization as the subscribers to Blue Cross-Blue Shield and indemnity plans. The hospital days per thousand for each of the three years for which reports have been published were: the group practice plans, 406, 455, and 433; Blue Cross-Blue Shield subscribers, 670, 826, and 865; indemnity plans, 660, 708, and 770. Experience with the Federal Employees Health Benefits Program is reported in the annual report of the U.S. Civil Service Commission, and reprinted separately.

The Labor Health Institute in St. Louis originally paid the same Blue Cross premium for its members' hospitalization as other Blue Cross subscribers. But experience showed much lower utilization (now about 765 hospital days per 1,000 members) and to reap the savings, LHI has operated its own hospitalization plan since 1949; hospital benefits have been increased three times since the change.

8 See the *Annual Reports* issued by the St. Louis Labor Health Institute, and occasional President's Report to the Members; Harold Gibbons, "How to Establish and Operate a Health Clinic"; *Textbook for Health and Welfare Trustees and Administrators,* Proceedings of the Third Annual Conference of Health and Welfare Plans, Trustees, and Administrators (Denver: 1957); Franz Goldman, M.D., and Evarts A. Graham, M.D., *The Quality of Medical Care Provided at the Labor Health Institute* (St. Louis: LHI, 1954); Henry G. Parish and Franz Goldman, *The Labor Health Institute: Quality of Service* (St. Louis: LHI, 1948); Nathan M. Simon, M.D., and Sanford E. Rabushka, M.D., *A Trade Union and Its Medical Service Plan* (St. Louis: LHI, 1948); *How Doctor Fees Were Determined at the St. Louis Labor Health Institute for the Fiscal Year July 1, 1952–June 30, 1953* (St. Louis: LHI, 1953); *Dental Care in a Group Practice Plan,* U.S. Dept. of Health, Education, and Welfare, Public Welfare Service (Washington, D.C.: Government Printing Office, 1959).

9 The information that follows is taken from Union Health Service, Inc., *Yearly Reports of Services,* 1955–66 (mimeo.).

10 See AFL Medical Service Plan, *Annual Reports,* 1955–65 (mimeo.).

11 The description that follows in the text emphasizes that portion of the co-operatives' efforts that is directed to reorganizing medical care. The co-operative movement, like labor, has been in some confusion about its ultimate goals—whether to emphasize insurance or medical services. It should be noted that some co-operatives are primarily interested in selling insurance—the Cooperative Health Association in Kansas City, the Nationwide Insurance Company, and Group Mutual in St. Paul are examples. Originally devoted to getting better medical services for lower income people, the co-operative insurance companies have successively dropped income limitations for enrollees, accepted groups (abandoning thereby the co-operative idea of "one member, one vote"), emphasized high cost hospitalization insurance rather than out-of-hospital bills, and, finally, promoted major medical insurance. But even as competition drew them into the ways of the commercial insurance business, the co-operative insurance companies have helped in the development of medical service centers by investing some of their assets in them and by making financial contributions to the former Cooperative Health Federation of America, which has consistently promoted medical services rather than indemnity insurance.

12 The most notable of these cases is United States v. American Medical As-

sociation, 110 F.2d 703 (D.C. Cir.), *cert. denied,* 310 U.S. 644 (1940). Another important one is Group Health Cooperative of Puget Sound v. King County Medical Society, 39 Wash. 2d 586, 237 Pac.2d 737 (1951).

13 It was here that the medical co-operative's fundamental principles took shape through the efforts of a lone wolf doctor named Michael Shadid. Concerned at the way farm people were butchered in proprietary hospitals run in competition with each other by doctors who practiced all types of medicine and promoted unnecessary surgery to improve their personal income, Dr. Shadid believed that the only way the farmers could save themselves was by banding together and building a co-operative hospital. Shadid and his hospital in Elk City, Oklahoma, survived the attacks of the medical society only because he had the support of the powerful Farmers' Union and the governor of the state. Shadid's four principles of cooperative medicine—group medical practice, periodic prepayment, consumer co-operative control, and preventive medicine—provided considerable inspiration, but only a handful of co-operative medical care programs has survived to realize them all. See Michael A. Shadid, M.D., *Principles of Cooperative Medicine* (Chicago: Cooperative League of the USA, 1946).

14 See George Strauss and Leonard Sayles, *The Local Union: Its Place in the Industrial Plant* (New York: Harper, 1953).

15 For a thorough description of obstacles and solutions to co-operative-union relations, see John Brumm, "Relating Cooperative and Community Prepaid Group Practice Health Plans to Labor Health Programs," speech before the Group Health Institute, Cooperative Health Federation of America, Annual Meeting, Seattle, Wash., July 28, 1955 (mimeo.).

16 Common purposes have merged the Cooperative Health Federation of America and the American Labor Health Association into the Group Health Association of America, but the practical demonstration of mutual goals is to be seen in merger at a local level.

17 This fund was established through collective bargaining by the National Capital Local Division 689, Amalgamated Association of Street, Electric Railway and Motor Coach Employees of America, AFL–CIO, and the District of Columbia Transit System, Inc. Unless otherwise indicated, the information in the rest of this chapter was obtained either from GHA, Inc. sources or from union sources. For the transition experience, see Walter J. Bierwagen, "Medical Care Under the Transit Employees Health and Welfare Plan," speech to the 1960 Annual Meeting, Industrial Medical Association, Medical Care Section, Rochester, N. Y., April 26, 1960 (mimeo.).

18 With capital obtained from the Home Owners' Loan Corporation in 1937, the founders equipped a clinic and hired doctors on a salaried basis, some of whom were promptly disciplined or expelled by the District of Columbia Medical Society. All GHA doctors were denied use of the hospitals in the District of Columbia, and in 1939 the Department of

Justice brought suit under the Sherman Anti-Trust Act against the AMA and the District Society. In 1943, the Supreme Court ruled for the government (American Medical Association v. United States, 317 U.S. 519 [1943]). In May, 1950, the District Medical Society gave formal and official approval to Group Health Association so long as it observes the "Twenty Principles" adopted by the House of Delegates of the American Medical Association as a guide to lay-sponsored medical care plans. Included in these "Twenty Principles" are provisions that the plan be genuinely non-profit, that it comply with the standards of medical ethics, that it be adequately financed, that it be devoted exclusively to health services, that it have high quality personnel and employ only licensed physicians.

19 Schwartz, "Consumer Sponsorship and Physician Sponsorship of Prepaid Group Practice Health Plans . . . ," p. 97.

20 For $12.66 a month per family, half paid by the company and half by the employee, the Transit Fund had been providing life, sickness, and accident insurance, Blue Cross and Blue Shield benefits, and in-hospital doctor visits up to $4 a day. In addition, the Fund had accumulated a surplus of $250,000 to capitalize a health center. After November, 1958, the employer agreed to pay an additional $2 per month for each employee. With matching employee contributions and with the $77,000 a year surplus, approximately $227,000 a year became available for the operating expenses of a health center.

21 Bierwagen, "Medical Care Under the Transit Employees Health and Welfare Plan," p. 5.

22 A formula for allotting costs to the Transit Fund roughly in accordance with their experience has been devised. The Transit Fund will bear the same proportion of total medical service costs as its utilization of those services bears to the total services rendered. This formula does not penalize GHA for increases in utilization that will come as Fund members learn how to use the services more effectively. How to allot the administrative costs was not so easily settled, but the union finally agreed to assume 30 per cent of these, the ratio of union membership to total membership.

23 E.g., the fourteen-year-old girl with a long history of ear infection and bad hearing who had had only the most haphazard treatment; under GHA, she received the necessary care to correct the ear drum. Bierwagen, "Medical Care Under the Transit Employees Health and Welfare Plan," p. 9.

24 E.g., a man whose chest X-ray showed a shadow but he did not return for additional X-rays in six months as prescribed by his doctor, allegedly because of their cost; he subsequently developed carcinoma. *Ibid.*

25 "We have had a case where acute mastoiditis was diagnosed by the private physician, who requested hospitalization. G.H.A. diagnosis showed the trouble to be a gland, acute lymphadenitis. The ears and mastoid were not involved. The child recovered with antibiotic therapy.

"There is a 51-year-old man who had had repair of a double hernia. He had chronic pyelonephritis, went into uremia and was doing very badly when G.H.A. was called in. He has recovered from the uremia and is doing moderately well. The nephritis is apparently under control.

"There was the case of the 58-year-old man being treated by a family physician for congestive heart failure and doing very badly before he was referred to G.H.A. The patient was immediately hospitalized. Diagnosis showed advanced pulmonary tuberculosis. He died within two weeks.

"A 55-year-old man was referred to G.H.A. who had had yearly X-rays for chronic bronchitis all his life; had a positive tuberculin test and skin test for histoplasmosis. Previous chest X-rays were reported showing a soft lesion. X-rays taken under our Plan showed a round lesion in the right lower lobe. Operation revealed cancer of the lung.

"One of the pensioners, 65 years old, had a history of diabetes which was not adequately controlled, a cardiac condition and high blood pressure, has been seen by G.H.A. sixteen times in six months. The improvement in his condition is marked; there is much better control both with respect to the diabetes and cardiac conditions. He is better able to get around and no longer has edema.

"One of our members, 49 years old, reported that he had had a cough for six months and had been seen during that time by his local physician several times. During the past three or four months he had not felt well and during the past month showed increasing weakness, loss of appetite and a weight loss of fifteen pounds. No X-rays had been made. X-rays and other tests by G.H.A. showed a solid lesion in the right lung. The diagnosis was abscess with cystic changes, requiring removal of part of the lung." *Ibid.*, pp. 9–10.

26 *Ibid.*
27 See Sidney R. Garfield, M.D., "A Report on Permanente's First Ten Years," *Permanente Foundation Medical Bulletin*, Vol. X, Nos. 1–4 (1952). For other information on the functioning of the Kaiser Plan see: Albert Deutsch, "The Kaiser Health Plan," *Consumer Reports*, Vol. XXII, No. 3 (March, 1957); Clifford Kuh, M.D., "Permanente Health Plan—Postwar," *Industrial Hygiene Newsletter*, Vol. VIII (Sept., 1948); Joseph W. Garbarino, *Health Plans and Collective Bargaining* (Berkeley: University of California Press, 1960); Avram Yedidia, "Types of Health Risk Bearers," in *Health Insurance Handbook*, ed. Robert D. Eilers and Robt. M. Crowe (Homewood, Ill.: Richard D. Irwin, 1965), pp. 272–94. The author has also drawn on unpublished material in the AFL–CIO files on Kaiser and other plans for this chapter.
28 Avram Yedidia, speech before Cooperative Health Federation of America, *Proceedings of the Sixth Annual Group Health Institute*, Aug. 22–24, 1956, Philadelphia, Pa. (Chicago: CHFA, 1956), pp. 119–20.
29 Some of the difficulties here were experienced when the Retail Clerks, Longshoremen, and Culinary Workers in Southern California attempted

to establish joint negotiations with Kaiser. The effort was not so successful as hoped because there were conflicting contract expiration dates involved and the Longshoremen's contract had been negotiated on a statewide basis with the Northern and Southern California Kaiser Plans.

30 Note this statement of Avram Yedidia: "We have always felt that voluntary enrollment was one of the important cornerstones of our Plan. We could not reconcile our concept of voluntary enrollment with a situation where 51 percent of a membership of a certain union could impose our Plan on the balance of the membership of that union." As a generalization or conclusion about the collective bargaining process, this statement reveals more about its source than about bargaining. Yedidia, speech before Cooperative Health Federation of America, p. 119.

31 Alternative choice proposals at first met with skepticism on the grounds that they would result in adverse risk selection for Kaiser. There was also a question whether other insurers would participate, and for a time Kaiser studied the possibilities of providing its own indemnity alternative to service benefits. However, other insurers are participating—although not enthusiastically and the actuarial objections have proved unwarranted, according to Kaiser officials. *Ibid.*

32 Solo practitioners who felt their practices threatened had urged the medical societies of San Francisco, Solano, and Multnomah to oppose the Kaiser Plan. The Los Angeles County Medical Association passed a resolution condemning "closed-panel procedure" for denying free choice of physician, interposing a "corporate overlord," and interfering with professional practices. (*Bulletin, Los Angeles County Medical Association,* LXXXVII [1953], 501.) Some participating physicians in the Kaiser Plan have been refused membership in the local medical society, and many Kaiser doctors have been ostracized by their colleagues. In recent years these attacks have slackened. The Kaiser Plan today boasts of excellent relations between the Alameda-Contra Costa Medical Association and the Kaiser physicians in Oakland. They also have a co-operative relationship with the Los Angeles and the San Bernardino County Medical Societies. Garfield, "A Report on Permanente's First Ten Years," p. 11.

33 About half of all the physicians in the health plan network are group partners. The rest are employed by the partnership on an annual basis. Employed doctors become eligible for election to partnership after three years of service. The medical group is paid a fixed amount each month according to the number of health plan members served in their area. In addition, there is an incentive increment based on the operating results of the total program in their region. Salaries of both partners and employed doctors are based on training, experience, seniority, and specialty rating. Partners generally get higher salaries than employees, and they share in the division of the medical group's surplus at the end of the year.

34 The criticisms noted are the more continuous ones heard in recent years in union circles.

35 This view has been expressed by Kaiser officials to union social security technicians and probably explains Deutsch's conclusion: "even at best, the continuing service one expects from a family physician is not always forthcoming, and this remains one of the major sources of Kaiser subscriber complaints." Deutsch, "The Kaiser Health Plan," p. 136.

36 Herbert Abrams, M.D., "Observations on Labor Health Planning—A Summary" (mimeo., n.d.). p. 3.

37 Much of the published material on HIP is written by persons associated with it in one capacity or another. The scholarly quality of the following make them particularly useful: Henry B. Makover, M.D., "The Quality of Medical Care," *American Journal of Public Health*, XLI (July, 1951), 824–32; George Rosen, M.D., "Health Education and Preventive Medicine—'New' Horizons in Medical Care," *American Journal of Public Health*, XLII (June, 1952), 687–93; E. F. Daily, M.D., and M. A. Moorhead, M.D., "A Method of Evaluating and Improving the Quality of Medical Care," *American Journal of Public Health*, XLVI (July, 1956), 848–54; Sam Shapiro, Louis Werner, and Paul M. Densen, "Comparison of Prematurity and Prenatal Mortality in General Population and in Population of Prepaid Group Practice, Medical Care Plan," *American Journal of Public Health*, XLVIII (Feb., 1958), 170–98; Paul M. Densen, Neva R. Deardorff, and Eve Balamuth, "Longitudinal Analyses of Four Years of Experience of a Prepaid Comprehensive Medical Care Plan," *Milbank Memorial Fund Quarterly*, XXXVI (Jan., 1958), 5–45; Paul M. Densen, Eve Balamuth, and Sam Shapiro, *Prepaid Medical Care and Hospital Utilization*, American Hospital Association Monograph Series No. 3 (Chicago, 1958); Commmittee for the Special Research Project in the Health Insurance Plan of Greater New York, *Health and Medical Care in New York City* (Cambridge, Mass.: Harvard University Press, 1957) [cited hereafter as *Health and Medical Care in New York City*].

The principles and aims of HIP have been eloquently stated many times by George Baehr, M.D., former President and Medical Director. Some of the following are illustrative: "Health Insurance," address to the Conference on Health and Welfare of the Chicago Federation of Labor, Jan. 9, 1951; "H.I.P.—An Alternative to National Compulsory Medical Insurance," *Connecticut State Medical Journal*, XVII (Jan., 1953), 29; "The Health Insurance Plan of Greater New York, The First Three Years," *Journal of the American Medical Association*, CXLIII, No. 7 (June 17, 1950), 637–40; *A Report of the First Ten Years* (New York: HIP, [1957?]); "The Quality of Medical Service Programs," *Papers and Proceedings, National Conference on Labor Health Services, Washington, D.C., June 16–17, 1958* (Washington, D.C.: American Labor

Health Association, 1958), pp. 35–40. For a summary of HIP, see E. F. Daily, M.D., "Medical Care Under The Health Insurance Plan of Greater New York," *Journal of the American Medical Association,* CLXX, No. 3 (May 16, 1959), 272–76. For the views of some outsiders, see Arthur M. Master, M.D., "Impact of Medical Care Plans on the Medical Profession," *Journal of the American Medical Association,* CL, No. 8 (Oct. 25, 1952), 766–70; Albert Deutsch, "Group Medicine, Part 2," *Consumer Reports,* XXII, No. 2 (Feb., 1957), 85–86; Michael M. Davis, *Medical Care for Tomorrow* (New York: Harper, 1955), pp. 235–37.

38 HIP provides medical and surgical care by family physicians and specialists, diagnostic and laboratory procedures, eye examinations, visiting nurse service, ambulance service between home and hospital, and periodic health examinations, immunizations and other measures of preventive medicine. The uniform standard contract calls for a monthly contribution of $4.50 for an individual subscriber, $9.00 for a couple, and $13.50 for a family. This is in addition to hospitalization insurance, which is a prerequisite for HIP membership.

39 Shapiro, *et al.,* "Comparison of Prematurity and Prenatal Mortality . . . ,"

40 *Health and Medical Care in New York City,* pp. 54–55, 62–63, 71–72, 170–79.

41 According to Blue Cross records, Blue Shield members in New York have a higher hospital admission rate than HIP members, 94.8 per thousand to 77.4 respectively. Densen, *et al., Prepaid Medical Care and Hospital Utilization.*

42 Group practice itself may contribute to a lower hospitalization rate. According to Blue Cross records, Group Health Insurance, Inc., members in New York, who have prepayment for the same range of services as HIP members but without group practice, have a higher hospital admission rate than HIP subscribers. O. W. Anderson and P. B. Sheatsley, *Comprehensive Medical Insurance—A Study of Costs, Use, and Attitudes Under Two Plans* (New York: Health Information Foundation, 1959), p. 36.

43 Makover, "The Quality of Medical Care." Dr. Makover argues that quality of care cannot be ascertained by such standards as the adequacy of the physical equipment, qualification of doctors, etc. These do not "directly establish the quality of medical care that is in fact rendered, but merely assumes that the quality of this care is or can be high if all the accepted standards are met. In place of relying on such an assumption, the present study seeks to determine the quality of the end product —the actual medical services rendered—on the basis of clinical performance" (p. 825). Dr. Makover found that the medical groups in HIP which achieved higher quality ratings by his method of studying clinical records were close to those that might be obtained using accepted standards. But he also found some significant differences and concluded "it would seem that further comparison of these two methods of rating is clearly indicated" (p. 850).

44 Baehr, "The Quality of Medical Service Programs," p. 38.

45 The method of this evaluation is reported by Daily and Moorhead, "A Method of Evaluating and Improving the Quality of Medical Care," pp. 848–54.

46 *Ibid.*, p. 854.

47 "Most significant in the H.I.P. program, however, is the fact that the involvement of the physician in subscriber-physician discussion groups and related activities point to a way of restructuring the patient-doctor relationship. When physicians sit down with a group of patients to discuss why a medical group is run in a certain way and to hear how their actions look from the patients' side, they cannot help being influenced in their behavior by the patient. The patient-physician relationship begins to approach more closely a relationship among equals. In effect, it is the beginning of a new, more democratic patient-physician relationship. This does not mean that we are completely out of the woods. Far from it. Much still remains to be done. Education of patients and physicians is a long, never-ending process. But we can see where we are going and that is important." Rosen, "Health Education and Preventive Medicine—'New' Horizons in Medical Care," p. 692.

48 See discussion of this question in UAW, "Revised Proceedings, Conference on Quality of Medical Care" (mimeo., 1957), pp. 78–81.

49 In Philadelphia, it was the unflagging efforts of Isadore Melamed, formerly with the ILGWU Health Center there, who brought the unions together in the AFL Medical Service Plan. Another multi-union plan (not sponsored by a city central body)—the Union Health Service in Chicago—was conceived by Olivia "Peg" Bautsch and T. J. Burke of Building Service Employees International Union Local 25. The activities of "Peg" Bautsch also served as the impetus of the Union Eye Care Center.

Chapter 14: Administering Medical Service Centers

1 AMA, "Guides for Evaluation of Management and Union Health Centers," in AMA, *A Survey of Union Health Centers* (Chicago: AMA, 1958), p. 56.

2 Dr. Russell V. Lee, Executive, Palo Alto Clinic, in UAW, "Revised Proceedings, Conference on Quality of Medical Care" (mimeo., 1957), p. 4.

3 AFL–CIO Committee on Social Security, Minutes, Dec. 15, 1959.

4 One of these was at a labor health center, The Amalgamated Meat Cutters' Center in St. Louis, allegedly over the hiring of an optometrist or ophthalmologist; the other was in a co-operative plan, the Group Health Cooperative at Puget Sound, involving dentists.

5 Michael M. Davis, "Setting Up Union Health Centers," *A.F.L.–C.I.O. American Federationist* (Nov., 1956).

6 The AMA's "Guides for Evaluation of Management and Union Health Centers" actually are not guides to quality; they are official views on cer-

tain organizational relationships, which will be discussed below. The AMA's 1958 survey of union health centers suggests the range of services but contains little else with which to evaluate the quality of care rendered. *A Survey of Union Health Centers.*

7 One of the most ambitious such meetings was arranged in Detroit by the UAW with forty-five doctors of local and national reputation. "Revised Proceedings, Conference on Quality of Medical Care."

8 Through the Group Health Federation of America, formerly, the American Labor Health Association.

9 "Many physicians hold back from joining a group because they still tend to regard their paying patients as personal property. But this attitude is, in fact, an anachronism, for in his hospital work every doctor today must foreswear his free-wheeling ways if he craves scientific recognition. Surgeons bow meekly to the tissue committee which checks on the removal of normal organs (hallmarks of venal or inept surgery). There is a like policing of Caesarean births and the high fees they command. The patient is no man's private preserve, for case records are kept in unit files subject to the official review of other professional eyes. The canniest diagnostician acknowledges his dependence on the laboratory and X-ray departments and his mistakes—like all others—are bared at clinical conferences." Marion K. Sanders, "Country Doctors Catch Up," *Harper's Magazine*, CCXVI, No. 1295 (April, 1958), 41–42.

10 Quoted by Herbert Abrams, M.D., "Quality of Medical Care," paper presented before Conference on Negotiation and Administration of Health and Welfare Plans of the Industrial Union Department, AFL–CIO, Washington, D.C., March 27–28, 1957 (mimeo., p. 3).

11 From conversation in August, 1955, with the late Dr. John McNeel, then Medical Director of LHI.

12 For a succinct review of the problems of measuring and controlling quality, see Walter J. McNerney, "Controls in the Medical Care Field," *Proceedings of the Thirteenth Annual Meeting of the Industrial Relations Research Association, December, 1960* ([Madison, Wis.]: IRRA, 1961), pp. 67–76.

13 Suggestion of Dr. Caldwell B. Esselstyn, "Revised Proceedings, Conference on Quality of Medical Care," p. 83. Dr. Esselstyn was Executive Director of the Rip Van Winkle Clinic, Hudson, New York.

14 The Labor Health Institute is the most "evaluated" plan; see Franz Goldman, M.D., and Evarts A. Graham, M.D., *The Quality of Medical Care Provided at the Labor Health Institute* (St. Louis: LHI, 1954); Henry G. Farish and Franz Goldman, *The Labor Health Institute: Quality of Service* (St. Louis: LHI, 1948); Nathan M. Simon, M.D., and Sanford E. Rabushka, M.D., *A Trade Union and Its Medical Service Plan* (St. Louis: LHI, 1948); *How Doctor Fees Were Determined at the St. Louis Labor Health Institute for the Fiscal Year July 1, 1952–June 30, 1953* (St. Louis: LHI, 1953) [cited hereafter as *How Doctor Fees Were Deter-*

mined at L.H.I.]; *Dental Care in a Group Practice Plan,* U.S. Dept. of Health, Education, and Welfare, Public Welfare Service (Washington, D.C.: Government Printing Office, 1959). A team of specialists has studied the Hotel Employees Health Center in New York City; see I. O. Woodruff, M.D., *et al.*, "Medical Survey of the New York Hotel Trade Council and Hotel Association of New York City," NYHTC and HANY Health Center, Inc., New York, N.Y., Jan., 1957 (mimeo.).

15 At HIP the clinical records themselves are studied to see whether the medical information recorded was accurate; how the patient was "handled" at each stage in diagnosis, therapy, and follow-up; whether preventive medicine was practiced; whether the laboratory service and special procedures were properly used; and, in general, the extent to which judgment and skill were employed in meeting medical problems. Dr. Makover, who conducted this study, was critical of the methodology in the LHI quality evaluation because it did not "directly establish the quality of medical care that is in fact rendered, but merely assumes that the quality of this care is or can be high if all of the accepted standards are met. In place of relying on such an assumption, the present study seeks to determine the quality of the end product—the actual medical services rendered—on the basis of clinical performance." Dr. Makover found that the medical groups in HIP which achieved higher quality ratings by his method of studying clinical records were close to those that might be obtained using accepted standards (as in the LHI study); he also found some significant differences and concluded, "it would seem that further comparison of these two methods of rating is clearly indicated." Henry B. Makover, M.D., "The Quality of Medical Care," *American Journal of Public Health,* XLI (July, 1951), 831–32.

16 Walter Reuther, "Revised Proceedings, Conference on Quality of Medical Care," p. 96.

17 Jerome L. Schwartz, "Participation of Consumers in Prepaid Health Plans," *Journal of Health and Human Behavior,* V, Nos. 2–3 (Summer-Fall, 1964), 74–84.

18 These are the proposals most commonly advanced by local medical societies when their opinions are asked. The AMA says simply that "the fee schedule should be acceptable to the local county medical society" (*A Survey of Union Health Centers,* p. 56).

19 Caldwell B. Esselstyn, M.D., when Director of the Rip Van Winkle Clinic, Hudson, New York, in discussions at the Seventh Annual Group Health Institute, Two Harbors, Minn., July 17, 1957. The discussion is very imperfectly summarized in *Proceedings of the Seventh Annual Group Health Institute, July 17–19, 1957* (Chicago: Cooperative Health Federation of America, 1957), pp. 26–27.

20 In this connection, the variance in going market rates for different specialties poses a difficult problem. In a letter to the author dated May 5, 1963, Dr. Herbert Abrams stated: "One of the problems which we and

other health centers have had, is the continuing pressure on the part of certain specialties, for example, surgery, to be paid at a higher rate than internal medicine. I have always insisted that physicians of equal qualifications should be paid equally. Once you give in to the pressure for differentials, there is no end to it and it cannot but have a poor effect on doctors' morale." The Labor Health Institute in St. Louis attempted to work out reimbursement schedules based on many measures of equity. *How Doctors Fees Were Determined at L.H.I.* But the effect of trying to weigh all factors was unsettling to the staff which demanded a simpler scale.

21 Abrams, "Quality of Medical Care," p. 3.
22 William A. MacColl, *Group Practice and Prepayment of Medical Care* (Washington, D.C.: Public Affairs Press, 1966), p. 109.
23 "The relative stability of Classes I and II [designation of samples by socioeconomic characteristics] as regards their use of the family doctor meant, therefore, that most of these families could have better medical care. In contrast, the relative instability of the physician-family relationship characteristic of Class III meant that the families of this class were seldom dealt with as a group of interrelated individuals whose several illnesses might have a common focus—the family milieu." Earl Lamon Koos, *The Health of Regionville* (New York: Columbia University Press, 1954), p. 63.
24 E. Richard Weinerman, M.D., "An Appraisal of Medical Care in Group Health Centers," *American Journal of Public Health,* XLVI (March, 1956), 308.
25 See Murray B. Hunter, M.D., and John H. Sloss, M.D., "Problems of Participation of the Family Physician in Medical Group Practice," paper presented before the Medical Care Section, American Public Health Association, Atlantic City, N.J., Nov. 15, 1956; also A. N. Kaplin and H. C. Daniels, "The Managing Physician in the Practice of Medicine," *Journal of the National Medical Association,* XLV (May, 1953), 196–200.
26 Nathan Simon, M.D., and Sanford Rabushka, M.D., "Membership Attitudes in the Labor Health Institute of St. Louis," *American Journal of Public Health,* XLVI (June, 1956), 720.
27 *Ibid.*
28 Abrams, "The Quality of Medical Care," p. 4.
29 Joseph A. Langbord, M.D., and George Shucker, M.D., "Problems Encountered in the Operation of the Health and Welfare Plan of the Philadelphia Male Apparel Industry," *Pennsylvania Medical Journal,* LIX (April, 1956), 457.
30 For example, the San Francisco Labor Council survey of 1952, published as *Labor Plans for Health;* and the Retail, Wholesale Local 688 study in St. Louis in 1945 that culminated in the Labor Health Institute.
31 See Harold Gibbons, "How to Establish and Operate a Health Clinic," *Textbook for Health and Welfare Trustees and Administrators,* Proceed-

ings of the Third Annual Conference of Health and Welfare Plans, Trustees and Administrators (Denver, 1957).

32 "When asked if they had ever received a detailed explanation of L.H.I. benefits and services, 61 per cent of the respondents answered yes and 39 per cent no. Of those who answered yes, about 45 per cent said they had received such an explanation at a union meeting, 37 per cent by reading a brochure, and the remainder had learned about the plan from the spouse, fellow-workers, or L.H.I. employees." Simon and Rabushka, "Membership Attitudes in the Labor Health Institute of St. Louis," p. 721.

33 Evaluation and comparison of health center utilization is very difficult because there are no generally applied ways of measuring it. Several indices are in use: (a) The percentage of the insured population or participants that visit the clinic each year. This is sometimes broken down to distinguish the number of old patients and the number of new ones. (b) The total number of patient visits per year, expressed as an average number of visits per patient. (c) The number of services rendered per patient or per covered population. This criterion is a common one, but suffers because of the confusion in the definition of what shall constitute a unit of service. This measure is too often used to create a magnified picture of the health center's usefulness. (d) Number of doctor visits per year, expressed as average number per patient or participant. The advantage of this criterion is that it does not weigh the utilization by counting all visits for minor laboratory tests not requiring a doctor's attention. (e) Number of doctor hours scheduled per patient or per participant. Doctors may do much advising over the telephone which is measured here but not in the other criteria. However, this criterion must be adjusted so as not to include time of doctors spent in research and administrative work. Although this measure could be criticized as weighing in favor of the inefficient health center that does not make sufficient use of auxiliary personnel, it is still probably the best measure of utilization.

These criteria are useful only in comparing two situations where all the actuarial variables are eliminated, such as age and sex distribution and extent of family coverage; employment factors—income level, job hazards, and occupational disease; and perhaps factors such as diet. If these independent variables could be eliminated, then utilization statistics could be used to measure the effect of health education, the efficiency of communications and the rapport between staff and patients. But it is difficult to compare the utilization of different centers and even the progress from year to year of one center because the actuarial character of the groups covered varies widely and is changing constantly.

In years to come the actuarial variables will fluctuate less, and it is important to develop new standard statistics in order to get at the intangible but fundamental attitudes that discourage utilization. Otherwise, health center administrators will not be able to learn much from either their own past experience or that of other health centers.

34 Weinerman, "An Appraisal of Medical Care in Group Health Centers," p. 308.
35 From conversation with Walter Bierwagen, President of Local 689, Amalgamated Association of Street, Electric Railway, and Motor Coach Employees of America. At the time (August, 1957), this local in the District of Columbia was working toward a medical care plan.
36 The following table shows the percentage of respondents in each social class who recognize specified symptoms as needing medical attention:

Symptom	CLASS I (N–51)	CLASS II (N–335)	CLASS III (N–128)
Loss of appetite	57%	50%	20%
Persistent backache	53	44	19
Continued coughing	77	78	23
Persistent joint and muscle pains	80	47	19
Blood in stool	98	89	60
Blood in urine	100	93	69
Excessive vaginal bleeding	92	83	54
Swelling of ankles	77	76	23
Loss of weight	80	51	21
Bleeding gums	79	51	20
Chronic fatigue	80	53	19
Shortness of breath	77	55	21
Persistent headaches	80	56	22
Fainting spells	80	51	33
Pain in chest	80	51	31
Lump in breast	94	71	44
Lump in abdomen	92	65	34

Koos, *The Health of Regionville*, p. 32.

37 *Ibid.*, p. 35.
38 *Ibid.*
39 *Ibid.*, p. 36.
40 Hyman J. Weiner and Shelley Akabas, "The Impact of Chronic Illness on a Union Population: Implications for Labor Health Programs," *Journal of Health and Human Behavior*, V, Nos. 2–3 (Summer-Fall, 1964), 103–7.
41 D. C. McElrath, "Prepaid Group Medical Practice: A Comparative Analysis of Organizations and Perspectives," unpub. Ph.D. Diss., Yale University, 1958, as reported by E. R. Weinerman, *Proceedings, 13th Annual Group Health Institute, Detroit, Mich., May 9–11, 1963* (Washington, D.C.: Group Health Association of America, 1963), p. 10.
42 *Ibid.*, p. 13.
43 Labor plans might take suggestions from others: the Group Health Co-

operative of Puget Sound holds a weekly orientation course for new members; slides are used to depict the services and facilities, as well as to explain their use. Group Health Association in Washington, D.C., sends out an extensive questionnaire to members every few years, and the results have proved of some value to the staff in improving services. HIP sends out a birthday card inviting the subscriber to give himself a present in the form of a physical examination.

44 William A. Sawyer, M.D., "Impact of Labor Health Plans on Occupational Health—The Opportunity," *American Journal of Public Health,* XLIV (May, 1954), 606.

45 F. Benedict Lanahan, M.D., formerly Medical Director of the AFL Medical Service Plan, Philadelphia, in *Proceedings of the Sixth Annual Group Health Institute, Aug. 22–24, 1956* (Chicago: Cooperative Health Federation of America, 1956), p. 79.

46 Abrams, "Quality of Medical Care," p. 6.

47 Weinerman, "An Appraisal of Medical Care in Group Health Centers," p. 307.

48 Two unions experimenting with this approach are the Distributive Local 65, New York City, and Teamsters Local 688, St. Louis.

49 Schwartz, "Participation of Consumers in Prepaid Health Plans."

50 Avram Yedidia, in *Proceedings of the Sixth Annual Group Health Institute,* p. 119.

51 Joseph W. Garbarino, *Health Plans and Collective Bargaining* (Berkeley: University of California Press, 1960), p. 223.

52 "This widening of the difference in the rates of [physician] contact as education increases seems to suggest that it is the people in the highest education class who avail themselves most readily of the benefits of prepaid medical care." Committee for the Special Research Project in the Health Insurance Plan of Greater New York, *Health and Medical Care in New York City* (Cambridge, Mass.: Harvard University Press, 1957), p. 53 [cited hereafter as *Health and Medical Care in New York City*]. See also Koos, *The Health of Regionville, passim.*

53 An HIP study shows that the higher the level of education of enrollees in a medical service plan, the less likely they are to use "outside" doctors. *Health and Medical Care in New York City,* p. 62.

54 Competitive pressures against HIP have been intense, from several sources, including the medical society, the commercial insurers, Blue Cross-Blue Shield, Group Health Insurance, Inc., and others all emphasizing free choice of physician. This has had its effect on city employees: first firemen wanted alternative choice, and then units of the American Federation of State, County, and Municipal Employees have decided for it.

55 A survey at HIP conducted before any alternative choice plans were available attempted to determine the extent to which non-HIP physicians were used by HIP enrollees, and the reasons for using "outside" doctors.

It was found that where more than one member of the family was covered by HIP, the HIP doctor was the family doctor in 82 per cent of the households; if only one member was covered by HIP, the HIP doctor was the family doctor only 32 per cent of the time. *Health and Medical Care in New York City*, pp. 61–62.

56 George Orwell observed in England in the middle 1930's this important feature of working class life: "This business of petty inconvenience and indignity, of being kept waiting about, of having to do everything at other people's convenience is inherent in working-class life. A thousand influences constantly press a working man down into a passive role. He does not act, he is acted upon. He feels himself the slave of mysterious authority and has a firm conviction that 'they' will never allow him to do this, that, and the other." *The Road to Wigan Pier* (New York: Berkley Publishing Corp., 1961), p. 52.

57 See Osler L. Peterson, M.D., Leon P. Andrews, M.D., Robert S. Spain, M.D., and Bernard G. Greenberg, "An Analytical Study of North Carolina General Practice, 1953–1954," *Journal of Medical Education*, Vol. XXXI, No. 12 (Dec., 1956), Part 2. In this study there were 7 physicians who ranked outstanding, 15 pretty good, 27 average, 23 poor, and 16 uniformly poor. " . . . In terms of medical education and training the physicians who participated in this study are not evidently different from general practitioners at large" (p. 71).

58 See Paul A. Lembcke, M.D., and Olive G. Johnson, *A Medical Audit Report, Comparison of the Findings in a 200-Bed Suburban Hospital With Those in University Teaching Hospitals* (Los Angeles: School of Public Health, University of California, 1963). According to this study, only a portion of major surgical operations were justified in the survey hospitals. The proportion of justified surgical operations varied greatly from none justified out of 37 cases of primary uterine suspension to 92 per cent of the exploratory laparotomy for suspected intestinal obstruction. The rates of justified operations in the University Teaching Hospital used for comparison were much higher (p. 285).

59 See the very readable account of the Kefauver drug hearings by Richard Harris, *The Real Voice* (New York: Macmillan, 1964).

60 A pioneering study of this sort has been done by Burton Wolfman of a United Auto Workers local in California—"Medical Expenses and Choice of Plans: A Case Study," *Monthly Labor Review*, LXXXIV, No. 11 (Nov., 1961), 1186–90.

61 Spencer Jones, Director of Planning at HIP, first suggested this pattern before the Eleventh Annual Meeting, Cooperative Health Federation of America, July 17–19, 1957, at Two Harbors, Minn. He reported that the pattern of choice in the HIP groups with alternative choice arrangements tended to support the hypothesis that previous affiliation and the preference of union leadership have an influence on the division. In a recent review of the evidence on choice, E. R. Weinerman suggests that "much

of the dual choice outcome depends upon which of the competing plans has the initial enrollment advantage and how well acquainted the group can become with the once strange health center method." "As Others See Us: The Patients' Viewpoint," *Proceedings, 13th Annual Group Health Institute,* p. 7.

62 Union leaders have influenced the choice in the New York Dress Joint Board of the ILGWU where Luigi Antonnini's Local 89 chose GHI because Mr. Antonnini has long been interested in GHI and promoted it, while those in Charles Zimmerman's Local 22 chose HIP by a big majority because it was his preference. Where the union emphasizes the benefits of a full-service program there will be an effect on the members' selection. The Longshoremen's local of the ILWU entered the Kaiser program in 1949; when an indemnity alternative was offered in 1954 under the new Kaiser policy for alternative choice only 3 per cent of the union members switched plans. Union members may wish to test the union's recommendations in the light of their own experience. When two warehousemen's locals of the ILWU negotiated their first welfare plan in 1953 and started out at the beginning with an alternative choice program, the members divided almost evenly; in the successive annual choices there has been a slight increase in the Kaiser proportion. UAW educational and promotional efforts plus word-of-mouth descriptions by those who had experienced Community Health Association in Detroit have steadily increased the number choosing it. In Washington, D.C., the Transit Workers after they had experienced Group Health Association, Inc., for several years were given full alternative choice, with the result that a very small percentage elected to leave for the indemnity choice. Had there been full dual choice from the beginning, there would undoubtedly be fewer in GHA today. Another consideration affecting choice may be the difference between an urban and small town setting. In the latter, effective leadership may be more able to encourage a large proportion to try a community health plan even under alternative choice conditions. At the Sault Ste Marie and District Group Health Association in Ontario, 80 per cent of United Steelworkers chose prepaid group practice initially.

Chapter 15:   Rationalizing the Medical Market

1 Indicative of the recent interest of economists in health and medical care are the following: Herbert E. Klarman, *The Economics of Health* (New York and London: Columbia University Press, 1965); *The Economics of Health and Medical Care, Proceedings of the Conference on the Economics of Health and Medical Care, May 10–12, 1962* (Ann Arbor: University of Michigan, 1964); Herman M. Somers and Anne R. Somers, *Doctors, Patients, and Health Insurance* (Washington, D.C.: Brookings Institution, 1961).

2 Milton Friedman and Simon Kuznetz, *Income from Independent Profes*

sional Practice (New York: National Bureau of Economic Research, 1945), pp. 136–37.

3 Klarman, *The Economics of Health,* p. 110.

4 John T. Dunlop, at the 1965 Health Conference of the New York Academy of Medicine, "Closing the Gaps in the Availability and Accessibility of Health Services," *Bulletin of the New York Academy of Medicine,* XLI, No. 12 (Dec., 1965), 1328.

5 "During the past five years, over a thousand disciplinary actions of state boards of medical examiners were reported; a large proportion of these were based on various forms of incompetence. . . .

"Despite the large number of medical regulatory bodies with varying degrees of authority and improvements in medical education, incompetent physicians still present a problem. Although they constitute a small minority of the profession, their potential dangers are disproportionate to their numbers. Particularly difficult to handle is the well-qualified specialist with borderline mental illness which may or may not be associated with alcoholism or drug addiction. Often the judgment of such a person becomes clouded gradually and he is not exposed until after disaster has struck. From a survey of state medical societies and medical practice laws, I concluded that neither provides the complete answer to the problem. The accredited hospitals, at least, have the authority to deal with incompetent physicians and the staffs of these hospitals are more and more accepting their responsibilities. The unaccredited fringe hospitals still provide refuge for incompetent physicians who have become outlaws after having been expelled from medical societies or the staffs of reputable hospitals. Great difficulties are encountered where there is no control. The boards of medical examiners are of little help because the licenses permit people to practice medicine and surgery with no limitations. . . ." Robert C. Derbyshire, M.D., "What Should the Profession do About the Incompetent Physician?" *Journal of the American Medical Association,* CXCIV, No. 12 (Dec. 20, 1965), 1287–90.

6 The Columbia School of Public Health and Administrative Medicine has completed two studies, one of patients hospitalized in 1959 (*The Quantity, Quality and Costs of Medical and Hospital Care Secured by a Sample of Teamster Families in the New York Area* [New York: Columbia University Press, 1962]) and one of patients in 1962 (*A Study of the Quality of Hospital Care Secured by A Sample of Teamster Family Members in New York City* [New York: Columbia University Press, 1964]) with generally similar findings.

7 Osler L. Peterson, Leon P. Andrews, Robert S. Spain, and Bernard G. Greenberg, "An Analytical Study of North Carolina General Practice, 1953–54," *Journal of Medical Education,* XXXI, No. 12 (Dec., 1956), Part 2, 1–165.

8 The infant death rate for Negroes is nearly twice that for whites; maternal

mortality is almost four times higher; and life expectancy 6.4 years less for males and 7.7 years less for females.

9 Osler L. Peterson, "Medical Care in the U.S.," *Scientific American*, CCIX, No. 2 (Aug., 1963), 19.

10 Anne R. Somers, "The Paradox of Medical Progress," *Pennsylvania Medical Journal*, LXIV (Jan., 1961) [p. 3 of 1961 reprint by the Brookings Institution].

11 Anne R. Somers, "Conflict, Accommodation, and Progress: Some Socio-economic Observations on Medical Education and the Practicing Profession," *Journal of Medical Education*, XXXVIII, No. 6 (June, 1963), 470–73.

12 From a study by H. Jack Geiger, as quoted by Peterson, "Medical Care in the U.S.," p. 21.

13 Reinhold Niebuhr, *Moral Man and Immoral Society* (New York: Charles Scribners, 1960), pp. xiv–xv, 234.

14 John R. Commons, "American Shoemakers, 1848–1895: A Sketch of Industrial Evolution," *Quarterly Journal of Economics*, XXIV (Nov., 1909), 39–81; John Kenneth Galbraith, *American Capitalism, The Concept of Countervailing Power* (Boston: Houghton Mifflin, 1952).

15 Milton I. Roemer, "Changing Patterns of Health Service: Their Dependence on a Changing World," *Annals of the American Academy of Political and Social Science*, CCCXLVI (March, 1963), 55.

Chapter 16: Community Health Bargaining

1 Paraphrase of a statement made to the author, Jan., 1957.

2 Statement made to the author in June, 1951, by John P. Burke, then President-Secretary of the International Brotherhood of Pulp, Sulphite and Paper Mill Workers.

3 Delegate Blumfield, Proceedings, Conference on Negotiation and Administration of Health and Welfare Plans, Industrial Union Department, AFL–CIO, March 27–28, 1957, Washington, D.C. (typescript at AFL–CIO headquarters), p. 209.

4 Albert J. Hayes, as quoted in Ruth Brecher and Edward Brecher, *How to Get the Most Out of Medical & Hospital Benefit Plans* (Englewood Cliffs, N.J.: Prentice-Hall, 1961), p. 118.

5 Nelson H. Cruikshank, "Labor's Interest in Medical Care," *New England Journal of Medicine*, CCLVII, No. 18 (Oct. 31, 1957), 866.

6 For a summary of American and foreign experience, see Eveline M. Burns, "The Role of Government in Health Services," *Bulletin of the New York Academy of Medicine*, XLI, No. 7 (July, 1965), 1–45.

7 My estimate. See Louis S. Reed and Ruth S. Hanft, "National Health Expenditures, 1950–64," *Social Security Bulletin*, XXIX, No. 1 (Jan., 1966), 13.

8 U.S. Congress, House of Representatives Committee on Ways and Means, *Executive Hearings on H.R. 1 and Other Proposals for Medical Care for the Aged,* 89 Cong., 1 sess. (1965), Part I, p. 376.

9 From "Policy Statement on the Role of Government Tax Funds in Problems of Health Care," adopted May 26, 1965, by the Trustees and Council of the New York Academy of Medicine, 2 East 103rd St., New York, N. Y.

INDEX

Abel, A. W., 54

Abrams, Dr. Herbert, 208, 213, 300n19, 301–2n20, 302n28,n30, 305n46

Administration of claims: ILGWU policies of, 16–17; by Amalgamated Clothing Workers, 24; in steel, 53, 58–59; grievance procedure in, 58, 71, 104; unions want role in, 104–6; difficulties in trusteed plans of, 113

Administration of health plans: in ILGWU, 14–17; by insurance companies in men's clothing, 23–25; in UMW, 36–39, 41–42; in steel, 55–59; in auto, 68, 70–71; summarized, 101–15; cost controls in, 114–15. *See also* "Management prerogative"

Algoma Steel Corporation, 64, 65

Allied Industrial Workers of America, International Union (AIW), 109, 271n41

Alternative choice arrangements: adopted by Dress Joint Board, ILGWU, 21; Steelworkers' plan for, in Pittsburg, Cal., 166–67; under Community Health Association, 182; of Kaiser Plan, 192–93; in HIP, 197; described and analyzed, 214–19; strategy of, 239–40; not adverse risk selection for Kaiser Plan, 296n31; adopted by units of State, County and Municipal Employees in HIP, 305n54; experience with, in labor plans, 307n62

Amalgamated Association of Street, Electric Railway and Motor Coach Employees of America. *See* Street and Electric Railway Employees.

Amalgamated Clothing Workers of America. *See* Clothing Workers, Amalgamated

Amalgamated Meat Cutters and Butcherworkmen of North America. *See* Meat Cutters

American Dental Association. *See* Dental Association, American

American Federation of Labor (AF of L): changing attitude on benefit plans, 4, 5, 247n9; requires annual audits of welfare funds, 108. *See also* Meany, George; Umhey, Frederick F.; Woll, Matthew

American Federation of Labor-Congress of Industrial Organizations (AFL–CIO): interest in prepaid group practice, 63; urged Medicare, 91–92; action on welfare irregularities, 108–9; suggests insurance reforms, 120–21; enforces ethical practice code, 121; attitude toward major medical, 126; critical of Blue Cross hospital policing, 134; emphasizes systematic hospital planning, 142–43; joint statement with American Dental Association, 173–75; Social Security Committee recommendation on medical centers, 205. *See also* Cruikshank, Nelson; Kirkland, Lane; Meany, George; Munts, Raymond; Shoemaker, Richard

American Federation of Labor-Congress of Industrial Organizations (AFL–CIO) Hospital Association, Philadelphia, 181–82

311

American Federation of Labor (AF of L) Medical Service Plan, Philadelphia: other health plans, paved way for, 168; includes city employees, 169; surmounts legal obstacles, 171; forerunner of AFL–CIO Hospital Association, 181–82
American Federation of State, County and Municipal Employees. *See* State, County and Municipal Employees
American Medical Association. *See* Medical Association, American
American Public Health Association. *See* Public Health Association, American
Antonnini, Luigi, 307n62
Appalachian Regional Hospitals, Inc., 43
Auto Workers, United (UAW): opposed employee benefit plans, 9; history of health bargaining, 48–52, 67–78; diagnostic center in Toledo, 75; Local 738 health plan, Baltimore, 75, 77; coverage for laid-off employees, 89–90; relations with Blue Cross, 132, 134, 142; negotiations with Blue Shield, 150; sponsor of Community Health Association, Detroit, 178, 182; and Union Health Service, 180; local option for direct–service plans, 190; health center in Toledo limited by medical society, 205; decision on alternative choice in Community Health Association, 215–16, 307n62; effect of national bargaining by, 237; contribution of UAW Conference on Quality, 239; advance groundwork for health bargaining, 249n23; *See also* Becker, Harry; Brindle, James; Esselstyn, Dr. Caldwell B.; Glasser, Melvin A.; Gosser, Richard; Mott, Dr. Fred; Pollack, Jerome; Reuther, Walter; Woodcock, Leonard

Baehr, Dr. George, 162
Bakery and Confectionery Workers, American, 271n41
Ball, Senator Joseph, 10
Barbash, Jack, 273n23
Barbers' Union, 4
Bautsch, Olivia "Peg," 299n49
Becker, Harry, 49, 261n12,n17
Benefits: bargaining on level of, 83–85; bargaining on employer contribution to, 84; inadequacy of, 98–99, 265n34; appraisal of, by administrative procedures, 114–15. *See also* Death benefits; Dental services; Disability benefits; Eye care service; Financing of benefits; Group life insurance; Hospitalization benefits; Medical benefits; Mental health service; Rehabilitation services; Surgical benefits
Bethlehem Steel Corporation, 53, 56
Bierwagen, Walter J., 186, 187, 188, 293n17, 294n21, 304n35
Bloch, Irvin, 149
Bloom, Dr. James, 19, 21
Blue Cross: services to Dress Joint Board, ILGWU, 21; rising costs, 57; Steelworkers and, 57, 59; comparison with Kaiser in steel plans, 61, 62; UAW experience with, 71–73; no union representation in Michigan Hospital Service, 72; entered coverage for retirees, 90; commercial insurance as an alternative to, 118; and competitive bidding, 124; effect on, of policies offered by commercial insurance, 125–26; union bargaining with, 132–40; improvements needed in regulation of, 139–40; Transit Fund attitude towards, 186; and Kaiser Foundation, 190, 191; weakness in hospital reform, 224; operating principles, 277n3
Blue Shield: United Medical Service and Dress Joint Board, ILGWU, 21; family income limits set by, 54, 94–95; rising costs of benefits, 57; Steelworkers' experience with, 60–61; UAW experience with, 71–73; Michigan Medical Service, 77; coverage for retirees, 90; commercial insurance as an alternative to, 118; doctors' commitment to, 147; origin and development, 148–52; and San Joaquin Foundation, 153; as alternative to Kaiser in Pittsburg, Cal., 166–67; and 1954 California Supreme Court decision, 170
Boone Commission (Admiral Joel T. Boone, Chairman), 33, 34, 35–36
Bowers, Paul E., 265n36, 269n25, 282n3,n7
Brand, Dr. Morris, 252n22, 287n9
Brewery, Flour, Cereal, Soft Drink and Distillery Workers of America, International Union of United, 105, 267n18
Bridges, Senator Styles H., 34

Brindle, James, 74, 261n15, 262n21,n30
Building Service Employees' International Union: murder of official leads to welfare investigation, 107; Chicago Local 25 initiated permissive statute, 171; founder of Union Health Service, 178, 299n49; innovating role, 236. *See also* Bautsch, Olivia "Peg"; Burke, T. J.
Burke, T. J., 299n49
Byrd, Senator Harry, 11

Cabinetmakers, Pennsylvania Society of Journeymen, 3
Carpenters and Joiners of America, United Brotherhood of, 4
Carrier selection: in steel, 57–58; in auto plans, 70–71; in single-employer plans, 102; problems of "switching," 123, 275n36
Central labor bodies: New York City Central Labor Council, 142, 163; Philadelphia, AFL CIO Medical Health Plan, 142; San Francisco Central Labor Council, 147, 168; New York City CIO Council, 164; New Haven, Conn., Central Labor Union, 169; Chicago Federation of Labor–CIO, 180; Philadelphia Central Labor Union, 181; San Francisco bay area AFL–CIO councils, 190; role in health center planning, 203; role in community health bargaining, 237
Chalk, O. Roy, 187
Chrysler Corporation, 52, 67–68
Cigar Makers' International Union of America, 4, 6
Cilento, Sol, 270n34
Claims administration. *See* Administration of claims
Cloakmakers' Union, International, 13
Clothing Manufacturers' Association, 22
Clothing Workers, Amalgamated: history, 22–27; Amalgamated Insurance Fund, 22; Amalgamated Social Benefit Association, 22, 23; Amalgamated Life Insurance Company, 23–24; Amalgamated Life and Health Insurance Company, 24; claims administration contrasted with ILGWU, 24; health centers, 25, 177; Pennsylvania diagnostic program, 25; Sidney Hillman Health Centers, 25–27, 168; comparison with ILGWU, 27–28; use

of self-insured funds, 127–28; health plan in Lehigh, Pa. opposed by medical society, 167; includes dental programs, 172; health plan in Rochester, N.Y., limited by medical society, 205; study of chronic illness, 212; innovation in New York and Philadelphia, 236; early health bargaining, 248n20, 249n22; *See also* Brand, Dr. Morris; Hillman, Sidney; Langbord, Dr. Joseph; Weiner, Dr. Hyman J.
Collisson, Captain A. T., 33
Commons, John R. 228
Communication Workers of America, 82, 83
Community Health Association, Detroit: early organization, 73–77; description of, 178, 182–83; included alternative choice, 215; local planning and national bargaining, 237
Community Health Foundation, Cleveland, 168, 178, 179
Community rating, 123, 136–37, 277n3
Competitive bidding, 121–22, 126
Congress of Industrial Organizations (CIO): avoided intra-union benefit programs, 5, 30; attitude toward employee benefit plans, 8; declared priority for health and welfare bargaining, 10; support for Blue Cross, 132
Consumer representation: on Blue Cross governing boards, 138–39; reluctance of dentists to grant, 174; in HIP, 196; recommended in governing body of medical service plan, 206; supported by Blue Cross official, 280n28
Conversion rights: Steelworkers, 54; reason UAW prefers Blue Cross, 71; definition, 98; none in self-insured plans, 128; under Community Health Association, 182–83
Cooperative health plans, 171, 183–84, 214
Countervailing power in medical market, 176, 228
Coverage of, dependents: not included in ILGWU New York Health Center, 18; Clothing Workers, 22, 26; Steelworkers, 53, 257n2; increase in, 88–89; in union health centers, 178; limitation of Union Health Service, 181; and alternative choice, 216
Coverage of laid off employees, 89

Coverage of retirees; in auto, 68, 71; costs of, borne by Ford and GM, 85; breakthrough in, 90–91; Blue Cross role in, 133; and life insurance in auto, 256n9

Coverage of, striking employees, 90

Cruikshank, Nelson, 264n17, 309n5

Culinary Workers. *See* Hotel and Restaurant Employees and Bartenders' International Union

Davis, Michael M., 206

Death benefits: ILGWU incorporates fund for, 14; Clothing Workers, 22; UMW Fund, 33, 40

Dental Asociation, American, 172, 173–75

Dental prepayment plans, 172–75

Dental services: UMW Fund, 40; extent of coverage, 96–97; quality of, 175; unique program at Labor Health Institute, 179; under Group Health Association, 185

Dental service corporations, 173

Derbyshire, Dr. Robert C., 225

Direct service plans. *See* Prepaid group practice

Disability benefits: Clothing Workers, 22; UMW Fund, 40; Steelworkers, 53, 54, 257n3; in auto, 68, 72, 256n9

Distillery, Rectifying and Wine Workers' International Union of America, 108–9, 270n34

Douglas Report, 103, 108

Draper, Dr. Warren, 34–47 *passim.*, 157, 160, 252n8, 253n28, 254n36, n40, 286n41

Dress and Waistmaker Joint Board, ILGWU, 21, 28

Dual choice arrangements. *See* Alternative choice arrangements

Dubinsky, David, 250n6

Dyers, Finishers, Printers and Bleachers of America, Federation of, 249n22

East Point Medical Center, Baltimore, 77

Eilers, Robert, 137

Electrical, Radio and Machine Workers of America, International Union of, 265n32

Electrical Workers, International Brotherhood of, 248n19, 271n41

Ellsworth, Ted, 274n26, 285n28

Employee benefit plans: started by employers, 8; and "management prerogative," 9; unilateral employer control of, ended by Inland Steel case, 12; in auto and steel, 48–50; as remuneration for work, 83; and administration of single-employer plans, 102; employers' control, where union is weak, 248n19

Esselstyn, Dr. Caldwell B., 77

Experience rating, 124, 136–37

Eye care service, 96–97

Falk, I. S., 64

Federal Employees Health Benefit Plan, 132, 185, 291n7

Fees, physicians': reimbursement by UMW Fund, 42; fee-for-service principle of, 44–45; traditional methods challenged, 144; schedule under Blue Shield, 144–45, 150; influence of payment method on group practice, 208; rising surgeons' fees, 224

Financing of health plans: Clothing Workers' experience, 24–25; by royalty in mining, 33, 34, 38; in steel industry, 54, 55–57, 257n2, 258n11, n12; non-contributory financing in auto, 70; trend to full employer financing, 85–88, 262n2, 263n6; analyzed by source, 86; in single-employer plans, 102–4. *See also* Benefits

Free choice of physician: by miners, 43, 44, 45; AMA attitude defined, 159; stipulated by state laws, 169–70; and alternative choice arrangements, 216–18

Ford Motor Company, 51, 52, 67–68, 71, 100

Furniture Workers of America, United, 127–28

Furstenberg, Dr. Frank, 242

Galbraith, John Kenneth, 228

Garbarino, Joseph, 164, 166

Garfield, Dr. Sidney, 188

Garment Workers' Union, International Ladies' (ILGWU): started tuberculosis benefits and medical care program, 4–5; opened New York City clinic, 6; history, 13–21; comparison with Clothing Workers' program, 24, 27–28; use of self-insured funds, 127–28; and medical societies, 167, 205; health centers in Philadelphia, St.

Louis, and Kansas City, 168; has sponsored eighteen health centers, 177; has limited power in medical market, 236; first health and welfare bargaining, 248n20; lower hospitalization rate in prepaid group practice than in indemnity plans, 291n7. *See also* Antonnini, Luigi; Bloom, Dr. James; Dubinsky, David; Held, Adolph; Minkoff, Nathaniel; Price, Dr. Leo; Sackman, Morris; Umhey, Frederick F.; Zimmerman, Charles

General Electric Corporation, 97

General Motors Corporation, 52, 67–68, 69, 71, 73, 103

Gibbons, Harold, 180, 302–3n31

Ginsburg, Woodrow L., 282n8

Glasser, Melvin A., 70, 261n3

Golberg, Ted, 64, 65, 260n46

Goldman, Dr. Franz, 74, 75

Goldsborough, Judge T. Alan, 34

Gosser, Richard, 75

Gotham Knife Cutters' Association, 13

Gottlieb, Sylvia, 83

Government health insurance, 8, 32, 148, 248n15. *See also* Medicare

Granite Cutters' International Association of America, The, 4

Greenberg, Bernard, 58, 259n15,n17, n18, 284n20

Gregg, Dr. Allen, 207

Group Health Association, Inc., Washington, D.C., 183, 184–88

Group Health Association of America, 172, 238

Group Health Cooperative of Puget Sound, 183

Group Health Insurance, Inc., 21, 163

Group Health Mutual, St. Paul, 183

Group life insurance: Montgomery Ward bought first plan of, 8; Steelworkers negotiate for, 53, 54, 55, 256n2; in auto, 68, 69, 72, 256n9; de-emphasized in collective bargaining, 124

Group practice: trend toward, 144; contrasting attitudes of labor and AMA, 159; patient education, 208–9; physician attitude toward patients, 212–13

Gunderson, Dr. Gunner, 159

Hallbeck, E. C., 265n32

Hanley, Edward Burnette, Jr., 176

Hansen, Horace, 170, 171, 172

Harrington, Dr. Donald, 154

Hart, Schaffner and Marx, 22

Hatters, Cap and Millinery Workers' International Union of America, United, 249n22

Hayes, Albert J., 155, 234, 286n36, 309n4

Health and welfare fund irregularities, 107–10, 250n6, 268n22,n25

Health centers. *See* Medical service centers and by name

Health education: Transit Fund experience in Group Health, 187; discussion of, 211–14; improved physician-patient relationship in HIP, 299n47

Health Insurance Plan of Greater New York (HIP): services to Dress Joint Board, ILGWU, 21; history, 162–64; description, 195–200; administrative problems, 205

"Healthmobile," 18, 19–20

Health plan administration. *See* Administration of health plans

Health planning, 201–3

Held, Adolph, 250n2,n8, 251n14,n19

Hill-Burton Act, 143, 241

Hillman, Sidney, 22

Hod Carriers' and Laborers' Union: and San Joaquin Foundation, 154; dental plans, 172; established Washington, D.C. health center, 184

Horelick, N. E., 272n1, 275n38

Hospital Council of Southern California, 141

Hospitalization benefits: in auto, 67–70, 71–73, 256n9; in steel contracts, 53, 55, 257n2; changing benefits, 93–94; in Blue Cross plans, 132

Hospitals: UMW early ventures, 29–30; Miners' Memorial, chain of, 42–43; in Detroit, purchased by Community Health Association, 77; union role in planning, 140–43; AFL–CIO Hospital Association, Philadelphia, 182–83

Hospitals, utilization of: excessive use and UMW Fund, 44, 46, 157; Steelworkers suspect excessive use, 63; excessive use, Michigan Hospital Service, 72; and commercial insurance principles, 125; Blue Cross role in preventing excessive use, 134–35; affected by hospital over-construction, 141–42; lower admission rate for HIP members, 197, 298n41,n42; studies on excessive use, 278n10

Hotel and Restaurant Employees and Bartenders' International Union (Hotel and Restaurant Employees): four health centers, 177; Culinary Workers and Kaiser Plan, 191, 295n96,n29; Chefs and Cooks Local 89 in HIP, 196; innovating role in New York, 236; early negotiated health plans, 249n22

Industrial medical care prepayment programs, 7
Industry-wide plans, 22–23, 69
Inland Steel case, 10, 11, 12, 49
Inland Steel Company, 52, 59–60
Insurance abuses, 107, 119
Insurance business: Steelworkers' attitude toward, 57; discouraged retiree coverage, 90–91; attitude on releasing cost data, 103; regulation of, 120–21, 240; early opposition to government health insurance, 248n15
Insurance, commercial group: early background, 117, union attitudes on buying, 121–24; union influence on programming, 124–27; evaluation and alternatives, 127–30; contrasted with Blue Shield, 144–45; guide for buyers, 273n24
Insurance commissions, 118–23 *passim*
Insurance companies, union, 23–25
Insurance companies, cooperative, 292-n11
Insurance, industrial, 116–17
Insurance Fund, Amalgamated. *See* Clothing Workers, Amalgamated
Insurance retentions: information needed by unions for bargaining, 105; excessive retentions revealed by investigations, 107; decline during health bargaining, 122–23; distinct from claims costs, 124
International Association of Machinists and Aerospace Workers. *See* Machinists (IAM)
International Brotherhood of Teamsters, Chauffeurs, Warehousemen and Helpers of America. *See* Teamsters
International Hod Carriers', Building and Common Laborers' Union of America. *See* Hod Carriers' and Laborers' Union
International Longshoremen's and Warehousemen's Union. *See* Long-

shoremen's and Warehousemen's Union
Investigations of welfare funds: described and evaluated, 107–9, 110; insurance abuses, 119–20; lessons for labor, 234; New York Insurance Department and Ives Senate Labor Subcommittee, 268n22
Iron Molders' Union. *See* Molders' Union, Iron

Jewelery Workers' Union, International, 249n22
Jones and Laughlin Steel Corporation, 56

Kaiser, Henry, 7
Kaiser Foundation Health Plan (Kaiser Plan): compared to other industrial plans, 7; Steelworkers' experience with, 60, 61, 62, 63, 165; and California medical societies, 151–52, 154; description of, 188–95; on alternative choice arrangements, 215; countervailing power in California, 229; three unions bargain with, together, 295–96n29; changing relations with medical societies, 296n32; contracts with doctors, 296n33
Kaiser-Frazer Corporation, 51, 52
Kaiser Steel Corporation, 54
Kestnbaum, Meyer, 22
Kirkland, Lane: 266n4, 275n40, 278n11, 279n22, 282n5
Koos, Earl Lamon, 211
Krantz, Goldie, 154, 285n30,n32
Krug, Julius A., Secretary of Interior, 33

Laborers' Union. *See* Hod Carriers' and Laborers' Union
Labor Health Institute, St. Louis: paved way for other health plans, 168, 255-n11; includes dental care, 172; described, 177, 179–80; outside study by experts, 206; pre-surgical review, 207; choosing family doctor, 210; educational efforts, 211; members' hospitalization rate, 292n7
Labor-Management Relations Act: legislative history, 10–12; invoked by Truman against UMW, 34; Congressional debates on, 37; and health plan administration, 101, 106–13; requires financial information for bargaining,

102, 104; and trusteed plans, 107–10; amendments proposed, 240

Lanahan, Dr. F. Benedict, 305*n*45

Landess, Dr. Ben, 163, 164

Langbord, Dr. Joseph, 210, 252*n*22, 302*n*29

Lathers', Plasterers', and Hod Carriers' Union, 154

Latimer, Murray, 258*n*7

Lee, Dr. Russell V., 205

Letter carriers, New York, 6

Lewis, John L., 20–43 *passim*, 86

Lewis-Krug Agreement, 33, 34, 35, 37

Liberty Mutual Insurance Company, 97

Life Insurance Company, Amalgamated. *See* Clothing Workers, Amalgamated

Life and Health Insurance Company, Amalgamated. *See* Clothing Workers, Amalgamated.

Local option, 64, 69, 190

Locomotive Firemen and Enginemen, Brotherhood of, 3

Longshoremen's and Warehousemen's Union (ILWU): arrangement with San Joaquin Foundation, 154; large membership in Kaiser Plan, 191; innovating role, 236; attempt to join other unions in dealing with Kaiser, 295–96*n*29; results under alternative choice at Kaiser Plan, 307*n*62

MacColl, Dr. William A., 209

McDonald, David, 54, 62, 63, 259*n*23, 260*n*35,*n*37,*n*38

Machinists (IAM): bargaining preparation, 82; dental coverage in Aerojet contract, 173; District Lodge 751 in Group Health Cooperative of Puget Sound, 183; District 15 in HIP, 196; employee benefit plan coexists with effective union at Cutler-Hammer, Milwaukee, 248*n*19; trusteed plan not coterminous with bargaining association, 271*n*41. *See also* Hayes, Albert J.; Sawyer, Dr. William A.

McLean, Dr. Basil C., 135

Major medical insurance: Steelworkers' attitude toward, 54; UAW attitude to Blue Cross proposal, 72; origin and union attitude toward, 97–98, 126–27

"Management prerogative": and employee benefit plans, 9; postwar issue in heavy industry, 48; scored by UAW, 50; and administration of single-employer plans, 102–3

Master, Dr. Arthur M., 162–63.

Meany, George, 91, 108, 155–56, 264-*n*18, 268–69*n*25, 286*n*37

Meat Cutters: Local 88 health center, St. Louis, 168; and Community Health Foundation, Cleveland, 168, 178; includes dental programs, 172; early participant in AF of L Medical Services Plan, Philadelphia, 181

Medical and Hospital Fund, UMW, 37, 38

Medical Association, American: and ILGWU health centers, 19; Appalachian medical care, 43; dealings with UMW, 43, 44, 45, 157; ten principles on prepayment, 148; and prepaid group practice, 159–62, 175; negotiations with labor, 160; and HIP, 164; and governmental intervention, 169; cautions local societies on disciplinary methods, 171; and medical control of health plans, 205; changing social role, 227

Medical benefits, 95–96

Medical care, attitudes toward, 209–12, 215

Medical care, costs of: stimulated union insurance demands, 10; effect of, on contributory issue, 87; union response to, 99; Blue Cross influence on, 140; savings by UMW hospitals, 141; surveillance of, 155–58; in Pittsburg, Cal., 164–65; medical pricing, 223–24; and utilization, 281–82*n*44

Medical care, quality of: surveillance by UMW, 47; union concern, 99; affected by indemnity insurance, 128–29; improved by UMW hospitals, 141; surveillance of, 155–58; under Kaiser Plan, 194–95; in HIP, 197–200; effect of part-time practice on, 202; in group practice, 207–11; analyzed, 224–26; planning for, better, 229

Medical service centers: co-operative-sponsored, 183–88, 293*n*13; grievance procedure, 193–94, 200; optimum size of, 290–91*n*3; and alternative choice arrangements, 215–19; criteria for measuring use of, 303*n*33

Medical service centers, union: ILGWU welfare funds invested in health centers, 16; ILGWU, 17–21; Clothing Workers, 25–27; operated by UMW, 46; Steelworkers in Ontario, 64–66,

UAW in Detroit, 73–77; UAW in Baltimore, 75; UAW in Toledo, 75; eye care centers, 96–97, 180, 181, 210; union-sponsored, 177–83; background of UMW centers, 255n41

Medical school faculties, 19, 168–69, 238

Medical societies: and ILGWU health centers, 19, 20–21, 167; and Sidney Hillman Health Centers, 26; and UMW, 44–45, 157; and Steelworkers, 63–64, 65, 164–67; and Community Health Association, Detroit, 76–77; sponsorship of Blue Shield, 145; Los Angeles County, and fee schedule, 147; San Francisco, negotiates with labor, 147; fee controls in Windsor, Ontario, 150; San Joaquin County, sponsors service program, 152–55; oppose HIP, 163; Lehigh County (Pa.), opposes Clothing Workers' plan 167; Milwaukee, opposes health plan, 167; discourage prepaid group practice, 170; limit scope of health centers, 205; and alternative choice arrangements, 218; opposition to government health insurance, 248n15; changing relations with Kaiser Plan, 296n32

Medicare: and retirement coverage in private plans, 91–93; implications of, 242–43; may mean savings for UMW Fund, 252n9

Melamed, Isadore, 289n39, 299n49

Mental health services: of Sidney Hillman Center, New York, 27; UAW pioneering, 70; extent of coverage, 96; in Blue Cross plans, 132; under Group Health Association, 185; in Kaiser Plan, 189; added to Steelworker coverage, 257n3

Metropolitan Life Insurance Company, 57, 59, 71, 103, 117

Mine, Mill and Smelter Workers, International Union of, 6, 249n22

Mine Workers, United (UMW): early prepaid hospital plans, 6; history of Welfare Fund, 29–47; medical centers, 46, 177, 255n41; coverage for laid-off employees, 89; use of self-insured funds, 127–28; outstanding hospital planning, 141; surveillance of medical quality and cost, 156–58; power in medical market, 236. *See also* Draper, Dr. Warren; Lewis, John L.

Minkoff, Nathaniel, 5, 247n7, 248n18

Molders' Union, Iron, 3, 4

Montgomery Ward and Company, 8

Mott, Dr. Fred, 77

Multiple choice arrangements. *See* Alternative choice arrangements

Munts, Raymond, 265n28

Murray, Thomas E., 33

Murray, Philip, 86

Mutual insurance companies, 4

National Labor Relations Board, 90, 248n17

Newspaper Guild, American, 82, 196

New York Academy of Medicine, 243

New York State Insurance Department, 108

Niebuhr, Reinhold, 227

Office of Economic Opportunity, 243

Painters, Decorators and Paperhangers of America, Brotherhood of, 181, 196

Petrillo, James A., 37, 106

Physician, personal: and ILGWU health centers, 19; at Sidney Hillman Centers, 27; little emphasis on, in Kaiser Plan, 194, 297n35; in medical service centers, 209–10; at Labor Health Institute, St. Louis, 210

Plasterers' and Cement Masons' International Association of the United States and Canada, Operative, 154

Plumbers' Union, 4, 108

Pollack, Jerome, 71, 127, 149, 256n7, 261n10,n16, 264n13, 265n32, 272n7, 276n49, 278n12, 284n17,n19

Postal Clerks, National Federation of, 265n32

Prepaid group practice: Steelworkers' policy toward, 61–64; AMA role, 160–62, 175; legal restrictions on, 169–72; and government policy, 241–42; and hospitalization rate, 291–92-n7. *See also* Medical service centers; Medical service centers, union

Preventive medicine: contribution of ILGWU, 18, 28; and commercial insurance principles, 125; in union health centers, 178

Price, Dr. Leo, 160, 251n15

Printers, 3, 4, 6

Printing Pressmen and Assistants' Union of North America, International, 249-n22

"Private social security," 32, 47
Prudential Insurance Company, 65
Public Health Association, American, 46
Public utility workers, Milwaukee, 6

Railway brotherhoods, 3
Reed, Louis, 43
Rehabilitation services: of ILGWU health centers, 17–18; of Sidney Hillman Center, New York; UMW Fund, 30; Boone Commission reports on need for, 36
Republic Steel Corporation, 52, 56, 57, 59
Retail, Wholesale and Department Store Union, 179, 196
Retail Clerks International Association: bargaining preparation, 82; and Kaiser, 96, 191, 295–96n29; sponsor of Community Health Foundation, Cleveland, 168, 178; innovating role in California, 236
Reuther, Walter, 51, 62, 156, 208, 256-n8, 286n38, 301n16
Roche, Josephine, 35
Roemer, Dr. Milton I., 230
Ross-Loos Medical Group, Los Angeles, 169
Rubber Workers: and doctors' fees, 99, 145, 146–47; attitude to employer claims administration, 104; experience with insurance companies, 119. *See also* Bowers, Paul; Ginsburg, Woodrow L.

Sackman, Morris, 215n16
San Diego Health Association, 183
San Joaquin Foundation for Medical Care, 152–55
Sault Ste Marie and District Group Health Association, 64–66, 177, 307-n62
Sawyer, Dr. William A., 160, 213, 305-n34
Sayers, Dr. R. R., 34
Schmidt, John, 105, 267n18
Schwartz, Jerome, 6
Seafarer's International Union of America, 177
Self-insurance: of ILGWU funds, 18; UMW Fund, 37–45 *passim.*; described and evaluated, 127–28
Shadid, Dr. Michael, 293n13
Shoaff, James J., 24
Shoemaker, Richard, 265n27, 289n42

Sidney Hillman Health Centers: New York, 25–27; Philadelphia, 25–27, 168
Sinclair, Upton, 8
Social Benefit Association, Amalgamated. *See* Clothing Workers, Amalgamated
Somers, Anne Ramsay, 137, 226
Somers, Herman Miles, 137
Southern Coal Producers' Association, 37
State, County and Municipal Employees, 169, 182, 305n54
State regulation: of insurance business, 120–21, 240; of Blue Cross, 133–34, 139–40, 240, 280n31; of medical service plans, 169–72, 241
Steel Factfinding Board, 51
Steelworkers of America, United: history of health bargaining, 48–66; and Kaiser Plan, 61–63, 164–67, 191; health center in Sault Ste Marie, 64–66, 177, 307n62; coverage of laid-off employees, 89; and claims administration, 104; negotiations with Blue Shield, 150; change in policy, 236; national bargaining, 237; lays groundwork for health bargaining, 249n23. *See also* Abel, A. W.; Goldberg, Ted; Greenberg, Bernard; Latimer, Murray; McDonald, David; Murray, Philip; Tomayko, John
Strasser, Adolph, 4
Street and Electric Railway Employees, 249n20. *See also* Transit Employees Health and Welfare Plan, Local 689
Surgical benefits: Steelworkers negotiate for, 53; in auto, 68, 69, 72; typical coverage, 93–94
Surgery, unneccessary, 19, 63, 169

Taft, Senator Robert, 11
Tax exemption on employer contribution: stimulated health benefits, 9; effect on contributory issue, 87–88; employee exemption proposed, 241
Teamsters: welfare irregularities and AFL–CIO expulsion, 109; opposed San Francisco health plan, 168; New York study of medical records of members, 225. *See also* Gibbons, Harold; Labor Health Institute, St. Louis; Tobin, Dan
Technicians, health: needed by unions, 82, 84; needed for astute insurance

buying, 123; professionalization of union staff, 235
Technology, medical, 226
Textile Workers' Union of America, 105
Thaler, Alan, 129
Tobacco Workers' Union, 4
Tobin, Dan, 5
Tomayko, John, 62, 259n16,n17, 260-n27,n29,n39
Transit Employees Health and Welfare Fund, Local 689: and Group Health Association, 184–88, 307n62. *See also* Bierwagen, Walter J.
Truman, President Harry S., 34
Trussel report, 139, 141
Trusteed plans: decentralized funds in ILGWU, 15; union administration in coal, 36–39, 41–42; administration of, 106–7; abuses in, 107–10; appropriate uses of 110–13; not coterminous with bargaining association, 271n4
Trust law, 109–110
Typographical Union, International, 3, 4, 6, 180. *See also* Printers

Umhey, Frederick F., 20, 160, 167, 287n6, 288n26
Union benefit plans, 3–6, 247n1,n9
Union Eye Care Center, Chicago: relation to Union Health Service, 180, 181; and patient education, 210; inspired by "Peg" Bautsch, 299n49
Union Health Service, Chicago, 178, 180–81
United Association of Journeymen and Apprentices of the Plumbing and Pipe Fitting Industry of the United States and Canada. *See* Plumbers' Union
United Automobile, Aerospace and Agricultural Implement Workers of

America. *See* Auto Workers, United (UAW)
United Mine Workers of America. *See* Mine Workers, United (UMW)
United States Steel Corporation, 53, 55, 56
Upholsterers' International Union of North America, 168, 271n41

Van Horn, Ezra, 33, 34

Wagner Act, 10, 11, 12
Warehouse and Distribution Workers' Union, Local 688, 236. *See also* Labor Health Institute, St. Louis
War Labor Board policy, 9, 32, 49
Weiner, Dr. Hyman J., 252n23, 304n40
Weinerman, Dr. Richard, 20, 210, 213
Welfare and Pension Plans Disclosure Act, 104, 109
Welfare and Pension Plan Investigation, Final Report. *See* Douglas Report
Welfare and Retirement Fund, UMW, 30–45 *passim*. *See also* Mine Workers, United (UMW)
"Welfare capitalism," 8, 117
Williams, Pierce, 6
Wilson, A. M., 127
Woll, Matthew, 5, 247n8
Woodcock, Leonard, 72, 73, 261n13
Woodruff Committee, 199
Workmen's Compensation, 31–32, 105, 241
W. W. Cross case, 49

Youngstown Sheet and Tube Company, 52

Zimmerman, Charles, 307n62